Humour,
Organiza

Humour, Work and Organization explores the critical, subversive and ambivalent character of humour and comedy as it relates to organizations and organized work. It examines the various individual, organizational, social and cultural means through which humour is represented, deployed, developed, used and understood.

The book considers the relationship between humour and organization in a nuanced and radical way and takes the view that humour and comedy are pervasive and highly meaningful aspects of human experience.

The richness and complexity of this relationship is examined across three related domains:

- How humour is constructed, enacted and responded to in organizational settings
- How organizations and work are represented comedically in various types of popular culture media
- How humour is used in organizations where there is a more explicit relationship between the comedic and work

An exciting and controversial text, *Humour, Work and Organization* will appeal to students of all levels as well as anyone interested in the full complexities of human interactions in the workplace.

Robert Westwood is Reader in Organization Studies at the University of Queensland Business School.

Carl Rhodes is Associate Professor of Organization Studies in the School of Management at the University of Technology, Sydney.

Humour, Work and Organization

Edited by
Robert Westwood and
Carl Rhodes

Routledge
Taylor & Francis Group

LONDON AND NEW YORK

First published 2007
by Routledge
2 Park Square, Milton Park, Abingdon, Oxon OX14 4RN

Simultaneously published in the USA and Canada
by Routledge
270 Madison Ave, New York, NY 10016

Routledge is an imprint of the Taylor & Francis Group, an informa business

Typeset in Perpetua and Bell Gothic by
HWA Text and Data Management, Tunbridge Wells
Printed and bound in Great Britain by
Antony Rowe Ltd, Chippenham, Wiltshire

British Library Cataloguing in Publication Data
A catalogue record for this book is available from the British Library

Library of Congress Cataloging-in-Publication Data
Humour, work, and organization / edited by Robert Westwood and
Carl Rhodes.
    p. cm.
Includes bibliographical references and index.
1. Humor in the workplace. 2. Work–Humor. 3. Organizational behavior–
Humor. 4. Organization in popular culture. 5. Organizational sociology.
I. Westwood, Robert Ian. II. Rhodes, Carl, 1967– III. Title: Humor, work,
and organization.
HF5549.5.H85W67 2006
302.3'5–dc22   2006021381

ISBN10: 0–415–38412–5 (hbk)
ISBN10: 0–415–38413–3 (pbk)

ISBN13: 978–0–415–38412–4 (hbk)
ISBN13: 978–0–415–38413–1 (pbk)

Contents

Notes on contributors

David M. Boje is Professor, and former Robert Owens Anderson Professor in Business Administration in the Management Department at New Mexico State University. His main research is the interplay of story, strategy and systemicity. He has published articles in the *Administrative Science Quarterly*, *Management Science*, *Management Communication Quarterly*, *Organization Studies*, *Leadership Quarterly*, and other fine journals. He is President of Standing Conference for Management and Organization Inquiry (Sc'MOI), editor of the journal *Tamara*, and associate editor for *Qualitative Research in Organization and Management (QROM)*. He serves on thirteen other editorial boards.

Yue Cai-Hillon is lecturer in the Department of Management at the University of Central Oklahoma. Her teaching and research interest include global strategic competence, storytelling/narrative strategy, business consulting and organizational behaviour. She published a number of articles in journals such as: *Metamorphosis*, *Tamara* and *Culture and Organization*. She is a member of the Academy of Management, as well as an active board member of Sc'MOI. Her current research involves the reconciliation of the predominant western strategy paradigm with the ancient traditions of the east.

Simon Critchley is Professor of Philosophy at the New School for Social Research and at the University of Essex. During 2006–7, he is a Getty Scholar in Los Angeles. He is author of many books; *On Humour* (Routledge, 2002) has been translated into eight languages. His next book is called *Infinitely Demanding*, forthcoming from Verso.

Stephen Fineman is Professor of Organizational Behavior in the School of Management, University of Bath. Recent interests focus on emotion in organizations, especially critical approaches. Publications include *Understanding Emotion at Work* (Sage, 2003), *Emotion in Organizations*, 2nd edn (Sage, 2000) and *Organizing and Organizations*, 3rd edn (Sage, 2005).

Heather Höpfl is Professor of Management at the University of Essex, UK. She has worked as a schoolteacher, a tour manager for a touring repertory company and in the R&D department of a large engineering company. She is editor, with Robert Westwood, of *Culture and Organization*, a former chair of SCOS, Visiting Professor at UvH Utrecht and the University of South Australia. She is interested in poststructuralist approaches to organizations, in theatre and performance and she has published widely in these areas. Recent relevant articles include 'Hitchcock's vertigo and the tragic sublime', *Journal of Organizational Change Management*, 'Organizations and the mouth of hell', *Culture and Organization*, and, with Georg Schreyoegg, a special issue of *Organization Studies*, on Theatre and Organizations.

Allanah Johnston is doing her PhD in the School of Business at the University of Queensland, Australia. Her thesis explores how humour is implicated in processes of gender identity construction within organizations. She is also interested in the theorization and practices of consumer culture, critical approaches to emotions in organizations and the organization of aesthetics. Currently she is concerned with exploring and sustaining any sense of humour she may have while writing her thesis.

Donncha Kavanagh is Senior Lecturer in Management at University College Cork, the National University of Ireland. He has published in the fields of management, marketing, organization studies and engineering. His research interests include the history of management thought, and the sociology of knowledge and technology. He is currently researching the translation of management technologies into higher education.

Stephen Linstead is Professor of Organization Theory and Critical Management at the University of York, UK. Ever since writing 'Doris, the Co-op Dairy Queen' and 'Hit Me with your Morris Stick' in the 1970s he has struggled to be taken seriously, though not too hard. Nevertheless, he has managed to publish edited and co-authored books on subjects including aesthetics, language, sex, textuality, philosophy, identity and the anthropology of management, and over a hundred book chapters and refereed journal articles. His current projects include the philosophies of Gilles Deleuze and Jacques Rancière, the politics of globalization, performance methodologies, the impact of post-punk pop culture on organizational thought and learning to be a grandparent. Yeah, we thought it was odd, too.

Meredith Marra is a lecturer in sociolinguistics within the School of Linguistics and Applied Language Studies and a Research Fellow for Victoria University of Wellington's Language in the Workplace project. Meredith's primary research interest is the language of meetings (including her PhD research which investigated the language of decision making in business meetings), but she has also published in the areas of humour and gender in workplace interactions.

Dennis Mumby is Professor in the Department of Communication Studies at the University of North Carolina at Chapel Hill, USA. His research focuses on the relationships among discourse, power, gender and organization. He has published in journals such as *Academy of Management Review*, *Communication Monographs*, *Communication Theory*, and *Management Communication Quarterly*. His most recent book, co-authored with Karen Lee Ashcraft, is *Reworking Gender: A Feminist Communicology of Organization* (Sage, 2004).

Damian P. O'Doherty is a lecturer in Organization Analysis at the Manchester Business School in the University of Manchester. His doctoral thesis examined the question of subjectivity and identity within the context of order and disorder in organization. Since the award of his doctoral degree Dr O'Doherty has published his work in a number of journals including *Culture and Organization*, *Sociology*, *Ephemera*, *Journal of Management Studies* and *International Studies in Management and Organization*. He has recently co-authored the collection *Manifestos for the Business School of Tomorrow* published by Dvalin Press in June 2005. He holds an ESRC research grant under the Evolution of Business Knowledge programme that is looking at the development of media and digital technologies and its impact on organization and its social relations. Dr O'Doherty is an executive board member of the Standing Conference in Organization Symbolism and sits on the editorial committees of a number of scholarly journals, including *Culture and Organization* and *Ephemera*.

Don O'Sullivan is a member of faculty in the Department of Management and Marketing, National University of Ireland, Cork. He has a long academic track record and is an internationally published author of numerous book chapters and journal articles. His marketing case studies are widely published and taught in business schools throughout Europe and the US. He recently returned to academia having spent four years as Director of Strategy at a marketing agency focused on the European technology sector. Clients included Microsoft, HP, Siemens, DoubleClick and Computer Associates. Don was responsible for multiple global award-winning marketing campaigns including an International ECHO Award from the MA and three ICON awards from ADWEEK's *Technology Marketing Magazine*. Don maintains close contacts with the marketing profession and is a member of the European Advisory Board of the Chief Marketing Officers Council. Don's interest in humour in marketing arose from his previous professional experiences as a script and joke writer for television.

Martin Parker is Professor of Culture and Organization at Leicester University Management Centre. He has published on various aspects of organizational culture and the culture of organization. His writing plans over the next few years include the mafia, angels, pirates, zombies and space rockets.

Alison Pullen is currently Senior Research Fellow at the University of Technology, Sydney. One day she will work as a fitter in a codpiece shop …

Carl Rhodes is Associate Professor in the School of Management at the University of Technology, Sydney (UTS). People have often told him that he is too serious. His involvement in this book is a futile and ironic attempt to prove them wrong. He has published books, articles, chapters, etc.

Grace-Ann Rosile is an Assistant Professor of management at New Mexico State University. Her primary interest is narrative approaches to organizational studies, including organizational theatrics, pedagogy, ethics and academic integrity. She received the Champion of Integrity award in 2005 from Duke University's Center for Academic Integrity. She has published in the *Journal of Applied Behavioral Science, Management Communication Quarterly, Organization Studies, Ephemera, Journal of Management Inquiry, Journal of Management Education, Journal of Organizational Change Management* and *Communication Research*, in addition to a book and several book chapters.

Esther R. Thomas is an Assistant Professor of management in the Department of Business Administration at the Jesse H. Jones School of Business at Texas Southern University. Dr Thomas has always had a passion for quality teaching, and focused her dissertation research on the enhancement of management education through use of non-traditional teaching methods with a primary focus on the use of improvisational theatre in the management classroom. Dr Thomas' research interests include, but are not limited to, organizational behaviour, organizational change and development, management education and development, and human resource management with a primary interest in international aspects of HRM. Dr Thomas is a member of the Organizational Behavior Teaching Society, Academy of Management, Southwest Academy of Management, and the Standing Conference for Management and Organization Inquiry (Sc'MOI).

Sam Warren lectures in Organizational Behaviour and Research Methods at University of Portsmouth Business School, UK. Broadly, her research interests centre on aesthetics and organizational life and, in particular, fun, play and 'artistic' management practices. She is also interested in the use of visual methodologies in qualitative management research. An executive board member of the Standing Conference on Organizational Symbolism (SCOS) and editor for the journal *Ephemera: Theory and Politics in Organization*, her work has appeared in the journals *Sociology*, *Administrative Theory and Praxis* and *Ephemera*.

Robert Westwood is Reader in Organization Studies at the University of Queensland Business School. He was educated in the United Kingdom receiving a PhD from Bath University. He has worked in the Asia-Pacific region since the mid-1980s. Bob has published widely in the areas of comparative and cross-cultural management and in various aspects of organization theory. His last book was *Debating Organization: Point/Counterpoint in Organization Studies*, edited with Stewart Clegg and published by Blackwell in 2003. He is co-editor of the journal *Culture and Organization* and on the board of three other journals. He is currently working on projects further related to humour and organization, on the representation of organization in popular culture, and on a postcolonial analysis of comparative management. Additional research interests include the meaning and experience of work, gender and language–power relations in organizations.

Chapter 1

Humour and the study of organizations

Robert Westwood and Carl Rhodes

12 May 2006 marked the twentieth day of the sixth season of the Australian version of the popular reality program *Big Brother*. An international phenomenon, *Big Brother* is a franchise that has been used on television in almost seventy countries around the world – from Albania to Argentina, Brazil to Bulgaria, Colombia to Croatia, and almost everywhere else around the globe varieties of the show can be found. Originating in Holland in 1999, the *Big Brother* concept has both developed and matured as a popular culture phenomenon. The basic format for the program is that a group of approximately twelve men and women are put in a house where they will live for about fifteen weeks. As fans know well, this is no ordinary house. Through a combination of two-way mirrors, hidden cameras and mandatorily worn microphones, the people in the house, or as they are known 'house-mates', are under constant surveillance. Broadcast on prime time television, the 'entertainment' offered by *Big Brother* is the opportunity to observe the activities of these people in the context of their most mundane everyday activities. The house is completely isolated from society – no newspapers, no television, no direct contact with the outside world.

As viewers look on through the voyeuristic frame of their television sets, the house-mates also have to undergo various ordeals as set for them by the voice of 'big brother' – a voice that regularly comes over a personal address system to give orders, administer punishments and provide information. The voyeurism is also one of competition. The house-mates are contestants, and each week one of them is evicted from the show based on audience voting of who viewers would like to stay and who they would like to go. The person who remains at the end wins a significant cash prize. But this is not the only mode of competition. In the sixth season of the Australian version there is also an activity known as the 'Friday Night Games'. Each Friday the house-mates participate in a competition against one another. The main prize is that the single winner can select another contestant and together they spend two nights in the 'rewards room' where they enjoy creature comforts denied them in the normal house – DVDs to watch, good food to eat, alcoholic beverages and the like.

One of these evenings of Friday Night Games occurred on 12 May 2006. On this night the games were dubbed the 'Office Olympics'. The competition involved four rounds. The first of these was an office chair race. There were six pairs of contestants. One sat on a wheeled office chair and was pulled around a pre-set course by the other. Completing five laps of the course in between being showered by cold water and having to dress in white collar garb, the contestants laughed their way through such abuse of office furniture in competition with each other. Eight people made it through to the second round. By round two, however, the laughter was growing. This round was dubbed 'Big Worker's Obstacle Course'. There were two teams of four people each. Each team had to wear giant inflated costumes made up to look like stereotypical office workers – somewhat resembling the iconic office nerd in Scott Adams's *Dilbert*. The costumes of each team were connected at the hands, and their sheer size made slapstick type body movements unavoidable. There was an uproar of laughter as each team had to walk up a slippery ramp and then down the other side, followed by completion of an obstacle course. The task seemed unachievable as the teams fell about looking impossibly exaggerated in terms of the size of their costumes, the clumsiness of their movements and their inability to fulfill their task. Eventually one team won, and its four members went on to round three – the penultimate round. Each of these four contestants was given a different office artefact – a telephone, a computer printer, a computer keyboard and a calculator. Their task was to provide a one-minute sales spiel on this item. The contestants who had already been eliminated ranked their performance on a scale of zero to five. Following the slapstick shenanigans of the giant office workers, the humorous effect here was more verbal. Michael particularly stood out in his sale of the printer. Barely a word could be understood as he went into super-salesman mode ranting and raving about the printer with bullshit extraordinaire. The other contestants couldn't contain their laughter. Another contestant, Krystal, also caused laughter when she took on the role of a television advertisement sales person extolling the virtues of the calculator. Bringing a sexual element into the proceedings she took off her tie and proceeded to use it to spank both herself and one of the other contestants.

Two people went through to the final round – Michael and Ashley. This was another obstacle course. They were each attached to a rope that was wound around various pieces of office furniture. They had to follow the course of the rope, around chairs, under desks and obstructed by other office paraphernalia and the winner was he who made it to the end first. To mark completion was a large picture of the 'boss' – smoking a cigar, overweight, and wearing a black suit, he was looking over his shoulder, with his massive backside featuring as the centrepiece of the image. On completing the course the leader marked their win by having to literally kiss the boss's ass. Michael won and as he reached the end he opened his arms, aimed his lips carefully and landed them enthusiastically on the image of this ass. The other contestants cheered and laughed uproariously. Meanwhile Ashley was still stuck trying to navigate past the water cooler.

Studying humour

Big Brother's Office Olympics is particularly interesting to us. Clearly the producers of the show fabricated these games with a view of providing humorous entertainment — something evidently hilarious to the people who participated in it, as much as to the vast numbers of home viewers tuned in. So why is this funny? We can only imagine that if the same set of activities was included without the office motif, the humour would have been severely muted — there would have been no water cooler to be trapped by, no boss's ass to smooch, no schmaltzy sales stereotype to hyperbolize. Indeed, there was something really funny about the layout and imagery of an office being used for fun. It was distinctly amusing to see the contestants, each dressed in conventional office attire, engaging in stupid and ridiculous competitions. The huge office worker outfits used in round two were particularly amusing as the expected seriousness of office work was pierced by excessive exaggeration. When Michael went into sales pitch over-drive, the other contestants were bent over in contortions of laugher as they wiped the tears from their eyes. The kissing of the boss's ass at the end wrapped it all up with a bow of hilarity and subversion.

A range of things were at play here — the use of work as a context for humour, the commercialization of humour in work, the possibilities of subversion of workplaces, a carnivalization of work for humorous effect, the humour of the misuse of workplace artefacts, the way that humour offers a potential window into the seriousness of work, relations between sex and gender at work, the role of humorous popular culture in parodying work and so on. Now, we'll come back to the Office Olympics shortly, but it is the sorts of issues presaged in the games that are rarely considered in the corpus of research on humour at work. To begin with interest and research on humour in organizations has had a patchy and intermittent history until relatively recently. Over the past twenty years or so, however, there has been burgeoning interest in the issue. Much of this research has been within clearly functionalist traditions wherein organizational humour has been associated with a range of presumed positive managerial and organizational outcomes. For example, research has explored the relationship between humour and the functioning of groups, indicating that through humour, group processes can be enhanced, and group communication, cohesiveness, and solidarity facilitated (Duncan 1982; Duncan and Feisal 1989; Duncan *et al.* 1990). Additional claims have also been made for humour's role in improving group problem-solving and in enhancing creativity and innovation (Consalvo 1989; Smith and White 1965). There has also been a significant amount of work relating humour and comedy to stress reduction, coping behaviour, and other types of adaptive behaviour (Buchman 1994; Martin and Lefcourt 1983; Yovitch et al. 1990). More recently, humour has been linked with effective organizational culture and culture change (Deal and Kennedy 2000; Dwyer 1991; Kahn 1989) and with effective leadership (Avolio et al. 1999; Crawford 1994). But still this all says nothing to the promise of resistant humour pointed to in the Office Olympics.

There is a danger of humour, as an enormously rich and complex facet of human behaviour, being appropriated by a managerialist discourse and subject to regimes of manipulation and control. There is already an emergent humour and management industry (Collinson 2002; Gibson 1994) in which humour is promoted as a viable tool for management (Caudron 1992; Malone 1980). Numerous popularist texts promulgating this functional application have appeared in recent times (e.g. Kushner 1990; Paulson 1989; Ross 1989).

The issue of the relationship between humour and power relations and hierarchical structures has been addressed in the literature and was present from a very early point (Coser 1960; Lundberg 1969; Traylor 1973). More recently this perspective has been narrowly focused on the role of humour in diminishing hierarchy and status (Duncan 1982), its role in smoothing power/authority relations (Dwyer 1991; Kahn 1989; Ullian 1976; Vinton 1989) or in enhancing social influence processes (O'Quin and Aronoff 1981; Powell 1977). Much of this remains under the umbrella of a functionalist paradigm.

There is a counterpoint to the functional view of humour indicated above. Although less dominant and pervasive, there is some research that suggests that comedy and humour can be deployed as resistance, challenge and subversion (Ackroyd and Thompson 1999; Collinson 1988, 2002; Linstead 1985). In line with such developments, researchers have explicitly investigated how humour can be deployed as a form of opposition or challenge to the status quo both in general (Jenkins 1994; Powell and Paton 1988) and in organizational contexts specifically (Ackroyd and Thompson 1999; Collinson 1988, 2002; Griffiths 1998; Grugulis 2002; Holmes 2000; Linstead 1985; Rodrigues and Collinson 1995; Taylor and Bain 2003). The subversive potential of humour and the attempts to control and police it strongly suggest that functionalist explanations are inadequate to account for the complexities and ambiguities of humour. Functionalist approaches treat the meaning of humour as self-evident (Collinson 2002).

In relation to the subversive and critical potential of humour, in this book we seek to examine in some detail the various organizational, social and cultural means through which such humour is represented, deployed, developed, used and understood. The book explores humour and comedy in organizational settings in a non-functionalist manner. It considers the relationship between humour and organization in a more nuanced and radical way, one which reflects the richness and complexity of the relationship in a broad variety of its manifestations. Further, it takes the view that humour and comedy are pervasive, entrenched and highly meaningful aspects of human experience and that they are as significant in organizational and work contexts as they are in any other domain of human activity.

The book starts with three conceptual chapters which consider, at a theoretical level, the general nature of humour and theories of humour. On this basis, the book then considers the relationship between humour, organizations and work in three different but related domains. First, it contemplates how humour is constructed, enacted and responded to in organizational settings. Second, it focuses on how organizations and work are represented comedically in various types of popular culture media – from television to the mass management textbook. Finally, it examines organizational and work situations where there is a more explicit relationship between the comedic and organization/work.

A funny thing happened on the way from the office (olympics) ...

As we noted in the previous section, when humour has been researched in relation to organizations, attention has most often paid to the way that it can enhance workplace functioning and support a broadly managerialist agenda. This managerial bias, however, is only one possible perspective and, when looking at the way that humour has been theorized more generally in the fields of philosophy, history, literary history, theology and history of religion, sociology and anthropology, the limitations of much of organization studies attention to humour becomes apparent. Simon Critchley examines this breadth of theory in the second chapter of the book. Attesting to how humour might be also used as a tool against management, Critchley discusses the critical and radical possibilities of humour. When humour has the potential to laugh at power – pointed to with Big Brother's Michael's hyperbolic kissing of the boss's ass – Critchley argues that it might also be a 'practically enacted theory' with emancipatory and elevatory potential. Through its ability to 'defamiliarize' the mundane, humour, as Critchely elaborates, can extract our understanding of life from the confines of 'common sense' so as to enable a questioning of the taken for granted operations of power.

While Critchley sets the theoretical ground for an examination of humour as a critical practice, Heather Höpfl, in Chapter 3, expands further the potentially disjunctive effects of humour as a phenomenological act that challenges the taken for granted. Drawing specifically on the treatment of humour by Umberto Eco (1986), Höpfl argues that humour's critical potential lies in its practices of violation – that is, the funniness resides in the way that it violates expectations and rules. As our brief review of *Big Brother* suggests, the laughter in the Office Olympics was engendered precisely because the serious expectations of what goes on in an office were both violated and mocked. Drawing on theoretical discussions of humour, often refracted through (and informed by) her own personal life experiences, Höpfl demonstrates how humour can subvert and parody power. For her, a positive view of humour sees it as subversive – it presents the possibility of alternatives such that the construction of management power might be undermined. Bad practices deserve derision, she argues, and humour might just be the best way to deride them.

In the final chapter of this section, Robert Westwood, like Critchley and Höpfl, considers humour's potential to laugh at power, but this time the power that is targeted is the power inherent in knowledge, or more specifically in theory. He argues that, if humour is actually derived from its capacity to construct and juxtapose alternative perspectives on reality, to intrude an alternate reality on a dominant one, then it is operating in the same manner as theory. In this sense, humour is considered to be theoretical because it threatens the paramount reality and creates a tension by disturbing the order of things. Alternatively, theory is considered as humour because of its intrusion of alternative realities into the dominant. Theory is funny when it is displaced by an alternative that is accepted as more plausible and legitimate, or when it makes claims that are defeated by a dominant explanation and fails to gain plausibility and acceptance. On this basis, the chapter explores the connections between theory and humour and the possibilities for theory participating in the comedic. It does so primarily through an exploration of theories of hysteria, the practices they engender and the effects, often gendered and negative, they visit upon people. This tracking of the trajectory of hysterical theory is intended to perturb both theory and its consequences. It is at least a cautionary tale against taking things too seriously.

Humour in organizations

Chapters 2–4 set the scene for what remains by opening up the possibility of a perspective on humour that exceeds focus on the maintenance of organizational social cohesion and the maintenance of established power relations. Here we have a humour that is regarded in terms of its function and potential for critique, resistance and change. An engagement with the nature of such critical potential as it might be played out within workplace and organizational settings is what forms the theme of the second part of the book entitled 'Humour in organizations'. This begins in Chapter 5 with Martin Parker's consideration of humorous workplace artefacts – as he clearly shows, if one examines the content of office spaces, a range of apparently humorous artefacts abound. Such objects, be they books, coffee mugs, cartoons, websites, stickers, toys or even a badge emblazoned with the imperative to *Fuck Work*, are omnipresent. Interested in a perspective he calls the 'culture of organization', Parker examines in detail the symbolism of humorous office artefacts – particularly those that are overtly critical of work. He too wants to know what it means to caricature the kissing of the boss's ass. Noting and documenting the ubiquity of comic artefacts, Parker illustrates how the culture of organizations is one that is marked most extensively by a form of critique embodied in the artefacts he surveys – for him they document a 'counter culture' to be found at work. He concludes on an ambivalent note, considering that such artefacts are both tragic and heroic and expands on how they play out the interpenetrative nature of power and resistance.

That the first round of *Big Brother*'s Office Olympics involved a race involving office chairs coincidentally relates to Sam Warren and Stephen Fineman's discussion of humour in the workplace in Chapter 6 – where a similar race took place as an unofficial response to attempts by the management to force fun on the organization. They discuss a case where humour was used by management as a deliberate workplace intervention to enhance the organizational culture of an office of a multinational information technology organization. Suggesting that contemporary organizations are increasingly using forms of 'designer fun', they examine how this played out in one organization. What they report is that, while the fun activities were put in place to improve the climate and culture of the organization, what occurred as a result of them was more complex. The employees in this organization not only engaged with the formal fun programs, but also responded to them in excessive ways – for example, racing around the office on a scooter in their very own Office Olympics. By examining the relation between the intentions of the program and its unintended consequences, Warren and Fineman conclude that simple dichotomies that promote a view of humour as being *either* managerialist *or* subversive did not hold. Instead, they propose that humour can be understood in four different ways, each of which can be present both in single organizations and within the responses of particular individuals. These four perspectives are that (1) organized fun is an oxymoron and therefore will inevitably fail, (2) organized fun is an oppressive means to silence dissent, (3) organized fun creates spaces for resistance and rebellion and (4) organized fun is a benign intervention that has become part of what is expected in contemporary organizations. Warren and Fineman conclude by noting that fun initiatives in organizations cannot be evaluated a priori as being *good* or *bad*. Similarly to Parker in Chapter 5, they suggest a broader and more ambivalent set of possibilities that may differ across and within both contexts and individuals.

If, as we have suggested so far, humour has a critical potential in terms of organizational power, one of its key dimensions is how this power relates to gendered relations at work. In Chapter 7, Allanah Johnson, Denis Mumby and Robert Westwood consider this important issue. The chapter shows how early research served to support and reproduce a gendered discourse about humour, even asserting that women lacked a sense of humour. Noting therefore the gendered nature of the discourses surrounding both organizations and humour, the chapter asks how women can construct and interpolate modes of humour that challenge rather than reproduce these discursive structures and the forms of power that support them. Indeed, it speculates on whether women can locate a form of humour that actually escapes the essentialisms and bifurcations of gender. The authors explore at least four issues. First, and looking at more recent research, they explore humour as a discursive resource through which gendered identities get played out in the context of organizational control, resistance, accommodation and transformation. Noting again the ambivalence of humour pointed to by Parker and Warren and Fineman, they consider how women's use of workplace humour can be a form of accommodation and/or resistance. Second, they consider the deployment of humour as a way of performing gendered organizational identity and of negotiating identity and relationships in the workplace. Third, they examine the potential of a feminine humour of excess, parody and irony to challenge and subvert gendered organizational order. Finally, they speculate on a feminist interrogation of humour that not only disturbs the dominion of hegemonic masculinity, but actually unsettles the essentializing binaries of gender.

The second part of the book closes with Meredith Marra's discussion of the goings on in workplace meetings – arenas which she presents as being distinctly and subversively humorous. By providing a critical discourse analysis of the transcripts of meetings that took place in a corporate organization in New Zealand, Marra demonstrates in some detail how humour was used to challenge hierarchical power relations and respond to inequality. Indeed, her claim is that humour is a central means by which those of low organizational status can achieve a degree of power in organizations. Humour is thus rendered central to a dynamic understanding of power that sees it as a shifting matrix relationally negotiated. As Marra is careful to note, however, humour might best be understood as being multifunctional. While humour acknowledges and challenges authority in workplace talk, it might simultaneously help make that authority more socially appealing and restore group harmony.

Humour of organizations

While the second part of the book examines various ways that humour is present within organizations, the study of humour and work does not end here. Indeed, as *Big Brother*'s Office Olympics illustrates, finding that organizations are funny is also the starting point for many humorous representations of work found in popular culture. It is the way that this is played out that provides the impetus for the third part of the book – the humour of organizations.

Part 3 begins with Rhodes and Pullen's discussion of humour and work found in the popular television program *The Simpsons*. Building on the themes of humorous subversion, Rhodes and Pullen examine *The Simpsons* as a carnivalesque critique of organizations – in particular a critique of work-based masculinity through a parody of the male body. Bringing together discussions of the body and its gendered inscription, and the analysis of carnival humour inspired by Bakhtin (1965/1984), they show how the grotesque realism of the bodies of the characters Homer Simpson and C. Montgomery Burns deeply undermine masculine stereotypes and render them ridiculous. Like the giant caricature of the boss in Big Brother, this is a humour of bodily exaggeration and degradation. Contrasting Burns's shrunken genitalia and Homer's gargantuan belly, Rhodes and Pullen claim that the subversive laugher of *The Simpsons* provides not only a raucous mockery and undermining of the fragility of masculinity, but also a means of understanding power and the potential to nourish the ability to conquer its terror. By confronting the cultural expectations of masculinity, Rhodes and Pullen argue, *The Simpsons* might just be a way to subvert the modes of knowledge that frame that culture and extend its domination.

While it is commonplace to regard popular culture representations as being confined to television programs, movies, fictional books and the like, it is also noteworthy that, with the rapid expansion of management education, the management textbook can also be regarded as a form of popular culture. From such a starting point, in Chapter 10, Damian O'Doherty considers the academic text in relation to humour. Situating his discussion within 'post-ironic' socio-political relations, O'Doherty radically questions the distinctions between the serious and funny. It is on this basis that he considers humour in relation to the massively popular textbook by Huczynksi and Buchanan (2001) called *Organizational Behaviour: An Introductory Text* – a phenomenon he refers to as *hucbuc*. On the one hand, as he notes, hucbuc contains within it many examples of humorous popular culture. It is, for example, filled with cartoons and references to Hollywood movies; indeed, a reference to *Big Brother*'s Office Olympics would not be out of place here. Pushing beyond such obvious connotations, and dubbing Huczynksi and Buchanan as the Laurel and Hardy of organizational analysis, O'Doherty goes further to characterize hucbuc as both an artefact and symptom of humour about organizations. This is a play of humour that exceeds location in the binary distinctions between humour as control *or* resistance, between humour as funny *or* serious ... and leaves us with the sheer meaninglessness of organization as we knew it.

The relations between the serious and the funny are also the subject of Stephen Linstead's discussion in Chapter 11. As he demonstrates, while humour might be funny, that does not mean that it cannot inspire a reflection of some of the deadly serious aspects of work. Linstead takes as his point of departure the massively successful American comedy television program *Seinfeld*. He begins by considering an episode of Seinfeld called *The New York Four* – this episode involves the main characters engaging in humorous repartee at the expense of a person they are observing being mugged in broad daylight. The humour this entails, he argues, is both funny *and* engages with serious moral questions – in this case the ethics of bystanding. Using the humour of Seinfeld as a springboard, Linstead extends into a discussion and elaboration of organization bystanding; something that he argues is a necessary condition for moral harassment in organizations. Through this discussion three main features of organizational bystanding are identified: ignoring what is going on in one's environment, the failure to recognize what is really happening and the refusal to act on injustice. Within such morally charged and complex predicaments, however, Linstead still maintains that it is shared laughter, both at ourselves and others, that might enable us to maintain a faith in humanity.

The organization of humour

While humour might be present in organizations, and while popular culture yields great effects from its treatment of humour, the fourth part of the book examines some different ways that humour is deliberately deployed for particular purposes: organizations which use humour to sell products, academics who use humour as a mode of organizational critique and comedians who use humour are the basis of their repertoire.

Some organizations deliberately try to make us laugh. This is particularly the case in terms of advertising – a medium of humour explored in Chapter 12 by Donncha Kavanagh and Don O' Sullivan. Focusing on television beer advertisements from the Unites States, Britain and Australia, they consider why humour is increasingly being used for advertising purposes by contemporary commercial organizations. Locating their discussion in the literature on humour and advertising, Kavanagh and O'Sullivan consider the way that humorous advertisements have increased in prevalence because they are in tune with the values of a romanticization of postmodernity – values such as intertextuality, reflexivity, self-referentiality, parody, paralogy and so forth. As an alternative to this, however, they also consider humour in advertising as a reaction against postmodernity. In this guise humour is a way of making reality tolerable and reducing anxiety. Humour in advertising can do this in a manner that creates a shared sociality through the presentation of a common exaggerated truth – a utopian vision that transcends the mundane. Such humour is again ambivalent: it might either liberate or entrap consumers.

If organizations can try to be funny, why can't academics do it? In Chapter 13 David Boje, Yue Cai-Hillon, Grace-Ann Rosile and Esther R. Thomas discuss a play that they wrote and produced entitled 'Grotesque Humor Regeneration of McDonaldization and McDonaldland'. The play is intended as an educational performance that examines and critiques the business behaviour of McDonald's in the global economy. Informed by the grotesque carnival humour of Mikhail Bakhtin, the 'Epic Theatre' satire of Bertolt Brecht, and Augusto Boal's 'theatre of the oppressed', the play is an example of how a combination of fictional and historical accounts of McDonald's were woven together in dramatic format that deliberately used humour for critical pedagogical purposes. As well as discussing the theoretical considerations that informed the play's development, the chapter also presents the full script of the play, and discusses its staging and reception at four academic conferences in 2004. The key point they make is that, as well as providing an arena for management and organization research, theoretical consideration of humour can also inform innovative forms of critical pedagogy. They conclude by asking whether management education is ready for a grotesque humour of global spectacle.

Even though organized work might be both the site of humour and the butt of jokes, there are some types of work whose very labour is being funny. In Chapter 14, Robert Westwood draws on field research and interviews with professional stand-up comedians to explore the organizational and managerial work that is involved in staging a comedic performance. In other words, he examines the organization of comedy and humour itself. Using Burke's dramatistic pentad as a heuristic device and taking that opportunity to incidentally critique the dramaturgical perspective, the chapter explores the performance of comedy in terms of Scene, Actor, Act, Agency and Purpose, with Goffman's notion of 'frame' also considered. The interviews and the analysis reveal the precariousness and vulnerability of comedic performance and focus particularly on those aspects of managing performance that have to do with managing self and managing the relationship with the audience. In examining these aspects of comedic performance, the chapter reflects on questions of self, authenticity and abjection and suggests that, while there is perhaps amplification in the case of comedians, their struggle to manage these issues in performance mirror the experience of many of us in our own work-related performance.

The chapters in this book have expressly eschewed a functionalist position with respect to humour. Indeed, the book looks with some alarm at the apparent appropriation of this most rich and elemental aspect of human behaviour for a functionalist, and within organizational studies, managerialist agenda. Such a trajectory vitiates a full consideration of humour in organizations, particularly its challenge to power and authority and its disruptive and subversive potential. What the chapters show is not only the fertile diversity of humour and its manifestations and significances within organizations, but also its complexities and ambivalences. We hope that the collection of chapters that make up this volume will contribute to a more open perspective of humour, work and organizations – one where the vast critical potential of humour in its myriad forms can come to be regarded both a pervasive and important part of organizational knowledge and workplace practice.

Let the games begin!

References

Ackroyd, S. and Thompson, P. (1999) *Organizational Misbehaviour*, London: Sage.

Avolio, B., Howell, J. M. and Sosik, J. J. (1999) 'A funny thing happened on the way to the bottom line: humour as a moderator of leadership style effects', *Academy of Management Journal*, 42(2): 219–27.

Bakhtin, M. M. (1965/1984) *Rabelais and his World*, tr. H. Iwolsky, Bloomington, IN: Indiana University Press.

Buchman, E. S. (ed.) (1994) *The Handbook of Humour: Clinical Applications in Psychotherapy*, Malabar, FL: Krieger Publishing Co.

Caudron, S. (1992) 'Humour is healthy in the workplace', *Personnel Journal* (June): 63–8.

Collinson, D. L. (1988) 'Engineering humour: masculinity, joking and conflict in shop-floor relations', *Organization Studies*, 92: 181–99.

Collinson, D. L. (2002) 'Managing humour', *Journal of Management Studies*, 39(3): 269–88.

Consalvo, C. M. (1989) 'Humour in management: no laughing matter', *Humour*, 2(3): 285–97.

Coser, R. L. (1960) 'Laughter among colleagues', *Psychiatry*, 23: 81–95.

Crawford, C. B. (1994) 'Theory and implications regarding the utilization of strategic humour by leaders', *Journal of Leadership Studies*, 1: 53–67.

Deal, T. T. and Kennedy, A. A. (2000) *The New Corporate Cultures*, London: Texere.

Duncan, W. J. (1982) 'Humour in management: prospects for administrative practice and research', *Academy of Management Review*, 7: 136–42.

Duncan, W. J. and Feisal, J. P. (1989) 'No laughing matter: patterns of humour in the workplace', *Organizational Dynamics*, 17(4): 18–30.

Duncan, W. J., Smeltzer, L. R. and Leap, T. L. (1990) 'Humour and work: application of joking behavior to management', *Journal of Management*, 16: 255–78.

Dwyer, T. (1991) 'Humour, power, and change in organizations', *Human Relations*, 44(1): 1–13.

Eco, U. (1986) 'The comic and the rule' (first published 1980, tr. William Weaver), in U. Eco, *Travels in Hyper-Reality*, pp. 275–7, London: Picador.

Gibson, D. E. (1994) 'Humour consulting: laughs for power and profit in organizations', *Humor*, 7(4): 403–28.

Griffiths, L. (1998) 'Humour as resistance to professional dominance in community mental health teams', *Sociology of Health and Illness*, 20(6): 874–95.

Grugulis, I. (2002) 'Nothing serious? Candidates' use humour in management training', *Human Relations*, 55(4): 387–406.

Holmes, J. (2000) 'Politeness, power and provocation: how humour functions in the workplace', *Discourse Studies*, 2(2): 159–85.

Huczynksi, A. and Buchanan, D. (2001) *Organizational Behaviour: An Introductory Text*, 4th edn, London: Pearson Education.

Jenkins, R. (1994) *Subversive Laughter: The Liberating Power of Comedy*, New York: Free Press.

Kahn, W. A. (1989) 'Toward a sense of organizational humour: implications for organizational diagnosis and change', *Journal of Applied Behavioral Science*, 25(1): 45–64.

Kushner, M. (1990) *The Light Touch: How to Use Humour for Business Success*, New York: Simon Schuster.

Linstead, S. (1985) 'Jokers wild: the importance of humour in the maintenance of organizational culture', *Sociological Review*, 33: 741–67.

Lundberg, C. C. (1969) 'Person-focused joking: pattern and function', *Human Organization*, 28: 22–8.

Malone, P. B. (1980) 'Humour: a double-edged tool for today's managers', *Academy of Management Review*, 5: 357–60.

Martin, R. A. and Lefcourt, H. M. (1983) 'Sense of humour as a moderator of the relation between stressors and moods', *Journal of Personality and Social Psychology*, 45: 1313–24.

O'Quin, K. and Aronoff, J. (1981) 'Humour as a technique of social influence', *Social Psychology Quarterly*, 44(4): 349–57.

Paulson, T. L. (1989) *Making Humour Work: Take your Job Seriously and Yourself Lightly*, Los Altos, CA: Crisp Publications.

Powell, C. (1977) 'Humour as a form of social control: a deviance approach', in A. J. Chapman and H. C. Foot (eds) *It's a Funny Thing, Humour*, pp. 53–5, Oxford: Pergamon.

Powell, C. and Paton, G. E. C. (eds) (1988) *Humour in Society: Resistance and Control*, Basingstoke: Macmillan.

Rodrigues, S. B. and Collinson, D. L. (1995) 'Having fun: humour as resistance in Brazil', *Organization Studies*, 16(5): 739–68.

Ross, B. (1989) *Laugh, Lead and Profit: Building Productive Workplaces with Humour*, San Diego, CA: Arrowhead.

Smith, E. E. and White, H. L. (1965) 'Wit, creativity, and sarcasm', *Journal of Applied Psychology*, 49: 131–4.

Taylor, P. and Bain, P. (2003) 'Subterranean worksick blues: humour as subversion in two call centres', *Organization Studies*, 24(9): 1487–509.

Traylor, G. (1973) 'Joking in a bush camp', *Human Relations*, 26: 479–86.

Ullian, J. A. (1976) 'Joking at work', *Journal of Communication*, 26 (Summer): 123–33.

Vinton, K. K. (1989) 'Humour in the workplace: it is more than telling jokes', *Small Group Behavior*, 20: 151–66.

Yovitch, N. A., Dale, J. A. and Hudak, M. A. (1990) 'Benefits of humour in reduction of threat-induced anxiety', *Psychological Reports*, 66: 51–8.

Part I

Theorizing humour, organization and work

Chapter 2

Humour as practically enacted theory, or, why critics should tell more jokes[1]

Simon Critchley

Imagine, if you will, a company called Humour Solutions International which endeavours to show how humour can produce greater social cohesion amongst the workforce and thereby increase efficiency and productivity. Some time ago, I was in Atlanta, staying at a huge hotel where one morning I had the occasion to observe such humour in action. About 50 people from the same company where engaged in collective hopscotch, frisbee and kickball under the guidance of some consultants. There was much yelping and clapping to be heard – the very soundtrack to happiness. After breakfast, I found a huddle of employees standing outside resolutely smoking in the Georgian drizzle and we exchanged a few words. I was enormously reassured that they felt just as cynical about the whole business as I did, but one of them said that they did not want to appear to be a bad sport or party pooper at work and that was why they went along with it. Also, he concluded, they were not really offered a choice. I think this incident is interesting for it reveals a vitally subversive feature of humour in the workplace. Namely, that as much as management consultants might try and formalize fun for the benefit of the company, where the comic punchline and the economic bottom line might be seen to blend, such fun is always capable of being ridiculed by informal, unofficial relations amongst employees. Anyone who has worked in a factory or office knows how the most scurrilous and usually obscene stories, songs and cartoons about the management are the very bread and butter of survival. Humour might be a management tool, but it can also be a tool against management.

That humour can be a tool against management is part of its broader social relevance. Of course with management and organizations being amongst the key institutions in contemporary society, it is not surprising that they are frequently the butt of jokes (as this volume demonstrates). So, despite how the managers might seek to appropriate humour for their own corporate purposes it also has much more critical and radical possibilities – possibilities that extend both within and beyond organizations. It is a theorization of the operation of these possibilities that I will look at in this chapter. In so doing I wish to explore humour's critical capacity in relation to everyday life.

Most humour simply seeks to reinforce consensus, as appeared to be intended by the management consultants. It in no way seeks to criticize the established order – if it toys with social hierarchies, it does so in a benign fashion that at best offers pleasurable yet transient relief. While recognizing the prevalence of such humour, in this chapter I am concerned mainly with another type of humour – one that, as was gestured to by the employees I briefly spoke to, works to serve a critical function. Such humour both reveals the situation by defamiliarizing it, and indicates how it might be changed. This humour is found in jokes that play with the accepted practices of a given society. Think of Charlie Chaplin in *Modern Times* where he satirizes the industrial machine by becoming a machine himself, in one memorable scene literally being ingested by the cogs of the industrial leviathan.

The incongruities of this humour speak both out of a massive congruence between joke structure and social structure, and against those structures by showing that they have no necessity. By laughing at power, we can expose its contingency, we can realize that what appeared to be fixed and oppressive is just the sort of thing that should be mocked and ridiculed. In other words, humour invites us to become philosophical spectators on our own lives; it is a practically enacted theory that might be said to be one of the conditions for taking up a critical position with respect to what passes for everyday life, producing a change in our situation which can be both liberating and elevating.

Theorising humour

Jokes tear holes in our usual predictions about the empirical world. We might say that humour is produced by a disjunction between the way things are and the way they are represented in the joke, between expectation and actuality. Humour defeats our expectations by producing a novel actuality, by changing the situation in which we find ourselves. Examples are legion, from boy bishops reciting learned sermons, to incompetent managers, to talking dogs, hamsters and bears, to farting professors and incontinent ballerinas, to straight linguistic inversion: 'I could wait for you until the cows come home. On second thoughts I'd rather wait for the cows until you come home'. Of course, this is hardly news. One already finds Cicero writing in *De Oratore*, 'The most common kind of joke is that in which we expect one thing and another is said; here our own disappointed expectation makes us laugh'. The comic world is not simply *die verkehrte Welt,* the inverted or upside-down world of philosophy, but rather the world with its causal chains broken, its social practices turned inside out and common-sense rationality left in tatters.

Of course, a similar tension between expectation and actuality might itself be claimed in the relation between the various objects of humour and any theoretical explanation thereof, the difference being that a theory of humour is not humorous. A joke explained is a joke misunderstood. In this case, what might make one laugh – albeit as dramatic irony – is the audacity or arrogance of the attempt to write a philosophy of humour. For example, persons who might not otherwise feel themselves to be experts in metapsychology or French spiritualism somehow feel confident in dismissing Freud's theory of jokes or Bergson's account of laughter because they are either not funny or simply miss the point. When it comes to what amuses us, we are all authorities, experts in the field. We *know* what we find funny. Nevertheless, the fact remains that humour is a nicely impossible object for a philosopher. But herein lies its irresistible attraction.

In an effort to approach this nicely impossible object, I have been filling much of my time lately reading books on humour and laughter. This is a surprisingly vast field, and much of the empirical research is extremely pleasurable. The further one looks, the more there is to see, not so much in philosophy, but more in the areas of history, literary history, theology and history of religion, sociology and anthropology.

There are many explanations of laughter and humour that John Morreall (1987) does well to distil into three theories: the superiority theory, the relief theory and the incongruity theory. In the first theory, represented by Plato, Aristotle, Quintillian and, at the dawn of the modern era, Hobbes, we laugh from feelings of superiority over other people, from 'suddaine Glory arising from suddaine Conception of some Eminency in our selves, by Comparison with the Infirmityes of others, or with our owne formerly'. Laughter is that 'passion, which hath no name', which would be forbidden to the virtuous guardians of Plato's imagined philosophical city. It is the superiority theory that dominates the philosophical tradition until the eighteenth century, and we shall have recourse to it in the discussion of ethnic humour. The relief theory emerges in the nineteenth century in the work of Herbert Spencer, where laughter is explained as a release of pent-up nervous energy, but the theory is best known in the version given in Freud's 1905 book *Jokes and their Relation to the Unconscious*, where the energy that is relieved and discharged in laughter provides pleasure because it allegedly economizes upon energy that would ordinarily be used to contain or repress psychic activity. Finally, the incongruity theory can be traced to Francis Hutcheson's *Reflections upon Laughter* from 1750, but is elaborated in related, but distinct, ways in Kant, as we shall see presently, Schopenhauer and Kierkegaard. As James Russell Lowell writes in 1870, 'Humour in its first analysis is a perception of the incongruous'. Humour is produced by the experience of a felt incongruity between what we know or expect to be the case, and what actually takes place in the joke, gag, jest or blague: 'Did you see me at Princess Diana's funeral? I was the one who started the Mexican wave'. Although I will refer to the other theories below, my discussion here is concerned mostly with the idea of humour as incongruity

So, can we describe what takes place in a joke? How might we give what philosophers call the 'phenomenology' of a joke? First, joking is a specific and meaningful practice that the audience and the joke-teller recognize as such. There is a tacit social contract at work here, namely some agreement about the social world in which we find ourselves as the implicit background to the joke. There has to be a sort of consensus or implicit shared understanding as to what constitutes joking 'for us', as to which linguistic or visual routines are recognized as joking. That is, in order for the incongruity of the joke to be seen as such, there has to be a congruence between joke structure and social structure – no social congruity, no comic incongruity. When this implicit congruence or tacit contract is missing, then laughter will probably not result, which can be the experience of trying – and failing – to tell a joke in a foreign language. Bergson (1980: 65) explains what he calls 'the leading idea in all our investigations' in *Le rire*:

> To understand laughter, we must put it back into its natural environment, which is society, and above all we must determine the utility of its function, which is a social one … . Laughter must answer to certain requirements of life in common. It must have a *social* signification.

So, in listening to a joke, I am presupposing a social world that is shared, the forms of which the practice of joke-telling is going to play with. Joking is a game that players only play successfully when they both understand and follow the rules. Wittgenstein (1980: 83) puts the point perspicuously,

> What is it like for people not to have the same sense of humour? They do not react properly to each other. It's as though there were a custom amongst certain people for one person to throw another a ball which he is supposed to catch and throw back; but some people, instead of throwing it back, put it in their pocket.

This is also what Mary Douglas (1975) has in mind in her groundbreaking anthropological work on the subject when she compares jokes with rites. A rite is here understood as a symbolic act that derives its meaning from a cluster of socially legitimated symbols, such as a funeral. But insofar as the joke plays with the symbolic forms of society – the bishop gets stuck in a lift, I spread margarine on the communion wafer – jokes are *anti-rites*. They mock, parody or deride the ritual practices of a given society, as Milan Kundera (1983: 232–3) remarks,

'Someone's hat falls on the coffin in a freshly dug grave, the funeral loses its meaning and laughter is born'.

Suppose that someone starts to tell you a joke: 'I never left the house as a child. My family were so poor that my mother couldn't afford to buy us clothes'. First, I recognize that a joke is being told and I assent to having my attention caught in this way. Assenting to having my attention caught is very important and if someone interrupts the joke-teller or simply walks away in the middle of the joke, then the tacit social contract of humour has been broken. This is bad form or simply bad manners. Instead of throwing the ball back, I put it in my pocket. In thus assenting and going along with the joke, a certain tension is created in the listener and I follow along willingly with the story that is being recounted. When the punchline kicks in, and the little bubble of tension pops, I experience an affect that can be described as pleasure, and I laugh or just smile: 'When I was ten my mother bought me a hat, so that I could look out of the window'.

What happens here is, as Kant (1952: 196–203) puts it in a brilliant short discussion of laughter from *The Critique of Judgement,* a sudden evaporation of expectation to nothing ('ein Affekt aus der plötzlichen Verwandlung einer gespannten Erwartung in nichts'). In hearing the punchline, the tension disappears and we experience comic relief. Rather than the tiresome and indeed racist examples of jokes that Kant recounts, involving Indians and bottles of beer, witness Philip Larkin (1974: 11) (that celebrated anti-racist!) in a characteristic flourish:

> When I drop four cubes of ice
> Chimingly in a glass, and add
> Three goes of gin, a lemon slice,
> And let a ten-ounce tonic void
> In foaming gulps until it smothers
> Everything else up to the edge,
> I lift the lot in silent pledge:
> *He devoted his life to others.*

The admittedly rather dry humour here is found in a combination of two features: conceptual and rhetorical. On the one hand, there is the conceptual disjunction between the wanton hedonism involved in preparing the gin and tonic, and the avowed altruism of the final line. But also – more importantly – there is the rhetorical effect generated by the sudden bathos of the final line in comparison to the cumulative and almost Miltonic overkill of what precedes it. Picking up on Hobbes's word, it is important to emphasize the necessary *suddenness* of the conceptual and rhetorical shift. Both brevity and speed are the soul of wit.

Mention of the suddenness of the bathetic shift that produces humour brings attention to the peculiar *temporal* dimension of jokes. As any comedian will readily admit, timing is everything, and a mastery of comic forms involves a careful control of pauses, hesitations and silences, of knowing exactly when to detonate the little dynamite of the joke. In this sense, jokes involve a shared knowledge of two temporal dimensions: of *duration* and the *instant*. What I mean is that when we give ourselves up to being told a joke, we undergo a peculiar and quite deliberate distention of time, where the practice of joking often involves cumulative repetition and wonderfully needless circumlocution. This is a technique brought to its digressive nadir in the 'shaggy dog' or 'cock and bull' story, such as *Tristram Shandy*.

> Digressions, incontestably, are the sun-shine – they are the life, the soul of reading, – take them out of this book for instance, – you might as well take the book along with them.
>
> (Sterne 1997: 58)

In being told a joke, we undergo a particular experience of duration through repetition and digression, of time being stretched out like an elastic band. We know that the elastic will snap, we just don't know when, and we find that anticipation rather pleasurable. It snaps with the punchline, which is a sudden acceleration of time, where the digressive stretching of the joke suddenly contracts into a heightened experience of the instant. We laugh. Viewed temporally, humorous pleasure would seem to be produced by the disjunction between duration and the instant, where we experience with renewed intensity both the slow passing of time and its sheer evanescence.

It is important to recall that the succession of tension by relief in humour is an essentially bodily affair. That is, the joke invites a corporeal response, from a chuckle, through a giggle to a guffaw. Laughter is a muscular phenomenon, consisting of spasmodic contraction and relaxation of the facial muscles with corresponding movements in the diaphragm. The associated contractions of the larynx and epiglottis interrupt the pattern of breathing and emit sound. Descartes puts the point much more exotically and powerfully in Article 124 of *The Passions of the Soul*:

> Laughter consists in the fact that the blood, which proceeds from the right orifice in the heart by the arterial vein, inflating the lungs suddenly and repeatedly, causes the air which they contain to be constrained and to pass out from them with an impetus by the windpipe, where it forms an inarticulate and explosive utterance; and the lungs in expanding equally with the air as it rushes out, set in motion all the muscles of the diaphragm

from the chest to the neck, by which means they cause motion in the facial muscles, which have a certain connection with them. And it is just this action of the face with this inarticulate and explosive voice that we call laughter.

It is just this interruption of breath that distinguishes laughter from smiling. As a bodily phenomenon, laughter invites comparison with similar convulsive phenomena like orgasm and weeping. Indeed, like the latter, laughter is distinguished by what Helmuth Plessner (1982: 185) calls 'A loss of self-control as the break between the person and their body' ('Verlust der Selbstbeherrschung als Bruch zwischen der Person und ihrem Körper'). In laughing violently, I lose self-control in a way that is akin to the moments of radical corporeal exposure that follow an orgasm or when crying turns into an uncontrollable sobbing. Picking up on a word employed by Descartes, and used by a whole tradition extending to Charles Baudelaire, André Breton and Plessner, laughter is an *explosion* expressed with the body. In a lovely formulation, Kant speaks of 'die Schwingung der Organen', 'the oscillation of the organs'. When I laugh vigorously, I literally experience an oscillation or vibration of the organs, which is why it can hurt when you laugh, if you engage in it a little too enthusiastically. Of course, as Jacques Le Goff (1997: 45) reminds us, the historical associations between laughter and the body cannot be overemphasized. It is this link to the body that was the reason for the Christian condemnation of laughter in the early Middle Ages, its careful codification in the later Middle Ages, before the explosion of laughter in the early Renaissance, in the work of Rabelais and Erasmus.

Critique and true humour

But is that an end to the matter? Hopefully not. For I want to claim that humour is not just comic relief, a transient corporeal affect induced by the raising and extinguishing of tension, of as little social consequence as masturbation, although slightly more acceptable to perform in public. I rather want to claim that what goes on in humour is a form of *liberation* or *elevation* that expresses something essential to what Plessner calls 'the humanity of the human'. But, as a provisional outline of the thought I am after, let me turn to the character of Eddie Waters, the philosopher-comedian from Trevor Griffiths's brilliant 1976 piece *Comedians*,

> A real comedian – that's a daring man. He *dares* to see what his listeners shy away from, fear to express. And what he sees is a sort of truth about people, about their situation, about what hurts or terrifies them, about

what's hard, above all, about what they *want*. A joke releases the tension, says the unsayable, any joke pretty well. But a true joke, a comedian's joke, has to do more than release tension, it has to *liberate* the will and the desire, it has to *change the situation*. (p. 20)

A true joke, a comedian's joke, suddenly and explosively lets us see the familiar defamiliarized, the ordinary made extraordinary and the real rendered surreal, and we laugh in a physiological squeal of transient delight, like an infant playing peek-a-boo: nurse to uncooperative patient, 'We have to see if you have a temperature'; uncooperative patient to nurse, 'Don't be silly, *everybody* has a temperature'. Humour brings about a change of situation, a *surrealization* of the real which is why someone like the great surrealist André Breton (1966) was so interested in humour, in particular the unsentimental subversions of what he baptized 'l'humour noir'.

This idea of a change of situation can be caught in Mary Douglas's (1975: 96) claim that 'A joke is a play upon form that affords an opportunity for realizing that an accepted pattern has no necessity'. Thus, jokes are a play upon form, where what is played with are the accepted practices of a given society. The incongruities of humour both speak out of a massive congruence between joke structure and social structure, and speak against those structures by showing that they have no necessity – of course, the social structure of work organizations is not immune here. The anti-rite of the joke shows the sheer contingency or arbitrariness of the social rites in which we engage. By producing a consciousness of contingency, humour can change the situation in which we find ourselves, and can even have a *critical* function with respect to society. Hence the great importance that humour has played in social movements that have set out to criticize the established order, such as radical feminist humour: 'How many men does it take to tile a bathroom?' 'I don't know'. 'It depends how thinly you slice them'. As the Italian Situationist street slogan has it, *Una risata vi seppellirà,* it will be a laugh that buries you, where the 'you' refers to those in power. By laughing at power, we expose its contingency, we realize that what appeared to be fixed and oppressive is in fact the emperor's new clothes, and just the sort of thing that should be mocked and ridiculed.

But before we get carried away, it is important to recognize that not all humour is of this type, and most of the best jokes are fairly reactionary or, at best, simply serve to reinforce social consensus. You will have noticed a couple of paragraphs back that, following Eddie Waters, I introduced the adjective 'true' into our discussion of humour. 'True' humour changes the situation, tells us something about who we are and the sort of place we live in, and perhaps indicates to us how it might be changed.

Most humour, in particular the comedy of recognition – and most humour *is* comedy of recognition – simply seeks to reinforce consensus and in no way seeks to criticize the established order or change the situation in which we find ourselves. Such humour simply toys with existing social hierarchies in a charming but quite benign fashion, as in P. G. Wodehouse's *The World of Jeeves*. This is the comic as sheer pleasing diversion, and it has an important place in any taxonomy of humour. More egregiously, much humour seeks to confirm the status quo either by denigrating a certain sector of society, as in sexist humour, or by laughing at the alleged stupidity of a social outsider. Thus, the British laugh at the Irish, the Canadians laugh at the Newfies, the Americans laugh at the Poles, the Swedes laugh at the Finns, the Germans laugh at the Ostfrieslanders, the Greeks laugh at the Pontians, the Czechs laugh at the Slovaks, the Russians laugh at the Ukrainians, the French laugh at the Belgians, the Dutch also laugh at the Belgians, and so on and so forth. Such comic scapegoating corresponds to what Hobbes means in suggesting that laughter is a feeling of sudden glory where I find another person ridiculous and laugh at their expense. Such humour is not laughter at power, but the powerful laughing at the powerless.

To talk, as I do, of true humour must presuppose some sort of normative claim, namely a distinction between 'good' and 'bad' jokes. However, such a claim must not be reduced to moral crispbread, but must be properly leavened and smeared with tasty examples. I will try and do this below when I make the distinction between *laughing at oneself* and *laughing at others*. In my view, true humour does not wound a specific victim and always contains self-mockery. The object of laughter is the subject who laughs. By way of preparation for this thought, we might cite a few of the closing lines from 'Verses on the Death of Dr Swift', an exquisitely bleak *apologia pro sua vita*,

> Perhaps I may allow the Dean
> Had too much satire in his vein;
> And seemed determined not to starve it,
> Because no age could more deserve it.
> Yet malice never was his aim;
> He lashed the vice but spared the name.
> No individual could resent,
> Where thousands equally were meant.
> His satire points at no defect,
> But what all mortals may correct;
> For he abhorred that senseless tribe,
> Who call it humour when they jibe:
> He spar'd a hump or crooked nose,
> Whose owners set not up for beaux.

> True genuine dullness moved his pity,
> Unless it offered to be witty.
>
> (Swift 1977: 85–6)

The critical task of humour, then, would not be sheer malice or jibing, but the lashing of vices which are general and not personal, 'no individual could resent, / Where thousands equally were meant'. Also, such lashing of vices does not point at a fundamental defect, 'But what all mortals may correct'. That is, true humour can be said to have a therapeutic as well as a critical function. The studied reversals of perspective and fantastical geographical displacements of Swift's (1967) *Gulliver's Travels*, offer, it is true, a devastating critique of the follies and vices of the modern European world, but the intent of the satire is therapeutic, to bring human beings back from what they have become to what they might be. Satire is often a question of scale, of the familiar becoming infinitely small or grotesquely huge, which can be seen in Gulliver's voyages from the littleness of Lilliput to the bigness of Brobdingnag. But, I would insist, from the studied savaging of modern mathematics, science and government in Laputa and the Academy of Lagado, through to the final descent into misanthropy caused by life with the fully rational animals of the land of the Houyhnhnms, Swift is offering a teaching of virtue that permits Gulliver and the rest of us to be reconciled to life amongst the vicious Yahoos. In my view, this is what Swift means when he complains to Alexander Pope in correspondence from 1725, 'I tell you after all that I do not hate mankind, it is *vous autres* who hate them because you would have them reasonable animals, and are angry for being disappointed' (cited in Price 1973) . For, after all, I am a Yahoo and you are too.

Humour both reveals the situation, and indicates how that situation might be changed. That is to say, laughter has a certain redemptive or messianic power. So, does this mean that true humour has to be religious? The argumentation linking humour to religion is impeccable enough and much great comic writing is Christian, particularly when one thinks of Pope, Swift and Sterne. The briefest glance at M. A. Screech's *Laughter at the Foot of the Cross* (1997) confirms the place of laughter in the Bible and in the self-understanding of Christianity through the ages. From the standpoint of the worldly wise, Christ appears to be a kind of madman. Where the world admires money, power and success, the Christian indifference to these values turns the secular world upside down. It is this folly of the cross that Erasmus understood so well, and which makes his *Praise of Folly* a powerful work of both comedy and confession. Christianity offers us a topsy-turvy world that inverts our worldly values. W. H. Auden (1973: 472) is therefore quite right when he says that:

The world of Laughter is much more closely related to the world of Prayer than either is to the everyday secular world of Work, for both are worlds in which we are all equal, in the first as individual members of our species, in the latter as unique persons … . In the world of Work, on the other hand, we are not and cannot be equal, only diverse and interdependent … those who try to live by Work alone, without Laughter or Prayer turn into insane lovers of power, tyrants who would enslave Nature to their immediate desires – an attempt which can only end in utter catastrophe, shipwreck on the isle of Sirens.[2]

If laughter lets us see the folly of the world in order to imagine a better world in its place, and to change the situation in which we find ourselves, then I have no objection to the religious interpretation of humour. True jokes would therefore be like shared prayers.

My quibble is rather the following: that the religious world-view invites us to look away from this world towards another in which, in Peter Berger's (1997: 210) words, 'the limitations of the human condition are miraculously overcome'. Humour lets us view the folly of the world by affording us the glimpse of another world, by offering what Berger calls 'a signal of transcendence'. However, in my view, humour does not redeem us from this world, but returns us to it ineluctably by showing that there is no alternative. The consolations of humour come from acknowledging that this is the only world and, imperfect as it is and we are, it is only here that we can make a difference. Therefore, the redemptive power of humour is not, as it is in Kierkegaard, the transition from the ethical to the religious point of view, where humour is the last stage of existential awareness before faith. Humour is not 'nuomenal' but phenomenal, not theological but anthropological, not numinous but simply luminous. By showing us the folly of the world, humour does not *save* us from that folly by turning our attention elsewhere, as it does in great Christian humour like Erasmus, but calls on us to face the folly of the world and change the situation in which we find ourselves.

Humour as practically enacted theory

Laughter is contagious – think of the intersubjectivity of giggling, particularly when it concerns something obscene in a context where one should be serious, such as listening to a formal academic paper or a management pep-talk. In such cases, and I am sure (or hope) that we all know them, the laughter can really hurt. One might say that the simple telling of a joke recalls us to what is shared in our everyday practices. It makes explicit the enormous commonality that is implicit in our social life. This is what Shaftesbury (1964) had in mind in the early eighteenth century when he spoke of humour as a form of *sensus communis*.

So humour reveals the depth of what we share. But, crucially, it does this not through the clumsiness of a theoretical description, but more quietly, practically and discreetly. Laughter suddenly breaks out in a bus queue, watching a party-political broadcast in a pub, when someone farts in a lift, or when listening to the false rhetoric of a self-aggrandizing CEO. Humour is an exemplary practice because it is a universal human activity that invites us to become philosophical spectators upon our lives. It is practically enacted theory. I think this is why Wittgenstein once said that he could imagine a book of philosophy that would be written entirely in the form of jokes.

The extraordinary thing about humour is that it returns us to common sense by distancing us from it. Humour familiarizes us with a common world through its miniature strategies of defamiliarization. If humour recalls us to *sensus communis*, then it does this by momentarily pulling us out of common sense, where jokes function as moments of *dissensus communis*. At its most powerful, say in those insanely punning dialogues between Chico and Groucho Marx, humour is a paradoxical form of speech and action that defeats our expectations, producing laughter with its unexpected verbal inversions, contortions and explosions, a refusal of everyday speech that lights up the everyday, showing it, in Adorno's (1974: 247) words, 'as it will one day appear in the messianic light'. Some sundry examples:

1   'What'll I say?' 'Tell them you're not here.' 'Suppose they don't believe me?' 'They'll believe you when you start talking.'
2   'Do you believe in the life to come?' 'Mine was always that.'
3   'Have you lived in Blackpool all your life?' 'Not yet.'
4   'Do me a favour and close the window, it's cold outside.' 'And if I close it, will that make it warm outside?'
5   'Do you want to use a pen?' 'I can't write.' 'That's OK, there wasn't any ink in it anyway.'
6   'Which of the following is the odd one out? Greed, envy, malice, anger and kindness.' *(Pause)* 'And.'
7   'Gentlemen, Chicolini here may talk like an idiot, and look like an idiot, but don't let that fool you. He really is an idiot. I implore you, send him back to his father and brothers who are waiting for him with open arms at the penitentiary. I suggest that we give him ten years at Leavenworth, or eleven years at Twelveworth.' 'I tell you what I'll do. I'll take five and ten and Woolworth.'[3]

To put it in a rather baroque formulation, humour changes the situation in which we find ourselves, or lights up the everyday by providing an *oblique phenomenology of ordinary life*. Let me quickly illustrate this claim by recalling the quotation from Epictetus, which provides the motto to volumes 1 and 2 of Sterne's (1997) *Tristram Shandy*: 'Human beings are troubled with the opinions *(dogmata)* they have of things, and not by the things themselves *(pragmata)*'. How is one to understand this epigraph in relation to Sterne's book? *Tristram Shandy* can evidently be viewed as an extended exploration of the fact that human beings are more troubled with *dogmata*, or their *hobby horses*, than with the things themselves. What Sterne calls 'the Shandian system' is entirely made up of digressions. For example, the digressions on the character and opinions of Mr Walter Shandy show him unable to view the world except through what Sterne calls his *hypotheses*: on names, on noses, on the best technique for birth in order to protect the delicate web of the cerebellum, and so on, and on, and on. And sweet Uncle Toby only sees things hobby-horsically through his obsession with the science of fortification and the attempt to reconstruct the precise dimensions of the siege of Namur where he received the terrible, but ever-obscure, blow to his groin.

Of course, the world viewed from a hobby-horsical, dogmatic perspective inevitably goes awry: Walter Shandy's son is given the wrong name, Tristram instead of Trismegistus, his nose is crushed following a forceps delivery, and the web of the cerebellum – seat of all wisdom – is irreparably crushed following a head-first birth ... And I almost forgot to add that Tristram is inadvertently circumcised by a window sash. Uncle Toby exchanges his heroic campaigns with Corporal Trim on the bowling green for his *amours* with the Widow Wadman, which end in disenchantment when the good Corporal explains to Toby that Mrs Wadman's interest in the wound upon his groin is not simply born from compassion. As Sterne remarks, 'Endless is the quest for truth'.

Yet, where do all these digressions lead? What cosmic truth does the Shandian system reveal to us? Perhaps this: that through the meandering circumlocutions of *Tristram Shandy*, the story of 'a COCK and a BULL ... and one of the best of its kind, I ever heard', we progressively approach the things themselves, the various *pragmata* that make up the stuff of what we call the ordinary life. That is to say, the infinitely digressive movement of Sterne's prose actually contains a contrary motion within it, which is progressive. We might think of this as a comic phenomenology which is animated by a concern for the things themselves, the things which show themselves when we get rid of our troubling opinions. Humourless dogmatism is replaced by humorous pragmatism. Although it is hardly a Cartesian discourse on the method, Sterne (1997: 58) writes of his procedure in the book:

> For in this long digression which I was accidentally lead into, as in all my digressions (one only excepted) there is a master-stroke of digressive skill, the merit of which has all along, I fear, been overlooked by my reader, – not

for want of penetration in him – but because 'tis an excellence seldom looked for, or expected indeed, in a digression; – and that I fly off from what I am about, as far and as often as any writer in *Great Britain;* yet I constantly take care to order affairs so, that my main business does not stand still in my absence ...

By this contrivance the machinery of my work is of a species by itself; two contrary motions are introduced into it, and reconciled, which were thought to be at variance with each other. In a word, my work is digressive, and it is progressive too, – and at the same time.

This is why, to recall my earlier citation from Sterne, digressions are the sunshine, the life and the soul of reading, 'take them out of this book for instance, – and you might as well take the book along with them'. Inasmuch as the book digresses, it also progresses by a contrary motion. In my view, it is this combination of these two contrary motions – progressive and digressive – that is at the heart of humour. That is to say, through the endless displacement of seeing the world through another's hobby horse, through the eyes of a Walter or a Toby Shandy, one is brought closer to the things themselves, to the finally laughable enigma of ordinary life.

Coda

If we think back to my anecdote at the beginning of this chapter, it is clear that the products and services offered by Humour Solutions International do not embody the type of true humour that I have been exploring. Instead we can say that the jokes and humour of the everyday serve as small anthropological essays. If one of the tasks of the anthropologist is to revise and relativize the categories of Western culture by bumping them up against cultures hitherto adjudged exotic, then we might say with Henk Driessen (1997: 227) that:

> Anthropology shares with humour the basic strategy of defamiliarization: common sense is disrupted, the unexpected is evoked, familiar subjects are situated in unfamiliar, even shocking contexts in order to make the audience or readership conscious of their own cultural assumptions.

The lesson that Driessen draws from this is that anthropologists are akin to comedians, tricksters, clowns or jesters. The lesson that we can draw from Driessen, and from the discussion above, is that humour is a form of critical social anthropology, defamiliarizing the familiar, demythologizing the exotic and inverting the world of common sense. Humour views the world awry, bringing us back to the everyday by estranging us from it. Humour then provides an oblique phenomenology of ordinary life. It is a practice that gives us an alien perspective on our practices. It lets us view the world as if we had just landed from another planet. The comedian is the anthropologist of our humdrum everyday lives. Moreover, it is humour's capacity for defamiliarization that, at its best, can help liberate us from the taken-for-granted structures and practices of power that can so easily dominate the seriousness of life.

Notes

1   This chapter is adapted from Critchley (2002).
2   My thanks to Peter Howarth for alerting me to this passage.
3   From various Marx Brothers' scripts, Chelsom's wonderful 1994 film *Funny Bones* and Samuel Beckett's *Endgame* (1958).

References

Adorno, T. (1974) *Minima Moralia*, London: Verso.
Auden, W. H. (1973) *Forewords and Afterwords*, London: Faber.
Beckett, S. (1958) *Endgame*, London: Faber.
Berger, P. L. (1997) *Redeeming Laughter: The Comic Dimension of Human Experience*, Berlin and New York: De Gruyter.
Bergson, H. (1980) *Laughter*, Baltimore, MD: Johns Hopkins University Press.
Breton, A. (1966) *Anthologie de l'humour noir*, Paris: Jean-Jacques Pauvert.
Critchley, S. (2002) *On Humour*, London: Routledge.
Descartes, R. (1649) *Les passions de l'ame*, Paris: Henry Le Gras.
Douglas, M. (1975) *Implicit Meanings: Essays in Anthropology*, London: Routledge.
Driessen, H. (1997) 'Humour, laughter and the field: reflections from anthropology', in J. Bremmer and H. Roodenburg (eds) *A Cultural History of Humour*, pp. 222–41, Malden, MA: Polity Press.
Freud, S. (1905/1976) *Jokes and Their Relation to the Unconsicous*, London: Penguin.
Griffiths, T. (1976) *Comedians*, London: Faber.
Hutcheson, F. (1750) *Reflections pon Laughter and Remarks upon the Fable of the Bees*, Glasgow: Baxter.
Kant, I. (1952) *The Critique of Judgement*, tr. J. C. Meredith, Oxford: Oxford University Press.
Kundera, M. (1983) *The Book of Laughter and Forgetting*, London: Penguin.
Larkin, P. (1974) *High Windows*, London: Faber.
Le Goff, J. (1997) 'Laughter in the Middle Ages', in J. Bremmer and H. Roodenburg (eds) *A Cultural History of Humour*, pp. 40–53, Cambridge: Polity Press.
Lowell, J. R. (1870) 'A Virginian in New England thirty-five years ago, I–IV', *The Atlantic Monthly*, 26(154): 158.
Morreall, J. (ed.) (1987) *The Philosophy of Laughter and Humour*, Albany, NY: State University of New York Press.
Plessner, H. (1982) *Mit anderen Augen: Aspekte einer philosophischen Anthropologie*, Stuttgart: Reclam.

Price, M. (ed.) (1973) *The Restoration and the Eighteenth Century*, Oxford: Oxford University Press.

Screech, M. A. (1997) *Laughter at the Foot of the Cross*, London: Penguin.

Shaftesbury, A., Earl of (1964) *Characteristics of Men, Manners, Opinions, Times*, vols 1–2, New York: Bobbs-Merrill.

Sterne, L. (1997) *The Life and Opinions of Tristram Shandy, Gentleman*, ed. M. and J. New, London: Penguin.

Swift, J. (1967) *Gulliver's Travels*, London: Penguin.

Swift, J. (1977) *Selected Poems*, ed. C. H. Sisson, Manchester: Carcanet.

Wittgenstein, L. (1980) *Culture and Value*, ed. G. H. Von Wright, Oxford: Blackwell.

Chapter 3

Humour and violation

Heather Höpfl

I am meeting my old friend Gerda Roper, Dean of the Faculty of Art and Media at the University of Teesside. Gerda is one of those rare people who seem always to be bathed in light. Not in the sense of an aura, you understand. More as if she is always in a moving spotlight. She is an artist and she talks like an artist. 'Darling,' she purrs, 'how absolutely delicious to see you'. We settle into conversation, but as we chat, her eye keeps travelling down to the Waterstones' carrier bag I have on the seat beside me. I have just bought Stephen Barber's book, *The Screaming Body*, a study of the works of Antonin Artaud, and it rests between us concealed, as if pornographic, in a black bag. 'Just a book on Artaud', I say thinking she is wondering what I have bought. But she picks up the bag and slowly begins to read, 'I cheated in the final of my metaphysics exam. I looked into the soul of the boy sitting next to me. Woody Allen', and we look at each other and laugh.

Humour

It is not my intention in this short essay to lay the theoretical foundations of the nature of humour in a way which makes it accessible to organization theory. I will leave this task to my fellow contributor, Simon Critchley, whose book, *On Humour* (2002), is an informative and concise introduction to the subject. My purpose in this chapter is more straightforward. The chapter seeks to examine the disjunctive effects of humour: to give attention to the way that humour functions to perform a phenomenological act, to challenge taken-for-granted meanings and understandings and to introduce disjuncture into the expectation of continuity. Humour violates trajectories, breaches the notion of inevitability and disposes of social convention. This is true whether the humour be crude and slapstick, like a custard pie in the face, or sophisticated and witty, like the insights of a Tom Stoppard play. Humour violates. *Monty Python's Flying Circus* always began by announcing this breach of expectation, 'and now for something completely different'. To this extent, humour is catastrophic (a. Gr. καταστ ροφη overturning, sudden turn, conclusion, f. κατα-στρεφειν to overturn, etc., f. κατα down + στρεφειν to turn). It involves a 'sudden turn' in the expectations of the way in which a scene is played out. From the embarrassed laughter caused by an inappropriate flatus, to the belly laughter provoked by Peter Kay's tales of a family wedding; from the smile of satisfaction at understanding a clever joke to the discomfiture brought on by an episode of *Fawlty Towers*: humour is recusant. It is a resistance to things as they are. It is irreverent and subversive. It deals in shared understandings of what is and what is overturned, and also of shared understandings of what is apposite about such overturnings. In producing this chapter, I have tried to work with Umberto Eco's writing on humour and his observations on the comic (Eco 1986) but I have also tried to write in a way which is sympathetic to Eco's own style of writing: self reflexive and sardonic. Consequently, this chapter draws on both Eco's work and personal observations.

Joke

It is often said that a joke which has to be explained is not funny. There is an elegance to the formulation of a joke. The *punchline* must deliver, must hit its mark. Otherwise, and this is a matter of timing as well as pertinence, the rhetorical trajectory of the joke will fail. Once when I was working in the theatre, one of the actors was telling me that she had had a cleaning firm round to clean her carpets. She had been flirting with the man from the cleaning firm and she leaned closer to intimate to me that she had discovered that the cleaner had an interesting hobby – 'muff diving'. She looked at me and threw back her head and laughed. Being an innocent in the land of sirens, I both betrayed my innocence and ruined her joke by saying, 'Does he need a lot of equipment for that?' She laughed both at my naivety and at my accidental extension of the joke. And then, when she explained, we both laughed. *She let me in on the joke*. Humour is consensual. When women naval officers complained about being molested by fellow officers at the infamous Tailhook Convention in Las Vegas in 1991, it was said that they 'couldn't take a joke', or as Faludi put it at the time of the subsequent report into the goings on at Tailhook, 'Feminism, we hear once again, is just a euphemism for Puritanism' (Faludi 1994). So, for example, one airman commented that the assaults were intended 'in a good-natured, lighthearted way' and when one woman officer reported her story to her superiors she was told, 'That's what you get when you go to a hotel party with a bunch of drunk aviators' (Boo 1992). Where such behaviour is not consensual, it is not funny. In this case, the assumptions about what was permitted were not shared *by all* participants. Hence, the first consideration to be carried forward is that humour rests on shared meanings.

Violations

In the argument that follows, I have tried to give attention to the notion of violation: the violation of the rule and its implications. In order to do this I have principally drawn on Umberto Eco's essay on 'The comic and the rule' (Eco 1986). This is because Eco examines both the comic and the tragic trope: the turn which renders one situation comic and another tragic. He sets the apparent universality of the tragic against the apparent specificity of the comic. This seems to be a useful distinction. However, Eco also makes a distinction between the comic and humour *per se*. The comic, he says, is concerned with the violation of the rule, humour with the attempt to understand the rule that has been violated. Humour then has an anamnesiac effect: it evokes a common and empathetic understanding. First then, it is necessary to give some thought to the nature of shared meaning.

Communities of meaning

Recently, Professor Jack Cohen, the well-known complexity theorist, came to the University of Essex to give a paper in the Department of Accounting, Finance and Management. As is usual on such occasions, he was taken out to dinner the night before his talk by myself and two of my colleagues. When we had finished the usual round of catching up on what we were all doing, mutual friends and colleagues, recent publications, conference stories and so forth, we moved to humorous incidents that had befallen us and then took to telling jokes. I had returned from Krakow earlier in the week. While I was there I had had lunch with a group of people that included Professor Stanislaw Obirek, a celebrated professor of theology. Over lunch, he had told a number of very mild Catholic jokes. For instance, he told the story of the aged Polish bishop who, on his death-bed, had called out for his favourite beer. To which, the two nuns who were keeping a bed-side vigil had responded, 'Ora pro nobis' (pray for us). Not a great joke as jokes go, admittedly, but a very Catholic joke and so I ramble on to tell my fellow dinner guests about the Holy Spirit deciding to take his holiday in Rome because he had 'never been there before'. Now at dinner with Jack Cohen I am telling these stories as travellers' tales and getting a response of polite amusement set in even more polite incomprehension. One colleague is a Scot, perhaps a Scottish Presbyterian, the other an agnostic Russian, Jack is Jewish, I am Catholic and, before this sounds like the beginning of another type of joke, let me explain my purpose here. There is no shared community of meaning. So Jack gamely takes on the next round and tells a series of Jewish jokes and we smile and laugh with the sense that we are missing something, that these acts of what Critchley calls an 'everyday anamnesis', or acts of recollection are not calling to mind any common memories or experiences. There is an absence of a common heritage (Critchley 2002: 86). We do not share enough context to appreciate the depth of the humour. 'We had the experience but missed the meaning', as Eliot says. So what about the man who asks the Jesuit and the Franciscan how many novenas he has to make in order to get a BMW? The Franciscan asks, 'What is a BMW?' and the Jesuit asks, 'What is a novena?' and secretly my fellow guests are saying and 'What is a Franciscan?', 'What is a Jesuit?', 'What is a novena?' and 'Why does it matter?' The point here is not only that there was a discontinuity in meanings but also that by telling this story I am creating a further community of meaning: a community of meaning where we share the joke about the absence of continuity. In the telling of the story, we are drawn into a wider community where what is shared is the knowledge of the rule and its violation.

Catharsis

In his essay, Umberto Eco seeks to draw out the relationship between the apparent universality of the tragic and the apparent specificity of the comic: to examine why the tragic appears to be universal in its effects, whereas the comic is 'bound to its time, society, cultural anthropology' (Eco 1986: 269). The tragic, according to Eco, survives over centuries. The tragedy of the battles of the First World War with their appalling loss of life, the atrocities of the holocaust, the horror of 9/11 and the daily litany of deaths and disasters seemingly crossing all boundaries of nationality, race or religion, serves to demonstrate the sense in which Eco invokes the notion of the universality of tragedy, especially when brought to the level of the individual victim. However, it should be noted that there is much to be said about the commodification of gratuitous violence which contradicts Eco's view. For example, in his powerful and persuasive article, *Passion of the Christ in Abu Ghraib*, Walter Davis (2004) comments on the commodification of brutality and its conversion into a recreational pursuit. Clearly, this is a different view from the compassionate and humanitarian position adopted by Eco. Davis draws parallels between Mel Gibson's controversial film *The Passion of the Christ* and the American depravity at the Abu Ghraib prison in Iraq.

> Both Mel Gibson's film The Passion of the Christ and Abu Ghraib are results of what I've shown elsewhere to be the condition of the American psyche: the deadening of emotion and the attempt to flee that inner state through violent acts which are needed to confer the momentary sense that one exists. The two … derivbe, however, from the same psychodynamic: sado-masochistic activity, extreme images of brutalization and suffering repeated, maximized in order to create in a mass audience the only feeling

of which the are capable: the overwrought glee that comes from spectacles of cruelty.

(Davis 2004)

Eco, in contrast, appeals to a notion of common humanity. In attempting to address this issue, Eco says that it is not merely sympathy for the fate of the other brought low by the violation of a moral or religious code, but also our terror that such fate might also strike us which gives the tragic its universal appeal. Consequently, in the tragic, the 'punishment' or fate befalling the individual is both a 'purification of his [sic] sin and of our temptations' (Eco 1986: 270). In this sense, according to Eco, the experience of the tragic performs an expiatory function. Of course, it could be said that the comic also has a universal element. Non-verbal, physical, rough and tumble, mime: these comic styles seem to have a broad appeal. However, the comic event tends to be of short duration. When I was a schoolgirl in the North-West of England in the 1960s, at the annual Speech Day presentation of prizes, the visiting speaker, a very 'county' and austere woman, came forward to the front of the stage to present the prizes. As she did so, she tumbled headfirst towards the auditorium and landed, tweed skirt over her head, long pink bloomers on full display to the assembled parents and pupils. The response from the audience was spontaneous but suppressed laughter. This was an incident on the cusp of the tragic and the comic (where most humour seems to reside). Like the Janus mask, these two faces appear to be entirely complementary. On this occasion, the poor woman was quite shaken, humiliated and dishevelled. One might say that when members of the audience recovered their composure, they *felt* for the *poor woman*. Eco says that 'the comic is the perception of the opposite; humour is the feeling of it' (Eco 1986: 276), that is to say, the perception of the unexpected outcome, the violation and the identification which permits us to become fellow-sufferers with the victim of the event. This was the empathetic reaction of the audience which transformed the response to the visiting speaker's *downfall* from comic to concerned.

Homoeopathy

Of course, Eco's well-known novel, *The Name of the Rose* (1983), also deals with humour. The novel itself purports to be about the quest for Aristotle's lost work on comedy and he uses references to Bakhtin's notion of carnival throughout the novel and to introduce disjuncture and disorder (Rose 1993: 247). However, it is in his two essays, 'The comic and the rule' (1986) and 'The frames of comic "freedom"' (1984) that he develops the idea of the violation of *frames of reference* as a cathartic purging of the ridiculous. So, just as tragedy achieves catharsis by 'arousing pity and fear' so comedy 'in inspiring the pleasure of the ridiculous

... arrives at the purification of that passion' (Eco 1983: 471; Rose 1993: 251). In taking up this position, Eco is aligning comedy with tragedy as *homoeopathic* in its functioning.

> Humour acts like the tragic, with perhaps this difference: in the tragic the reiterated rule is part of the narrative universe ... in humour, on the other hand, the description of the rule should appear as an intrusion, though concealed, of the author, who reflects on the social scenarios in which the enunciated character should believe.

Thus, in tragedy, the social rule is a part of the narrative, rehearsed and repeated so that the audience will experience its breach all the more acutely. In the comic, the breach is not presaged by announcement. To work as a comic effect it is important that a notion of propriety is maintained up to the point at which the continuity is breached, when the normal rules of social engagement fail and their fragility is revealed. Eco's standpoint contrasts with the more usual view of comedy as *allopathic*, that is to say, comedy is normally regarded as drawing on the opposite emotions to those observed. For example, just as in tragedy, fear and pity achieve a cathartic effect; so with comedy, according to Eco, catharsis is achieved by and through a homoeopathic response (Rose 1993: 251). Consequently, Rose contends that Eco offers a more complex and postmodern view of the comic as the purging of the ridiculous (Rose 1993: 252). Tragedy offers a moral exhortation to improvement. Comedy, in contrast, ridicules and reduces. However, according to Eco, each, tragedy and comedy, is concerned with the purification of the passions they arouse.

Theory

In tragedy, we are saved, or perhaps more aptly spared, by the sufferings of others. Indeed, Lacoue-Labarthe argues that in the face of the tragic one can only 'attempt to circumscribe it theoretically, to put it on stage and theatricalize it in order to try to catch it in the trap of (in)sight [(sa)voir])' (1989: 117). The presentation of the tragic renders the spectator powerless and helpless, and in the face of tragedy, s/he can only speculate. The only possible response to such 'theatre' is theorization (where theatre and theory are etymologically cognate). But theorization is a necessary abstraction, a reaction and a construction. Tragedy produces introversion and renders the observer speechless. As a sociology student in the late 1960s, I had to study the holocaust. It was fashionable at that time to use the artefacts of the holocaust – bureaucratic records of transportations, accounts of appalling experiments on living human beings, unbelievable stories of products made with human tissue – to teach about the logic of production and about the nature of authority and response. It is nearly 40 years since I read those accounts and I am still distraught. I have never been able to theorize my way out of the horror of those records. After all these years, I still feel myself vicariously complicit in these acts of failed humanity. Such things are unspeakable. Such acts of violation leave a deep scar and endure. The important point here is that, following Lacoue-Labarthe's (1989: 100) translation of Socrates, to gaze into the face of tragedy – here taken to mean not suffering but terror, the terror of absence of resolution – is to experience a 'corruption of judgement of all listeners who do not possess as an antidote [*pharmakon*] a knowledge of things as they are' (Plato, *Republic,* 10. 595b). Lacoue-Labarthe uses the notion of 'corruption', translated from the Greek word *lobe* to mean outrage, shame, ruin, destruction and, not least, madness He argues that the only response to such devastation is insightful theory (Lacoue-Labarthe 1989: 101). In other words, the response to the madness induced by terror is *(sa)voir.*

Therefore, unless we are truly outrageous and without shame, we tend not to share our deepest pains or relate our most reprehensible acts. Humour, in contrast, is extrovert. It delights in being shared and so people besiege each other with humorous stories, jokes, incidents and tales which draw them closer to each other. To this extent, humour is amiable. This is not to say that tragedy is not also binding; people are held together in common grief, for example. So, overall, there are differences between the tragic and the comic which seem to require different release mechanisms; but behind this, and Eco seems to be right here, both the tragic and the comic seem to produce a commonality and a community, however transient, and at the same time to perform an expiatory role in social behaviour. However, as Westwood (2004) rightly points out, humour has also been used to construct and perpetuate boundaries and power asymmetries. This is apparent for example in the work of Davies on humour and ethnic boundaries (e.g. 1998) and in those who pursue a superiority theory of humour.

Erection

What then are the constructions which are violated? For the purposes of this chapter, I would prefer to use the term *erection.* There are a number of reasons for this choice of terminology. First, the root of the word erection is the Latin *e-regere* meaning *to direct.* Second, there is the more straightforward association of the word with something built, erected. Third, there is the more supplemental idea of the erection of social structures, rules, behaviours and so forth – in the argument presented here, a concern with the rules which maintain order and a sense of place. These erections *direct* the transmission of the structure and its content. Therefore, the erections are the means of achieving order. The erection is the means by which patterns of social life are effected. Erections are authoritative because they lay claim to an anterior authority and create the world by verbal fiat and if in saying this I reify the erection it is to transgress the way in which the erection reifies me. So, just as it is impossible, so I hear, to maintain a physical erection in the face of laughter, so theoretical and social structures, patterns, order are destabilized by humour. Order is violated by the comic. Theorization itself, as erection, 'cracks under the pressure of seeking with all its power to complete or accomplish itself' (Lacoue-Labarthe 1989: 138). It is this cracking which is at the heart of both the tragic and the comic.

Hypothetic/hypothermic

It is just before Christmas 2002 and I am travelling on the Newcastle Metro. I am on my way to the office staff Christmas dinner. It is early in the evening and the train is not crowded. It is the lull between the time when people go home from work and when they go out for the evening. Beside me, holding on to one of the uprights is a young girl: 16 or 17. She is incredibly thin, to the point of being emaciated. In common with Newcastle's passion for Balearic dress codes, she is wearing next to nothing: loose top with thin shoulder straps, a short skirt, high-heeled golden shoes. She is not wearing tights or, indeed, much of anything else. She is standing beside me, holding onto the pole and swaying slightly with the movement of the train. Her right hand hangs down on a level with my head. Her finger-tips are dark blue. Her hands are purple with pink blotches: a pattern which extends up her arms. Her feet show a similar discolouration. Mentally noting this cyanosis, I look up. She is lazily chewing gum and her purple lips move mechanically to complete a look of affected boredom. She is on her way to join the hundreds of revellers who will move from club to club along the quayside this evening. Outside the temperature is below zero. I know that if she drinks to excess and stays outside in these temperatures she will be close to death. Everyone else in the compartment is dressed for winter with warm boots, scarves, gloves, big coats. She is different. The woman sitting opposite me makes eye contact. She looks at the girl then she looks at me and rolls her eyes: 'Mad' she is saying. Monument Station: the girl gets off here and we watch her, not without sympathy, as she totters off down the platform.

But what if, hypothetically, in the tradition of *l'humour noir*, the woman opposite to me had said, 'Did you see the shade of blue she was turning? It really didn't go with her dress'.

Doing a turn

What then of the comic? There are many theories of comic behaviour, of the dynamics of the comic, of bathos and of types of humour. Eco puts forward the view that in the comic the rule is usually violated by a person of lower order than the person violated. A person over whom the spectators can feel 'a sense of superiority so that we do not identify ourselves with his [sic] downfall' (Eco 1986: 270) and nor do we feel moved by the fate of this character except perhaps in the most superficial way that the comic figure carries a degree of pathos. Well, of course, there are many obvious cases of the comic in which this is not the case. However, what is of interest is what Eco has to say about violation. Eco argues that the comic violation rests on an absence of identification with the transgressor which produces both a sense of security – a standpoint from which to observe the violation – and a sense of impunity because the character is so different from ourselves. This resonates with the notion of the Fool: the Fool as Other. The comic violator also performs an expiatory function because he/she permits 'the vicarious pleasure of a transgression that offends a rule we have secretly wanted to violate, but without the risk' (Eco 1986: 271), which, again, echoes the role of the fool/jester. However, Eco goes further (and this provides what is perhaps the first most obvious link to the study of the function of humour in organizations). In the tragic, he argues, it is repetition and emphasis of the rule of the tragic which sets the experience of the tragic into context. The rules of the tragic are drummed into characters and the spectators. The warnings of the consequences of violation are frequent and emphatic. The tragic abounds in monitory rhetoric. In fact, this is precisely the disposition for theorization and *sa/voir*. In contrast, the comic works by taking the rules of the situation for granted and violating them by a range of extensions, excesses, inversions and subversions. Eco says that the best results are achieved where the rule is not cited but assumed to be implicit. Here the spectator knows what should happen and the comic effect is achieved when an alternative ending is substituted. Of course, this effect is entirely dependent on common understanding and shared experiences.

I was not brought up by my natural parents so I was rather surprised when, in 1982, just after I had completed by PhD at Lancaster University, I was contacted by my birth mother who wrote to me to say, 'I was really disappointed that you didn't invite me to your graduation ceremony. I have always wanted to see Princess Alexandra'. Well, no problem. I got her tickets for the ceremony and for the wine reception in Bowland Senior Common Room afterwards. Lancaster, of course, is one of the universities built in the UK in the 1960s. It has more of formica than woodpanelling about it and the Common Room was far from grand. With her neat hat and handbag pulled in under her ribs in a style later adopted by Margaret Thatcher, she stood inspecting her surroundings. At this point, one of the science professors came over to be sociable. 'You must be awwwfully proud of her' he said plummily and put out his hand to greet her. 'Oh', she said, 'Did you do your degree here?' 'No', he replied with a magnanimous smile, 'actually, I' (he paused for dramatic effect) 'was at Cambridge'. My mother eyed him carefully and then replied, 'Cambridge, I've not heard of that. Is it nice?' I cringed from head to foot as he looked at her with disdain and went off to find other, more appreciative people to speak to. It was almost two years before I saw her again. My embarrassment still smarted a little. 'I have been meaning to ask you', I said, 'do you remember at my graduation ceremony, you told that professor that you hadn't heard of Cambridge. You have, haven't you?' She looked at me without a hint of irony or discomfort and said, 'Indeed, I have love, but I thought he was a silly bugger'. My affection for her was greatly increased by this story. Her disregard for his construction of the situation and her confidence in her own and in the face of this filled me with admiration. And here is the comic turned into humour. Her behaviour, admittedly painful to me at the time, endeared me to her when she revealed her own comic rule, her awareness of the social convention she had violated. Her sharing the story *let me in on the joke* and I respond homoeopathically.

In a similar way, the final story which I want to relate involves someone being *put in their place*. This time it is a story from an organization. It demonstrates all the characteristics which Eco discusses. There is a situation where a manager has an inflated view of himself. His staff seek revenge. They choose their moment carefully. They execute the joke and then they share the satisfaction of a violation both enacted and observed. This story appears in Yiannis Gabriel's (2004) book, *Myths, Stories and Organizations*, but I would like to repeat it here because it demonstrates so well the relevance of the study of humour for the analysis of the organization.

Comic relief

In the early 1990s I was working with Stephen Linstead at Lancaster University on a management development programme for a major UK company. As part of the programme, we explored issues of emotional labour and asked participants to provide examples drawn from their experiences of the workplace. One story concerned a newly appointed manager who was 'very full of himself'. This young man was apparently very quick to assume what he saw as the managerial role and this had obvious consequences for his staff who were expected to demonstrate appropriate deference to his self-importance. For about three weeks after his promotion they reluctantly and grudgingly gave him the approbation he demanded of them but then they began to formulate a plan for revenge. One afternoon, this pretentious and narcissistic new manager had an important meeting in his office. One of the company's senior managers was coming to hear his plans for the development of his area. He was not to be disturbed at any price. He would go down to reception himself to greet his guest. Did they all realize how important this was for him? He planned the visit with meticulous care. Reports and graphics were prepared but he would present them. He did not want his staff to damage his opportunity to make a big impression on the visitor and he made this clear to them. He arrived in the morning smartly dressed, a spring in his feet, a confident air. Unfortunately, what he could not have anticipated was that his staff, now thoroughly disaffected by his posturing, planned to bring him down. His glass-walled office beautifully ordered and polished with fresh flowers on his desk, he responded to the call to reception to greet his guest. However, while he was out of the office, his staff arranged for a colleague with an unenviable but practised capacity for expressing bodily wind, to enter the office and emit a foul and obnoxious flatus. Then, the unsuspecting manager returned to his office, proudly opened his office door and ushered in his guest to be greeted by the fetid smell his staff had left for him. The glass walls of the office made a theatre of this event and as the new manager looked round at his colleagues he was met by their various faces regarding him with a strange mixture of affected innocence, contempt and satisfaction at achieving some degree of retaliation.

Pride goes before a fall, as they say. He got his 'come-uppance'.

Violation/affirmation

This chapter has looked at violations and their comic value. Specifically, I have tried to say something about the ways in which comic/comedic behaviour functions to subvert and parody established social order and also to give attention to the force of such behaviours and their effects. If Eco is right, then the tragic rule is enforced by repetition and definition. The comic, in contrast, is local and short-lived. The argument here has attempted to explore the relationship between the maintenance of the universal and its incidental subversion by the comic. For example, according to the *Catechism of the Catholic Church*, the Feast of Fools, which was held on or around the Feast of Circumcision (1 January), arose from a pagan custom which gave slaves and serving maids a day on which they might notionally invert the power relations with their masters in the celebration of a common festivity (Knight 2003). The Feast of Fools involved a series of inversions which poked fun at authority figures, the priesthood, the church. However, undoubtedly it confirmed these figures as much as it ridiculed them. Not surprisingly, this feast of buffoonery and excess was permitted and regulated by the church authorities who retained mastery of this apparent celebration of liberality. Eco (1984) has written about how violation works in Bakhtin's notion of carnival. In his 'The comic and the rule', he says, 'carnival can take place only once a year. It takes a year of ritual observance for the violation of the ritual precepts to be enjoyed'. Quite so. Order is affirmed by the breach. I will not explore this here.

Humour pricks pomposity, reminds us of our excesses and the constraints which 'order' imposes upon them. Humour reminds us of the possibility of being excessive, shows our foibles and follies and reminds us of our frailties, but it also draws people together on the basis of their shared understandings, gives us a common form of expression, breaks down social barriers (but, of course, can also erect them), creates friendships and creates targets – the butt of jokes, enemies, stereotypes. In an organizational sense, humour reminds workers that there is an alternative, that bad practice deserves derision, and that management as *erection* cannot be sustained in the face of ridicule.

References

Boo, K. (1992) 'Universal soldier: what Paula Couglin can teach American women', *Washington Monthly* (Sept.).

Critchley, S. (2002) *On Humour*, London: Routledge.

Davies, C. (1998) *Jokes and their Relation to Society*, Berlin: Mouton de Gruyter.

Davis, W. A. (2004) *The Passion of the Christ in Abu Ghraib*, counterpunch.org, <http://counterpunch.org/davis06192004.html>, accessed 10 Feb. 2006.

Eco, U. (1983) *The Name of the Rose*, tr. William Weaver, London: Secker & Warburg.

Eco, U. (1984) 'The frames of comic "freedom"', in T. Sebeok (ed.), *Carnival!*, pp. 1–10, Berlin: Mouton Publishers.

Eco, U. (1986) 'The comic and the rule' (first published 1980, tr. William Weaver), in U. Eco, *Travels in Hyper-Reality*, pp. 275–7, London: Picador.

Eliot, T. S. (1944) *The Four Quartets*, London: Faber and Faber.

Faludi, S. (1994) *Going Wild*, PBS website, <http://www.pbs.org/wgbh/pages/frontline/shows/navy/tailhook/debate.html>, accessed 5 Dec. 2005.

Gabriel, Y. (2004) *Myths, Stories and Organizations*, Oxford: Oxford University Press.

Höpfl, H. (2004) 'The Hymn to Demeter: the curse of insatiable consumption', in Y. Gabriel (ed.), *Myths, Stories and Organizations*, pp. 192–204, Oxford: Oxford University Press.

Knight, K. (2003) *The Catholic Encyclopedia*, vol. 6, originally published in 1909 by Robert Appleton Co. Online Edition © 2003, <http://www.newadvent.org/cathen/06132a.htm>, accessed 5 Dec. 2005.

Lacoue-Labarthe, P. (1989) *Typography*, Stanford, CA: Stanford University Press.

Rose, M. (1993) *Parody: Ancient, Modern and Post-Modern*, Cambridge: Cambridge University Press.

Westwood, R. I. (2004) 'Comic relief: subversion and catharsis in organizational comedic theatre', *Organization Studies*, 25(5): 775–95.

Chapter 4

Theory as joke
A hysterical perturbation

Robert Westwood

Theories have four stages of acceptance: i) this is worthless nonsense; ii) this is an interesting, but perverse, point of view; iii) this is true but quite unimportant; iv) I always said so.

(J. B. S. Haldane)

When did God make men? When she realized that vibrators couldn't dance.

(Roz Warren)

The sexual life of adult women is a 'dark continent' for psychology.

(Sigmund Freud, *The Question of Lay Analysis*)

Hysteria, rhythmotherapy and the Chattanooga

In late May 1906, Beatrice Webber visited her favourite 'spa' in Connecticut hoping for some effective treatment for her 'vapours'. Her good friend, Mrs Marchand, had recommended the establishment, telling her that just one visit had left her feeling 'quite, quite rejuvenated dear'. At the spa that May, Beatrice, after settling herself into her rooms, had an appointment with Dr Wesley the resident physician and part owner of the establishment. After a thorough examination, Dr Wesley suggested some adjustments to her diet, a regime of exercise and a course of treatment of electro-vibrotherapy. After a particularly restful night, a light breakfast and an hour taking the waters in the spa, Beatrice was introduced to the Chattanooga,[1] the veritable 'Cadillac of vibrators' (Maines 1999: 15). Beatrice was able to lie on a tall divan whilst the 125lb electro-mechanical device was wheeled up to her, the nodes applied to the appropriate place, and the machine switched on. She was then left to the pleasant sensations for twenty minutes or so. After the treatment Beatrice retired, flushed and languid, to her room for some recuperative rest. She might well have stayed longer but the nurses had been given careful instructions not to allow the female patients to linger on the divans with that apparatus. Indeed, none other than George Taylor, the physician who had patented a steam-powered vibratory apparatus in 1872, had expressly warned fellow physicians to properly supervise the use of his 'Manipulator' machines to ensure that there was no 'overindulgence'.

(Maines 1999: 15)

The above might strike you as exceedingly odd – odd that a somewhat refined middle-class woman such as Beatrice should, a mere 100 years ago, seek out such a treatment, odder still that a medical physician might legitimately prescribe mechanized masturbation to orgasm for such a woman. However, you should know that the use of electrical and electromechanical vibrators had become a standard medical procedure since their first patented introduction by Dr Joseph Mortimer Granville in the 1870s, particularly for the treatment for hysteria or similarly diagnosed 'female' conditions. It is reported that the first medical use of electromechanical vibrators – for the treatment of hysteria – was at the esteemed Salpêtrière in Paris, the clinic of the celebrated Charcot.[2] It was supported as a treatment for hysteria by leading medical practitioners of the time such as William Goodell (1890) who maintained that electrotherapy was useful for the release of fluids congesting the uterus of women as a result of unsatisfactory intercourse. Although the language is sometimes elliptical it is obvious that the devices are being used to induce female orgasm. As Maines (1999: 3) states:

Massage to orgasm of female patients was a staple of medical practice among some … Western physicians from the time of Hippocrates until the 1920s, and mechanizing this task significantly increased the number of patients a doctor could treat in a working day.

Indeed, these electromechanical devices were simply the latest and more efficient versions of a long line of masturbatory devices and techniques used to treat women for hysteria and related conditions going back to Hippocratic times. Predecessors to electromechanical devices, from just the recent past, included hydrotherapy, water-powered hydro-massage and 'pelvic' douches, 'jolting chairs', devices powered by foot-pedal and foot-powered 'concussors', pneumatic vibrators, spring-driven wind-up 'percuteurs', and various steam-driven machines. Electrotherapeutic devices quickly became big business with 66 companies generating $1 million of goods in 1905, rising to $2.6 million by 1914 (cited in Maines 1999: 87). It is of historico-sociological interest to note:

The first home appliance to be electrified was the sewing machine in 1889, followed in the next ten years by the fan, the teakettle, the toaster, and the vibrator. The last preceded the electric vacuum by some nine years, the electric iron by ten, and the electric frying pan by more than a decade, possibly reflecting consumer priorities.

(Maines 1999: 100)

Demand was fed at least in part by the recognition by physicians that the electromechanical vibrator was a labour saving device *par excellence*. Administering the required massages by hand was labour-intensive and time-consuming, and not an activity most physicians relished. Even if delegated to a midwife or nurse it would still be absorbing labour time and thus incurring costs. As Samuel Wallian (1906: 56) noted in advocating the use of the electromechanical vibrator for his 'rhythmotherapy', a manual massage 'consumes a painstaking hour to accomplish much less profound results than are easily effected by the other [the vibrator] in a short five or ten minutes'. For physicians and spa operators this was a significant boon to business. One business sought to further maximize this by linking several separate vibrators to one steam engine thereby enabling one machine to service several patients in serried rows simultaneously. The spa had effectively constructed a kind of assembly line of the orgasm. The vibrator is a proven technology and its efficaciousness was recognized at the outset: 'No human hand is capable of cummunicating [sic][3] to the tissues such rapid, steady and prolonged vibrations, and certain kneading and percussion movements, as the vibrator' (Matijaca 1917: 134) These practices and the theories behind them that deem to explain aspects of women's bodies and health, hysteria in particular, have been controversial for their gendered structures and discourses. However, as Reynolds (1971) notes, electrotherapy was used with men and was said to be efficacious, particularly in treating impotence. It was also used as a treatment for 'nymphomania', an association that leads Reynolds to comment that:

Presumably the treatment for nymphomania differed from that for impotency – perhaps a reversal of polarity. The responsibility of the nineteenth century physician in treating impotency and nymphomania with electricity was awesome. A mix-up in the leads could result in personal tragedy in one patient – a social menace in another.

(Reynolds 1971: 6)

In the entrepreneurial climate of the US it is not surprising that the opportunity of marketing the vibrator as a domestic product for personal use was seized upon. From around the turn of the century magazines such as *Needlecraft*,

Woman's Home Companion,[4] and *Modern Priscilla* were carrying advertisements for personal vibrators (Maines 1999). At about the same time they started to appear in pornographic films. This domestication of the vibrator and the obvious sexual rather than medical uses to which it was being put was the death knell for their use by respectable physicians. Once the sexual and demedicalized use of the vibrator to stimulate orgasm sheerly for pleasure was out in the open, as it were, the medical camouflage that had legitimated doctors' manipulation of women's sexual organs was lifted and the boundary between the medical and the sexual was construed as breached. This occurred very rapidly, so that by the end of the 1920s the vibrator had virtually disappeared from respectable doctors' surgeries. It was not long before the taint of overt sexuality associated with the vibrator meant that respectable magazines also stopped carrying advertising. The vibrator went 'underground' and did not re-emerge, fully demedicalized as a *bona fide* sex toy or aid, until the 'sexual revolution' of the 1960s.

These enlightening aspects of medical-sexual history notwithstanding, it is the theories behind such medical practice that are of most significance here. By way of an initial, small example, Samuel Wallian, cited above promoting the benefits of the vibration through 'rhythmotherapy', promoted a general theory of vibration to support his practice. Indeed, he declared that all life is based on vibration and that variations in vibration rates gave rise to variance in the matter and substance of material existence, including organic creatures. Thus 'A certain rate begets a *vermis*, another and higher rate produces a *viper*, a vertebrate, a *vestryman*' (Wallian 1905, emphasis in the original). However, to explore the theoretical base that more fully underpinned the practices described above we need to go right back to the supposed birth of modern medicine with Hippocrates (460–370 BC) in Ancient Greece. Before doing so I will reflect on why the above story might have caused amusement and why more generally some theories, at some points in time, appear comic – as a form of joke.

Incongruity, humour and theory

I cannot know if you all found Beatrice Webber's encounter with the Chattanooga and worthy doctors saving their energies through the deployment of a linked row of steam-driven vibrators funny – humour is variable and idiosyncratic – but I would guarantee that some of you did. The question then is 'why is it funny?' More importantly, do we find the underlying theory funny? Do we now find Wallian's general theory of vibration and, as I hope to show, many other theoretical accounts, funny? In order to explore this I venture briefly into some core theories of humour.

For many, incongruity is the basis for humour, and indeed, incongruity theory constitutes a dominant theoretical perspective on humour (Deckers and Buttram

1990; Morreall 1987; Nerhardt 1996; Palmer 1994). Essentially incongruity theory maintains that humour arises from the surprising, unexpected and/or illogical juxtaposition of two events, ideas, values, perspectives that are normally not co-located. Humour is generated through the experienced incongruity of the surprising intrusion of something other, different and not normally expected into the normal, expected and mundane. The incongruity might be experienced cognitively, but it might also be experienced emotionally, a felt response to a jarring juxtaposition. Schopenhauer expressed the former narrowly and formalistically when arguing that all humour can be 'traced to a syllogism in the first figure with an undisputed major and an unexpected minor which to a certain extent is only sophistically valid' (cited in Munro 1988: 352). Mulkay (1988) expresses the more general principle when he suggests that humour emerges in the juxtaposition of two or more elements wherein a more expected, dominant and typical element is unsettled by a less expected, less familiar and minor element, thereby precipitating a surprise, an interpretative shift and a cognitive realignment.

Morreall (1987: 130) puts incongruity into a broader philosophical context, arguing that 'We live in an orderly world where we have come to expect certain patterns among things, properties, events etc. When we experience something that doesn't fit these patterns, that violates our expectations, we laugh'. This resonates with Berger's interesting variant of the incongruity perspective. In *Redeeming Laughter* (Berger 1997) he maintains that humour arises through the interpolation of an alternate reality into the 'paramount' reality of ongoing, mundane existence. All such alternate realities, and dream states, child's play, fictive worlds (especially theatre), extreme types of aesthetic or spiritual experience, and drug-induced states are cited as examples, adhere to their own logics, but are internally coherent. They do, however, engender a different mode of engagement, form of consciousness, and possibly different conception of time and sociality (Berger 1997: 8–9). The comedic, Berger maintains, works by playing along the margins between mundane reality and the possibilities of other realities. Humour constructs an alternate world, one at odds with our normal way of viewing things. It takes us sideways away from the well-worn path of common sense and known reality towards something odd and different. This alternate world challenges paramount reality and hence a frisson is established, a psychological uncertainty that is at some level actually threatening. Elsewhere (Westwood 2004) I have used the example of the circus clown. In a typical routine the clown points a gun at the audience. He pulls the trigger. A flag pops out the end of the gun with the word 'BANG' emblazoned upon it. There is enough residual apprehension in the symbolic space surrounding guns for the frisson of uncertainty to be constructed. The limp 'bang' is experienced as relief ('comic relief') and we laugh at the incongruity between gun and the flagged 'bang'. This is (mildly) funny, but what if, when the clown pulls the trigger, the brains of the nearest five year old are splashed into the crowd? Then we have not comedy, but horror. The humour depends upon tension created by the presence, however tenuous, of this other horrific reality. Such a fine line between the two realms is reflected in theory and research. Research on the structure of jokes shows that, as the joke develops, the incongruity needs to be moderate: if too weak there is no tension, if too extreme it will precipitate anxiety and stress (Kuhlman 1985). Some go further and suggest that humour is not merely about incongruity *per se*, but about the resolution of incongruity. The comic intrudes as an alternate 'take' on reality and thus as a threat to the mundane world we take for granted. However, the frame of the comedic shows that the threat is not material or substantive, it is only there in potentiality. Humour works by implying this threat but dissolving it through resolving the incongruity by showing that mundane reality is not 'seriously' challenged – the challenge is not in serious mode. We can laugh with relief as the threat of the alternate reality is shown to be 'only a joke' and the world as we know it is, at least for now, restored to us.

If humour derives from the juxtaposition of alternate perspectives on reality, then theory, as the contemporary explicator of realities *par excellence*, presumably at times participates in the comedic. Theory presumes to present a particular view of reality, to model it, and aspires to make that the dominant, even exclusive, view. There is an assumption that the 'reality' under consideration is non-obvious: the theory presumes to offer a model or explanation of 'reality' beyond the level of common sense, beyond the mundane apprehension of those inhabiting it. In that sense theory is an intrusion into the mundane reality of 'lay people's' normal lived experience through being different from and excessive to their everyday, common-sense understandings. It is also an intrusion in another sense, through interpolating a different account of 'reality' from that offered by existing and accepted theory. In both senses, such an intrusion constitutes a surprising juxtaposition of the type underpinning incongruity theory. If there is no surprise, one might assume that there is no differentiation from mundane experience and the theory is adding nothing to common sense nor challenging existing theory. New theory, then, is a threat to either common sense, mundane reality, or to extant theories – or both.

Humour, then, arises when an alternate reality intrudes on dominant reality, poses a threat, but is seen to not be a serious contender. We can therefore expect, logically, humour to be potentially inherent whenever a theoretical claim intrudes upon an already dominant explanation of any particular piece of reality. This might occur in relation to common-sense 'lay' understanding, or to extant theories that claim to explain for that particular 'reality'. In the latter case, humour might be potentially present if the existing theory assumes a position of dominance, has become widely accepted as *the* account and become part of paramount reality. In other terms we might say that it has achieved a dominant paradigmatic position as the relatively uncontested cornerstone of a normal science before the interruption of a revolutionary alternative. When an intruding theory enters the fray it threatens paramount reality and creates a tension by disturbing the order of things. Humour arises when this threatening alternative is taken or shown to not seriously challenge the dominant version of reality and falls away into nothing. I think we can hear at least the chuckles of the proponents of the dominant theory as the pretender withers away. There is also humour, though, when the challenging alternate reality is shown to not be viable and is then seen as ridiculous or absurd, laughingly dismissed as not serious. New theories are often greeted in this manner. Some theories are originally treated with derision, but in the end displace older theories which may themselves become a source of bemusement. The cases of the former are legion throughout the history of scientific theory: Copernicus's *Little Commentary*; Galileo's challenge to the Inquisition; Arrhenius' (1859–1927) theory of molecular dissociation; John Logie Baird's development of television cameras (1925–6); Chandrasekhar's theory of Black Holes (1930); the Doppler Effect (1842); Harvey's notions on blood circulation (1628); Rous's theory of cancer-causing viruses (1911); Wegener's theory of continental drift (1912); the Wright brothers' theories of flight (*c.*1903); Zweig's quark theory (1964). I could go on … and on. Of those that remained at the level of the absurd, many in recent times have been collated by Abrahams (1997, 2003) in his *Annals of Improbable Research.*[5]

On the 'wetness' of women, the wandering womb and the suffocation of the mother

Hilaria, the 18-year-old, unmarried daughter of Kopris, lay on the daybed with an apparent fever; she was shivering, grinding her teeth and very short of breath. She had complained of this malaise earlier in the day, but had now been rendered speechless. These were the classic symptoms of *hysterike pnix* (suffocation caused by the womb) as identified by the physician Soranus in his *Gynecology* (Soranus 1956). Being a man of some influence, Kopris arranged to have his daughter ministered to by a latter-day acolyte of Hippocrates, someone who knew that a fumigation of the womb was required as set out in the Hippocratic text the *Diseases of Women* (2. 133):

Take an earthenware pot with two-sixths capacity, put on it a dish, and fit them together so that no air can get in. Then pierce the bottom of the dish and make a hole. Put in the hole a reed, about a cubit long … place the dish

on the pot and plaster it round with clay. [Then] dig a hole in the ground
… large enough to make room for the pot. Then burn firewood, until you
have made the hole red-hot … When the pot is heated up and vapor rises
… she is to sit on the end of the reed, and pass it into the mouth [of the
womb], then fumigate … In the pot you should put dry garlic, and pour in
water so that it rises two digits above, and soak it well, and pour in seal oil
too. Heat this. The fumigation must go on for a long time … On the next
day, if she is weak from the fumigation, intermit that day: if not, go back to
the fumigation. While she is being fumigated, if she is able to examine it,
order her to touch the mouth [of the womb]. The fumigation itself inflates
the womb, makes it more upright and opens it.

Again, this treatment for *hysteria pnix*[6] may appear funny, or at least unusual,
from the purview of today. It was, however, based upon a theory[7] that
was more or less coherent at the time and that remained influential for a
substantial period. The term *hysteria* comes from the Greek meaning 'that
which proceeds from the uterus' (Maines 1999: 21). For the Hippocratics, as
for Plato, the womb was disconnected and capable of wandering around the
body. Indeed, Plato spoke of the womb almost as if it were an independent
creature within the body of the woman; 'an animal inside an animal' as some
translate a passage from *Timaeus* (Lee 1972). The womb is envisaged as being
capable of moving around the body, uncontrolled and wreaking havoc as it
went. Thus, *hysterike pnix* was a real, *physical* condition, understood to result
from movements of the womb, specifically upwards within the body towards
the diaphragm, resulting, literally, in a form of suffocation – the suffocation by
the womb, or 'suffocation of the mother' as it became known colloquially. The
treatment, as in Hilaria's case, is designed to encourage the womb to move
back to its proper place.
    What would induce the womb to go 'walkabout'? There are intimations
in Plato of a voraciousness about the 'animal inside the animal'; perhaps
metaphorically linked to male fear of rampant female sexuality and desire. The
Hippocratic texts cite, and this becomes significant for hysteria throughout
its history, menstrual suppression and/or sexual abstinence. This can induce
changes in the condition of the womb, making it, for example, 'dry' or 'light'
(King 1993: 14). In addition to the fumigation technique, ministrations at the
time included the use of various odorous herbs and other substances which were
applied to the nose in an attempt to repel the uterus downwards, whilst sweet-
smelling, fragrant substances, such as perfumed oils, were applied to and around
the vulva to entice the womb down and back to its proper place. For example,
Soranus (1956: 140) urged paying attention to the groin and pubic area and the
need to 'moisten these parts freely with sweet oil, keeping it up for some time'.

However, it was also common to prescribe marriage or pregnancy. It is clear that what is being recommended is sexual activity and intercourse, with marriage deemed the appropriate context for that to occur. Behind this diagnostic and treatment regime are theories about radical gender differences, sexuality and the nature of women's bodies.

Part of the theoretical rationale maintains that the flesh of women is different to the flesh of men. The *Diseases of Women,* 1. 1 (L 8. 10–14) states that women's flesh has a looser texture than men's, and an analogy likens women's flesh to sheepskin and men's to a rug:

> If a fleece and a rug of equal weight are placed over water or in a damp place for two days and nights, the fleece will be found to have become much heavier than the rug. This is because sheepskin has a greater capacity to absorb water: a capacity shared with female flesh.

Consequently, women are 'wetter' than men: the loose texture of their flesh absorbs and retains more fluid. This can be potentially unhealthy and excess fluid needs to be expelled. Menstruation, in part, accomplishes this and is seen as an essential process for mature feminine health and well-being. Suppression of menstruation leads to an excess of fluid with potentially harmful effects. Pregnancy and childbirth are also deemed to be conducive to female health. A woman who has not given birth will have a tighter, more densely packed fleshy texture with fewer spaces for fluids to flow. Menstrual flow might become obstructed. Childbirth helps to 'break down' the fleshy body, making it more favourable to the passage of fluids. So, a childless woman

> due to the lack of spaces in her body in which moisture can be stored, is at particular risk, above all if she abstains from the 'moistening' activity of sexual intercourse. In such a woman, the 'dry and light' womb may suddenly 'turn around' … and move up in search of moisture.
>
> (King 1993: 18)

The wandering womb, then, is in search of moisture. Such movements cause the 'suffocation of the mother' and engender the symptoms that Hilaria displayed. Intercourse is often recommended since it moistens the womb and from the time of Soranus right through to the twentieth century, sexual activity was advocated for the treatment of hysteria – as we saw in the opening story.

Treatments using odoriferous substances at the nostrils and vulva rest on another theory. This gynaecological theory posits the existence of a *hodos* or 'way' from the nostrils and mouth to the vagina (King 1993: 25). One application of the theory is the testing of a woman's fertility by placing a strongly scented substance at one end of the *hodos* and then to sniff at the other end – if the odour carries through the 'way' is clear and the woman is in a state to conceive.

In addition to anatomical theories about the different structure of women's bodies, humoral theory was also prominent. A version of humoral theory already existed in Plato and Aretaeus, but it was Galen of Pergamum (*c*.AD 129–200) who comprehensively articulated the theory, and so successfully that it remained a dominant model until the eighteenth century. Galen held, with Hippocratic physicians, that the womb was mobile and the cause of many a malaise in women, including *hysteria*. He explicitly maintained that often the cause lay in sexual deprivation which caused the uterus to engorge with unexpended 'seed', thereby impelling it to move from its proper location. Treatments, all designed to entice the womb back to its proper place and expel the excess seed, were consistent with Galen's humoral theory (Temkin 1973).

Humoral theory remained a cornerstone of scientific and medical explanation right through the medieval and Renaissance periods and subsequently evolved into a theory of personality type (Kiple 1993).[8] It has equivalents in the knowledge systems of ancient China, Indian *unani* medical practice and Arabic culture. Based originally on Anaximander's (*c*.610–510 BC) more abstract philosophical realism and the principles of the balance of opposites, it was transformed into a theory of four elements – fire, air, water and earth – and associated qualities. Empedocles substituted these four opposing elements with the four 'humours': phlegm, blood, yellow bile and black bile. For Plato, Aristotle and Hippocrates, disease was caused by 'isonomia', an imbalance in the humours. Hippocrates, for example, in *The Sacred Disease* maintains that what we would now call epilepsy was caused by phlegm congesting the airways inducing convulsions as the body struggled to clear itself, whereas black bile caused melancholy. The four humours and their various relationships and imbalances became associated with states of health and, through Theophrastus, with character disposition and personality. Personalities were held to be shaped by vapours arising from the humours, affecting our brains and the way we think and act. Treatments to restore humoral balance such as blood letting, purges and emetics were at the cornerstone of medical practice from Galen through to the eighteenth century (Nutton 2004).

We might smile at this 'inaccurate' model of the functioning of the human body, but we should note that Hippocratic medicine was based on observation, diagnosis and prognosis (Longrigg 1998). Hippocrates stated in *On Ancient Medicine* that medicine was not philosophy and cannot be based purely on general principles, but must rest upon case-by-case observation. He posited natural causes to human illness and disease, thus instigating the replacement of ideas that such conditions resulted from divine interventions and punishments (King 1993). There are principles and methods derived from Hippocratic thinking that have profoundly shaped Western and Middle Eastern medicine and science.

Cunning midwives

Leda, whose aging husband was kindly, but not much given to sexual activity anymore, informed him that she was hysterical and suggested that the standard treatment was necessary. Thus, young doctors were summoned and required to perform sexual intercourse with Leda in order to effect a cure and settle her symptoms.

(Related in Martial's *Epigrams*, 11. 71 and retold in King 1993: 42)

The recommendation of including sexual activity in the treatment of hysteria is more explicit in Galen than Soranus and others. He talks of retained female 'seed' and the need to expel it, otherwise it can rot releasing noxious humours that might affect the rest of the body through 'sympathy' (King 1993: 43). As King relates, Galen discusses the case of a widow of long standing who, exhibiting signs of *hysteria*, was told by the midwife that her womb was 'drawn up' and applied remedies to her external genitalia precipitating a flow of thick 'seed' in what appears, King suggests, to be an induced orgasm. As we have just seen in the case of Leda, it was not always the midwife who conducted such ministrations.

Arabic physicians, much influenced by Galen, were also explicit about sexual cures for hysteria. In the *Paradise of Wisdom*, Ali ibn Rabban at-Tabari (810–61) also talked about the 'wetness' of women, the retention of fluids that give off the vapours causing hysteria, and the value of intercourse to release the fluids. Both Ibn al Jazzar in the *Viaticum* and Avicenna (Ibn Sina) similarly talk of suffocation caused by vapours given off by retained 'seed' and recommend rubbing scented oil into the vulva to release it. Such teachings were the basis for medical treatment across much of Europe during the Middle Ages and into the Rennaisance. In the thirteenth century in Europe, Pseudo-Albertus Magnus (1992) reiterated Arabic physician advice suggesting a midwife rub oil into the genitals of women to release the build-up of 'seminal humours'. He felt menstrual fluids were particularly noxious, in fact suggesting that fumes emanating from menstruating women could 'poison the eyes of children lying in their cradles by a glance' (Pseudo-Albertus Magnus 1992: 129). Drawing on humoral theory, his advice on inducing conception noted that

if the womb and intestine of a hare are dried and pulverized they become very hot, and similarly a pig's liver is hot in itself, and these will generate heat sufficient for conception. This should be administered in the end of the menstrual period, because the womb is dry in this time, and somewhat hotter than usual because of the retreat of menstrual cold.

(Ibid.: 140)

Conversely, he said, drinking the urine of men will impede conception. About a century later, writing 'On the diseases that deprive man of his reason', Philippus Theophrastus Bombastus von Hohenheim (1528/1996) said that hysteria – or 'chorea lascivia' – was manifest in contractions of the uterus and vagina. A further century on and similar theories and remedies are being bandied about:

> Womb-Furie is a sort of madness, arising from a vehement and unbridled desire of Carnal Imbracement, which desire disthrones the Rational Facul[ty] so far, that the Patient utters wanton and lascivious Speeches … [Although it mainly affects virgins and young widows,] it may also betide married women, that have impotent Husbands, or such as they do not much affect, whereby their seminary vessels are not sufficiently disburthened … [If marriage fails as a remedy] some advise that the Genital Parts should be by a cunning Midwife so handled and rubbed, so as to cause an Evacuation of the over-abounding Sperm.
>
> (Eccles 1982: 82, quoting *Rivererius*, cited in Maines 1992: 27)

By the late Middle Ages orgasm had come to be seen as necessary for good health and, still under the influence of Galen, lack of sexual activity meant the build-up of harmful fluids whose vapour caused all sorts of disturbances, including hysteria. It had also become commonplace to recommend intercourse as a curative. Normally this was expected within the confines of marriage and with one's partner. However, medical necessity legitimized the intervention of midwives, physicians or others. An eminent doctor of the time, Pieter van Foreest (1653), gives expression to these views and practices, whilst noting their authoritative antecedents:

> When these symptoms indicate, we think it necessary to ask a midwife to assist, so that she can massage the genitalia with one finger inside, using oil of lilies, musk root, crocus, or [something] similar. And in this way the afflicted woman can be aroused to the paroxysm. This kind of stimulation with the finger is recommended by Galen and Avicenna, among others, most especially for widows, those who live chaste lives, and female religious, as Gradus [Ferrari da Gradi] proposes; it is less often recommended for very young women, public women, or married women, for whom it is a better remedy to engage in intercourse with their spouses.

Into the eighteenth century the theory and treatments continued in much the same vein. Bernard Mandeville (1711) recommended massage for hysterical young women of up to three hours daily. He also recommended horse riding. There was discussion about the effects of sexual deprivation as a cause of hysteria, sometimes still linked to notions of engorgement and retention of fluids and/or 'seed'. Cullen (1791) said that hysteria often occurs in young widows 'especially in those females who are liable to the Nymphomania; and the Nosologists have properly enough marked one of the varieties of the disease by the title of *Hysteria Libinosa*' (cited in Maines 1999: 33). The harmful effects of sexual deprivation and the association with hysteria were commented upon by Culverwell in his *Porneiopathology* in 1844 wherein he said that 'continence' in females – considered the 'brightest ornament they possess' – had pathological consequences manifest not least in the 'miseries of hysteria'. Inducements of orgasm, although not often discussed in those terms, continued to be an outcome of a range of 'treatments'.

Women on the edge of nervous breakdown

Mary Glover's parents were extremely anxious; their daughter was behaving in an increasingly odd and disturbing way. The 'attacks' were becoming more frequent and fearsome and these 'fittes' were now 'so fearful, that all that were about her, supposed that she would dye' (MacDonald 1990).[9] As if this was not worrying enough, at times she would be rendered speechless, and then, by turns, apparently blind. The development of a form of paralysis, all down Mary's left side, completed the utter consternation of her loving parents. John Glover, her father, who had become wealthy through the manufacture of gunpowder, was able to secure the services of the best doctors at the Royal College in London. These worthy physicians were intrigued by the case. At first they were confident, seeing in Mary's condition some classic symptoms that they proceeded to treat with the prescribed herbal remedies and other preparations. However, Mary failed to respond and the 'fittes' and other symptoms grew worse. The doctors of the Royal College pronounced that there was something 'beyond naturall' in the case. This caused as much fear in her parents as the symptoms themselves since there was not much of a step from this pregnant statement to the assumption of some demonic involvement. If such an assumption was made and Mary labelled a 'witch' then her parents knew that a calamitous fate might await her, not to mention the ignominy that would descend on the family. One of the attending physicians, Edward Jorden, did not agree with the others and asserted that Mary was indeed suffering from the 'suffocation of the mother'. He saw her condition as simply symptomatic of a medical pathology with a uterine cause and invoked treatments based on the old notions of the balance of opposites. He rejected any 'un-naturall' or demonic cause. The case went before Justice Anderson, renowned for his witch-finding rulings, who over-ruled Jorden's diagnosis. Jorden felt compelled to defend his position and this led to the publication of *A Brief Discourse of a Disease Called the Suffocation of the Mother.*

(Jorden 1603, cited in Rousseau 1993: 114–15)

Jorden's 'normalization' and medicalization of hysteria took place in the context of religious fundamentalism that had seen Galileo silenced and within which hysteria and such conditions were held to be a result of demonic or satanic intervention. The notorious purges of supposed witches of the sixteenth and seventeenth centuries were often connected with hysteria, and indeed, with forms of mass hysteria[10] (Allison and Roberts 1994; Bronfen 1998; Rousseau 1993). Indeed, Veith (1965), a historian of hysteria, maintains that a study of the *Malleus Maleficarum*, which documents many cases of dealing with witchcraft in the fifteenth century, clearly shows that most of the so-called witches as well as many of their victims were actually 'hysterics', some suffering from sexual delusions. Note, however, that in resisting the reactionary demonic explanation, Jorden calls upon the 'wondering womb' theories of Hippocrates and Galen, on humoral theory and the passage of vapours, through 'sympathy', that linked the womb to the imagination, the senses and the 'animal soul'. Treatments too were traditional, including the application of 'evil smells to their nostrils, and sweet smells beneath' (Jorden 1603: G3. 3). Ultimately though, the dryness, and subsequent derangement of the womb, was best cured by the reception of male seed through intercourse, thereby providing the necessary moisture to the womb. For young Mary – she was only 14 years old – the knowledge systems of the time presented a Hobson's choice; either be condemned as a witch and perhaps have the 'treatments' described in the *Malleus Maleficarum* visited upon her, or be 'diagnosed' as a victim of the 'mother' (as hysteria was colloquially called) and have actions taken to rehydrate her wandering womb – perhaps through therapeutic massage, but most certainly through advocacy of marriage at the earliest possible moment. At the level of these outcomes there is obviously more tragedy than comedy.

It is apparent, however, that a significant theoretical change emerged in the seventeenth century. Jorden was part of a process that 'naturalized' hysteria and retrieved it from the demonic and the supernatural and that saw its renewed medicalization. From the mid to late seventeenth century and into the early eighteenth, although the symptomology and treatment remained similar, hysteria was increasingly considered a 'nervous' condition. For some this still entailed a physical connection to humoral distortion but now not affecting the womb, but the brain. However, as Rousseau suggests, 'Once medicalized, hysteria became the deviant sport of Renaissance and Enlightenment doctors who justified any therapy in the name of calming female fits and faints'.

Of significance is Sydenham (1624–89) who developed different theoretical ideas about hysteria. He maintained there was no simple or single cause for hysteria, rather it emanated from a range of both 'bodily derangements' and 'mental emotions', but most significantly, the effects were communicated around the body through a neural network. He suggested that women had a weaker nervous constitution and were susceptible to 'nervous' disorders. This neurological discourse and the practices it gave rise to were to become pervasive not only in the medical treatment of women, but in broader gender discourse and politics from that point down to the present. His conceptualization of hysteria is highly significant in enabling it increasingly to be thought of as nervous disorder and thence a mental or psychological disorder. Another key part of Sydenham's conceptualization was that hysteria is mimetic: that it imitates other illnesses and conditions. This presages the possibility of a somatization thesis, but Sydenham had a broader view maintaining that 'hysteria imitates culture'. He was of the opinion that the 'nervous' conditions presenting in the symptoms of hysteria were induced by the tensions and stresses generated by the new socio-cultural conditions confronting people in the 'modern' era. Given this mimetic quality – in both senses – Sydenham maintained that hysteria was a condition that both men and women were susceptible to, and that it was the most common of all diseases (Rousseau 1993: 140). The nervous model took hold, supplanting a uterine, humoral or vaporific model, and a whole new language developed in which 'hysteria' became synonymous with 'nervous'. As Rousseau (1993: 154) says, 'all cases [of hysteria] were deemed to result from deviant physiologies of the nervous system that could be understood only by Newtonian or other mechanical analyses'.

The theoretical history of hysteria, then, passes from states inflicted by the gods, to a physical condition induced by the wondering womb, to a disturbance caused by humoral imbalance, to a satanic visitation, to a physical disease emanating in the womb but disseminated through the nerves, to a mimetic condition with a significant mental/psychological component, to a mechanico-neurological dysfunction. However, these are not discrete or mutually exclusive theories; there is a good deal of overlap, circling back and reiteration. Sydenham's more enlightened thinking notwithstanding, the notion that hysteria is caused by some form of 'congestion' induced, at least in part, by sexual abstinence was still pervasive into the early twentieth century as the redoubtable Chattanooga is brought to bear on women's nether regions. It was noted in commenting on the opening story about Beatrice that electromechanical vibrators were first used for the treatment of hysteria at the Salpêtrière clinic of Charcot in the late 1880s.

Charcot's gaze and the spectacle of the hysteric

The occasion is one of Charcot's renowned 'Tuesday Lectures' inside the 'museum of living pathology', as Charcot referred to the Salpêtrière (Guillain 1959: 10), March 1876. An audience comprised of physicians, interns, scientists, politicians, artists and the curious[11] look on as a young girl of about 15 is brought into the theatre and seated on a wooden chair. The girl is 'blond, tall and strong for her age, and gives every appearance of a pubescent girl. She is active, intelligent, affectionate, impressionable, but capricious, loving to attract attention. She is coquettish …' (Bourneville and Regnard 1876–80: 2. 127). She is dressed only in a simple white slip. One of Charcot's assistants induces hypnosis in the girl, as was normal practice, since this allowed Charcot to bring on a hysteria attack through hypnotic suggestion. Charcot, both thumbs hooked in his waistcoat, head thrown back, addresses the audience:

CHARCOT: Let us press again on the hysterogenic point. Here we go again. …
  Look at the arched back, which is so well described in the text-books.
PATIENT: Mother, I am frightened.
CHARCOT: Note the emotional outburst. If we let things go unabated, we will
  soon return to the epileptoid behavior. Now we have a bit of tranquility, of
  resolution, followed by a type of static contracted posture. I consider this
  latter deformity as an accessory phenomenon to the basic attack.
  (The patient cries again: 'Oh! Mother')
CHARCOT: Again, note these screams. You could say it is a noise over nothing.
  True epilepsy is much more serious and also quiet.

(Cited in Goetz 1987: 105–6)[12]

What is noticeable here, as de Marneffe (1991)[13] notes, is that Charcot does not respond to or interact with the patient. Indeed, de Marneffe argues that Charcot's conception of hysteria is constructed in an expressed avoidance of the talk of his patients and that he 'regularly overruled his patients' pronouncements about actual predisposing experiences in favor of his own hereditary explanations' (1991: 75). I will return to this shortly.

Charcot was enamoured of the 'clinico-anatomic' method which involved analysing and categorizing 'clinical phenomena into "archetypes"' and seeking to detect their anatomical bases through careful observation of cases. Behind the method, the theory supposed that disease resulted from anatomical lesions caused by trauma or hereditary defect that affected the central nervous system leading to the epileptiform symptoms. The approach had enabled Charcot to make significant advances, but hysteria was more of a challenge – one that increasingly preoccupied him. Since there was no obvious pathological lesion to explain hysteria, Charcot constructed the notion of the 'dynamic lesions', conceived of as psychologically traumatic events that were responsible for triggering a hereditary proclivity for nervous disease (de Marneffe 1991: 75). He was insistent on a physical cause and wanted to dismiss any religious or demonic explanation. He did also link the symptoms to the womb, or more specifically the ovaries. Reflex theory, popular at the time, suggested that perturbations in the ovaries could send signals via the spinal cord to other organs. He claimed that pressure on the ovaries could impact hysterical symptoms and reduce a hysterical seizure. He developed apparatus to do that. He tried to do the same for men, compressing the testicles to try and induce a 'hysterogenic' seizure. However, as Showalter observes, 'Unsurprisingly, the procedure did not always work, and some doctors discovered that squeezing the patient's testicles actually made the convulsions stronger' (1997: 33).

The method was heavily dependent on careful observation, something Charcot thought he was particularly equipped for, holding, as he did, the conceit that he was something of an artist with an attuned artist's eye (Bogousslavsky 2004; de Marneffe 1991): a persona befitting a leading figure in the Belle Époque. Charcot incorporated art directly into his clinical work, publishing *Les demoniaques dans l'art* in which he discusses an extensive catalogue of artwork which depicted 'the external manifestations of hysteria', even though they may have been referred to as 'possessions by the devil' or 'ecstatic states' in other times (Charcot and Richer 1972). He uses these representations to show that hysteria was not confined to women nor contemporary times. This artistic pretension together with his valorization of the visual led him to develop photography as a method of documenting the disease. The three volumes of the *Iconographie* are a visual record with drawings and photographs capturing women supposedly manifesting aspects of the disease. These were ordered, as was Charcot's whole nosography of hysteria, around four stages: 1) tonic rigidity – seizures sometimes preceded by an aura; 2) 'clownism' or *grands mouvements* – odd and exaggerated gestures and postures; 3) *attitudes passionelles* – in the form of emotional gestures and vocalizations; 4) a final delirium – accompanied by sobs, tears, or perhaps laughter. Charcot had inscribed order onto a 'wastepaper basket' (Goldstein 1987) of disparate symptoms and inscribed that onto the bodies of women. Augustine was a favoured subject in the *Iconographie* where a series of 17 plates map out Charcot's hysterical nosography. The first photograph shows Augustine properly attired and in a 'normal state'. Then in turn she is pictured

> 'Debut de l'attaque' (beginning of the attack) and two manifestations of 'Tetanisme' (tetanism). The next ten plates represent the 'Attitudes passionnelles': 'Menace' (threat) (two), 'Appel' (call), 'Supplication

amoureuse' (amorous supplication), 'Erotisme' (erotism), 'Extase' (ecstasy) (two), 'Hallucination de l'ouie' (auditory hallucination), 'Crucifiement' (crucifixion), and 'Moquerie' (teasing). (The eleventh plate, not in sequence, depicts another aspect of the 'Debut d'une attaque', the extension of the tongue.) The final two images show the contractures of limbs.

(de Marneffe 1991: 79)

There are odd and ironic aspects of this photographic record. The first is that it is clearly a representation of *Charcot's ordering* of the disease, a constructed sequencing that appears to have little relationship to the way the 'illness' actually manifested itself in Augustine or actual experiences witnessed in the clinic. The clinic's documents recording Augustine's case clearly show 'a more frenzied and chaotic expression than is depicted by the orderly sequence of photographs' (de Marneffe 1991: 80). It is apparent that the photographs are posed and there is evidence of them being 'touched up' with paint. Suggestions that the behaviour of Charcot's patients, especially in these public sessions, was staged have been repeatedly made (Goldstein 1987; Justice-Malloy 1995; Showalter 1997). The use of hypnosis to induce symptoms reinforced this impression. There was unquestionably a theatrical quality to the Tuesday demonstrations and other lectures.[14] Indeed, a frequent observer, Pierre Janet, said that 'Everything in his lectures was designed to attract attention and to captivate the audience by means of visual and auditory impressions' (quoted in Guillain 1959: 55). There are suggestions that he was 'inventing' hysteria and that patients were learning to 'perform' hysteria. Some accused Charcot and his aides of coaching the patients how to act, but even without that a degree of 'suggestion' seems likely, with patients mirroring what they saw and performing to meet the expectations of the powerful. As Goldstein argues:

> The 'iconography' of hysteria as defined by Charcot – with all its vividly theatrical contortions and grimaces – seems to have been so widely publicized … in both pictorial and verbal form, as to constitute for that historical moment a reigning 'cultural preconception' of how to act when insane.
>
> (1987: 330)

Augustine even reportedly experienced periods of colour blindness with everything appearing in the monochrome of photography! One of his most widely discussed (and displayed) patients, Blanche Wittman, subsequently denied any staging, but ironically Wittman's 'attacks' receded after Charcot left, and she remained at the Salpêtrière working in the photography department and later the radiography unit (Harris 2005).

The second odd aspect is the obviously sexual semiotics used in the captions and other language deployed by Charcot and his team, even though he repeatedly denied that hysteria was a sexual disease (Showalter 1997: 34). The captions and 'staging' of the photographs and the pictures, especially the 'attitudes passionnelles', have a distinctly erotic tone. This is doubly odd since Freud famously reports overhearing Charcot clearly imply a sexual cause for the condition (Freud and Breuer 1893: 13–14). We know too that electromechanical devices were used at the clinic to massage women in a sexual manner.

The third oddity is related and concerns the lack of attention paid to the verbal data provided by the female patients themselves, as noted earlier. Charcot seemed obsessed with the power of the visual and gave no credence to the women's spontaneous verbalizations, their own accounts, or their (sexual) histories. In addition to photographs and drawings, the *Iconographie* includes detailed transcriptions of the often anguished utterances of these women, and many times these allude to past traumas such as rape or abuse. However, these verbal accounts were not discussed or apparently used in any analysis. The clinic's own records also show that Wittman, admitted when she was 15, had been subjected to a rape attempt by an employer. The husband of a woman Augustine knew attempted to rape her whilst she was at religious school. Back home she was molested by an acquaintance of her mother, with her mother's connivance. She was housed in a small back room of his house and she was further abused, raped and threatened with a knife. She was only 13 and complained of pain and bleeding from her genitals, but her doctor simply concluded she had started her period. Her 'hysterical' attacks begin soon after. She was then placed with an old woman to work as a chambermaid. Whilst in service her brother introduced her to two of his friends and both of them had sex with her. So having been procured for sex by her mother she was now procured by her brother. As well as the hypnosis, Augustine was treated with drugs but also placed in strait-jackets and solitary confinement (Showalter 1997: 35). She tried to escape and – another irony – finally succeeded by dressing up as a man. This information was on the records at the Salpêtrière, but appears to have been discounted in favour of the power of Charcot's own observational and diagnostic skills.

The events befalling Augustine are horrific and I am certainly not trying to belittle them in any way by implying there is anything funny about them. There is, I would submit however, a deep irony in the pomposity and certitude of Charcot, his claim to scientific rigour, his obsessive observational practices, and the supposed logic of his analysis when contrasted with the absolute failure to pay any attention to evidence right under his nose, indeed, recorded in this own clinical documentation. There is something very odd about him being absorbed in a fastidious observation of his patients – with eyes wide open – whilst remaining studiously oblivious to their voices as they scream their condition and its cause into his ears closed shut. One can almost visualize him leaning forward, looking at his patient and describing to his adoring audience, 'See how she moves and shouts, a classic example of the *grands mouvements* phase that I have seen so often. This is evidence of a neurological lesion of the type I have described …' whilst his patient is shouting out that she has been deeply traumatized by being raped by her father. It is farcical that Charcot made no systematic connection between patients' traumatic sexual experiences and their clear and graphic expression of that experience, and the types of symptoms they exhibited. But then Charcot's is only one example in a long line of patriarchal displays of power in which men write women's biology, psychology, experience and history and inscribe their bodies with the consequences of that misogynistic myopia.

Picking over Anna O and Emma's otorhinolaryngological catastrophe

> Emma Eckstein was finally referred to Dr Freud's clinic for her persisting problems of menstrual irregularity, stomach pains and headaches. Freud felt that hers was a case of hysteria and originally held the opinion that the cause was masturbation (Showalter 1997: 39). He discussed the case with his friend and colleague Wilhelm Fliess. Given Fliess's otorhinolaryngological expertise, theories on reflex nasal neurosis, and the connection between sexuality, sexual dysfunction and the nose, it was decided that Fleiss would operate on Emma's nose. Early in 1895 he removed the turbinate bone from her nose. The operation was not a success. The wound became infected and when a second surgeon investigated a piece of gauze left behind by Fliess during surgery was discovered. Emma had nearly bled to death and she was left with permanent facial disfigurement. Freud persisted in his hysterical diagnosis and held that even these post-operative haemorrhages and other effects were hysterical manifestations. He engaged in the 'talking cure',[15] getting Emma to discuss her masturbation practices. This seemed to have little positive effect on her so Freud encouraged her to locate and talk through other 'memories'. This resulted in 'an account of sexual abuse when she was eight, and even a story about satanic ritual female circumcision'.
> (Showalter 1997: 40)

Freud had, as noted, attended Charcot's clinic and was a student of Charcot's methods during 1885–6. He took up and developed Charcot's hypnosis methods, believing that hypnosis could induce hysteria. He also agreed with Charcot that pressing on and massaging the 'hysterogenic' zones around the womb could help with hysteria. But it was Fliess's theories that had influenced Freud's initial treatment of Emma. In addition to his theories of reflex nasal neuroses,

Fliess also developed a theory he called vital periodicity, which supposed that all vital processes were based on biorhythms lasting 28 days in women and 23 days in men. This was related to some unusual numerological theories he had developed, particularly located around the significance of the numbers 23 and 28. In a letter dated 1 January 1896, Freud joins with Fliess in speculations of an otorhinolaryngological nature:

> The question of the source of the states of stimulation in the nasal organs now arises. The idea suggests itself that the qualitative organ for olfactory stimuli may be Schneider's membrane and the quantitative organ ... may be the *corpora cavernosa*. Olfactory substances – as indeed, you yourself believe, and as we know from flowers – are breakdown products of the sexual metabolism; they would act as stimuli on both these organs. During menstruation and other sexual processes the body produces an increased Q of these substances and therefore of these stimuli. It would have to be decided whether these act on the nasal organs through the expiratory air or through the blood vessels; probably the latter, since one has no subjective sensation of smell before migraine. Thus the nose would, as it were, receive information about *internal* olfactory stimuli by means of the *corpora cavernosa*, just as it does about external stimuli by Schneider's membrane: one would come to grief from one's own body.[16]

Anna O was the pseudonym given to Bertha Pappenheim in Freud and Breuer's *Studies on Hysteria* (1895) and she is the 'most famous patient in the annals of hysteria' (Micale 1995: 27). Indeed, it is no exaggeration to say that the whole edifice of Freudian psychoanalysis is built upon a handful of cases of female hysterics. Anna O was a patient of Breuer who presented a range of symptoms – persistent cough, headaches, sleepwalking, loss of voice and contractures of her right-side limbs – indicating hysterical conversion.[17] Breuer put her under hypnosis and encouraged her to talk about her past, memories and feelings. Breuer and Freud developed a theory suggesting that hysteria was induced by trauma, not, as with Charcot, necessarily physical or hereditary traumas, but rather events in the patient's past that had been repressed and that manifested as symptoms through symbolization. The traumas, often sexual, occurred when the person was in a 'hypnoid' state and the experience repressed into the unconscious to emerge as conversions into physical symptoms (Showalter 1997: 39). In a link to the 'suffocation of the mother', Freud suggested that negative emotional energy led to a 'strangulation effect' with the memories unconsciously converted into somatic representations (Micale 1995: 27). The 'talking cure', developed primarily through dealing with Anna O, consisted of getting the patient to retrieve these repressed memories, often through hypnosis in the early days, bringing them into consciousness and resolving them. Breuer claimed to have alleviated Anna O's condition through this methodology. Her case became an exemplar of not only the theory but of psychoanalytic practice. It was a theory and practice that quickly established itself as the new paradigm, but one subject to much revision and reinterpretation in the years since; indeed, Freud made numerous adjustments himself, mostly to strengthen the purely psychological and defensive nature of the condition.

In the post-Freudian years it is no exaggeration to say that Anna O has suffered from an excess of theorizing as her case has been picked over by successive generations of psychoanalysts and psychotherapists. Some reaffirm the Freud/Breuer diagnosis and model, but there has been a concatenation of competing accounts. These include the claim that these were cases of misdiagnosed schizophrenia, or that Anna O exhibited the symptoms of multiple disorder personality, major depression, tubercular meningitis, encephalitis. Still others claimed that she suffered a toxic psychosis as a result of being given too much morphine (Micale 1995: 60). In a different vein, Hollender (1980) argued that it was the intensity and intimacy of the patient–doctor relationship that was at issue, with Breuer being infatuated with his charge and Anna seeking something from a charismatic older man beyond the stultifying confines of her domestic situation. The excesses of Anna O reached their peak in 1984 with the publication of *Anna O: Fourteen Contemporary Reinterpretations* (Rosenbaum and Muroff 1984), which, unsurprisingly, offered 14 different accounts of Anna's case, including *inter alia* her poor psycho-sexual development, a biochemical cause, conflicted relations with the mother, her father, her brother (three different interpretations), and even that she suffered from 'Viennese Jewish Princess syndrome'.

There are again ironic elements to Anna O's tale. The first is that the much lauded treatment was not, in fact, successful. Anna (Bertha) continued to suffer, indeed showing signs of more severe pathology than that indicated by Breuer, spent periods within sanatoriums over the next few years, became addicted to the drugs administered to her and attempted suicide. A particular irony is that Pappenheim went on to become a prominent figure in German early feminist and political movements, actually authoring a play called *Women's Rights*. Some, such as Israel (1979), still sought to attribute this successful career to the effect of hysteria, a sort of drive to succeed through self-abnegation resulting from sublimating her real frustrations. A second irony is that it was Bertha who terminated the treatment with Breuer when she began to hallucinate about giving birth to his baby! This 'transference' does not appear to be founded in any actual illicit relations. Thirdly, the case again reveals the arrogance of the scientist in ignoring a patient's own biography, narrative and voice, in preference to their own interpretation. As Breuer acknowledges, Bertha was very intelligent, but came from a conservative family with puritanical morals. That familial context and the prevailing social mores of the time placed severe restrictions on Bertha and she spoke about the major frustrations she felt at not being able to realize her intellectual ambitions. Hunter (1983), invoking Lacan, argues that Bertha's linguistic symptoms were in fact an unconscious rejection of the patriarchal world and its language in which she felt trapped.

As we move closer in time to the present the risks inherent in what I am doing in this chapter increase and that is because we are entering zones where contemporary theories, with their attendant certainties, presumptions and supportive knowledge-power networks, prevail. We are less able to give ourselves the perspective of time through which to view current theories and which humour needs. They will have their attachments and will be taken seriously. Their defeasibility and risibility are less apparent. I could, for instance, pursue the hysterical peregrination into the contemporary era and look at current ideas and theories about hysteria, but am wary of doing so given the inherent dangers just intimated. A natural trajectory, for example, would be to further pursue Freud and in particular to look at the 'celebrated' case of Dora, the details of which have been copiously reported. When looked at in bare descriptive terms, that is detached from analytical and theoretical ruminations, the case actually reads like a concept pitch for a lurid prime-time soap opera, but the truth is that Dora's case and Freud's analysis of it are at the very heart of psychoanalytic practice and have been analysed, reanalyzed and repositioned *ad nauseam* ever since Freud constructed his account. Once again, the theorist silences the patient's account, overriding it with his own.

From there, the hysterical journey could continue into the present with Dora's resistance becoming a source of celebration for those seeking to critique Freud from a feminist perspective and where hysteria has a new theoretical space in feminism and in literary and cultural studies. Hélène Cixous, for example, asked 'What woman is not Dora?' (Cixous and Clement 1986), implying that Dora's positionings and frustrations within patriarchal structure, culture and language were those of every woman. She valorizes the hysteric as 'a suffering and sumptuous sister of modern feminists' (cited in Evans 1991). Hunter (1983: 485) goes further, constructing an isomorphism between feminism and hysteria such that 'feminism is transformed hysteria, or more precisely, that hysteria is feminism lacking a social network in the outer world'. The parallels are elaborated by Showalter (1985) and she envisages both feminism and hysteria as violent responses by women to patriarchal dominance – one a private, internal violence, the other a public, external form. Showalter (1997: 57) says that Dora has become 'a saint in the pantheon of feminist martyrs'.

It has been argued that hysteria has declined, if not disappeared (Veith 1965) and certainly the American Psychiatric Association ruled out the term in 1952. However, others argue that it still exists, either under different labels and guises or that it has gone underground. Showalter (1997) sees it as a pervasive phenomena manifest in a host of contemporary hysterical epidemics including tales of alien abduction, chronic fatigue syndrome, Gulf War syndrome and the resurgence of repressed memories in psychotherapy. There has also been a contemporary increase in scholarly interest in the history and, one might say, social philosophy of hysteria across a range of disciplines including literary studies, medical history, sociology, feminist theory, art theory, as well as the perhaps more obvious psychiatry, health sciences, clinical psychology and medicine – a scholarly interest that Micale (1995: 5) refers to as 'the new hysteria studies'. But I dare not venture into that theoretical field. Their time for being funny has – perhaps – not yet come.

Taking the piss

And so to finish. This chapter is about theory, it is therefore metatheoretical. But it is also anti-theory. It sees theory as funny, and as repeatedly funny. It does not want to be theoretical. It decries the claims made on behalf of theory and the damage caused in the name of theory. It notes in particular the damage inflicted on women – through male theory. How have you reacted to the stories of hysteria and the theories that have underpinned them and driven the consequential practices that inform them? Some of you might not have found anything funny or amusing in the chapter. It will depend upon who you are, your situated identities and experiences, and the theoretical locations you find comfortable. But don't get too comfortable – the ideas you hold as true may soon become the object of derision. I might have chosen something less sensitive or controversial to focus upon than hysteria, indeed, that might have been safer. In a sense almost any theorized terrain would probably have served. But, the choice is appropriate in that it has an area of extensive, long-standing and diverse theory, one that is still unresolved theoretically. It is also an effective choice because, like humour in general, it is complex, ambiguous and confusing. If the theories and their applications do now give rise to humour, they also give rise to pain, anger and suffering, and humour always functions with those adjacencies and juxtapositions, and necessarily so. I expect some people might also take offence at some, or perhaps all, of this, but that's OK. Humour is offensive sometimes, quite often in fact. Indeed, another ambiguity of humour, and one made abundantly clear throughout this book, is that humour can be unsettling and even subversive, but it can also serve to provide a containment of subversion within the safe confines of the 'merely comic' – comic relief, not serious and therefore not transformative. Reflexively it might well be that this chapter suffers the same fate. It might, at one level, be subversive with respect to theorizing and to professional practices reliant on those theoretic discourses, but will also be dismissable as 'just a bit of fun'. Indeed, the location of this chapter in a scholarly academic book, produced from within the academy, by an established and establishment publishing house constitutes a location within the extant power structures that largely militates against the possibility of subversion and transformation.

A final theory as joke – I can't resist. A medieval *physic* would demonstrate his 'craft' by peering into a vessel containing the urine of his patient.[18] This scrutiny attempted to make a 'reading' of the urine; best done whilst it was still hot, but good practice required two subsequent examinations. A judicious evaluation of the colour – and some thirty shades were deemed discernible – and consistency of the emission provided the grounds for a diagnosis of what ailed the person. The good doctor would look for a bright gold colour, signalling a healthy constitution. The content of the urine was also at issue – with some 19 types of things potentially present in the urine. Certain sediments might indicate problems with the kidneys or gout. Some also advised tasting the urine to determine its acidity levels. Such uroscopy had been practised in Europe since the time of Hippocrates and indeed, medieval *physics* relied upon texts summarizing the thoughts of Galen and Hippocrates on the matter, such as those derived from the tome compiled by the Byzantine scholar Theophilos Protospatharios. The knowledge system required to provide a proper diagnosis was not just dependent on the symptomology of, for example, the colour of the urine, the doctor would also have recourse to the Theory of Everything. There was a holistic cosmology prevalent at the time which suggested that everything was composed of the same elements – earth, water, fire and air. Everything reflects the elemental motions of the celestial bodies, themselves impelled by God. 'Man' is a microcosm of that universe and the digestive system must reflect the same balance and harmony found in the elements in the universe. Urine is the best indicator of this balance. Because in studying urine one is studying the universe in microcosm; one is, in fact, studying the universe and gaining access to the theory of everything. It might be said that by taking the piss one can discover the meaning of life, the universe, and everything.

Notes

1 The Chattanooga vibrator was produced by the Vibrator Instrument Company of Chattanooga, Tennessee and retailed for around $200 in 1900 (Maines 1999: 16, 95).

2 We shall have cause to return to Charcot later. We might note for now that Freud was a frequent visitor to the Salpêtrière and developed much of his psychoanalytic theory from the analysis of hysteria.

3 It is not clear if this is a Freudian slip, a joke, or a simple typographic error.

4 Despite the title this was a general women's magazine and not one devoted to the personal vibrator.

5 The Ig Nobel Awards are made every year at Harvard University for 'achievements that cannot or should not be reproduced'. Dan Quale was given an Ig Nobel Award for Education for 'demonstrating, better than anyone else, the need for science education'.

6 *Hysterike pnix* evolved into a complex (and here we have a linguistic and semantic problem; do we apply the label disease, conditions, syndrome, complex, illness or something else?) 'condition' that came to be labelled *hysteria*. Hysteria has an incredibly long and complex evolution dating back even beyond the time of Hippocrates in the fourth century BC. Indeed, Micale (1995: 3) suggests that references to something akin to hysteria are inscribed on Egyptian papyri of 1900 BC.

7 It is perhaps more accurate to say that a series of theories was involved.

8 There have been contemporary advocates such as Rudolph Steiner, and Eysenck's theory of personality was informed by humoral theory.

9 Cited in Rousseau (1993), from where this story is reconstructed.

10 Mass hysteria has its own history, mythology and curious theoretical trajectory that is beyond the scope of this chapter.

11 Included among those known to have attended were Henri Bergson, Emile Durkheim, Guy de Maupassant, Georges Gilles de la Tourette, Paul Richer, Edmond de Goncourt and Sigmund Freud.

12 This particular quoted text does not refer to Augustine, who will be discussed later in this chapter, but it might well have done.

13 Much of the illustration and discussion of Charcot here draws particularly on de Marneffe's paper, but also on Micale (1995) and Showalter (1997) and others.

14 Charcot had a new amphitheatre built that could seat 500, had a stage, footlights, props and other theatrical accoutrements. He scripted and presented his presentations and liberally sprinkled them with quotes from the likes of Racine and Shakespeare (e.g. see Justice-Malloy 1995).

15 An expression provided by Anna O (Bertha Pappanheim) to describe the process of talking about her past experiences and traumas to Breuer – a method Freud would subsequently label catharsis.

16 Freud had, at a later stage, asked that his correspondence with Fliess be destroyed, but they were preserved by Marie Bonaparte and were published in English (Freud 1954, more recently translated as Freud 1985).

17 As hysteria had by now come to be called.

18 I am indebted to the work of Harvey (1998) for this observation and much of the discussion of urinalysis that follows.

References

Abrahams, M. (1997) *The Best Annals of Improbable Research*, reissue edn, New York: W. H. Freeman.

Abrahams, M. (2003) *The Ig Nobel Prizes: The Annals of Improbable Research,* New York: Dutton/Penguin.

Allison, D. B., and Roberts, M. S. (1994) 'On constructing the disorder of hysteria', *Journal of Medicine and Philosophy*, 19(3): 239–51.

Berger, P. L. (1997) *Redeeming Laughter: The Comic Dimension of Human Experience*, Berlin: Walter de Gruyter.

Bogousslavsky, J. (2004) 'Charcot and art: from a hobby to science', *European Neurology*, 51(2): 78–83.

Bourneville, D. M. and Regnard, P. (1876–80) *Iconographie photographique de la Salpêtrière*, 3 vols, Paris: Au Bureau du Progres Medical, V. A. Delahaye & Cie.

Bronfen, E. (1998) *The Knotted Subject: Hysteria and its Discontents,* Princeton, NJ: Princeton University Press.

Charcot, J. M. and Richer, P. (1972) *Les Demoniaques dans l'Art*, reprinted from the original 1887 edn, Amsterdam: B. M. Israel.

Cixous, H. and Clement, C. (1986) *The Newly Born Woman*, Theory and History of Literature, 24, Minneapolis, MN: University of Minnesota Press.

Cullen, W. (1791) *First Lines of the Practice of Physic*, Edinburgh: Bell, Bradfute.

Culverwell, R. J. (1844) *Porneiopathology: A Popular Treatise on Venereal Diseases of the Male and Female Genital System*, New York: J. S. Redfield.

Deckers, L. and Buttram, R. T. (1990) 'Humour as a response to incongruities within or between schemata', *Humour: International Journal of Humour Research*, 3(1): 53–64.

de Marneffe, D. (1991) 'Looking and listening: the construction of clinical knowledge in Charcot and Freud', *Signs*, 17(1): 71–111.

Eccles, A. (1982) *Obstetrics and Gynaecology in Tudor and Stuart England*, London: Croom Helm.

Evans, M. N. (1991) *Fits and Starts: A Genealogy of Hysteria in Modern France*, Ithaca, NY: Cornell University Press.

Freud, S. (1954) *Origins of Psychoanalysis: Letters to Wilhelm Fliess, Drafts and Notes, 1887–1902*, ed. Marie Bonaparte, Anna Freud and Ernst Kris, tr. Eric Mosbacher and James Strachey, London: Imago Publ. Co.

Freud, S. (1985) *The Complete Letters of Sigmund Freud to Wilhelm Fliess, 1887–1904*, tr. Jeffrey Moussaieff Masson. Cambridge, MA: Belknap Press of Harvard University Press.

Freud, S. and Breuer, J. (1893/1955) *The Standard Edition: Studies on Hysteria*, vol. 2, tr. James Strachey, London: Hogarth Press.

Freud, S. and Breuer, J. (1895/1966) *Studies on Hysteria*, New York: Discus Books.

Goetz, C., annotator and tr. (1987) *Charcot, the Clinician: The Tuesday Lessons*, New York: Raven.

Goldstein, J. (1987) *Console and Classify: The French Psychiatric Profession in the Nineteenth Century*, New York: Cambridge University Press.

Goodell, W. (1890) *Lessons in Gynecology*, 3rd edn, Philadelphia, PA: Davis.

Guillain, G. (1959) *J.-M. Charcot, 1825–1893: His Life and Work*, New York: Hoeber.

Harris, J. C. (2005) 'A clinical lesson at the Salpêtrière', *Archives of General Psychiatry*, 62(5): 470–3.

Harvey, R. (1998) 'The judgement of urines', *Canadian Medical Association Journal*, 159(12): 1482–5.

Hollender, M. H. (1980) 'The case of Anna O: a reformulation', *American Journal of Psychiatry*, 137: 797–800.

Hunter, D. (1983) 'Hysteria, psychoanalysis, and feminism: the case of Anna O', *Feminist Studies*, 9(3): 464–88.

Israel, L. (1979) *L'hysterique, le sexe et le médicin*, Paris: Masson.

Jorden, E. (1603) *A Brief Discourse of a Disease Called the Suffocation of the Mother*, London: John Windet.

Justice-Malloy, R. (1995) 'Charcot and the theatre of hysteria', *Journal of Popular Culture*, 28(4): 133–8.

King, H. (1993) 'Once upon a text; hysteria from Hippocrates', in Sander L. Gilman, Helen King, Roy Porter, G. S. Rousseau and Elaine Showalter (eds), *Hysteria Beyond Freud*, pp. 3–65, Berkeley, CA: University of California Press, <http://ark.cdlib.org/ark:/13030/ft0p3003d3/>.

Kiple, K. F. (ed.) (1993) *The Cambridge World History of Human Disease*, Cambridge: Cambridge University Press.

Kuhlman, T. L. (1985) 'A study of salience and motivational theories of humour', *Journal of Personality and Social Psychology*, 49(1): 281–6.

Lee, D. (tr.) (1972) *Timaeus and Critias*, London: Penguin Books.

Longrigg, J. (ed.) (1998) *Greek Medicine: From the Heroic to the Hellenistic Age*, New York: Routledge.

MacDonald, M. (1990) *Witchcraft and Hysteria in Elizabethan London: Edward Jorden and the Mary Glover Case*, Tavistock Clinic Reprints in the History of Psychiatry, London: Routledge.

Maines, R. P. (1999) *The Technology of Orgasm: 'Hysteria', the Vibrator, and Women's Sexual Satisfaction*, Baltimore, MD and London: Johns Hopkins University Press.

Mandeville, B. (1711/1981) *A Treatise of the Hypochondriack and Hysteric Passions*, Hildesheim, reprinted, New York: G. Olms.

Matijaca, A. (1917) *Principles of Electro-Medicine, Electro-Surgery and Radiology*, Tangerine, FL: Benedict Lust.

Micale, M. S. (1995) *Approaching Hysteria: Disease and its Interpretation*, Princeton, NJ: Princeton University Press.

Morreall, J. (1987) 'A new theory of laughter', in J. Morreall (ed.), *The Philosophy of Laughter and Humor*, pp. 128–38, Albany, NY: State University of New York Press.

Mulkay, M. J. (1988) *On Humour: Its Nature and its Place in Modern Society*, Cambridge: Polity Press.

Munro, D. H. (1988) 'Theories of humor', in L. Behrens and L. J. Rosen (eds), *Writing and Reading across the Curriculum*, 3rd edn, pp. 349–55, Glenview, IL: Scott, Foresman & Co.

Nerhardt, G. (1996) 'Incongruity and funniness: towards a new descriptive model', in A. J. Chapman and H. C. Foot (eds), *Humour and Laughter: Theory, Research, and Applications*, pp. 55–62, New Brunswick, NJ: Transaction.

Nutton, V. (2004) *Ancient Medicine: Sciences of Antiquity*, London: Routledge.

Palmer, J. (1994) *Taking Humour Seriously*, London and New York: Routledge.

Pseudo-Albertus Magnus (1992) *De Secretis Mulierum (On the Secrets of Women)*, tr. Helen Rodnite Lemay, Albany, NY: State University of New York.

Reynolds, D. V. (1971) 'A brief history of electrotherapeutics', in D. V. Reynolds and A. E. Sjoberg (eds), *Neuroelectric Research: Electroneuroprosthesis, Electroanesthesia, and Nonconvulsive Electrotherapy*, pp. 1–22, Springfield, IL: Thomas.

Rosenbaum, M. and Muroff, M. (eds) (1984) *Anna O: Fourteen Contemporary Reinterpretations*, New York: Free Press.

Rousseau, G. S. (1993) 'A strange pathology: hysteria in the early modern world, 1500–1800', in S. L. Gilman, H. King, R. Porter, G. S. Rousseau and E. Showalter (eds), *Hysteria Beyond Freud*, pp. 91–186, Berkeley, CA: University of California Press, <http://ark.cdlib.org/ark:/13030/ft0p3003d3/>.

Showalter, E. (1985) *The Female Malady: Women, Madness, and English Culture, 1830–1980*, New York: Pantheon.

Showalter, E. (1997) *Hystories: Hysterical Epidemics and Modern Culture*, New York: Columbia University Press.

Soranus of Ephesus (1956) *Gynecology*, tr. Owsei Temkin, Baltimore, MD: Johns Hopkins University Press.

Temkin, O. (1973) *Galenism: Rise and Decline of a Medical Philosophy*, Ithaca, NY: Cornell University Press.

van Foreest, Pieter (1653) *Observationem et Curationem Medicinalium ac Chirurgicarum Opera Omnia*, Rouen: Bertherlin.

Veith, I. (1965) *Hysteria: The History of Disease*, Chicago, IL and London: University of Chicago Press.

von Hohenheim, Philippus Theophrastus Bombastus (1528/1996) 'On the diseases that deprive man of his reason', in H. Sigerest (ed.) *Four Treatises of Theophrastus Von Hohenheim*, Baltimore, MD: Johns Hopkins University Press.

Wallian, S. S. (1905) 'The undulatory theory in therapeutics … first paper', *Medical Brief* (May).

Wallian, S. S. (1906) *Rhythmotherapy: A Discussion of the Physiologic Basis and Therapeutic Potency of Mechano-Vital Vibration, to which is Added a Dictionary of Diseases with Suggestions as to the Technic of Vibratory Therapeutics*, Chicago, IL: Oaellette Press.

Westwood, R. I. (2004) 'Comic relief: subversion and catharsis in organizational comedic theatre', *Organization Studies*, 25(5): 775–95.

Part II

Humour in organizations

Chapter 5

The Little Book of Management Bollocks **and the culture of organization**

Martin Parker

Executive summary[1]

Don't just be an enabler, be a proactive, innovative and risk taking enabler! Explain to your team that in a project-driven matrix organisation, where organisational sub-systems provide enhanced double-loop learning paradigms, the challenging of structural assumptions is as inherent to strategic planning as an enhanced implementation analysis is to forward visionary thinking.

Illustrate this point by asking everybody to work over the weekend.

(Beaton 2001)

The Little Book of Management Bollocks (Beaton 2001) contains a hundred or so management clichés, nostrums and homilies. It is presumably the sort of thing that you might give to one of your colleagues at work. You might even give it to a manager who, for whatever reason, would be unlikely to retaliate. Or perhaps you would give them a coffee mug which claims 'You don't have to be mad to work here, but it helps'; rear view mirrors for their PC; a '52 ways to have fun at work' pack of cards; a poster that says 'Sarcasm. Just one more service we offer'; a Dilbert cartoon; office voodoo kit; or a David Brent screensaver. Giving work the finger, in a wide variety of ways, is the small act of revolution which makes these artefacts work. The assumption that work is boring and degrading, and satirizing it can be fun, is one part of a culture that simultaneously celebrates and denigrates management and organizations. This is the culture of organization, and it doesn't look much like the sort of excellent corporate culture that is supposed to characterise twenty-first-century western workplaces.

In this chapter I will begin by collecting and considering the sort of artefacts that start off decorating offices and are later found in car boot sales and charity shops. Offices (and factories[2]) are often personalized in this way, and the decorations very often have an 'anti-work' theme. I will then expand the illustrations in order to relate these things to a wide variety of popular and cynical representations of work organizations that are often found in advertising, TV programmes, websites and so on. All are meant to provoke a little ironic laugh, perhaps a shared smile. Given the context of this book, it is important to note that these satirical representations might be understood as resistance being produced at the point of power, or a challenge to hegemonic managerial ideology, or a form of 'safety valve', or a collision between the real and the possible, or whatever. I won't be exploring these sorts of theories and arguments here because I don't really want to sponsor any particular general theory of humour and work organizations. The book as a whole explores these ideas well enough. In this chapter, I just want to be a minor anthropologist, and describe some of the things that are pinned to notice boards in the hope that it encourages other people to notice them too. Or to put it another way, I want to share some things that have really made me laugh a lot.

Mikroman fights back

Mikroman is an intricate and incredible creation designed by Sam Buxton for the Worldwide Company. Mikroman 04 is called 'Office'. Beginning with a credit-card-sized thin sheet of metal that has been cut by machine, in two minutes you can fold out a minute creation. A headless man, seated at a desk, with a laptop computer, CD Rom, mobile phone, anglepoise lamp, wastepaper bin and digital clock. Mikroman is only possible because of technology, and his shiny metal body is conjoined with the desk/chair/computer assemblage. Poor Mikroman.

In a critical tradition of representation that we inherit from what might be called 'organizational gothic', workplaces could be seen as places of repetitive violence. This is a black and white world, one in which the only laughter at work is that of the monomaniac tycoon who wishes to control the world. Bored bodies serve machines, lowering mills and office blocks, rows of heads bent in sullen silence. Whether in Marx, Dickens, Weber or Kafka, the image is one of repeated acts of indignity, leaving hidden injuries that last a lifetime. The monotonous rhythms of crashing metal, or clicking keys, gradually stamp the souls of people into the shape of silent workers. Tin men, with no heart.

I have argued elsewhere that these sorts of images can be seen as a form of representational criticism, a way of redescribing the turgid familiarity of work in shades that highlight its horror (Parker 2005). This is also one of the things that social science can do too – take the everyday and defamiliarize it. Much of what passes for critical social science elevates this estrangement into a political virtue, as if showing people their reflections in a different mirror would be enough to make them realize that the promises of organized modernity have not been fulfilled. So, for example, the 'realist' stories of misery, intrigue and megalomania sometimes told by those who write critical work on organizations sometimes shares a certain conspiratorial glee, or sad superiority. 'Look how limited your lives are!', they might say. 'You don't see the bars of the cage that traps you!' But the authors know, because they have peeped behind the curtain and have seen that the booming voice of the Wizard of Oz is a trick.

In this chapter I intend to perform a related, but slightly different trick. For reasons I will explain below, I am interested in the idea of a 'culture of organization', which is condensed way of indicating a culture in which a wide variety of images of work and organizations are traded as routine symbols and understandings. I will expand upon this notion below, but it is worth remembering that this concept is meant to have a much wider scope than the idea of 'organizational culture'. It is intended to include all sorts of representations of work, from adverts to business guru texts. Some of these representations are very positive indeed, and it is these that have often been the butt of critical work. Airport management books, recruitment advertising, popular management magazines, MBA texts, business school PR, careers guidance, management skills training, government propaganda and even papers in *Administrative Science Quarterly* (generally seen to be the 'top' journal in the field): these are precisely the sort of shameless horrors that critical academics have (rightly in my opinion) attempted to shame. But let's try to find a little balance here, because this wide-eyed madness of management seems to be less than half of the story, and there is a real danger of overstating its effects and reach. In fact, in a wide variety of other domains, the positive representations are being continually reframed, and often actively contested. I have elsewhere suggested that business ethics, critical management studies, popular film and anti-corporate protest constitute different elements of this contest (Parker 2002), but here I want to concentrate on some more mundane aspects of the 'counter culture' of organization: the coffee cup, the notice board, the TV show.

Instead of presenting work organizations as gothic places, all about intrigue and misery, I wish to reframe them as profuse symbolic jungles that spread their subversive post-it notes, scornful laughter and email spam like spores. The teddy bear-covered computer, executive stress relievers and the 'ihatemyboss.com' websites surfed at work, as well as the toys, books and films enjoyed outside work: all these things can speak against work and all that it represents, though they are clearly also part of the culture of organization. To be clear here, my intention is not to ironize these things by being 'clever' about them, but instead to celebrate their sarcastic ubiquity. As I said, I also find a lot of this material very funny indeed.

(Mikroman is still sitting there. It is 5.47 on his digital clock, so he is working late. He has no head, so we have no idea what he is thinking. But if we look at his laptop, we can see an image of someone kicking a ball. Perhaps he is not working after all.)

'Bit of fun for a Friday!!!!'[3]

THE IMPORTANCE OF HUMOUR

> Humour is an under-used tool. Impress other people by taking out your under-used tool at unexpected moments.
>
> If other people don't like your under-used tool, put it away quickly.
>
> (Beaton 2001)

Negative representations of the world of organizations are actually very common, even if we usually overlook them. For example, in blockbuster feature films such as *Bridget Jones' Diary*, *American Beauty* and *Fight Club* we have plots that are organized around the idea that it is impossible to be true to yourself at work. In countless other films, the organization is the problem, populated by heartless bureaucrats or hungry careerists (or even vampires). Redemption is to be found in telling your boss to stick it, or placing a stake through his heart, and then walking out of the door to freedom, the beloved, the child or even the dog. Yes, even the dog is better than work. In part, this is no more than the deployment of common stereotypes. If you want a bad guy, whether in *Spiderman* or the latest James Bond, then make him a millionaire tycoon.

But what is missing from this account are all the small ways in which the same scepticism is routinely deployed in endless micro acts of constrained creativity. For example, there is something chasteningly illustrative about the selling of a *Fuck Work* sticker ($1.49, plus postage and packing, and an extra 99¢ if you want it magnetized). Someone imagined it, someone financed it and then other people designed it, marketed it, optimized the production schedule, pressed the button that made the machines run, packed it, distributed it, sold it and finally collected the profit, or the interest from their investment. Someone else bought it with money that they earned from working, but can probably never stick it up at work for fear of the consequences.[4] So it goes.

Whilst the *Fuck Work* example is rather extreme, a lot of money has clearly been made through selling humorous opposition to management. Why not try '250 Dumb Dares for the Workplace', 'guaranteed to keep the office entertained'? Your colleagues might also be entertained if you threw the office dice, giving you six chances: 'Have a meeting', 'Make a phone call', 'Work late', 'Send an e-mail', 'Resign' or '**** the secretary'. Or, you could play 'Boss Toss' with a tub of 72 mini executives, 'dressed for success and ready to make their way up the corporate ladder'. You could collect 'The Cubes', a set of action figures that includes bosses, employees, a sensitivity consultant and even a 'corporate protester'. All, apart from the last one, come with their own cubicle, filing cabinet and office posters. Or you might choose 'Voodoo Lou's Office Voodoo Kit' containing a corporate doll (with male and female sides), pins and 'Executive Spellbook'. The book explains what is wrong with bosses (playing golf, eating big lunches, driving a Lexus), as well as their assistants, the computer nerd and so on. It then proposes various voodoo remedies which will deal with them, and provide the owner with 'your ticket to the corporate high life'. The same is probably not true of the Office Profanity Kit, containing a mini talking punchbag which swears at you when you hit it, and three stamps with the mottos 'This is F**CKING URGENT', 'Complete and Utter BULLSHIT' and 'I haven't got time to read this CRAP'.

Or if you fancy something a little more educational *The Little Book of Management Bollocks* is merely one example of a long line of work-related satirical books. *The Organization Mad* (Feldstein 1956),[5] C. Northcote Parkinson's *Parkinson's Law* (1958), *Up the Organization* by Robert Townsend (1970), *Managers and Magic* (Cleverley 1971), Martin Page's *Company Savage* (1972) and Raymond Monbiot's *How to Manage your Boss* (1982) are all book-length articulations of a view of organizations as inept bureaucracies populated by pompous and stupid executives. More recent examples are *The Official Rules of Work* (Dickson 1996), which has collected a wide range of management related 'principles, maxims and instructions'; the self-explanatory *Bluffer's Guide to Management* (Courtis 2000); *How to be a Sincere Phoney* by Jim Boren (2003), which contains Machiavellian advice for bureaucrats; and *Office Wit and Wisdom* (Turner 2004).[6]

The small screen is another place to find such satire made routine.[7] In the UK in 2003, the ITV network screened a show called *Office Monkey*. Each half an hour episode performed a reality TV version of giving the boss the finger.

> Offices are dull dreary places where nothing ever happens. That's why we bribed two members of offices around the country to disrupt their work places in the funniest ways possible. The winner gets a holiday, and the right to call themselves: Office Monkey.
>
> (http://www.princess.uk.com/programmes/individual/recent/office. htm#)

The sniggering, squirming embarrassment that accompanied victory was painful to watch, but tapped into some deeply rooted assumptions about what work is, and what it does to people. Office humour is generally spiteful, a form of vengeance that generalizes the hypocrisy and pomposity found in so many workplaces. Many British situation comedies have exploited this in their portrayal of figures of authority. *On the Buses* (1969–73), *Are You Being Served?* (1972–83), and the remarkable *Reginald Perrin* (1976–9) shows all contain various supervisory or management characters whose vacuous vanity is regularly exposed. Perhaps iconically, in the latter we have the pompous CJ (the CEO of Sunshine Desserts) pronouncing pearls of managerial wisdom – 'I didn't get to where I am today by ... ' Often, these dramas were also post-war satires of social class in an era of accelerated social mobility, particularly of the 'jobsworth'[8] who is acting up in terms of status and authority. So, Captain Mainwaring, the bank manager in *Dads' Army* (1968–77), the prison warder Mr Mackay in *Porridge* (1974–7) or the leisure centre manager Gordon Brittas in *The Brittas Empire* (1991–7) are claiming airs and graces which they clearly don't possess. Nowhere was this better satirized recently than in the mock reality TV show *The Office* which ran for two series on the BBC between 2001 and 2003. The banal vanity of David Brent (a vile middle-aged middle manager) and his ordinary organization made the show a cult hit, and a substantial amount of merchandising (DVDs, books, scripts, notepad, pen and pencil, sticker, mug, badge, ruler, mouse mat, calendar) was rapidly spun off from the series, as well as an official Office website which encourages the submission of pictures and stories about work.

Of course the other iconic anti-work satire of the last decade has been the Dilbert cartoons by Scott Adams. Co-opted by an entire generation of management academics and trainers, Adams's syndicated strip explores the endless stupidities of office life through the eyes of a naïve junior. The first collection was beautifully titled *Build a Better Life by Stealing Office Supplies*. As Adams says in the introduction:

> To research this book I spent nearly two weeks working at a large American company. This was long enough to become an expert by American standards, but not so long that the life force would be sucked out of me.
>
> (1991: 3)

His later work has covered just about every management fad, and skewered management hypocrisies with considerable skill (see, for example, Adams 1997). Many episodes of *The Simpsons* picked up on similar themes concerning Homer's work at Mr Burns's power plant (Rhodes 2001), and these themselves had been prefigured in Matt Groening's 1980s cartoons such as the *Work is Hell* collection (2004). In Groening's marvellous world, senior managers read articles titled 'How to Make the Veins in your Forehead Throb Alarmingly' in a magazine called *Lonely Tyrant*. An even more surreal portrayal of work is the collection *My New Filing Technique is Unstoppable* (Rees 2004) which contains assorted employees abusing each other about their filing systems, computers that call you a stupid motherfucker, and Dr Niles Fanderbiles from the Quality Perfection Department who delivers self-righteous homilies in a Chinese accent.

Given its easy access at most workplaces, it is hardly surprising that the internet has become a home for a great deal of anti-work culture. Surfing during work time is, of course, a problem for organizations in itself, and various snooping technologies have been developed to prevent it, just as other counter technologies have been developed to allow rapid movement between illicit web trivia and 'real' work on the computer. After all, if you were forwarding email messages which claimed to be from the Personnel Department about 'Special High Intensity Training (S.H.I.T)', or warning about the 'Worm-Overload-Recreational-Killer (WORK)' you might not want your boss to know. They certainly wouldn't like it if you were playing 'Hate Boss', a downloadable game that lets you execute hateful photos of 'your boss or somebody who makes you crazy' (http://www.downlinx.com/proghtml/303/30334.htm). You might also have fun forwarding attachments that pretend to be staff opinion surveys, but only allow you to vote for more work and less money. Or new pull down menus for 'Word for Windows' which say things like 'Take Back Flippant Comment', 'Extend Deadline', 'Read Boss's Mind', 'Reclaim Wasted Evenings' and so on.

Bored with this (because so much of this is all about negotiating boredom) you might go and have a look at fake company websites such as huhcorp.com, Bonk Business Inc. (www.bonkcentre.fi), Despair, Inc. (www.despair.com), and the Australian International University (www.aiu.name). Slightly more risky at work might be looking at mybossisatosser.co.uk, ihatemyboss.ca, fthisjob.com, fuckthatjob.com, or even ihatemydamnjob.com.[9] The latter contains the following categories for you to mail in your own stories.

- General Workplace Stories and Crap. Come here to bitch about all the above.
- My Boss, The Idiot. Do you have one of THOSE bosses?
- Who has the Crappiest Job? You think your job has what it takes to have the crappiest job?
- What I Hate the Most … What's the one thing you can't stand at work?
- Tales from the Cubical Farm.

The website workorspoon.com has a particularly delightful origin. SpoonMan was 'preparing to grind another thin shard of his life away at "that place"', and on the way to the shower, picked up a spoon from the kitchen. He then proceeded to stare in the mirror, deciding whether to go to work or gouge one of his eyes out with the spoon. 'This site is your chance to bitch and complain to the whole world about how fucking stupid your company really is'. Moving to iworkwithfools.com, we even find a delightful mission statement that nicely captures the combination of satire and raging angst that characterizes many of these sites.

1. To show the world what a complete bunch of morons we all work with.

2. To rant since we would all love to rip someone a new one.
3. To realize we are not alone in our futility.
4. To try and stop the madness from spreading.
5. To teach others that there is no hope.
6. To use the words 'WTF' since it is always an appropriate answer.
7. To share with others your misery.
8. To let others know you are smarter than your boss.
9. To tell others how easy they have it since you have it worse.
10. To not be able to quit since the economy sucks.
11. To share tricks with others you use to get through the day.
12. To want to knock some fool unconscious because of their stupidity.
   To know this list is endless and you are NOT a fool!

All these examples work precisely because anti-work humour is embedded in so many assumptions about what work is and what it is not. Indeed, almost any leisure related product can make a useful reference to the repressive structure of the working week, such as the restaurant chain 'TGI Friday' (Thank God It's …), the TV show *TFI Friday* (Thank Fuck It's …), or the hundred and one pop songs that have Friday on their mind, and celebrate that the weekend is here. In 2004, the vodka bar chain 'Revolution' was advertising 'P45' office Christmas parties;[10] the Vauxhall Tigra was advertised with a guide to avoiding the office idiot; and EasyJet were advertising using the strapline: 'Tell the boss to stick it … where the sun don't shine'. Perhaps the oddest recent example was the website ihatework.co.uk of the English theme park Alton Towers, which encouraged employees of other organizations to 'escape the workplace rat-race' by printing off a coupon for a cheap day at the theme park. The clear implication of the site was that you might pretend to be ill that day, and this provoked a small media storm in May 2004 with the Confederation of British Industries claiming that the park management was acting irresponsibly in encouraging unauthorized absences. The PR people from the theme park of course denied this was the case, but one might wonder how tolerant Alton Towers management might be if other organizations encouraged their employees to go shopping when they should be working. Perhaps the fictional National Society for the Prevention of Cruelty in Offices should become involved (www.nspco.org.uk).

I suspect that most of the examples in this section have not surprised you, though I hope that they have made you laugh. I haven't needed to do much work with the list of artefacts and ideas above because they reflect common elements of a set of wide cultural assumptions, and do not need to be explained in order to make sense. They are not, in the precise sense of the term, *sub*-cultural. Nonetheless, what might puzzle you at this point is just what unifies this rather odd list of artefacts, and just why I think it is worthwhile bringing them to your attention.

Culture in organizations, and of organization

The previous section is a sketch of one aspect of the culture of organization. This is clearly a contested culture, one in which images of clever knowledge workers enthusiastically pointing at each other's laptops contrasts with images of bored spotty cubicle drones surfing for porn. As I have suggested above, I think that a great deal of attention has been paid to the former set of images by those doing critical work on organizations, but that there has been relatively little attention paid to the latter. This is rather odd, given the very substantial increase of interest in organizational culture over the past two decades, but perhaps that tells us something rather interesting about the temporally and spatially restricted ways in which culture has been conceptualized within parts of organization studies. If culture, following Raymond Williams (1976), is the *whole* way of life of a people, then it seems that studying the culture of organization might not end in the reception area. Of course another discipline that has not suffered from these restrictions is cultural studies, which finds its origins in the radical humanism offered by Williams. But, despite the canonical beginnings offered by Willis (1977), attempting to understand the relation between lived culture and lived economy seemed to become less important as cultural studies developed. As has been commonly observed, contemporary cultural studies has been more at home studying representations of leisure rather than work, consumption rather than production. A recent 'definitive guide' to popular culture (Guins and Cruz 2005) contains essays on music, fashion, Barbie, Disney, pornography, *Star Trek*, cities and queers, but nothing on work. All too often, cultural studies has ended at 9.00, and begun again at 5.30, or missed the structure of the working week altogether in order to celebrate the agency of the weekend.[11]

But there is nothing intrinsic to a cultural studies approach that would make it ignore work organizations. So what might a cultural study of organization look like? It might begin with Smircich's (1983) dismissal of the idea that organizations *have* cultures, and her sponsoring the idea that organizations *are* cultures. Not a new move in itself, given the century-long interest amongst those who study organizations in atmosphere, informal structure, personality, climate and so on, but an articulation that licensed a resurgence of interest in participant observation and ethnographic work within the business schools. Studies of symbolism, photocopier stories, resistance, narratives, rituals and ceremonies became quite common enough, and much quasi-anthropological terminology was used to bring back tales from these strange organizational tribes (Parker 2000). Yet, despite this wonderful series of accounts, the idea of the organization as a container still tended to be the dominant one. So, what was being studied was culture *in* organizations, with all the boundaries that implied. But very little of what I have covered in the previous section can reasonably be included in such a narrow definition of culture. Indeed, I would argue that that is precisely why it has so often been left out. It is too much like leisure for theorists of work, and too much like work for theorists of leisure. But think about an example that confuses such simple categories. What about sex at work? Julianne Balmain's *Office Kama Sutra* (2001) is a book that is about getting a good position in the office. It is the very ambivalence of that joke that is important. It is not just a book about a leisure activity, or a book about how to get promoted by having sex with people. It is both.

Hence the suggestion here is to study the culture *of* organization. Or perhaps to practise cultural studies of organization, if cultural studies is understood as including economy. The key question would be a simple one, one that in various ways concerned Marx, Weber and Durkheim: 'what does it mean to live in an organized society?' A broad question certainly, but one that assumes no particular divisions between economy and culture. That question, in this chapter, has become an account of cultural representations of contemporary economy, or economic representations of contemporary culture. It doesn't particularly matter which, as long as both are assumed to be absolutely intertwined. One of the elegant things about such a question is that its materials necessarily cut neatly through a variety of dualisms which have been manifested across the human sciences – structure/agency, culture/economy and material/human.

First, most of these TV shows, books and novelties are meant to make money. Even the *Fuck Work* sticker is being sold for money.[12] So this production of culture through ironizing the economic is itself one element of the economy. Rehn expresses this nicely when he points out that popular culture can be taken seriously, whether that involves the massively profitable business of selling toys (both for adults and children), or rap artists singing about how wealthy they are (Rehn 2004; Rehn and Sköld 2005). Secondly, all these artefacts make their meaning by commenting on the constraints that work constructs, whether temporal, emotional, financial or whatever. In some sense they exemplify the tragedy of mass culture, of selling dope to the dupes who are enslaved by the iron cage. There is little heroic agency in these portrayals of microserfs, McJobs and netslaves, but a great deal of disgust and self-pity. But this very acknowledgement is itself an indication that the people who produce and consume this stuff are (at the very least) reflexive agents who can see the bars of the cage. All the materials that I have gathered together in the previous section are subversive, whether the subversion is badmouthing the boss, taking a holiday, or laughing knowingly at the stupidities of organizations. Whether this makes them romantically resistant, or inevitably co-opted, is something that I will return to in the final section.

The final element that I want to briefly comment upon is that my list of artefacts above has largely been based on 'materials', on objects (both real and virtual) that human beings can use to make meaning with. As any phenomenologist would tell you, the meanings that particular objects can provide does not reside only in the objects themselves, but has a great deal to do with the way that people understand the world. Yet, as any materialist would also tell you, the things in themselves can also be actors in this process, and they can translate understandings into concrete forms. Warren (2004) points out that even the personalization of office space can be a subversive act, even if it is merely to place teddy bears on the computer monitor. So, depending on the context, a 'Thank God it's Friday' mug could be a deeply felt condemnation, a barely noticed cliché or a piece of junk in a car boot sale. As actor network theorists might say, it depends on what network of actants the mug happens to be located within (Latour 2005).

So the so-called 'dualisms' of culture/economy, and structure/agency, and human/material seem to be nicely dissolving here. Or, to put it another way, their tensions and inter-relatedness are necessarily exposed. Savage satire and dull powerlessness are co-constituted, because *Fuck Work* is still work. But what kind of work is it, and who benefits?

Difficult questions

> DIFFICULT QUESTIONS
> During important presentations, use humour to defuse difficult questions. For example, if somebody asks you something you can't answer, just smile and say:
> 'Hey, that's a tricky one – too tricky for me!'
> or
> 'That's a very good question. Wish I knew the answer!'
> or
> 'Fuck off, smart-ass'
>
> (Beaton 2001)

As I suggested above, I think that the culture of organization is co-constituted by (at least) two powerful and opposed currents. One is market managerialism, and all the marketing that goes along with it. The Bill Gates world of self-actualized managers in a dynamic global economy is one that is told and sold from the minarets of corporate consultancies the world over. But it is not unchallenged. The other current is a multitude of critical representations of this ideology – critical management studies, business ethics, trade unionism, anti-corporate protest, film sub-texts, satirical books, fucktheboss websites, fake notices about a 'New Toilet Policy' and so on. It seems to me helpful to think of these cultural currents as engaged in a contest for a form of representational hegemony. This is a cultural economic struggle that is being carried out on many different levels.

The organized pressure groups who wish to encourage ethical investing for pension funds might be at one extreme, whilst the *Fuck Work* sticker might be at the other. Both are important.

In that sense then, documenting elements of the 'counter culture' of organization is to give them a certain voice, and perhaps suggest that these practices and materials are actually rather central to constituting a sense of an oppositional identity at work. Some of this work has been carried out within the organizational culture and symbolism tradition and some within cultural studies. For example, Warren (2004) has studied the resistance to hot-desking by personalizing office space, whilst Lupton and Noble (2002) looked at the appropriation and decoration of office PCs. Whilst this is certainly relevant, it occupies only a small part of the counter culture, and I think this is largely because fucktheboss websites fall between disciplines, between culture and economy. So it might well be that, despite what I have said about dualisms above, this chapter is simply read as a statement about humour as resistant agency. That would be misleading.

I don't want to romanticize 'resistance' any more than I want to fetishize power. There has been a fair amount of writing about dissent, misbehaviour and resistance at work (see, for a summary, Ackroyd and Thompson 1999), but much of it tends to fall into an either/or trap. Either dissent is a marvellous example of human agency when confronted with dehumanizing situations, or resistance merely confirms the power of that which it pushes against. In terms of humour, this would be the distinction between humour as a pin to prick the balloon, or humour as a plaster to stop the air escaping. But how could we choose between these two positions? It is the very ambivalence of anti-work culture that I think is so important to keep in mind. It bites the hand that feeds it, and very often knows this all too well. It would also bite any hand that attempted to analyse it, explain it or account for it.

I was told about the colleague of a friend, a lecturer in a further education college, who keeps a clock on his wall stopped permanently at five to five. A workplace ethnographer told me about designers who had parodied their organizational logo by redesigning it in 'inappropriate' ways. A poster on the back of an office door read 'Everyone Brings Joy to this Office. Some when they enter. Some when they leave.' A distant senior manager in the National Health Service forwarded fake PowerPoint slides which parodied a lesson in corporate strategy. Rubbed into the dirt on the back of a lorry was an unhappy face with MON underneath it and a happy face with FRI underneath it.[13] In all these cases, the juggernaut of the organization is still there, and the humour can just as easily be understood as resignation rather than revolution. Like the scratches on a prison wall, they confirm the existence of the wall. But like the scratches on the prison wall, they demonstrate that the wall is not all that there is.

So I don't know whether *The Little Book of Management Bollocks* is a tragic gesture or a heroic one, and I think the answer is that it is both. Always both. Indeed, only the simple-minded could insist that it was one or the other. If you need further convincing, imagine a world where *The Little Book of Management Bollocks* did not exist. It would either be a utopia where work was always joy, or totalitarianism, where you are told that work is always a joy.

Recommendations

Mikroman would smile, if he had a face, because he likes playing his football game on his computer. Being at work gives many small pleasures, and he would rather not leave his desk. He is afraid that there is nothing outside his flat shiny world, but he is wrong.

Notes

1　Thanks to Peter Armstrong, Phil Hancock, Simon Lilley and the editors of this book. Earlier versions of the paper were presented in Turku, Amsterdam, Paris and Sunderland. A paper which develops the 'counter culture' and 'cultural studies' elements of this argument appears as Parker (2006).

2　Though factories do display various forms of subversive or personalizing decoration, this paper concentrates on offices. The iconography of the office seems to be the dominant one, which is hardly surprising given the collapse of the primary and secondary sector in the global north since the late 1970s.

3　This header was used on a spam email satirizing work. Thanks to Julie Ball for this.

4　You can also buy a 'fuck it' button for your PC, which is probably easier to hide than the sticker. I have a 'Fuck Work' badge, but I only wear it at the university around people below the level of dean.

5　The title of which parodies W. H. Whyte's book *Organization Man* published in the same year.

6　A recent French example was Corinne Maier's *Bonjour Paresse* ('Hello Laziness') which celebrates doing nothing at work, and prompted her employer (Electricité de France) to attempt to discipline her (Gentleman 2004).

7　In 2004 a story line in the English television soap opera *Coronation Street* (about a serial killer businessman) provoked Digby Jones, the Director of the Confederation of British Industry, to complain to ITV that 'business people are portrayed as greedy or crooks' (Sherwin 2004: 22).

8　An English term for someone who, if asked to do something unusual, would reply 'it's more than my job's worth'. In other words, a dull bureaucrat.

9　All these sites were visited around May 2004. If they aren't there anymore, I'm sure you can find plenty more like them.

10　A 'P45' is the tax form you get in the UK when leaving, or being sacked from, a job.

11　The turn to 'cultural economy', mostly coming from sociology rather than cultural studies, does begin to indicate some shifts here, but the emphasis is primarily on 'cultural labour', not the culture of labour. See Ray and Sayer (1999), du Gay and Pryke (2002), Amin and Thrift (2004).

12 The co-optation of resistance was nicely illustrated when the telecommunications company NTL bought the domain name for the protest site ntlhell.co.uk. They turned it into a customer complaints site masquerading as something vaguely anti-corporate.

13 Thanks to Paul Grivell for the first example, Sam Warren for the second, Wendy Brown for the third, Jude Courtney for the fourth, and *The Idler* (2005) for the fifth.

References

Ackroyd, S. and Thompson, P. (1999) *Organisational Misbehaviour*, London: Sage.

Adams, S. (1991) *Build a Better Life by Stealing Office Supplies: Dogbert's Big Book of Business*, London: Nicholas Brealey.

Adams, S. (1997) *The Dilbert Future: Thriving on Stupidity in the 21st Century*, London: Boxtree.

Amin, A. and Thrift, N. (2004) *The Cultural Economy Reader*, Oxford: Blackwell.

Balmain, J. (2001) *The Office Kama Sutra*, San Francisco, CA: Chronicle Books.

Beaton, A. (2001) *The Little Book of Management Bollocks*, London: Pocket Books.

Boren, J. (2003) *How to be a Sincere Phoney: A Handbook for Politicians and Bureaucrats*, Whitsboro, TX: Birdcage Publications.

Cleverley, G. (1971) *Managers and Magic*, London: Longman.

Courtis, J. (2000) *The Bluffer's Guide to Management*, London: Oval Books.

Dickson, P. (1996) *The Official Rules at Work*, London: Robson Books.

du Gay, P. and Pryke, M. (eds) (2002) *Cultural Economy*, London: Sage.

Feldstein, A. B. (ed.) (1956) *William M. Gaines's The Organization Mad*, New York: New American Library.

Gentleman, A. (2004) 'Hello indolence, goodbye job', *Guardian* (28 July).

Groening, M. (2004) *Work is Hell*, London: HarperCollins.

Guins, R. and Cruz, O. (2005) *Popular Culture: A Reader*, London: Sage.

Latour, B. (2005) *Reassembling the Social: An Introduction to Actor Network Theory*, Oxford: Oxford University Press.

Lupton, D. and Noble, G. (2002) 'Mine/not mine: appropriating personal computers in the academic workplace', *Journal of Sociology*, 38(1): 5–19.

Monbiot, R. (1982) *How to Manage Your Boss*, London: Corgi.

Page, M. (1972) *The Company Savage*, London: Cassell & Co.

Parker, M. (2000) *Organisational Culture and Identity*, London: Sage.

Parker, M. (2002) *Against Management*, Oxford: Polity.

Parker, M. (2005) 'Organisational gothic', *Culture and Organization*, 11(3): 153–66.

Parkinson, C. (1958) *Parkinson's Law, or the Pursuit of Progress*, London: John Murray.

Ray, L. and Sayer, A. (1999) *Culture and Economy After the Cultural Turn*, London: Sage.

Rees, D. (2004) *My New Filing Technique is Unstoppable*, New York: Berkeley Publishing Group.

Rehn, A. (2004) *The Serious Unreal*, Helsinki: Dvalin.

Rehn, A. and Sköld, D. (2005) 'I love the dough: rap lyrics as a minor economic literature', *Culture and Organization*, 11(1): 17–31.

Rhodes, C. (2001) '"D'Oh": *The Simpsons*, popular culture and the organizational carnival', *Journal of Management Inquiry*, 10(4): 374–83.

Sherwin, A. (2004) 'TV accused of badmouthing the bosses', *The Times* (16 Nov.).

Smircich, L. (1983) 'Concepts of culture and organizational analysis', *Administrative Science Quarterly*, 28: 339–58.

The Idler (2005) 'War on work', issue 35, London: Ebury Press.

Townsend, R. (1970) *Up the Organization*, London: Michael Joseph.

Turner, T. (2004) *Office Wit and Wisdom*, London: Prion.

Warren, S. (2004) *Hot Nesting: A Visual Exploration of the Personalisation of Work Space in a Hot-Desking Environment*, Portsmouth: Portsmouth Business School.

Whyte, W. H. (1956) *The Organization Man*, New York: Simon & Schuster.

Williams, R. (1976) *Keywords*, London: Fontana.

Willis, P. (1977) *Learning to Labour*, Farnborough: Saxon House.

Chapter 6

'Don't get me wrong, it's fun here, but ...'
Ambivalence and paradox in a 'fun' work environment

Sam Warren and Stephen Fineman

> A number of books written within the last few years have been telling employers and employees to have fun at work. Whether it is throwing a fish, squirting each other with water guns, or throwing a pie in the CEO's face. A problem with a number of these 'fun' books is that they do not define what fun is before letting the dogs loose. Rule number one is to clearly explain to the employees what fun is and what it is not.
>
> ('Workplace Tips' found at employer-employee.com)

For this management consultant, fun at work is not as straightforward as it seems. The 'wrong' sort of fun contains seeds of danger as the 'dogs' (i.e. employees) do things they should not do, disrupting the managerially legitimated order. Therefore, employees (and employers) need to be instructed on what does and does not constitute appropriate fun at work. This is an intriguing perspective on what has become a mini industry of *prescribed* fun at work (Warren 2005a). Fun, of course, may be more or less formally organized – such as 'fun' parties, learning events or recreational 'experiences'. But fun programmes at work add a particular dimension of control and morality to the kinds of fun or mirth that employees *ought* to experience. Is this a mark of neo-humanism at work, aimed at increasing the overall sum of happiness, health and, presumably, productivity at work? If so, then some celebration of 'the childishness in us all' could be considered a good thing. Or, more critically, is such organized fun a new form of managerial control, a way of engineering employees' compliance to monotonous or stressful work through mood-elevating distractions? Viewed from this perspective, structured fun represents an attempt to colonize the 'affective zone' of work and workplaces, so as to neutralize the impulse for dissent.

In this chapter, we address the questions posed above by drawing insights from an ethnography of a corporate fun programme where participants try to make sense of their feelings and experiences. This initiative consisted of an 'aestheticization' of the web-design department of a multinational IT firm, in the face of an otherwise traditional – even staid – organizational culture. For example, the office was decorated in bright, funky colours; meeting rooms were decked out with foam blocks and soft furnishings more usually seen in a children's nursery; and toys and games were provided by management which staff were encouraged to use. These fun activities, described in more detail in the case study below, constitute a subtle interpretative arena that belies a simple analysis of structured fun. Participants often debunked or subverted the instruments of fun, while the very existence of a fun programme seemed also to contribute to employees' feeling of wellness; indeed they felt special and valued because of the provision of the 'fun zone'.

After presenting some examples from the research, the implications of the study are discussed in terms of four possible, different and not necessarily mutually exclusive, conceptual positions: (1) that 'managing' 'fun' is an oxymoron – they are mutually contradictory terms, so fun events must fail; (2) that prescribed fun at work is oppressive, silencing important, negative, voices; (3) that fun programmes might create spaces for collective rebellion – making fun of the fun programme is what is really fun; (4) and finally that fun at work is a benign intervention, an incremental addition to wider social expectations about warm, friendly, conditions of work and the importance of 'all things fun' in everyday life – 'it's just part of being nice to work here'. In conclusion, we suggest that the introduction of structured fun at work is a potentially ambivalent phenomenon – one that can register a range of both positive and negative responses from those who participate in it.

'Work should be fun'

One impact of the Industrial Revolution was that work was rendered as heavy toil and regimented performance. Fun and play were to be squeezed into whatever time was left after long and exhausting periods of work, paced by the relentlessness of factory machines. European Protestantism added an ascetic dimension to the seriousness of work: fun had no place in the redemptive role of hard toil and solemn application (Weber 1958). Early nineteenth-century America witnessed a growth in mass, family, leisure facilities, a form of fun regarded by the establishment of Protestant ministers as a wholesome contribution to a 'rounded' moral and physical character (Uminowicz 1992). It also seeded the 'work hard, play hard' mantra, to become robust shorthand for self-improvement and achievement in capitalist societies. In such conditions, play was to be quite separate from the working environment, a divorce that was not seriously challenged until the late twentieth-century interest in corporate culture. We see here, for example, Deal and Kennedy's (1982) influential claims that the success of many blue chip American corporations could, in large measure, be put down to their organizational cultures that *intermix* work and play. 'Appropriate' fun, play, humour and jokes should, therefore, be seen as managerial resources that could be used positively to energize and motivate employees. Play should be a legitimate facet of the *manifest* culture of the workplace.

Today, Deal and Kennedy's legacy can be detected in a wide range of managerialist publications from 'humour consultants', prescribing regimes and techniques of play at work. These authors, typically, underscore claims about the performance and bottom-line benefits of fun, also asserting that fun can improve workers' emotional and physical health (Blumfled 1994; Conte 1998; Segal and LaCroix 2000; Yerkes 2001). This literature also connects with work that seeks to demonstrate humour's apparent health benefits and positive effect on perceived well-being (see e.g. Thorson *et al.* 1997, and more critically, Martin 2001). Humour's apparent qualities as panacea have been adopted enthusiastically by companies across different sectors, ranging from engineering and airlines to photographic processing and banking (Caudron 1992; Collinson 2002; Meyer 1999; Thomas 1999). Particularly noteworthy are companies that rely on virtual communications served through call centres. For example Alferoff and Knights (2003) describe how games and fancy dress are used by call centres in financial services, telecommunications and mail-order shopping. The humour is intended to ameliorate or palliate the often highly regulated and controlled environment of call centre work. Likewise, an Australian, multi-agency, call centre, has celebrated its '3Fs' ('Focus, Fun, Fulfilment') with events such as theme-dress days, team-building exercises, alcohol periods, open flirting and exhortations to 'be yourself' (Fleming and Spicer 2004). Kinnie *et al.* (2000) report on a call centre of a major UK bank where team bonding is encouraged through themed dressing-up days, raffles and prizes for 'good ideas'. Indeed, at the call-centre headquarters of Egg, a UK bank, play areas are interspersed amongst the open-plan work stations. An Egg employee explains:

> The places we work in are kitted out with designated chill out areas. So if you need to get away from the grindstone, there's somewhere to go and sit. You can even take in a game of pool or table football. On top of that, we have a relaxed, informal dress code – we want to get to work feeling comfortable.
>
> (Bogdan *et al.* 2005: 143)

The 'fun at work is good for you' discourse has been recently elevated by 'positive organizational scholarship' (Cameron *et al.* 2003; Fineman 2006). This American-led neo-humanist movement is committed to understanding and promoting the 'upside' of working life. It is interested in the personal ingredients and circumstances that contribute to positive moods, well-being and happiness at work. In application, the approach endorses organizational development programmes that foster positive thinking, appreciation and fun. Amongst their 'positive' exemplars is Southwest Airlines' 'corporate culture of fun' (Bernstein 2003), an airline that seeks out 'positive people' to create a 'Positively Outrageous Spirit' (Deal and Kennedy 1999; Sunoo 1995). Such initiatives, according to positive scholars, humanize organizations by enhancing the mood, creativity and well-being of employees, and by reducing turnover and absenteeism (Ford *et al.* 2004).

The infantile turn we see in many of these initiatives sits oddly with the image of grown-ups at work. Yet some observers regard this as more than simply a quirky or ephemeral addition to the armoury of management (Bogdan *et al.* 2005; Pinault 2003). Rather (and arguably) it reflects a wider cultural predilection towards play as a new ethical ingredient of a 'fulfilled life in Western consumer cultures', and the 'growing cultural obsession with self-work and personal well-being in the West' (Bogdan *et al.* 2005: 142). It is no longer confined to the idiosyncrasies of a particular organizational culture, *à la* Deal and Kennedy, but is something that workers of all grades and callings should expect. The spirit of uninhibited play, therefore, in its purest form, is seen to touch an ever-receptive audience because it provides affective and productive energy, not the destructiveness feared by the commentator in our opening citation.

Elided by the 'fun at work' approaches described above is the extent to which designer fun can operate alongside, or even displace, the *realpolitik* of humour and fun in the workplace. Our attention here is drawn to the 'unmanaged' political and psychodynamic arenas of work life (Gabriel 1995). Such arenas are where humour operates within essentially schismatic labour processes, characterized by power imbalances within and between levels of employees (Edwards 1990). Humour in these circumstances is seen to act as a countervailing force, temporarily soothing the effects of workplace humiliations and subjugations. Jokes, satire and poking fun can score symbolic victories, evening out the emotive territory. Importantly for our purposes here, this kind of humour is self and group authored and carefully coded for relevant audiences by the participants themselves, in stark contrast to the surface jollity, clowning and bubbly demeanour which saturates the pages of manuals offering prescriptions for structured fun.

The subversive and survival role of humour is a theme in critical writings in the field (e.g. Rodrigues and Collinson 1995; Westwood 2004). Workgroup fun, at management's expense, can directly or indirectly weaken managerial authority. Moreover, an individual's or group's identity can be defined through the humour it directs towards itself, and the deprecating jokes it aims at others (Collinson 1988, 2002; Taylor and Bain 2003). Indeed, such community humour can be all that separates a barely tolerable job from an intolerable one. It is a survival mechanism, well illustrated by Taylor and Bain (2003) in their ethnography of UK call centres. As one employee in their study comments: 'People are unhappy – lots of things but mainly the calls ... This place does your head in, if it wasn't for the jokers here it wouldn't be tolerable' (2003: 1495). Both management and customers were targets for the 'jokers', the latter silently mocked in non-verbal gestures during telephone conversations, or openly satirized with the 'mute' button pressed – ironically beneath a banner proclaiming the company's 'first commitment to meeting its customers' needs'.[1]

Against this overall background, understanding the role of organized or 'designer' fun at work is clearly complex. The strands of thought we have outlined provide contrasting theoretical purchases. Organized fun can be seen to be a reflection of the growth of the 'feelgood factor' in life, so even intrinsically routine or mundane tasks can be experienced as acceptable when there is a playful, positive, culture to the workplace. By engineering work in this manner, managers and organizational consultants can be seen as simply reflecting the 'self-expressive' spirit of the age. Indeed, the importance of 'the good life' in contemporary Western culture is well illustrated by the incredulity that meets anyone who questions the premise that fun might not *prima facie* be a 'Good Thing' (Billig 2005). As Gabriel and Lang (1995: 100) similarly note, 'if we fail to enjoy life, it may be that we are failing to look after ourselves, weighed down by self-inflicted hang-ups and inhibitions'.

The second perspective we discussed is less charitable towards the motives of the fun's instigators. It suggests that managers control the content and boundaries of fun as an essentially manipulative and diversionary device to entice greater productive value from employees. Workers may or may not engage willingly in 'having fun' and their responses are as likely to be cynical or ambivalent as positive. Fun events, therefore, become sites to rehumour and subvert. They are ironic emotional zones where grievances, dissatisfactions and identity are voiced. We take these thoughts forward in considering a specific case of organized fun at work.

Department X – a fun workplace

At the time of the research, Department X was the web-design department of a global IT firm (MCS) headquartered in the south of England. Its management had recently instigated a programme of change to create an environment to stimulate the creative powers of the staff working there, whilst at the same time communicating the innovative internet capabilities of the company to existing and potential clients. MCS were/are not generally known for their innovative approach to internet business, instead being more readily recognized as a traditional and rather staid (albeit prestigious) organization. This made the organization a particularly interesting case study because the changes at Department X were seemingly such a radical departure from their regular business practices.[2]

More specifically, and as briefly noted in our introduction, the changes centred on the physical working environment. The departmental office space was redesigned incorporating, among other things, a shiny floored, blue-lit elliptical corridor that diagonally bisected the space, glass-walled offices and a room kitted out like a child's playroom: lined with padded blocks in primary colours, wipe-clean surfaces and unusual neon lighting. The office itself was redecorated in bright 'funky' colours, designer lockers were installed and the space was populated with toys, games, sculptures and art objects. All of this, it was hoped, would foster the desired external image and internal climate – one of wild, wacky, playful innovation. In other words the workplace was designed to look and be fun.

The data presented here were gathered during a three-month ethnography of Department X carried out by one of us between March and May 2001 (Warren 2005b) in order to explore the increasing importance of aesthetics in organizational settings. Broadly speaking, the research turned on the question: 'How does it feel to work in an environment aesthetically manipulated to "be fun"?' An ethnographic approach was adopted incorporating semi-structured interviewing as a research method. Respondents were also asked to take and discuss photographs of their workplace (Warren 2002, 2005b, 2005c). The images included here are drawn from this data.

The most striking thing about the data we will discuss is that they are characterized by paradox, ambivalence and apparent contradiction – as the title of this chapter suggests. The respondents held conflicting views about the changes to their organization, their work and the workplace. These were not, however, just differences between individuals as one might expect, but

Figure 6.1

conflicting views *within* individuals' own accounts. That is, ambivalent and/or contradictory views were often held by the same respondent about the same issue. This was substantively interesting and intriguing, as illustrated below, but also raises important issues of interpretation because, as El-Sawad *et al.* (2004) point out, contradictory statements do not necessarily mean that the respondent who makes them *experiences* them in any way as contradictory (although of course they may do).

As we sketched out earlier, commentators on structured fun seem to fall into one of two opposing subject positions – either fun programmes are oppressive or they are humanizing. From this, we might expect that employees required to participate in them would either hate or love them. However, as we are interpreting them, the data presented below indicate that fun at work for the employees involved is a manifold experience. For many of the people of Department X, at least, fun at work was loved, hated, valuable *and* unimportant – all at once.

'It's SO embarrassing ...'

For several of the department members, and particularly the graphic design staff, being associated with the 'fun office' was deeply humiliating. A close-knit community, they shared a professional identity that was built upon pride in their expertise and the work that they produced. For them, the management's public insinuation that a brightly coloured 'playroom' could get their 'creative juices flowing' was insulting, embarrassing and just plain wrong. Shortly before the research was carried out, the Department had been featured on a local television news programme and subsequently reported in the national press. Members of staff had been asked to get down and 'play for the camera' with a range of toys – including Lego bricks – pretending that they were in the process of designing a website for a client. Deb, a graphic designer, explained how she felt about this in the following excerpt from her interview transcript:

> I don't think I'll ever be able to make the transition with playing with toys at work ... We had this TV crew in and [our manager] was encouraging us to do this metaphor thing playing with Lego as a brainstorm for overcoming some sort of [problem]. We made up this brainstorm off the cuff that was just totally, total fluff and nonsense. And we were pretending that we use Lego in order to brainstorm customer ideas. [*Cringes*] We don't use Lego for that. It's nonsense and in fact I think [the producers of the TV programme] used it as a stick to take the piss with – beat us with – really.

These opinions, and others like them within the data, suggest that the infantilizing effect of the programme, coupled with its public 'promotion', was something which respondents felt belittled their status as professional people and, moreover, something which was simply not necessary. Having to act out their manager's fantasies about the programme simply reinforced their resentment.

There were other sentiments expressed about the incongruity of the fun programme with working life. When the office was first occupied, plastic 'nerf guns' were particularly popular. They could fire soft-tipped missiles at high speed over surprisingly long distances. Many 'battles' took place (predominantly among the male members of the Department) by firing these projectiles up and over the central corridor in an attempt to hit unsuspecting passers-by beyond the partitions. After a short while, the use of the guns was curtailed after complaints from other – mostly female – staff as to the hazardous nature of the game. Slightly less dramatic, but still significant, was the extent to which respondents reported that fun meant a noisy office in which it was difficult to work and a significant proportion of people reported taking work home so they could concentrate.

All for show?

Some of the respondents spoke of the superficiality of the whole programme, claiming that management's intentions were not really to provide a more pleasing working environment but, instead, the whole campaign was a marketing gimmick. There was a strong feeling that the revamped office was a surface attempt to rejuvenate working conditions without paying attention to issues that mattered most to employees, such as the way that many staff felt unnecessarily micro-managed. Likewise, limited involvement in the design of the office and choice of 'fun objects' also led to dissatisfaction and poor relationships with management.

Figure 6.2

The most notable example of this centred on a set of oversize 'Russian dolls' that had been commissioned for the reception area at a rumoured cost of £10,000. The dolls were decorated to look as if they were wearing business dress or, as one sceptical respondent put it, to resemble 'a stupid fucking politically correct family'. There was a large white male doll, a female, black and Asian males and one painted to look older than the rest. The dolls arrived in the office unannounced, coinciding with budget cuts for other, employee-favoured, aspects of the office. For example, the staff had requested a kitchenette so they could prepare food and drinks on occasions when looming deadlines meant they needed to work late into the night. This was deemed too expensive to provide. Even their request for a kettle was not honoured. Consequently, hot water had to be purchased from a vending machine. The following passage is Jason's response when asked if there was anything he did not like about the new office:

> certain things like these stupid Russian dolls which there's so much fuss going on about at the moment. They're kind of a centre of gossip. They [sigh, laugh] ... there's so much to say... . I can say there is a general feeling of complete dissatisfaction with the Russian dolls because of the way they were, [the way their arrival] was executed. It was forced down our throats. It was something that was [management's] concept not anybody else's. Now whilst he's the creative director, um and it goes without saying that his direction is the direction that the [department] should take, there is definite feeling of being railroaded into something that nobody wanted ...

The perceived superficiality of the changes also meant that employees just didn't 'buy in' to management's ideas. They failed to engage in the fun that had been envisaged because, for them, the fun was political, or at the very least not really intended for them. It is a sentiment is evident in computer programmer Guy's account of what he saw as the importance of the 'marketing' element of the Department:

> it's the right environment to be advertising as I don't know whether that necessarily means it's the best place to work but it's good to bring customers into, customers think, wow isn't this nice, you know they must be real hi-tech and everything and the fact that most people [here] have never actually used a flat screen or anything like [*laughs*] we've all got big and bulky monitors and stuff but it looks nice!

Many of the respondents recounted similar sentiments during their interviews, their voices tinged with amusement because they regarded the whole 'fun' initiative as mildly farcical and laughable, partly because they considered the rationale for the 'fun' environment was, above all else, to create the right impression on clients. They found this amusing because their reality of working in Department X was quite different.

Poking fun at the fun

When the dolls first arrived, several members of staff started playing with them – having fun. For example, and with much amusement, respondents told stories about the dolls appearing in unexpected places throughout the office after persons unknown had moved them when no one was looking, or after hours when the office was empty. One story recounted how a female member of staff had called security because she was convinced there was a man in the ladies' toilets. When the security officer peered over the top of the toilet cubicle, however, the offending 'man' was one of the dolls, 'sitting' on top of the toilet seat. Another example was the whole 'family' of dolls being placed in the elevator when clients were due to visit. When the elevator doors opened one can imagine the clients' surprise at being greeted by five enormous dolls.

Such events tested the boundaries of 'acceptable fun'. Management were not impressed with the ways the dolls were being used, complaining that they were being damaged in the process. They instructed staff not to play with them any more. This further angered those who had not wanted the dolls in the first place. Consequently, person(s) unknown took it upon themselves to punch one of the dolls in the 'face', leaving an indented fist mark in its surface. This escalated the rift with management, and the act interpreted as a malicious attempt to damage company property – an offence which, if repeated and the culprit caught, would result in summary dismissal. Two days later, a CCTV camera was installed to 'watch' the dolls to prevent a recurrence. I asked Jason to explain how it happened:

> What the punch? Oh it was deliberate, yeah! It was just because they are stupid things! [uncontrollable laughter] … sorry, sorry … I know at least five other people who have done it [they] line up and take turns. It's just so so funny [still laughing] and I know that we will now get sacked on the spot if we are caught doing it … [management have installed] a CCTV system to watch them.

Another fun, but unintended, consequence of the new office involved a microscooter which the staff had been allowed to purchase with company money. The scooter was very popular amongst staff for running errands and the like. We could surmise that their enjoyment was, in part, because they had some control over the choice and use of the scooter; it lacked the imposed character

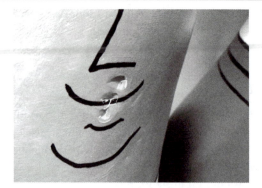

Figure 6.3

of other toys and games. But it was after hours when the scooter came into its own – as a vehicle for 'round the office races' against the clock. One evening, during one such race, a health and safety official happened to walk past, colliding with the scooter and its rider. This resulted in an administrative furore, as well as an unusual entry in the accident book (no risk assessment had ever been done for the use of a scooter in an office). Yet it was also the cause of much hilarity, as this excerpt from Deb's interview shows:

> we had a laugh on the microscooter awhile back, we got told off by the site services guy [because] we had a race around the [department] with the microscooter. There was only one person on it but there was a crash and it all got really ugly! [*laughing*] ... we got a whiteboard and somebody with a stopwatch and we had to go round the circuit and see who could do it quickest. And about half way through one of the site services guys came round – who's a very very miserable man and has no joy ... and someone was going a bit too quick to make the corner and did a huge sort of like falling action over the settees and stuff [*mimes slow motion falling*] over the end and this guy jumped out and said 'Stop! Health and Safety!' and we were all [*much laughter!*], we dissolved into fits of laughter on the floor and er so the most the biggest laugh I've ever had in the office came out of the microscooter.

The item was banned from use. However, instead of resignedly accepting this, the staff suggested they display warning signs on all entrances to the office so as to comply with health and safety legislation. This took the form of a drawing of a microscooter in the centre of a red 'prohibited' triangle with the words 'Warning! Microscooter in use' written above and below. The sign does represent legislative compliance, but is also highly ironic, designed with tongue firmly in cheek.

Figure 6.4

'But don't get me wrong ...'

The data presented so far suggest that the fun environment was perceived negatively by the employees. Indeed, almost every respondent articulated dissatisfaction, scepticism and/or insult concerning *some* aspect of the new office and its operation. However, this negativity was countered by the potential for 'real' fun that the environment offered, as exemplified by the dolls and the scooter – even though (perhaps because) such subversive fun carried with it a real risk of sanction.

Alongside the sense of cynicism about the 'effectiveness' of the new office as a 'creative space', respondents expressed the view that 'at least management are trying to change things, even if they are going about it the wrong way'. This was a curious sentiment – best characterized as a mixture of 'patronizing pride' – and often came from the same respondents who had spoken with bitterness about the whole programme. The tone of these conversations was condescending but benevolent, suggesting some deference to the power asymmetries. Respondents seemed mindful of what they saw as management's inability to 'do any better', but they were still 'proud' of them for trying in the first place. Giles and Deb express it in their own words:

> This one [photograph of a curvy bookshelf] I'd say was a 'like' because they are attempting to [keep] the creative promise they were suggesting way back when ... and every now and then you see it pops out in ... very small subtle places. So ... I like it because OK they were trying... . Bless! Lack of budget and the wrong people calling the shots [meant] it didn't happen everywhere else. So this was like a little oasis of 'almost creativity' really.
>
> (Giles, designer)

Figure 6.5

> When the pool table first arrived I played on it a couple of times and then I've not played on it since and I loved the fact that it's there because I think um it gives other people. It lifts the morale generally in the office and I think it probably tempts people to stay later umm even just to play on it, or it makes them happier to be working later in the evening knowing that there's been some thought put in by the management and the people who run the [department].

> (Deb, designer)

The sense of 'being valued' is suggested here. People felt attached to MCS because they had been allowed a fun, funky office – moreover, one that was overtly designated as 'special' because it was accessible only by swipe-card or 'badge locks'. Russell, a producer, echoes such sentiments – despite remarking earlier in the interview that 'such silliness' had no bearing on his working life whatsoever:

Figure 6.6

> That's something I like … the feeling that this area's special because it's … extra secured and I quite like [the] idea that I'm working … somewhere that's prized by [MCS] we're worth something, which is good. It's the best place to be and I like the kudos …

For Scott (also a producer), the company's fun setting also held contradictory meanings, his cynicism mixed with feelings of goodness about being in a comfortable workspace:

> [The company is] still a monolith of a dinosaur underneath – just tarted up to look a bit younger! But as I say I'm still glad to be here! Yeah and it's not just a case of I'd rather be here than somewhere else. It's not making a comparison – it's I like it here, compared to nothing. I like it. Like it here.

Kate, a designer, also reflects on her mixed emotions:

> I don't know … It's nice – I like it, don't get me wrong! I'm not sure that it really improves my work because er, I'm still kind of at a desk, I'm still stuck to my PC so the only time I ever really take advantage of [the environment] is [when I'm] walking down the corridor to get a drink or go to the loo … I think it probably has uplifted my spirits sort of thing as in like, it would probably make me stay here, you know longer than I would have normally in a company. If anything it's a plus isn't it? I mean it's treating employees well and you know giving them an environment that would be nice to come to and I think that's important …

Discussion

Although the data we present here are not generalizable, in the sense that their idiosyncrasies can be directly mapped onto other locales, we do suggest that they offer tentative insights into fun programmes in other workplaces. Williams (2002) has used the phrase 'moderatum generalisation' to refer to this kind of speculative association, reminding us that:

> If characteristics point to particular structures in one situation, then one can hypothesize that the existence of such structures in a further situation will lead to at least some similar characteristics … Though there may be evidence of a shared reality as experienced, or shared underlying structures, the complexity of these structures and the possibility of agency to transform them, means that generalizations can be only moderate ones.
>
> (Williams 2002: 138)

With this in mind, we offer four non-competing conceptualizations of structured fun at work that draw upon our case study. The first is that that 'managing' 'fun' is an oxymoron; the second that prescribed fun at work is oppressive; the third that fun programmes might create spaces for collective rebellion; and the fourth that fun at work is a benign intervention.

Managed fun – an oxymoron?

Is there such a thing as unmanaged fun? As implied at the start of this chapter, fun can be more or less spontaneous, more or less self-authored, more or less subject to the rules of feeling and expression imposed by others (Bolton 2004; Fineman 2003). Yet we cannot envisage a situation where feelings of fun and joy are somehow free from any sort of social context or presentational norms. In other words, even in situations where fun and laughter appear spontaneous, there are social and cultural conventions that shape what is felt, what is expressed and what is shared. However, it is clear from the present case that the fun-ness of a supposed fun working environment is complex and multifaceted. Where fun is 'required' and its structure imposed, where it is heavily 'managed', the frisson of self-authorship and surprise are lost; feelings of fun are muted, heavily bounded or effectively extinguished. In these circumstances people may still laugh and smile, but hollowed of any feelings of pleasure; they behave in ways that appear socially acceptable. This is the emotional labour of keeping up appearances (see Critchley 2002: 12; Ashforth and Tomiuk 2000).

Managing others' fun in an organization rubs against pre-existing perceptions of trust or distrust in management, as well as employee expectations about participation in decisions that will directly affect them. As the example of the scooter accident and sign exemplifies, 'real' fun in organizations can be subversive and counter-establishment. If fun is instructed, predetermined and its outcomes highly controlled, then it can cease to engender fun – as the example of the Russian dolls shows. The dolls were *supposed* to be fun, so therefore they were not, exposing an 'unmanageable' dimension to work organizations that Gabriel (1995) identifies.

Fun as oppression

Discourses of control pave the way for the possibility that structured fun may actually be an oppressing experience for those involved. As noted in the case study, all respondents expressed dissatisfaction to some degree with the fun programme because they felt that other aspects of their working arrangements were more worthy of managerial attention. This is oppressive and silencing in several ways. First, the 'fun' itself can be read as oppressive because it is difficult for an employee to refuse to participate. As Eadie (1999) notes, those who refuse to join in can be stigmatized, branded as having 'no sense of humour'. Moreover, as much of the structured fun in the present case was male-oriented (and designed by men), we might reasonably expect women to feel especially pressured by such initiatives. We see this especially in the tale of the nerf guns. Second, fun programmes can bury more important considerations (to employees) under 'gaily painted aesthetic gloss' which (one assumes) is hoped will curry favour with employees without actually changing anything substantive. Third, assuming that the programme does engender *some* feelings of fun, this may serve a 'safety-valve' function whereby employees are able to 'let off steam' in a safe manner that does not threaten the organizational status quo, thus silencing militant voices (e.g. Radcliffe-Brown 1940; Collinson 2002). Finally, the very fact that management have benevolently bestowed the 'gift' of fun on their employees can be seen as device to diffuse, rather than directly confront, disaffection amongst employees.

Fun as collective rebellion

One outcome of the management/structuring of fun is that humour arises not from the intended, but from the unintended consequences of programmes. Programmes can be the target of employee rebellion, and this irony can be a source of mirth to those involved. We would argue that both the punching of the Russian dolls and the designing of the scooter sign are fertile ground for fun, but not the sort of fun that was intended by management. The organizational consequences of this can be read in, at least, two ways: either management will attempt to control employees' behaviour (as in the installation of CCTV to 'watch' the dolls after their assault), or they will 'turn a blind eye' and allow the subversive fun to continue. Further, some potentially problematic outcomes can occur; rebellious fun is rarely kind to all involved – somebody is often at the butt of the joke. Relatedly, 'harmless fun' to one person can easily be interpreted by others as a vehicle for racial, sexual or other harassment (Collinson 2002; Warren 2005a).

Fun as benign intervention

Finally, there exists the possibility, as strongly suggested by these data, that fun is increasingly an *expected* element of working life. It is this possibility that we will explore in more detail. The desire for working environments that excite and delight can be conceptualizd using two bodies of theory: which both centre on the growing normalization of fun, pleasure and positivity more generally in contemporary culture – aestheticization and positive psychology.

The first of these (aestheticization) is connected to the rise of the aesthetic in everyday life and the way all aspects of life seem increasingly subject to 'styling', or as Böhme (2003) puts it, 'staging', in order to remain valuable and/or worthwhile. Various explanations are given for the rise of aestheticization such as increased affluence leading to a rise in consumerism; blurring of boundaries between 'high' and 'low' culture under postmodern conditions; and the prevalence of mass media with a predilection for slick aesthetic presentations and reliance on image (for summaries see Featherstone 1991; Hancock 2003). From shopping precincts to hospitals this trend is recognizable, we suggest, in almost all public spaces – including workplaces. Bauman (1998) argues that work is increasingly valued on account of its capacity to offer or generate aesthetic pleasure, rather than its potential to fulfil a sense of duty or 'calling', and/ or offer moral ennoblement. Instead of gaining dignity and a sense of self-worth from one's work (no matter how menial the task involved), Bauman proposes that employees in contemporary consumer society choose their occupations and employers according to whether they promise exciting, stimulating activities carried out in fun environments, brimful of opportunities for new and varied experiences. In short, he suggests that the same aesthetic-hedonistic principles that drive our desire to consume are also beginning to govern the choices we make about our work.

Bauman views late capitalism as producing a *new* work ethic – one that is based on aesthetics and not ethics, and one which leads to the conclusion that work is no longer to be endured or avoided. Rather, it should be enjoyed as a leisure activity itself – or at the very least embraced as a vocation. He notes that these kinds of work are reserved for a privileged few in contemporary society and therefore asks, what of everyone else? He also observes that there is nothing especially new about some jobs affording aesthetic engagement and the opportunity for self-fulfilment and others not. There have, of course, always been jobs that are monotonous, dull, routine, tedious, low status, banal and the like. But crucially, as he also tells us:

> the point was from the ethical perspective, no job could be seriously argued to be deprived of value and demeaning; all work equally served the cause of moral propriety and spiritual redemption.
>
> (Bauman 1998: 33)

Whilst there are many critical voices on such social development (questioning whether the elevation of surface over substance is a good thing – see Welsch 1997 in particular), there can be little doubt that aesthetic considerations are now of prime social and organizational importance. For our purposes, however, we wish only to note that the 'culture of beauty and fun' that aestheticization brings (or results from it, depending on which explanation one prefers) is likely to be permeating organizational boundaries for the reasons we outline above. As Strati (2001) also notes, this is likely to be inevitable given that organizations are inextricable parts of wider cultural milieux; they are 'without walls'.

From the above discussion, it is a logical step to suggest that organizations will increasingly have to offer (or at least appear to offer) work that can generate these aesthetic possibilities if they are to entice people to work for them. We might also surmise that pay, under these conditions, will not work alone as a compensatory measure – since it is intrinsic satisfaction and the thrill of experience that people are demanding as their reward.[3] Could it be that structured fun programmes as aestheticization practices (and others like them) are organizational responses to a socio-cultural demand for aestheticized work? Put another way, if we accept that fun is increasingly assuming a central role in life then, as we indicate here, it may be reasonable to assume that employees will expect their *working* lives to offer opportunities for fun too. Thus, structured fun might be seen more positively as a fairly benign organizational response to employee expectations and, importantly, as something that is *enjoyed* by employees. Moreover, we might extrapolate that if organizations can offer environments where dull work can at least be carried out pleasurably, as a 'bolt on' to the job itself, they might just stand a chance of attracting and retaining relatively committed staff. If the reality of boring, monotonous and tightly controlled work can be smothered in a kitschy blanket of manufactured beauty and fun, then employees-cum-consumers might be persuaded to do it willingly – at least for a little while.

The recent, US-inspired, turn to positive organizational scholarship takes this argument a step further. Ducking the postmodern turn towards splintered ethics, positive scholars take the production of positive feelings, such as joy, happiness and well-being, as a key moral imperative for 'virtuous' workplaces (see Cameron *et al.* 2003a). They celebrate hedonistic work experiences such as 'engagement' and 'flow', and steer away from what they see as a preoccupation with negative experiences and problem-fixing at work. Like aestheticization, these ideas have attracted some solid followers as well as sharp criticism, the latter focusing on the extent to which they are framed within a North American 'positive' culture, while also making few concessions to differences in ethnicity or gender (see Fineman 2006). Furthermore, bracketing off positive feelings for special attention neglects the symbiotic, interactive, nature of positive, negative and ambivalent emotions. However, the positive verve does lend ideological and rhetorical support to the notion that fun programmes should generate a 'motivating', 'feelgood', factor to workplace experiences.

Conclusions

In the discussion we have presented four ways that can make sense of the phenomenon of structured fun and the case study data. We have done this collectively so as not to assume a priori that such management initiatives are necessarily *either* good *or* bad. Instead we hope to have shown that the lived reality of fun at work can be far more complex and plural, invoking a range of possible political, ethical, aesthetic and emotional responses and characterized by ambivalence and paradox. Our contribution to the important work already under way in relation to fun regimes in the workplace is to destabilize this positive/negative dichotomy and to suggest alternative interpretations that seek to nuance the debate based on empirical data. In doing so we hope to have shown that a number of lenses might be usefully employed through which to explore the topic further.

Notes

1 Of course humour as a coping mechanism still serves a managerialist agenda by making time at work more palatable and enabling its continued performance.

2 Attempts have been made to establish links between humour and creativity (e.g. Murdock and Ganim 1993) which have been influential in organizational thinking around innovation and creative behaviour, although we are unaware if MCS's rationale for the programme included such studies.

3 A need for intrinsic satisfaction is, of course, reminiscent of classic motivation theories which have repeatedly established this. What does seem to be a new departure here is the notion of 'thrilling experience' or 'excitement' and indeed 'fun' as a dimension of satisfaction.

References

Alferoff, C. and Knights, D. (2003) 'We're all partying here: targets and games, or targets as games in call centre management', in A. Carr and P. Hancock (eds), *Art and Aesthetics at Work*, pp. 70–92, London: Palgrave Macmillan.

Ashforth, B. E. and Tomiuk, M. A. (2000) 'Emotional labour and authenticity: views from service agents', in S. Fineman (ed.), *Emotion in Organizations*, 2nd edn, pp. 194–203, London: Sage.

Bauman, Z. (1998) *Work, Consumerism and the New Poor*, Milton Keynes: Open University Press.

Bernstein, S. D. (2003) 'Positive organizational scholarship: meet the movement', *Journal of Management Inquiry*, 12(3): 266–71.

Billig, M. (2005) *Laughter and Ridicule: Towards a Social Critique of Humour*, London: Sage.

Blumfled, E. (1994) *Humor at Work: The Guaranteed Bottom-Line, Low Cost, High Efficiency Guide to Success through Humor*, Atlanta, GA: Peachtree.

Bogdan, C., Norman, C. and Holm, J. (2005) 'Dionysus at work? The ethos of play and the ethos of management', *Culture and Organization*, 11(2): 139–51.

Böhme, G. (2003) 'Contribution to the critique of the aesthetic economy', *Thesis Eleven*, 71–82.

Bolton, S. (2004) *Emotion Management in the Workplace*, London: Routledge.

Cameron, K. S., Dutton, J. E. and Quinn, R. E. (2003) 'Foundations of positive organizational scholarship', in K. S. Cameron, J. E. Dutton and R. E. Quinn (eds), *Positive Organizational Scholarship: Foundations of a New Discipline*, pp. 3–13, San Francisco, CA: Berrett-Koehler.

Caudron, S. (1992) 'Humor is healthy in the workplace', *Personnel Journal*, 71(960): 63–7.

Collinson, D. (1988) '"Engineering humour": Masculinity, joking and conflict in shop-floor relations', *Organization Studies*, 9(2): 181–99.

Collinson, D. (2002) 'Managing humour', *Human Relations*, 39(3): 269–88.

Conte, Y. (1998) *Serious Laughter: Live a Happier, Healthier, More Productive Life*, Rochester, NY: Amsterdam-Berwick.

Critchley, S. (2002) *On Humour*, London: Routledge.

Deal, T. and Kennedy, A. (1982) *Corporate Cultures*, Harmondsworth: Penguin.

Deal, T. and Kennedy, A. (1999) *The New Corporate Cultures*, London: Textere.

Eadie, A. (1999) 'Fun at work can be no laughing matter', *The Financial Times* (21 Nov.): A20.

Edwards, P. K. (1990) 'Understanding conflict in the labour process: the logic and autonomy of struggle', in D. Knights and H. Willmott (eds), *Labour Process Theory*, pp. 125–52, London: Macmillan.

El-Sawad, A., Arnold, J. and Cohen, L. (2004) '"Doublethink": the prevalence and function of contradiction in accounts of organizational life', *Human Relations*, 57(9): 1179–203.

Featherstone, M. (1991) *Consumer Culture and Postmodernism*, London: Sage.

Fineman, S. (2003) *Understanding Emotion at Work*, London: Sage.

Fineman, S. (2006) 'On being positive: concerns and counterpoints', *Academy of Management Review*, 31(2): 270–91.

Fleming, P. and Spicer, A. (2004) '"You can checkout anytime, but you can never leave": spatial boundaries in a high commitment organization', *Human Relations*, 57(1): 75–94.

Ford, R. C., Newestom, J. W. and McLaughlin, F. S. (2004) 'Making workplace fun functional', *Industrial and Commercial Training*, 36(3): 117–20.

Gabriel, Y. (1995) 'The unmanaged organization: stories, fantasies and subjectivity', *Organization Studies*, 16(3): 477–501.

Gabriel, Y. and Lang, T. (1995) *The Unmanageable Consumer: Contemporary Consumption and its Fragmentations*, London: Sage.

Hancock, P. (2003) 'Aestheticizing the world of organization: creating beautiful untrue things', in A. Carr and P. Hancock (eds), *Art and Aesthetics at Work*, pp. 174–94, London: Palgrave Macmillan.

Kinnie, N., Hutchinson, S. and Purcell, J. (2000) 'Fun and surveillance: the paradox of high commitment management in call centres', *International Journal of Human Resource Management*, 11(5): 967–85.

Martin, R. (2001) 'Humor, laughter and physical health: methodological issues and research findings', *Psychological Bulletin*, 127(4): 504–19.

Meyer, H. (1999) 'Fun for everyone', *Journal of Business Strategy*, 20(12): 13.

Murdock, M. C. and Ganim, R. M. (1993) 'Creativity and humour: integration and incongruity', *Journal of Creative Behaviour*, 27(1): 57–70.

Pinault, L. (2003) *The Play Zone: Unlock your Creative Genius and Connect with Consumers*, Cambridge: Cambridge University Press.

Radcliffe-Brown, A. R. (1940) 'On joking relationships', *Africa: Journal of the International African Institute*, 13(3): 195–210.

Rodrigues, S. and Collinson, D. (1995) 'Having fun? Humour as resistance in Brazil', *Organization Studies*, 16(5): 739.

Segal, R. and LaCroix, D. (2000) *Laugh and Get Rich: How to Profit from Humor in Any Business*, Burlington, MA: Specific House.

Strati, A. (2001) *Theory and Method in Organization Studies*, London: Sage.

Sunoo, B. P. (1995) 'How fun flies at Southwest Airlines', *Personnel Journal*, 74(6): 62–71.

Taylor, P. and Bain, P. (2003) '"Subterreanean worksick blues": humour as subversion in two call centres', *Organization Studies*, 24(9): 1487–509.

Thomas, R. (1999) 'Humour as the new weapon in the business wars', *Observer* (21 Feb.): 8.

Thorson, J. A., Powell, F. C., Sarmany-Schuller, I. and Hampes, W. P. (1997) 'Psychological health and sense of humour', *Journal of Clinical Psychology*, 53(6): 1–15.

Uminowicz, G. (1992) 'Recreation in Christian America, 1869–1914', in K. Grover (ed.), *Hard at Play: Leisure in America, 1840–1940*, pp. 8–38, Boston, MA: University of Massachusetts Press.

Warren, S. (2002) 'Show me how it feels to work here: the role of photography in researching organizational aesthetics', *Ephemera: Theory and Politics in Organization*, 3(2): 224–45.

Warren, S. (2005a) 'Humour as a management tool? The irony of structuring fun in organizations', in U. Johannson and J. Woddilla (eds), *Irony and Organizations*, pp. 174–99, Koege: Copenhagen Business School Press.

Warren, S. (2005b) 'Consuming work: an exploration of organizational aestheticization', unpublished PhD thesis, University of Portsmouth.

Warren, S. (2005c) 'Photography and voice in critical, qualitative, management research', *Accounting, Auditing and Accountability Journal*, 18(6): 861–82.

Weber, M. (1958) *The Protestant Ethic and the Spirit of Capitalism*, New York: Scribner.

Welsch, W. (1997) *Undoing Aesthetics*, London: Sage.

Westwood, R. I. (2004) 'Comic relief: subversion and catharsis in organizational comedic theatre', *Organization Studies*, 25(5): 775–95.

Williams, M. (2002) 'Generalization in interpretive research', in T. May (ed.), *Qualitative Research in Action*, pp. 125–43, London: Sage.

Yerkes, L. (2001) *Fun Works: Creating Places Where People Love to Work*, San Francisco, CA: Berrett-Koehler.

Chapter 7

Representing the unrepresentable

Gender, humour and organization

Allanah Johnston, Dennis Mumby and Robert Westwood

Daughter: Ma, do you think I can be a feminist and still like men!
Mother: Sure. Just like you can be a vegetarian and like fried chicken.

(Nichole Hollander)

Q. How many feminists does it take to change a lightbulb?
A. None. It's not the lightbulb that needs changing.

(Sasha Wasley, Murdoch University, Western Australia)

And I do offensive things ... That's who I am. That's my act.

(Roseanne Barr)

If evolution really works, how come mothers only have two hands?

(Milton Berle)

Pro-male males [i.e. males whose definition of themselves coincided with traditional conceptions of masculinity] found pro-male anti-female jokes funnier than pro-female anti-male jokes; pro-female females [i.e. women whose views coincided with feminism] found pro-female anti-male jokes funnier than pro-male anti-female jokes.

(La Fave 1972: 205)

We don't believe that La Fave intended to be humorous in penning the above and the fact that we found it so perhaps reflects more on us than him. We contend, however, that there is something at least vaguely comical about two things: the language deployed and the obviousness of what is expressed by that language. The passage also, in a way, offers a reminder of a common folly that we, presumably the editors of this book, and many other scholars who venture into the field experience: the potential absurdity of taking humour seriously and writing about it in a serious 'academic' manner. But we do – and we will ...

Despite the folly, humour research is by now extensive, multidisciplinary and multifaceted, although, oddly perhaps, research on humour in organizational contexts and from a sociological perspective remains relatively impoverished. Further, despite recent attention on gender issues in humour, 'The interfaces between women, femininity and comedy are desperately under-developed fields of research' (Porter 1998: 67). While functionalist accounts dominate the literature on humour in organization, there have been a growing number of studies focusing on the relationship between humour and issues of power, control, resistance and identity in organization. More critical approaches have demonstrated the complex nature of humour as part of social interaction and have treated humour as a discursive practice. Considering humour as part of 'naturally occurring' verbal conversation, it is argued, construes it as implicated in the 'performance of social identities' (Erickson and Schultz 1982) such as, for example, class, race and gender (Holmes et al. 2003). Conceiving of humour as a discursive practice brings it into the ambit of the language games we deploy in mounting, sustaining, protecting and changing the (social) identities we adopt within the complex, fragmented and shifting social contexts with which we increasingly engage. Studies of humour have also focused on the resistive qualities of humour and how humour may function to challenge or even subvert existing power relations (Taylor and Bain 2003; Grugulis 2002; Rodrigues and Collinson 1995; Griffiths 1998; Holmes 2000). These studies also tend to focus on aspects of identity and how humour may challenge perceived threats to identity via organizational control or be used to protect certain identity positions from such threats. For example, humour has been associated with practices of resistance among employees in relation to management. Thus, organizational humour studies have increasingly recognized the imbrication of humour within discursive practices and inevitably, then, with issues of power and identity.

A key study exploring how humour functions as a mode of resistance is Collinson's (1988) ethnographic study of male shopfloor workers. However, Collinson demonstrates that, while humour can be used as a form of resistance to organizational control, it can simultaneously operate to reinforce lines of authority and even serve to control fellow workers. Within the context of a highly masculinized working-class culture, workers were so preoccupied with sustaining their working-class male identity that their humour sometimes operated to reinforce the extant organizational hierarchy and, more broadly, the dominant patriarchal discourse within the culture. Indeed, the majority of critical accounts of humour in organization highlight this ambiguity around resistance and reconstruction of power structures and relationships (e.g. Grugulis 2002; Holmes 2000; Taylor and Bain 2003). Holmes (2000), for example, shows how humour was used both as a resource by those with organizational power to assert and consolidate their power and authority – to 'do power' – but also 'contestively' to challenge and subvert authority and generate solidarity.

Despite the increasing recognition of humour as discursive and resistive, there have been surprisingly few studies that have examined the *gendered* character of humour in organizational contexts. Surprising particularly given the clear exposition of gendered organizations/organizing emergent over the past couple of decades (Aaltio and Mills 2002; Acker 1990; Ashcraft and Mumby 2004; Mills and Tancred 1992); surprising too, given that gender–humour issues have received increasing attention in other areas of study (Barreca 1991; Finney 1994; Hengen 1998; Kotthoff 2006; Sochen 1991). The majority of studies have focused on men's use of humour in the workplace, with a relative neglect of women's humour and how this might be implicated in processes of resistance and identity formation. Indeed, if we are to assume that humour is linked to issues of power, then a focus upon a social group that has historically been marginalized from circuits of power would seem imperative.

Increasing rates of female labour force participation and women in positions of power in organizations have significantly eroded neither the radically gendered character of organizational forms and practices nor the dominance of patriarchal discourses and masculinized cultures (Ashcraft and Mumby 2004; Ely *et al.* 2003; Gherardi 1995). In such a space, women's gender identities are insecure, fragile and contested, and work, particularly interactional work, is needed to mount and sustain their identities. As part of everyday interaction and discourse, humour can be considered as an element in gender identity work. The question then becomes 'how do women use humour as part of "doing gender" in their everyday interaction and discourse?' Further, how do they do so within that male-dominated space? Can humour be enacted to resist, challenge, deconstruct or at least render ironic the gender relations, subject positionings and identity formations that organizations constitute within patriarchal power structures and practices? If humour can be considered in this manner can it be done without falling into the trap of much existing critical humour-in-organization literature of essentializing the constructs of masculine and feminine, thereby reinforcing stereotypical notions of 'gender'? Indeed, perhaps the most radical question concerns humour's potential role in actually overcoming the conflation of gender with the masculine/feminine binary and in stepping outside of the power systems that sustain it. This chapter, then, examines humour as a gendered practice embedded in practices of power, resistance and identity construction. We adopt a feminist perspective to interrogate the critical literature on organizational humour and to highlight the complex and gendered character of humour.

Gender and humour: the recursive construction of difference

Much of the extant research and literature on humour and gender works on of the assumption of difference, the effect of which is to reconstruct gender difference with respect to humour. Current research locates humour through research practices embedded in male dominant discourse and presumptions of gender difference and reproduces the gender bifurcations and essentialisms that the dominant discourse already instantiates. As noted, gender–humour relationships in non-organizational contexts have gained increasing attention among researchers. The fields of psychology, psychoanalysis, sociology, linguistics, culture studies and literary studies have all explored differences and similarities between women and men in their initiation, use and consumption of humour. Research has variously proposed gender differences in participation in humour and joking activities, overall 'sense of humour', the use of forms of humour and in humour skills.

The body of research investigating the appreciation of humour has a relatively long history and the bulk of it has promulgated the (mis)conception that women 'lack' a sense of humour. Deploying the notion of 'a sense of humour', researchers have typically essentialized it as a stable trait and proclaimed it to be a trait women lack. For example, experimental psychological studies have claimed gender differences in the enjoyment of humour (Cantor 1976; Bruner and Kelso 1980; Jenkins 1985). In an influential but much disputed study, Lakoff (1975: 56) bluntly stated that 'women don't tell jokes' within their routine language or conversational style. Several other studies claim females to be significantly less positive than males in responding to humorous stimuli (Chapman and Gadfield 1976; McGhee and Goldstein 1983; McGhee 1979). Such findings have led others to theoretically account for the presumed 'fact' that women do not use humour.

In responding to the thesis that women don't have or need a sense of humour, it has been argued that humour is dominated by a masculinist discourse in which the subject content and interactional context of humour are male-dominated. It is not surprising, therefore, that women struggle to participate in such a discourse in ways other than through those subject positions the discourse provides. Further, the discourse tends to locate them as the object of humour and circumscribes their participation in and reactions to humour (Hay 2000). Hay further notes that such locations mean it is more likely that women recognize the joking interests of males rather than vice versa. Kramarae (1981) suggests that this structural asymmetry is the primary basis for the assertion that women have no sense of humour. Put bluntly, within existing power asymmetries, women have to understand male humour; men do not have to understand women's.

The asymmetry constructs conditions for the gendered character of humour and this recursively helps to constitute what is appropriate male and female behaviour with respect to conversational style generally and humour specifically. Joking performance becomes part of doing masculinity, whereas not displaying humour becomes part of doing femininity. Since humour has a generally positive value, the blanket attribution of no sense of humour is thoroughly negative and thus we find no nuanced accounts of women's sense of humour – particularly their ability to produce humour. The discourse vitiates the notion of female producers of humour, and even when it is allowed that women respond to and appreciate humour, they are positioned as passive recipients (and objects) of masculine humour (Coser 1960; McGhee 1979; Barreca 1991).

The literature also purports to show that women are absent from certain forms of humour and effectively silenced in relation to others. It has been argued, for example, that sexual humour is less likely to be appreciated by women (Terry and Ertel 1974), especially when it conforms to dominant notions of masculinity (Chapman and Gadfield 1976). It is also argued that women are absent from 'slapstick' and 'horseplay' as well as from 'verbal duels and ritual insults'; in other words, from those humour modes considered most aggressive and masculine within the culture (Palmer 1994: 71). However, such difference is, as Palmer suggests, 'more to do with forms of social control than with any "universal" or "natural" features of either gender' (p. 71), a view reinforced by counterfactuals – the slapstick and physical humour of Lucille Ball and the aggressive and physical humour of Jennifer Saunders in *Absolutely Fabulous*, for example.

Mirroring work which suggests that there are significant sex differences in conversational style in general, it has been further argued that conversational humour is experienced, practised, received and transmitted differently by men and women (Mulkay 1988; Crawford 1995). The most consistent general interpretation is that women tend to be more supportive in their conversational style, and men more competitive (Fishman 1983; Coates 1986), findings with which studies of gender and humour show correspondence. For example, Jenkins (1985) says that men's humour tends to be more performance-oriented than women's, is characterized by self-aggrandizing one-upmanship, and more often uses formulaic jokes which are detached from the surrounding discourse and which involve a performance and display. These aspects of male humour provide an opportunity through which they can establish themselves as credible performers and thereby sustain a sense of identity as 'male'. Male joke telling is thus part of masculine gender identity work – part of performing gender. Conversely, women are said to rely more on the context in the creation of humour and to use humour in ways that are supportive of others in the social context (Hay 2000).

There has been a significant challenge to these earlier studies and concomitant theories purporting to deny or limit women's humour. The methodology and the validity of the experimental studies have been subject to critique (Kotthoff 2000; Palmer 1994). The artificiality and decontextualization inherent in laboratory and survey studies of humour has been criticized, particularly as they fail to grasp the interactional quality of humour in everyday conversation and the variable enactment of humour by individuals across situations. Crawford (1989) also notes that many functionalist empirical studies have also been subject to systematic bias through being, for example, predominantly devised and conducted by men, and relying on women's responses to humorous stimuli constructed by men: the latter are weak methodologically through dependence upon the assumption that a (female) respondent sees the stimuli as humorous in the same way as the (male) person constructing the stimuli (Hay 2000). Furthermore, research has focused on forms of humour more typically associated with men (such as structured/canned jokes) (Hay 2000; Jenkins 1985; Goodwin 1982), and on humour in public male domains. As Hay (2000) notes, women's humour is more routinely exhibited in the private domain.

Although the majority of research has relied on artificial settings and scripted jokes, there are a small number of studies exploring women's and men's use of humour in more naturalistic settings. For example, Boxer and Cortés-Conde (1997) analysed informal conversations between both strangers and family members (mostly status equals) in a variety of natural settings. They found that women tended to use bonding forms of humour irrespective of their relationship to other participants, whereas men tended to engage in more biting forms that often negated bonding. Women also regarded jokes at their own expense as funnier than men, whilst men used these joking situations to make more definite 'identity displays' (p. 291) and within the social mores this meant making distinctly masculine identity displays.

Another suggested gender difference is that women tend to use self-deprecating humour more than men (Boxer and Cortés-Conde 1997; Zillman and Stocking 1976). Reincke (1991: 34) claims that when women laugh at self-deprecating humour they are laughing at themselves and reinforcing 'male bonding and denying female knowledge'. However, Kotthoff (2000: 75) argues that by making jokes about their own experiences, the women 'confirm(ed) themselves and their individual identity'. Rather than treat self-deprecating humour as an indication of a weakness or lack of self-respect, as maintained by some psychologists, Kotthoff suggests it confirms the intimacy of the discourse between participants and builds on personal identity work rather than 'positional' or status-based identity work. Bing argues further that female humour's emancipatory potential resides in it being humour for and about women: 'As long as women's jokes focus on men, male definitions, and male behaviour, women are marginalizing females, even if their jokes target males' (2004: 22). She points to the effectiveness of certain lesbian humour which circulates within the interests and preoccupations of lesbian women and does not bother to make men and masculine culture the target. Reincke (1991: 34) adds,

> When they are laughing for themselves, they create female bonding. This is the crux of the threat to male dominance. The male is displaced from the center of knowledge and meaning as well as from the center of gender relations when girl-gets-girl.

Kotthoff (2000: 75) further explores how women use humour as part of their 'personal identity politics'. For example, she argues that female narrators organized their 'presentations' so that other people did not laugh 'at *their* expense' but rather 'at the expense of the norm which they mock' (emphasis in original, p. 55) – centred around gender relations and women's self-image. The concept of humour as a form of 'image politics' (Kotthoff 2000) has also been explored by Hay (2000), who found that in friendship groups women are more likely to share funny personal stories to create solidarity, whereas men used other strategies. However, it needs to be noted that Hay's study, like others, focuses only on friendship groups and that other studies conducted in the context of status differences demonstrate humour more closely tied to an expression of power.

An underlying and general criticism of these empirical studies is that most of them tend to essentialize gender and the use of humour by 'men' and 'women'. There has been a tendency to use the categories 'men' and 'women' in homogenized, undifferentiated and essentialized ways and to then assert or assume that each category only uses one form of humour. The (stereo)typical depiction is to suggest that men use a more aggressive style while women use a more supportive style of humour. There is no consideration of how various contexts may affect the style of humour used, nor of how the use of humour may vary if a more differentiated view of gender is taken. For instance, it could be that women in all-female contexts may not use 'supportive' humour so much, and may even use humour in ways more akin to that attributed to men (Palmer 1994). Conversely, we cannot assume that all men will always use humour in a performative, aggrandizing style. There is clearly a need for more research that explores the varieties of humour used by both men and women in different contexts, particularly in situations where there are status differences – such as the workplace.

Humour and the doing of gender

Much of the above work on humour and gender difference rests on the assumption of prefigured gender polarities and hence it tends to reproduce and reconstitute the traditional and stereotypical gender bifurcations that the dominant masculinist discourse constitutes. Gender is simply deployed as a taken-for-granted resource and utilized as a variable through which to explore and hence reproduce difference. In adopting functionalist paradigmatic positions, decontextualizing empiricism and the assumptions of difference, this work essentializes gender and reproduces the restrictive categories of 'men' and 'women'. Equally restrictively, it locates humour-related behaviour differences under those categories. It is work that pays scant attention to the social construction of gender and the location of gender identity work within the discursive relations of power. It is apparent that much of the extant research suggesting gender differences in humour is flawed and inconclusive. Critiquing it has suggested that humour can be part of gendered identity work. More interpretivist research practices have highlighted how humour is implicated in the everyday 'doing of gender' (West and Zimmerman 1987). Indeed, Crawford (1995) contends that humour offers an important site through which to examine the construction of gender identities because it can be analysed from a number of levels. In the context of gendered organizing (Acker 1990), how members 'do humour' to both reproduce and resist the gendered workplace is an under-researched but valid and valuable issue.

We want to turn, then, to a consideration of humour in gender identity work. In doing so we draw on those conceptual trajectories that take gender as a discursive accomplishment taking place within the context of already gendered discourses and the power relations that inform and sustain them. In the more specific space of organizations, we take the view that gender identity work is a process of social construction accomplished through the interactions of organizational members but within the context of gendered organizational forms, discourses and power relations. Under this rubric, humour is an interactional resource that may be invoked in performing gender and, as such, may take forms which produce/reproduce prevailing and dominant gendered discourses and power relations, and/or, conversely, take forms that resist and subvert them. Humour can be part of the discursive contestations over organizational meanings and identities and part of the complex social dynamics through which gender identities are formed, reformed and transformed.

We wish to explore these aspects of humour in doing gender first in relation to the construction of masculinities, before turning to humour's role in resisting restrictive gender positions within organizations and finally to the problematizing of gender itself as a particular effect of the discourse–power nexus.

Masculinities, patriarchy and hierarchy

As noted earlier, Collinson's (1988, 1992) study of a working-class male-dominated organizational culture shows that humour can take the form of resistance, but that it can also manifest as an element of conformity and even of control. Shopfloor joking was used to resist boredom, but was also found to embody considerable social pressure to conform to a preoccupation with working-class masculinity. Workers were required to display a willingness, for example, to give and take a joke, to swear, to be dismissive of and objectify women, and to retain their domestic authority as 'breadwinner' and 'provider' – failure to display these signifiers of class-related masculinity was to fail as a 'real man'. The ability to be 'the provider' for one's family was of particular concern given the context of impending threats of job loss. Rather than encouraging a form of collective action, the relationships among the men were 'largely defensive and superficial' (1998: 198). Therefore, Collinson argues, the workers' preoccupation with sustaining their gender identity meant that most of the humour they used was deployed to do that rather than to subvert or challenge managerial actions or power asymmetries.

Within these processes of gender identity formation, women and the 'feminine' are afforded a particular space. It is largely a space of absence; women are treated as the 'absent other' against which men construct their identities. Otherwise women are represented by male workers as either highly sexualized or as passive dependants who must be controlled. There is no space for the real women – the wives and girlfriends (off-stage at home) – and no space for their voice. We do not know how the process of identity construction in the masculinized workplace is affected by the men's relationships with their female partners, nor how parallel identity construction work is conducted in the domestic context. Indeed, Collinson's study shows the contradictory features of the organizational location of the men and their constructions of 'masculine identity' in relation to women. On the one hand many male workers' identities were constructed in terms of being the responsible 'family man' and 'breadwinner', which detracted from collective worker action. However, the men leavened this apparently inclusive, nurturing, 'provider/family man' identity location by also asserting a 'masculine' identity location through, for example, retaining control of the family finances. Furthermore, there was a juxtaposition of paternalistic 'taking care of her' with the predatory male dominating the woman as sexual object. Humour played a part in all these identity moves, yet the profound influence of the 'absent female' on this identity work is not explored.

A different social space was also marked out and contested through humour. While the workers represented their own jobs as embodying 'real men's work' and this was part of their identity work, they often sought to feminize 'management'. The workers' (joking) talk ridicules managers as effeminate and managerial work as not 'real men's' work. This reinforces their own masculine identity in relation to a different other – the feminized male manager as opposed to female partners. It is a move that reinforces the political and structural polarization between themselves and management.

While not focusing on humour *per se*, a study by Alvesson (1988) centred on an advertising agency demonstrates how humour can be used to reinforce stereotypical elements of masculinities and femininities. The study found that aspects of 'traditional' masculine identity were strained within a context not necessarily favouring traditional notions of masculinity. While the agency was structured along traditionally gendered lines (predominantly males in senior positions and 'attractive', 'younger' women in the 'helping roles'[1]), there were elements of both work roles and the profession which did not correspond with typical notions of masculine identity. Being part of what Alvesson terms a 'soft (semi) profession' centred around compliance to client demands and a work role that requires the use of 'soft', 'creative' skills, challenged the symbolic construction of masculine identity. Alvesson argues that males in the agency engaged in forms of defensive 'masculinity enabling identity work' which involved 'using gender relations to repair and support self-identity' (p. 999). For example, he discusses how sexual jokes were used by the male employees, usually alluding to the sexual availability of female employees (e.g. 'That one. With butter on!'), and argues that this is part of their identity work in creating a sense of fellowship and gender affiliation. Thus, humour and joking were used to construct and confirm (stereotyped) gender identity.

While Alvesson cautions against essentializing the categories of men and women and detracting from the agency of women, there is no reporting of women using humour to challenge these gender constructions. Only one female manager is quoted as saying that having a sense of humour is important in order to cope with the male-dominated management and culture of advertising. As with Collinson's study, the voices, and in particular the humour, of women goes uninvestigated and is largely absent. However, Alvesson's study does show that gender-supporting work that constructs stereotypical formations may be expressed in 'privileged, well-paid, and creative workplaces' (Alvesson 1998: 999), as well as in low-status, low-pay and routinized work contexts such as industrial shopfloors.

These studies demonstrate that the construction of gender identity, in these cases masculine identity, can be a highly complex and nuanced process that is dependent on the context within which the identity work occurs. They also show that, irrespective of context, male identities are not homogeneous and need to be constructed. It is apparent that traditional and stereotypical notions of masculinity are frequently challenged in organizational contexts and either require repair work or the construction of alternate masculine identities. Importantly, both studies demonstrate how humour is used to deal with these challenges by facilitating or challenging gender identity constructions. They show how humour and joking helped sustain a masculine culture and were central to certain masculine identity formations. Humour is especially apparent in constructing notions of identity against the 'other', particularly women, and thereby reinforcing gender stereotypes.

Being female, doing humour, doing gender

Collinson's and Alvesson's work clearly demonstrates the interconnection of gendered identities, organizing, and humour. It also shows, however, that such processes occur within the frame of gendered discourses and the power relations that privilege certain discursive forms and arrangements. Work exploring women's use of humour in the workplace is very limited and mostly focuses on 'professional' or managerial women; nonetheless, they throw further light on the 'doing of gender' and on humour's role in the politics of gender identity and resistance.

The first thing to note is that exploring women's use of humour in a 'professional' (i.e. non-working-class) context, reveals that women are far from 'humourless', unable to tell jokes, or unable to appreciate others' humour as some earlier functionalist work suggested. Holmes *et al.* (2003), for example, found that women managers tended to use humour more than male counterparts, particularly in mixed-gender meetings. Humour was also a resource that women managers used to give directives or even reprimands to staff in order to 'smooth over' these actions. These female managers tended to initiate and encourage supportive humour and collaborative humour sequences which contributed to workplace solidarity (Holmes *et al.* 2003: 422). Yet as Holmes shows in another study, while humour might be used by female managers in order to maintain 'good relations' with those of lower status, within a power-differentiated context humour can also be interpreted as a form of 'repressive discourse' (Holmes 2000: 175) through an implicit disguising of power differences. A study by Mullany (2004) reveals similar findings. In this study the female chairs of meetings used a type of repressive humour to gain compliance from subordinates. Humour, then, can be deployed by women managers to 'do power' – to reaffirm and reconstruct power relations – as well as foster inclusive relations. Such studies have significant implications for understanding women's use of humour when in positions of organizational authority. They suggest that women too may have recourse to using humour in order to sustain hierarchy.

In a study investigating how female middle managers use humour to negotiate the 'multiple paradoxes' arising from their structural and gendered location,

Martin (2004), like Holmes *et al.*, also found women engaging in humour more than male counterparts. Not only did they use humour more frequently, they were also mindful of the types of humour they used and its effects on others. It is suggested, though, that humour also assisted women managers in 'blurring and transcending artificial boundaries between the feminine and the managerial' (Martin 2004: 162), therefore offering the possibility for the reversal of the 'symbolic order' of gender relations (Gherardi 1995). Thus, the study helps not only further dismantle the myth that women are not funny, but also contributes to an extension of the identification of what is humorous to include 'women-identified humorous discourse' (Martin 2004). This challenges the circumscriptions that the dominant (male) discourse has sought to impose that limits women's use of humour in certain contexts. Rather than fearing that humour initiation would mean they would not be taken seriously or that their gender identity would be put in question, these female managers regularly initiated humour. Nevertheless, the study also found an additional contextual factor that appeared to still constrain the women's enactment of humour initiation and appreciation, evidenced by their unwillingness to reciprocate deprecating humorous discourse initiated by subordinates. Martin argues that social conventions and gender role expectations still constrained female managers to undermine their own aggressive humour, such as sarcasm, with apologia, thus restoring the symbolic order of gender. While feminist scholars such as Gherardi (1995) argue that humour can be used to negotiate the paradox of gender roles, it also appears that humour can be deployed to simultaneously affirm the gendered order of work. It is shown to be used both in the construction of gender identity positions that are traditional/expected, but also to challenge these identity positions and construct alternatives. Humour thus appears as part of the resources available in gender politics and the processes of gender identity construction.

There has been little research exploring how women use humour as part of their 'identity work' in *non-managerial or non-professional* contexts. A rare exception is Sykes's (1966) study of how jokes were used in a Glasgow printworks. The study showed differences in the nature and intensity of joking behaviour at work compared with at home and between those considered as potential sexual partners and those not. A second exception is Spradley and Mann's (1975) ethnographic study of waitresses, which, among other things, considers the role of humour in their relationships with barmen. The thesis is that such humour essentially functions as a benign safety-valve in a tension-laden situation: the demands of the workplace entail that waitresses be simultaneously cooperative with the barmen and subordinate to them. But Mulkay (1988) suggests that this overlooks the inherent power relations in the situation, and that the humour, in the end, actually serves to reinforce those power relations and is oppressive to the waitresses. The women were not, in fact, able to initiate and close out their own humorous themes.

A study conducted by Bell and Forbes (1994) looks at female university office workers' use of 'office folklore' such as cartoons posted on walls, parodies of letters and memoranda. Here the workers used gendered artefacts to subvert the discourses of organizational control, and in particular, to resist, in an ironic way, female stereotypes. Through these images the women, individually and collectively, constructed symbolic forms that challenged the 'feminisation of work and the reductionism of bureaucracy' (Bell and Forbes 1994: 195) – doing so 'safely' within the guise of humour. Compared to Collinson's study on male workers, it is interesting how these women used stereotypical notions of gender identity and 'played' with these to create their own form of critique. It is a mode of appropriation and ironic reversal open to those captured by and enfolded in a dominant discourse, as a means of resistance. Indeed, as Bell and Forbes comment, the women did not attempt to 'destroy' the logic and practices they endured, but instead deployed humour interstitially to create something different and meaningful to them 'as women' in that particular organizational and social location. Studies such as this and Martin's on women managers demonstrate how humour can be used to accommodate, negotiate and (potentially) transform organizational control processes.

(Un)doing gender through humour

Functionalist research on gender and humour accepts the gender divisions within extant discourses and provides studies which essentialize gender differences. It reinforces and reproduces the discourses that position women as lacking a sense of humour and/or excludes their participation in humour. The domain of humour, particularly certain types of humour such as joke-as-performance, slapstick and physical humour, sarcasm and aggressive modes of humour, are held to be a masculine domain. Indeed, the extant discourse(s) on humour, including the academic variants, are male constructions and thus humour, its forms, locations and effects are defined within these masculine and patriarchal locations. As Palmer (1994: 71) notes, 'such studies indicate very clearly ... that there is a link between women's absence from many forms of humour and the forms of social control exercised over them'.

Given that much humour is used by those in powerful positions in relation to those in less powerful ones to sustain hierarchical arrangements, the very gender asymmetries in organizations and other social formations already explain women's relative absence or silence in public displays of humour (Bing 2004). As Stott (2005) points out, the sexual in much comedy is another reason for women's exclusion since it has been deemed culturally inappropriate for women to be involved in overt and public expressions of sexuality. Indeed, Barreca (1991: 50) goes so far as to suggest that 'in communities throughout the world ... women who tell jokes are regarded as sexually promiscuous'. Furthermore, in much humour women are objectified; they are made the passive object of humour, the 'handmaiden of laugher, not its creator' (Stott 2005). Just as feminist film theory has argued that women in mainstream cinema are coded to-be-looked-at (Mulvey 1981) so in the domain of humour women are coded as to-be-laughed-at. The male-dominated domain of humour is central to men's control and sexual domination of women. As such, women's lack of participation is hardly surprising, for it would simply reproduce and reinforce the male discourse and its negative and derogatory representations of women (Mulkay 1988: 141–2).

It is untenable to maintain, as do some studies cited here, that women lack a sense of humour and don't engage with the humorous. However, in resisting the notion of women as absent from humour, a difficulty still exists if we acknowledge that the domain of the humorous and the discourses around humour and comedy are male-dominated – at least in the public sphere. Even if women are to participate in humour, not just as passive receivers but as active producers, a dilemma persists. As Mulkay (1988: 149) says:

> Women operate as cultural producers within the context of a dominant discourse and a pattern of social relationships which are premised on a male view of the world. Consequently, although the humour used by and circulated among women will tend to have certain distinctive features, it will also resemble men's humour in many ways and will draw upon similar interpretative resources.

How do women get outside of or traverse the boundaries of this discursive formation that has become sedimented in social arrangements and recursively reproduced through humour? How can women be producers of humour outside the male-dominated discourse and produce humour that does not reproduce gendered differences and asymmetries?

This is the dilemma faced by any oppressed or marginalized group captive to the totalizing effects of dominant discourses, and it is precisely this dilemma that feminist theory has wrestled with, and postcolonial theory has taken up in relation to the colonized and ethnically marginalized – vividly captured by Spivak's (1994) question, 'Can the subaltern speak?' The issue here though is not 'Can women be funny?' – the evidence by now makes it abundantly clear that they can – rather it is 'Can women be funny on their own terms, in ways that do not reproduce male-dominant discourses and their concomitant subject positions, and that reflect women's interests and promotes their emancipation and well-being?' A feminist humour needs to challenge the male-dominant discourse around humour, to resist its codes and subject positions, begin to play with and transgress those codes and the boundaries of the discourse, and generate alternatives.

As with other modes of resistance to dominant discourse, feminist humour can at least strategically draw attention to the (male-dominated) discourses and codes that position women as the passive object of jokes. It can surface what is normally left implicit and unspoken, namely the codes, methods and forms that are used in humour to exclude or to position women in humour in particular ways. As Merrill (1988: 279) suggests, it 'empower[s] women to examine how we have been objectified and fetishised and to what extent we have been led to perpetuate this objectification'.

An entry into a feminist humour practice is offered by an interrogation of Freud's account of jokes (1960) in which he constructs a triangular relationship between a male joker, an object of the joke (typically a female object) and a male listener or audience. Flieger (1983) interrogates that structure, asking whether women can come to occupy the first position – of active constructer of the joke – or at least that of complicitous listener. She deconstructs Freud's arrangement, arguing that the gendered structure is not inherent to joking relations and that there is no logical reason why women cannot occupy the other positions. Historically it may have been difficult in practice, but today it is apparent that women can occupy those positions. Even so, the dynamics and effects of the humour may not be the same.

Feminist scholars have focused on the exclusion of women from humour, with some focusing on the exclusion from the pleasure it offers. Modleski (1987) suggests, however, that there is a possible position of pleasure for women even when women remain the subject and butt of humour; the pleasure derived from 'getting' the joke and from a form of righteous anger at apprehending the power effects enabling masculinist humour to objectify women. It is, as Reincke (1991: 27) suggests, 'the pleasure of the oppressed coming to consciousness of the way that oppression works'. Modleski sees this as liberatory, or at least cathartic, through offering a way for women to come to consciousness of the conditions of their oppression and to work through their anger. One can imagine workplace humour being a vehicle to animate these dynamics. The knowing listener is a feasible subject position for women within the discourses of humour and it may be liberatory or palliative, but the transformatory potential is limited. Modleski's other strategy – of feminists telling male jokes to other women – also has limitations, although the value of recontextualization as a mode of deconstruction can be acknowledged.

There would seem to be more subversive and transformative potential in women adopting the active role of humour producer. It is a role women have increasingly adopted. In the clearest, public sense, there has been a steady increase in the number of professional female comedians. However, some female comedians continue to locate women as the object of humour – and often such that the woman-as-object is actually the comedian herself using self-disparaging, self-deprecating humour. Phyllis Diller, for example, made self-deprecation the core of her comedy. In an interview she revealed that:

> I think that started in high school, when I realized I was not going to be Queen of the May. And I thought, well, I – I'll get them – I'll tell them about it before they tell me. So I always made jokes, about my appearance and what I was wearing … I think it started in – as a defense mechanism … Because I was not a beauty.
>
> (Dana and Matz 2005)

Ms Diller makes herself the target of her own jokes and it is precisely her 'femaleness' that is the source of that. She talks about her appearance and implicitly she knows that this is working against an idealized image or model of femininity constructed though masculine discourse. However, there is a kind of 'stage one' appropriation here. Diller and other women who assume the role of producers of humour have deconstructed Freud's gendered triangle and insinuated themselves into the active role. Additionally though, they have (partly) reappropriated their own bodies and identities. There is a degree of resistance to masculine domination in the fact that it is women talking about women's appearance, body, sexuality and identity, not men. It might be argued that humour that keeps women positioned as the focus of jokes is really reproducing gendered asymmetries and male dominance. With Diller, and others, there is, however, an additional line of subversion and resistance through appropriation and parody. It has less to do with a direct critique of the structures and systems of dominance than about holding up a distorting mirror reflecting a parodied, distorted and grotesque image of the cultural and identity codes that the mainstream constructs. Diller takes the codes of femininity that the dominant patriarchal system constructs and projects back a parodied, distorted and unruly version. Diller reputedly said that 'Elegance isn't funny' and that more particularly it was good taste that was at issue. She suggests that her comedy pushes good taste over the edge. It is an assault on good taste; it is also a critique of the traditional, valorized codes of femininity.

As noted earlier, Reincke (1991) sees self-deprecating humour as women laughing at themselves and thereby reproducing the male dominance inherent to much humour in society. She maintains that when women laugh *for themselves*, in ways not framed by male interests and discourse, they pose a genuine threat to male dominance by displacing men and their interests from the centre of knowing and knowledge, a displacement of men and masculinity that is subversive. This is especially so when female humour is not directed at men, since that is a mirror that retains male dominance, but when the humour is within and about female interests. The challenge, of course, is to locate a discourse and a discursive space that manages to detach itself from the dominant male discourses in society. Even if such a space can be located, if it even exists, can the construction of a purely female discourse and accompanying humour, whilst pleasurable and reassuring, be transformational without engagement with male-dominant discourse? Is a disengaged, parallel female discourse able to offer emancipatory potential?

There is a version of contemporary female comedy that strongly engages in reappropriative and parodying strategies exemplified by the comedy of Roseanne Barr in the USA and Jo Brand in the UK. Both deliberately play with and project back the image of women and femininity that the orthodox, male-shaded world constructs, in a manner that resists the stereotypes and male desires embedded therein. They resolutely resist the alignment of femininity with a decorous, slim, quiet, inoffensive, humourless woman. It is a mode of humour also apparent in the comedy of French and Saunders, Margaret Cho, and to some extent Victoria Wood. Dawn French revels in and sexualizes her large body in ways not typical of media representations. The female body, so persistently objectified in male humour and discourse, has unsurprisingly become a focus for feminist theorizing and much contemporary women's comedy, often focusing on the pressures and anxieties women are subjected to in the constant promulgation of idealized and narrowly sexualized female bodies. Commenting on Victoria Wood and Jo Brand, Porter (1998: 79) suggests that by reappropriating their own bodies, by 'placing their bodies and sexuality at the centre of their humour', they escape the objectification of women and women's bodies so apparent in male humour and discourse. Comedy offers a mode of articulation and emotion in relation to female bodies that is an alternative to the impossible representations recycled through dominant discourses. As Porter suggests, 'Comedy with its essential anarchism is perhaps the most appropriate tool to mock canonical attitudes towards the female body' (1998: 81).

The parodying and subversive effects of contemporary female humour are not confined to the body. In her *Absolutely Fabulous* creation, Edina Monsoon, Saunders constructs a grotesque figure, but in so doing allows women to be represented as unabashedly vain, selfish, greedy, narcissistic, un-nurturing, and – most challenging of all perhaps – thoroughly bad mothers. This is carnivalesque, an inversion of female stereotypes. As such, it is a challenge to the dominant order and potentially subversive. Rowe (1997: 75) sees 'Roseanne' as a contemporary exemplar of the 'unruly woman' – 'a topos of female outrageousness and transgression from literary and social history' – who deploys a 'semiotics of the unruly' to counterpoint the expectations, abstractions and affectations of white, middle-class feminism of the 1970s and 1980s with the humdrum realities and struggles of life for working-class women in the 1990s. She also, of course, constructs a counterpoint to (other) stereotypical constructions of the feminine emanating from patriarchal discourses. Margaret Cho is another exemplar. She used to declare in her act that she was 'very inappropriate' – a self-description reflected in her frank and graphic discussions of the female body and its functions such as florid descriptions of childbirth, masturbation and of soiling her own pants. There is an anarchic play with the body and the discourses that accompany it that challenges the narrow and limited (and limiting) subject positions typically made available for women. Roseanne Barr pursues a similar strategy. She also self-consciously creates offence – 'I do offensive things … that's who I am. That's my act' (quoted in Rowe 1997: 79). The lack of clear differentiation between Roseanne the character and Roseanne the person is part of the strategy. It means that what she does cannot be shrugged off as merely performance, as playing a part, as non-real. She declares that she wants to 'break every social norm … and see that it is laughed at. I chuckle with glee if I know I have offended someone because the people I intend to insult offend me horribly' (in Rowe 1997: 79).

The stand-up comedian Sarah Silverman represents an interesting example of transgression and subversion of women's traditional roles and their relationship to humour precisely by, in many ways, embodying a traditional form of femininity that appeals to hegemonic masculinity. Her on-stage persona signifies a very conservative femininity – she is self-absorbed, obsessed with her weight and looks, and views the world via an extremely egocentric lens; her persona is sorority-girl-meets-Jewish-American-Princess. However, Silverman uses this persona to gleefully address taboo topics such as rape, racism and dead grandmothers. A typical example of her humour involves her own idiosyncratic account of the events of 9/11:

> They were devastating. They were beyond devastating. I don't want to say especially for these people, or especially for these people, but especially for me, because it happened to be the same exact day that I found out that the soy chai latte was, like, nine hundred calories. I had been drinking them *every day*. You hear soy, you think healthy. And it's a lie.
>
> (Quoted in Goodyear 2005)

The transgressive character of Silverman's humour derives specifically from the fact that she delivers these missives via an innocence, obliviousness and earnestness that is shocking and jarring to the audience: 'Everybody blames the Jews for killing Christ', Silverman says. 'And then the Jews try to pass it off on the Romans. I'm one of the few people that believe it was the blacks' (quoted in Goodyear 2005). Such humour is not racist, but functions rather as a comment on, and critique of, racism. As with Hannah Arendt's 'banality of evil', Silverman shines a spotlight on the ways in which racism and sexism are embedded in the glib everydayness of the unreflective worldview.

Mellencamp (1997) argues that Gracie Allen (in *The George Burns and Gracie Allen Show*) and Lucille Ball (in *I Love Lucy*) represent earlier versions of unruly women in US popular culture challenging the dominant gender order through being 'out of control', Gracie via language and Lucy the body – neither of them conformed to the stereotypical image of the quiet, obedient and tidy housewife expected at the time. In this sense, Mellencamp invokes Baudrillard's notion that 'The witticism, which is a transgressive reversal of discourse, does not act on the basis of another code as such; it works through the instantaneous deconstruction of the dominant discursive code' (1981: 184). This offers a possible solution to the problem of women obtaining a space for autonomous articulation in the context of male-dominated discourses; humour can deconstruct and subvert from *within* a discourse. This is of great significance for organizational life since it means that humour can become a vehicle for the interrogation, challenge and subversion of hegemonic masculinity encoded in organizational discourses.

The difference between Lucy/Gracie and, say, Roseanne is that Roseanne controls the process and asserts her authority to construct an unruly woman on her own terms. She, like Margaret Cho and Jennifer Saunders, deals in excess – their bodies, attitudes and behaviours are in excess of the expected and accepted limits of the stereotypical feminine. By being the producers of comedy, especially with the level of control they exhibit, they are already in excess. An excess is a challenge to the status quo; it spills over and resists containment, but it also suggests a supplementarity that points to a lack or deficiency in that to which it is a supplement – namely the dominant discourse and the status quo. What is revealed as supplement is women's desire, knowledge and power – precisely those things that are deficient in the patriarchally defined status quo and it is the surfacing of those as excess in this mode of humour that is a challenge and a potential subversion.

These comedians also subvert by surfacing and confronting taboos and transgressing the boundaries constructed to house women and the feminine in particular ways. The taboos of bodily function, female sexuality, motherhood and nurturing and of female unruliness are surfaced, transgressing the boundaries of accepted behaviours and discourse. The comedic surfacing of such taboos opens up the dominant discourse and creates spaces to interpolate new and different meanings. As Rowe (1997: 77) argues, 'the parodic excesses of the unruly woman and the comic conventions surrounding her provide a space to act out the dilemmas of femininity, to make visible and laughable what Mary Ann Doane describes as the "tropes of femininity"'. The standard tropes of femininity that have held women in restricted meaning frames and subject positions are challenged and inverted by this humour; it opens up new tropological spaces and, potentially, new positions of intelligibility and subjectivity. It is the traditions of humour and the conventions of comedy that permit this type of subversion. There is more legitimized space to play and challenge with humour than there might be in more serious modes of challenge and subversion which are also more likely to engender counter-resistance and counter moves.

In organizational contexts it might be effective or valuable to engage in deconstructions and taboo transgressions of the type these comedians enact, but there are other tropes of femininity that are pervasive and restrictive in organizational contexts that could be also be targets for female humour. Simply assuming the role of humour producer in an organizational context already provides an opening. The point is the potential to use humour to challenge existing tropes, meaning frames and discourses and in so doing open up alternative spaces. Trethewey (2004) provides a compelling example of the possibilities for such opening up of alternative spaces in her discussion of the relationships among laughter, eros and pedagogy. While she is specifically discussing the classroom space and the relationship between teachers and students, her argument seems broadly applicable to organizational life. She suggests laughter as both a literal and metaphorical way to rethink the place of sexuality and the erotic in organizational contexts such as the classroom. While sexuality (particularly women's sexuality) is typically excised from organizational life, laughter is an embodied experience that allows us to rethink what sexuality might look like outside of a frame of (masculine) dominance and (feminine) subordination. Trethewey argues, quoting Davis (1990: 12), that 'The laughter metaphor redeems the experience of women's sexuality. Actively engaged laughter is contextual, emotional, physical, interactive, and by no means passive' (2004: 37). She suggests that the erotic aspects of laughter are derived from its ability to make meaningful connections with others, and to be energized by such connections. Laughter, then, becomes one way to explore and reflect upon organizational experience in a shared, engaged manner. She uses the example of relating to a class the experience of being a nursing mother in a professional environment to illustrate how she was both

> materially and ideologically positioned betwixt and between discourses of home and work, public and private, and struggled to negotiate an appropriate identity. As a class, we laughed together about my awkward experiences and identity(ies), but in so doing we began to critique taken-for-granted assumptions about work, family, sexuality and their relationship to current understandings of professionalism. (p. 38)

From a feminist perspective, then, it is perhaps worth stating that the corollary of humour is laughter. While this may seem absurdly obvious, discussions of humour and (generally male) comedians focus mainly on the performative aspects of humour and say little about the audience that the humour engages. Using Trethewey's metaphor of laughter, we might suggest that, following Cixous (1981), laughter becomes a form of organizational disorder that allows for the exploration of alternative ways of thinking and spaces for action. Humour is not just wry commentary on the world; it engages people in physical ways that can either confirm 'common sense' thinking and reproduce the status quo, or produce self-reflection and foment transgression, subversion, and resistance. In this sense, humour is fundamentally dialectic and dialogic. Laughter is both medium and outcome of (humorous) dialogue and reflective engagement with others. As Stott (2005) notes, the sheer physicality of laughter itself dislodges the notion of women as quiet, refined and calm. It displays a more bodily, animalistic aspect that men, he suggests, find fearful. Cixous (1981) herself offers a nearly audible claim that 'laughter that breaks out, overflows, a humor no one would expect to find in women' challenges and reflects upon the dominant social order, for '"she who laughs last" ... [must] laugh at herself'. One way to reclaim this voice is to reclaim the Medusa. Cixous (1975) insists that 'in fact, you only have to look at the Medusa straight on to see her. And she's not deadly. She's beautiful and she's laughing'.

Conclusion: toward representing the unrepresentable

Deetz (2005) has recently argued that engaging in critical theory as a way of life involves three moments: being filled with thought, being filled with care and being filled with good humour. The first moment invokes the need for careful critique and analysis of hidden systems of domination. The second recognizes the importance of attending to the differences of others and recognizing how those differences challenge one's own sense of self. The third moment rejects mere cynicism and

> works toward the acceptance of the lack of certainty and the recognition that we make it up as we go. Vocabulary and answers are not final but rather are 'resting places' ... as we move into worlds where they no longer work, where their partiality is shown, where a different response is needed. The righteousness and pretense are gone, and we must act without knowing for sure. The grand narratives are dead, but there is meaning and pleasure in the little ones.

> (2005: 105)

Perhaps, then, 'representing the unrepresentable' means starting by laughing at ourselves; recognizing the profound absurdity and whimsy of life in an organizational world. The articulation of feminism and humour is one way to bring irony to bear on the mundane aspects of organizing (Trethewey 1999), and provides a potential mechanism for subverting the gendered social order from within the halls of hegemonic masculinity. Bell and Forbes's (1994) study suggests one way in which this ironic 'laughing at ourselves' might occur, although one might argue about the extent to which the appropriation of feminine stereotypes by the female office staff subverts the gendered order of things rather than reifying it. There is something subversive about laughter in the workplace, particularly if it is about engagement with others through a process of self-reflection.

Of course, 'being filled with humour' ideally moves beyond a masculine/ feminine dichotomy that identifies men's and women's forms of humour to adddress the ways in which gendered institutions and practices are maintained, transformed and reproduced through humour. For example, how might gay humour in the workplace subvert masculine/feminine dichotomies and challenge the hegemonic masculinity of the workplace? While not directly addressing gender issues, Taylor and Bain's (2003) study of humour as subversion in a call centre illustrates how an openly gay employee used anti-management humour and performed identity work that management seemed ill-equipped to handle. Using his 'campness' to 'undermine management' and 'win people over', the employee was able to 'push' what was permissible to the limits. He could 'get away' with this 'because he could exploit both his own popularity and managers' stereotypical expectations of a gay man' (p. 1503). Being openly gay is not inherently subversive in the workplace, but it is interesting to note how, in this context, humour as a means of 'laughing together' created a workplace environment that, at times, bordered on the carnivalesque.

Another interesting issue that moves us beyond the masculine/feminine humour dichotomy addresses the question of how men might use humour to transform hegemonic forms of masculinity and create hybrid identities/ masculinities (Connell 1995). The self-described 'executive transvestite' comedian Eddie Izzard is perhaps the most obvious example of such a hybrid identity – a heterosexual man who wears women's clothing and makeup and engages in surreal, self-referential monologues that critique imperialism (amongst many other things) and promote transnational identity (for example, he once described himself in a political debate on TV as 'British-European').

A perhaps less obvious example is the US comedian Stephen Colbert's development of a comedic persona that parodies the right-wing, hyper-masculine talking heads that are a staple of US news television. Modelled principally on Bill O'Reilly, the right-wing host of *The O'Reilly Factor*, Colbert's character hosts his own show called *The Colbert Report* (pronounced 'reporr'). He has coined the term 'truthiness' to describe a form of truth that one believes emotionally rather than intellectually and with scant regard for available evidence. He has deployed this term in a devastating manner to skewer the Bush administration and its penchant for using 'truthiness' rather than evidence in policy decisions. From a feminist perspective, Colbert's character is interesting in its articulation of a particular form of hegemonic masculinity (egotistical, dogmatic, bullying, bigoted, anti-intellectual, etc.) with a political perspective that is insular, religiously fundamentalist, racist and jingoistic in the extreme. His character speaks truth (or 'truthiness'!) to power in the sense that he allows us to see the disastrous consequences of the marriage of hyper-masculinity, anti-intellectualism, political power, and therefore serves to critique hegemonic forms of masculinity.

In sum, a feminist interrogation of humour allows us to explore ways in which humour – as an everyday discursive practice – can be deployed as a means to unsettle and subvert the gendered organizational order. While much of our discussion has focused on feminist/women's alternatives to masculinist forms of humour, a useful way to understand the intersection of feminism and humour is to investigate the ways in which humour/laughter is simultaneously a form of engagement with others and a subversive discursive practice that introduces disorder into the apparently seamless patina of institutional and organizational life. In this sense, humour is a serious thing; it can be dangerous to those in power precisely because it is a means by which to remove the veil and expose the emperor's empty wardrobe.

Note

1   These were terms deployed in the organization and reported in the article.

References

Aaltio, I. and Mills, A. J. (eds) (2002) *Gender, Identity and the Culture of Organizations*, London: Routledge.

Acker, J. (1990) 'Hierarchies, jobs, bodies: a theory of gendered organizations', *Gender and Society*, 4: 139–58.

Alvesson, M. (1998) 'Gender relations and identity at work: a case study of masculinities and femininities at an advertising agency', *Human Relations*, 51(8): 969–1005.

Ashcraft, K. L. and Mumby, D. K. (2004) *Reworking Gender: A Feminist Communicology of Organization*, Thousand Oaks, CA: Sage.

Barreca, R. (1991) *They Used to Call me Snow White ...But I Drifted: Women's Strategic Use of Humour*, New York: Penguin.

Baudrillard, J. (1981) 'Requiem for the media', in *For a Critique of the Political Economy of the Sign*, tr. Charles Levin, St Louis, MO: Telos.

Bell, E. L. and Forbes, L. C. (1994) 'Office folklore in the academic paperwork empire: the interstitial space of gendered (con)texts', *Text and Performance Quarterly*, 14: 181–96.

Bing, J. (2004) 'Is feminist humour an oxymoron?', *Women and Language*, 27(1): 22–33.

Boxer, D. and Cortés-Conde, F. (1997) 'From bonding to biting: conversational joking and identity display', *Journal of Pragmatics*, 27: 275–94.

Bruner, E. and Kelso, J. P. (1980) 'Gender differences in graffiti: a semiotic perspective', *Women's Studies International Quarterly*, 3: 239–52.

Cantor, J. (1976) 'What is funny to whom?', *Journal of Communication*, 26(3): 315–21.

Chapman, A. and Gadfield, N. (1976) 'Is sexual humour sexist?', *Journal of Communication*, 25: 141–53.

Cixous, H. (1975) 'The laugh of the Medusa', 1975, tr. Keith Cohen and Paula Cohen, *Signs* 1 (1976): 875–93.

Cixous, H. (1981) 'Castration and decapitation', tr. A. Kuhn, *Signs: Journal of Women in Culture and Society*, 7 (autumn): 41–55.

Coates, J. (1986) *Women, Men and Language: A Sociolinguistic Account of Sex Differences in Language*, London: Longman.

Collinson, D. (1988) 'Engineering humour: masculinity, joking and conflict in shop floor relations', *Organization Studies*, 9(2): 181–99.

Collinson, D. (1992) *Managing the Shopfloor: Subjectivity, Masculinity, and Workplace Culture*, New York: De Gruyter

Connell, R. W. (1995) *Masculinities*, St Leonards, NSW: Allen & Unwin.

Coser, R. (1960) 'Laughter among colleagues', *Psychiatry*, 23: 81–95.

Crawford, M. (1989) 'Humor in conversational context: beyond biases in the study of gender and humor', in R. K. Unger (ed.), *Representations: Social Constructions of Gender*, pp. 155–66, Amityville, NY: Baywood Publishing.

Crawford, M. (1995) *Talking Difference: On Gender and Language*, London: Sage.

Dana, B. and Matz, J. (2005) 'Interview with Phyllis Diller', Boston, MA: Emerson Comedy Archives Oral History Project, Emerson College, <http://www.emerson.edu/comedy/histories/index.cfm>, accessed Nov. 2005.

Davis, K. E. (1990) 'I love myself when I'm laughing: a new paradigm for sex', *Journal of Social Philosophy*, 21: 5–24.

Deetz, S. (2005) 'Critical theory', in S. May and D. Mumby (eds), *Engaging Organizational Communication Theory: Multiple Perspectives*, pp. 85–112, Thousand Oaks, CA: Sage.

Ely, R. J., Scully, M. A. and Foldy, E. G. (eds) (2003) *Reader in Gender, Work and Organization*, Oxford and New York: Blackwell.

Erickson, F. and Schultz, J. (1982) *The Councillor as Gatekeeper*, New York: Academic Press.

Finney, G. (1994) *Look Who's Laughing: Gender and Comedy*, Langhome, PA: Gordon & Breach.

Fishman, P. (1983) 'Interaction: the work women do', in B. Thorne, C. Kramarae and N. Henley (eds), *Language, Gender and Society*, pp. 89–101, Rowley, MA: Newbury.

Flieger, J. A. (1983) 'The purloined punchline: joke as textual paradigm', *Modern Language Notes*, 98(5): 943–67.

Freud, S. (1960) *Jokes and their Relation to the Unconscious*, tr. James Strachey, New York: W. W. Norton & Co.

Gherardi, S. (1995) *Gender, Symbolism and Organizational Cultures*, London: Sage.

Goodwin, M. H. (1982) 'Instigating storytelling as social process', *American Ethnologist*, 9(4): 799–819.

Goodyear, D. (2005) 'Quiet depravity', *The New Yorker*. Online at <http://www.newyorker.com/fact/content/articles/051024fa_fact>.

Griffiths, L. (1998) 'Humour as resistance to professional dominance in community mental health teams', *Sociology of Health and Illness*, 20(6): 874–95.

Grugulis, I. (2002) 'Nothing serious? Candidates' use of humour in management training', *Human Relations*, 55(4): 387–406.

Hay, J. (2000) 'Functions of humour in the conversations of men and women', *Journal of Pragmatics*, 32: 709–42.

Hengen, S. (ed.) (1998) *Performing Gender and Comedy: Theories, Texts and Contexts*, Amsterdam: Gordon & Breach.

Holmes, J. (2000) 'Politeness, power and provocation: how humour functions in the workplace', *Discourse Studies*, 2(2): 159–85.

Holmes, J., Burns, L., Marra, M., Stubbe, M. and Vine, B. (2003) 'Women managing discourse in the workplace', *Women in Management Review*, 18(8): 414–24.

Jenkins, M. (1985) 'What's so funny? Joking among women', in S. Bremmer, N. Caskey and B. Moonwomon (eds), *Proceedings of the First Berkeley Women and Language Conference*, pp. 135–51, Berkeley, CA: Women and Language Group.

Kotthoff, H. (2000) 'Gender and joking: on the complexities of women's image politics in humorous narratives', *Journal of Pragmatics*, 32: 55–80.

Kotthoff, H. (2006) 'Gender and humour: the state of the art', *Journal of Pragmatics*, 38: 4–25.

Kramarae, C. (1981) *Women and Men Speaking: Framework for Analysis*, Rowley, MA: Newbury.

La Fave, L. (1972) 'Humor judgments as a function of reference groups and identification classes', in H. Goldstein and P. E. McGhee (eds), *The Psychology of Humor: Theoretical Perspectives and Empirical Issues*, pp. 81–100, New York: Academic Press.

Lakoff, R. (1975) *Language and Women's Place*, New York: Harper Row.

McGhee, P. E. (1979) *Humour, its Origin and Development*, San Francisco, CA: Freeman.

McGhee, P. and Goldstein, J. (1983) *Handbook of Humour Research*, vol. 1, New York: Springer-Verlag.

Martin, D. M. (2004) 'Humor in middle management: women negotiating the paradoxes of organizational life', *Journal of Applied Communication Research*, 32: 147–70.

Mellencamp, P. (1997) 'Situation comedy, feminism, and Freud: discourses of Gracie and Lucy', in C. Brunsdon, J. D'Acci and L. Spigel (eds), *Feminist Television Criticism: A Reader*, pp. 60–73, Oxford: Clarendon Press.

Merrill, L. (1988) 'Feminist humor: rebellious and self-affirming', *Women's Studies*, 15: 271–80.

Mills, A. J. and Tancred, P. (1992) *Gendering Organizational Analysis*, Newbury Park, CA: Sage.

Modleski, T. (1987) 'Rape versus mans/laughter: Hitchcock's *Blackmail* and feminist interpretation', *PMLA* (May): 304–15.

Mulkay, M. J. (1988) *On Humour: Its Nature and its Place in Modern Society*, Cambridge: Polity Press.

Mullany, L. (2004) 'Gender, politeness and institutional power roles: humour as a tactic to gain compliance in workplace business meetings', *Multilingua*, 23: 13–37.

Mulvey, L. (1981) 'Afterthoughts on "visual pleasure and narrative cinema" inspired by duel in the sun, frameworks', *The Journal of Cinema and Media*, Summer.

Palmer, J. (1994) *Taking Humor Seriously*, London: Routledge.

Porter, L. (1998) 'Tarts, tampons and tyrants: women and representation in British comedy', in S. Wagg (ed.), *Because I Tell A Joke Or Two: Comedy, Politics and Social Difference*, pp. 65–93, London and New York: Routledge.

Reincke, N. (1991) 'Antidote to dominance: women's laughter as counteraction', *Journal of Popular Culture*, 24(4): 27–37.

Rodrigues, S. B. and Collinson, D. L. (1995) 'Having fun: humour as resistance in Brazil', *Organization Studies*, 16(5): 739–68.

Rowe, K. K. (1997) 'Roseanne: unruly woman as domestic goddess', in C. Brunsdon, J. D'Acci and L. Spigel (eds), *Feminist Television Criticism: A Reader*, pp. 74–83, Oxford: Clarendon Press.

Sochen, J. (ed.) (1991) *Women's Comic Visions*, Detroit, MI: Wayne State University Press.

Spivak, G. C. (1994) 'Can the subaltern speak?', in P. William and L. Chrisman (eds), *Colonial Discourse and Post-Colonial Theory: A Reader*, pp. 66–111, New York: Columbia University Press.

Spradley, J. P. and Mann, B. (1975) *The Cocktail Waitress*, New York: John Wiley & Sons.

Stott, A. (2005) *Comedy*, London and New York: Routledge.

Sykes, A. J. M. (1966) 'The joking relationship in an industrial setting', *American Anthropologist*, 68: 188–93.

Taylor, P. and Bain, P. (2003) '"Subterranean worksick blues": humour as subversion in two call centres', *Organization Studies*, 24(9): 1487–509.

Terry, R. L and Ertel, S. L. (1974) 'Exploration of individual differences in preferences of humor', *Psychological Reports*, 34: 1034–7.

Trethewey, A. (1999) 'Isn't it ironic: using irony to explore the contradictions of organizational life', *Western Journal of Communication*, 63: 140–67.

Trethewey, A. (2004) 'Sexuality, eros, and pedagogy: desiring laughter in the classroom', *Women and Language*, 27(1): 34–9.

West, C. and Zimmerman, D. (1987) 'Doing gender', *Gender and Society*, 1(2): 125–51.

Zillman, D. and Stocking, S. H. (1976) 'Putdown humor', *Journal of Communication*, 26(3): 154–72.

Chapter 8

Humour in workplace meetings

Challenging hierarchies

Meredith Marra

Within the scope of workplace interactions, corporate business meetings invoke images of serious talk about serious issues. However, the frequency of humour that can be found in such meetings challenges stereotypical preconceptions about the appropriateness and place of humour at work. As Vuorela notes, 'humor would appear to be risky in business' (2005: 106). Nevertheless, in our large database of recorded meetings (collected as part of the Wellington Language in the Workplace Project), humour is endemic. In our recent research, even the most humourless of meetings averaged an instance of humour every six minutes (Holmes and Schnurr 2005).

Many have argued that this pervasive occurrence of humour in the workplace reflects humour's value as a solidarity device, building a sense of team and cohesion within an organization (e.g. Vinton 1989; Holmes 2000; see also the review in Westwood 2004). Adopting this approach, humour is often described as a managerial tool intended to smooth the path for effective interaction (e.g. Consalvo 1989; Duncan *et al.* 1990). However, it is important to recognize that organizational humour occurs in settings characterized by power asymmetries, both imposed and implicit; the workplace, like any institutional setting, is typically hierarchical.

There is a growing body of research which recognizes these asymmetries and examines the use of humour as resistance, subversion or challenge to the status quo (e.g. Collinson 2002; Ackroyd and Thompson 1999; Rodrigues and Collinson 1995). In my own collaborative research with Janet Holmes, the frequency of subversive humour in business meetings was compared with its occurrence in the conversations of friendship groups (Holmes and Marra 2002a). In the workplace context, the data contained extensive use of humour which functioned to subvert. Overall, subversive humour amounted to 40 per cent of the total instances of humour, with rates per minute at levels ten times above the levels identified in friendship group interactions (a context where participants enjoy greater equality). Identifying and interpreting this 'darker' side (Austin 1990) of humour at work seems important, especially in societies where democratic processes are overtly promulgated as desirable.

The analysis of subversive humour has typically been concerned with the ways in which subordinates exploit the distancing function of humour. Making light of situations allows them to challenge or criticize their superiors through the mitigating effect of the humour. By contrast, the analysis that will be presented here focuses on the way humour draws attention to and challenges organizational hierarchies. My interest in this perspective arose from a retort delivered by a manager in a corporate organization. After her team made humorous remarks about the way she presented a controversial decision with little regard for their opinions, she quipped back 'did you feel disempowered by that?' This example is analysed in greater detail below (example 1). The analysis highlights the ways in which both the more and less powerful participants in the decision use humour to instantiate the inevitable tension arising from status differences within workplace teams. These hierarchies may be a necessary outcome of the degrees of accountability and responsibility assigned to particular roles (Marra 2003), but they are problematic within a society such as New Zealand with low tolerance of power inequalities (Hofstede 1997).

Adopting a critical discourse analysis (CDA) framework with the overt aims of exposing and questioning patterns of dominance, this chapter examines the relationship between systemic power differences and the distribution of humour in workplace talk. The examples included in the investigation are extracted from recordings of the everyday business meetings of an established workplace team. Through close and critical analysis of the interaction, humour which might be analysed as functioning to maintain and develop solidarity is reanalysed as an implicit challenge to behaviour which actively constructs the imposed status differences in the workplace. Focusing on the specific meeting task of decision-making, the distribution of humour within the structure of decisions suggests that humour may be interpreted as a response to inequality; humour signals awareness by both managers and subordinates of the hierarchical roles they play at work, particularly in the light of the democratic practices subscribed to by the wider society. Thus, we see managers and other dominant participants humorously drawing attention to their overt displays of power, as well as subordinates using humour to expose the limits on their power because of their lower organizational status. The aim of this analysis is to present an alternative to a functional approach which privileges one interpretation of the humour, for example as a solidarity device, or even as a strategy for subversion. Presenting humour as a solidarity strategy ignores other plausible explanations for its frequency in interaction. To question this approach, I present an additional lens through which to view humour at work, one which focuses on the structural distribution of the humour and provides another account for its occurrence.

Undoubtedly the orientation chosen plays a role in this interpretation; hence the premise of the critical standpoint used in this analysis is discussed in the next section.

Critical discourse analysis

Within linguistics, two theoretical frameworks have dominated workplace studies, namely conversation analysis and ethnomethodology (see e.g. Boden 1994, and the articles in the volume by Drew and Heritage 1992). Increasingly, however, CDA, with its acute focus on power asymmetry, has established a central place in workplace research (e.g. Wodak 1997; Iedema 1999; Candlin and Maley 1997; Scheuer 2003). CDA recognizes that workplaces typically operate with an enforced and visible institutional structure, with managers explicitly positioned in high-status roles in relation to their subordinates. The result is asymmetric power relationships which, I argue, play an overt but under-recognized role in the communicative behaviour of workers.

Critical social research has many offshoots, for example, critical feminist theory (e.g. Buzzanell 1994) and critical applied linguistics (e.g. Pennycook 2001). CDA, as one such critical school, shares with others a common concern with social inequality. Originating in studies of discrimination, CDA aims to make explicit the 'taken for granted' assumptions that allow the powerful to dominate the powerless, and makes use of the analysis of text as a way of revealing and exposing dominance. It addresses the Foucauldian call that we should take 'forms of resistance against different forms of power as a starting point' (Foucault 2000: 329). CDA is thus a 'top–down' approach, revealing how the dominant are controlling the dominated.

A critical perspective does not focus solely on the explicit exercise of power. The thrust of Foucault's aims was to instill a sense of the reflexive into the way people think and act. With this in mind, it is clear that the notion of power also includes implicit, conventionalized inequality and hegemony. My own stance emphasizes the dynamic nature of power and characterizes it as a negotiated construct (see Marra 2003, for a fuller description). The status assigned to managers is legitimized by the dominated who allow themselves to be controlled (Gramsci's coercion and consent); indeed, Foucault argues that without resistance to such power, there is no power (Hindess 1996: 101).

This notion of power which includes both explicit power and naturalized dominance underpins the CDA framework. As a theoretical approach, CDA views language as 'a form of social practice' (Titscher et al. 2000: 147), whereby the linguistic forms and discourse strategies that we use reveal our societal and cultural norms. A critical discourse analysis approach describes the way power and dominance are produced and reproduced in completely unremarkable interactions, such as the meetings which form the basis of the analysis described below. Within this framework, humour, as a frequently employed discourse strategy, can provide insights into how status differences are ratified, negotiated and also questioned and challenged. The context of the business meeting is a setting in which the construction of power asymmetries can be particularly clearly observed.

The data: the Language in the Workplace project[1]

The meetings used in this analysis have been drawn from the larger corpus collected by the Wellington Language in the Workplace project (LWP). LWP is a large-scale sociolinguistic research project investigating workplace communication through the analysis of authentic interactions collected in a variety of New Zealand workplaces. For close to a decade, the research team (located in the School of Linguistics and Applied Language Studies at Victoria University of Wellington) has collaborated with many different workplaces, asking volunteers to record their everyday interactions at work. Workplace communication is an important topic for research because of the practical contributions that can emanate from analysis. Boden (1994) claims organization *is* talk; Sarangi and Roberts argue 'workplaces are held together by communicative practices' (1999: 1); and Wodak and Iedema describe organizations as being 'continuously created and re-created in the acts of communication between organizational members' (1999: 7). However, despite this emphasis on communication at work, research based on genuine workplace data and focused on workplace talk is noticeably sparse.

The philosophy behind LWP's methodology is to hand over total and final control of what is recorded to the volunteers in workplaces; so participants record their own interactions.[2] We use an appreciative enquiry methodology (Fry *et al.* 2002; Hammond 1998). Hence we approach only those workplaces and communicators who have been identified as effective by their colleagues, and by positive organizational and business outcomes (i.e. there is an independent measure of the quality of the communication we collect and analyse). Participants typically report surprise at how quickly they become accustomed to the recording process, and the result for our purposes is a high proportion of useable quality data with little evidence of interactions being affected by tape awareness or shyness. Statistically, the database now incorporates several thousand interactions from approximately 500 participants in more than 20 different workplaces (see Holmes and Stubbe 2003, for a description of the methodology and constitution of the corpus).

Business meetings are a particular type of interaction which we are keen to capture in these workplaces. Although workplace communication continues to develop as a field, research which focuses specifically on meetings is still relatively scarce (Tracy and Dimock 2004; Chan 2006). Within linguistic research, meetings are seldom distinguished from other types of workplace interaction (for example, none of the papers in Drew and Heritage's important 1992 collection on talk at work specifically focuses on meetings), although there is limited but useful literature in the areas of floor management and turntaking (e.g. Edelsky 1981; Morgenthaler 1990; Larrue and Trognon 1993), as well as topic management (e.g. Hanak 1998). Meetings are, however, an important part of workplace communication: '[b]lending talk and task, meetings also tie up innumerable organizational hours and thus resources, a further reason why they merit careful attention' (Boden 1994: 81).

To capture large group meetings audio recordings will not suffice because not only is speaker identification almost impossible, but the gestures, gaze and body movement vital to interpreting the interaction are not recorded. In each workplace we have used video cameras to record a series of meetings from workplace teams. Again the aim is that the meetings should be as 'normal' as possible, so the research team takes measures to avoid any unnecessary disruption caused by the recording process. Cameras are set up on tripods at two corners of the room before meetings begin and are removed by the team after the participants have finished. Meetings are always collected as a series so participants become more accustomed to the process, and selection for analysis excludes sections where the recording process appears to be interfering with the authenticity of the talk.

The examples discussed in this paper are taken from recordings made in one particular corporate organization from within the larger LWP corpus.[3] The case study approach was chosen so that the analysis could incorporate more contextual information and therefore build a more detailed picture of the meeting group and its various power dynamics. As a result the extracts are taken from a series of weekly meetings of a project team charged with the responsibility of setting up a new telephone call centre for the local branch of a large multinational corporation. The project team members (total 14) have been brought together from a larger department managed on a day-to-day basis by Clara Banks, sometimes jokingly referred to as 'Queen Clara'. The project which is the focus of the meetings is being led by Jock 'Smithy' Smitherson who chairs the meetings and to whom the subproject leaders that make up the rest of the meeting team report. Smithy reports to Clara, who in turn reports to the senior management team.

This information is important to an understanding of the interaction. The way we interpret utterances relies on our understanding of the rules and norms for the setting: 'The situational context is crucial in understanding any *text*, any piece of language' (Brugman 1995: 61, emphasis in original). Just as society has norms for behaviour (Brugman's 'cultural context'), groups develop norms for the way they interact in meetings (Bettenhausen and Murnighan 1985). The analysis aims to contribute towards Blommaert's (2005) call for CDA to consider context in greater detail and in different ways, by taking account of the context of the group's norms.

The examples described below have been identified as instances of decisions made by the group. Decision-making is an important and frequent task in the workplace. Tannen comments that 'making decisions is a crucial part of any workday' (1994: 30). For participants in a meeting, as a task-oriented group, I posit that reaching decisions is one of their primary goals, a claim supported by Sollitt-Morris who argues that decision-making is 'integral' to the meeting genre (1996: 165). An initial quantitative analysis of the amount and distribution of humour in meetings indicated that a common position for humour, and one which is therefore worthy of particular attention, is the point where a group reaches a decision.

Figure 8.1 provides a visual representation of the position where humour typically occurs. The distribution of humour in these decisions could be interpreted as humour acting as a valve to release tension built up during the decision-making process (cf. Consalvo 1989; Pizzini 1991).[4] The tension these authors describe seems to develop out of disagreement between individual group members (or subgroups) as they fight to get the result they favour. In the analysis below, it is argued that this tension is not due to this fraught negotiation, but results from an awareness of the status differences which directly affect the outcome: the tension is an indication that power has been exercised in reaching the decision. In a great majority of the decisions found in the meetings of this team and others, the highest status member of the team controls the decision outcome (see Marra 2003, for a more detailed description). Where the controller is not the meeting chair or group manager, the decision is typically dominated by the person with 'expert power' of some kind (French and Raven 1959; Thomas 1995). In either case, this participant may in fact be the only

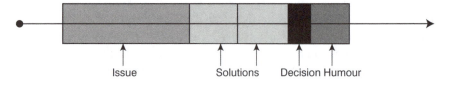

Figure 8.1 The structural components of a typical decision made in a New Zealand business meeting (adapted from Marra 2003)

person who verbally contributes to the decision. For other team members, their participation in the discussion seems almost irrelevant.[5] If this is the case, one may legitimately ask 'are subordinates involved in the decision-making process only in order to provide the appearance of democracy?' In the analysis below, humour is identified as one signal of the impotence experienced by these dominated group members.

Analysis

In the opening sections of the chapter, I referred to the example which first drew my attention to the challenge signalled by humour. In this example, team members raise a contentious issue regarding the call centre staff's request that their on-screen instructions be printed out as reference materials (i.e. that they be allowed to 'screen dump'). In a previous meeting the group had decided to restrict users to an online version of the instructions in order to avoid the need to replace out-of-date printed material. After consultation with the people who will use the programme, Harry and Rob bring what they consider to be legitimate concerns to the group, requesting that they reconsider the earlier decision. However, Clara, the chair and section manager, has no qualms about ignoring these concerns and sticking to the previously ratified decision.

Example 1[6]

1. HARRY:	looks like there's been actually a request for screendumps
2.	I know it was outside of the scope but people (will be) pretty
3.	worried about it maybe if you=/
4. ROB:	/=we can quickly show you that
5. CLARA:	no screendumps
6. ROB:	we-
7. CLARA:	no screendumps
8. ROB:	( )
9. PEG:	thank you clara
10. CLARA:	no /screendumps\
11. ROB:	/we know\ we know you didn't want them and we /
12.	we've\ um er /
13. CLARA:	/that does not\ meet the criteria …
14.	thanks for looking at that though
15. SMITHY:	so that's a clear well maybe no
16. CLARA:	it's a no
17. SMITHY:	it's a no a royal no
18. CLARA:	did people feel disempowered by that decision

19. PEG: [sarcastically]: no:
20. CLARA: [laughs]

Despite the fact that on paper this example makes Clara seem callous with her uncompromising and repeated response 'no screendumps', she is in fact considered a fair and good leader by her team, a team which is lively, quick-witted and friendly (see Holmes and Marra 2002b, for a description of their workplace culture). Clara herself uses various strategies to lighten what seems like a bald on record act (Brown and Levinson 1987); she repeats her decision without any attempt to change the construction of the response (lines 5, 7 and 10), and then adds 'that does not meet criteria' with a humorously intended robot-like delivery (line 13). The humour develops further in the next utterance where she incongruously and ironically thanks the men for bringing the problem to the group for discussion. Throughout this, her status as the most powerful participant with the ability to make a unilateral decision is forefronted.

The challenge to this established and visible hierarchy comes from Smithy, Clara's second-in-command. He ironically quips that they are struggling to understand her viewpoint: 'so that's a clear well maybe no'. After her humorous clarification, Smithy then draws attention to the nickname given to his boss, 'Queen Clara', by referring to her decision as 'a royal no' (line 17). The effect of this remark, which is supposedly intended to amuse, is to draw attention to the overt status difference that Clara is exploiting in order to override the concerns of her team. In support of this interpretation, note that Harry indicates awareness of his lowly position in his presentation of his concerns: he deflects personal responsibility by assigning the blame to the endusers, and uses discourse features such as hedges ('actually') to soften his request (line 1). By raising this contentious issue, he and Rob signal a level of concern which indicates that they consider that the idea deserves a serious hearing, something which Clara ignores.

However, Clara is not insensitive and appears to pick up and react to the covert challenge present in Smithy's humour. Her comment (line 18) that this decision has the potential to make the others feel disempowered explicitly focuses on issues of status. (The humour derives from the tone she uses when choosing a 'PC' term and concept that the team find amusing, indicated particularly by Peg's sarcastic response.) In this one short extract, then, we see Smithy (as the highest ranking subordinate) challenge the power inequalities in the team, and Clara respond with her own humour which likewise signals her recognition of the power differential (and perhaps her acknowledgement of the dispreferred nature of hierarchical relationships within a team).

In example 2, the absolute power that Clara has the right to exercise is evident again. In this excerpt even the preferences of Smithy, her second-in-command, are ignored in reaching a decision. As project manager for the call centre, a position which carries its own high status, Smithy wants the group to decide which form of greeting the telephone operators will use. Will they use the standard greeting 'Welcome' or will they use the Maori greeting 'Kia ora'?[7]

Example 2[8]

1. SMITHY:	we were going to have a vote on it's um welcome
2.	or is it kia ora
3. CLARA:	oh it's welcome
4. VITA:	yeah
5. SMITHY:	you sure
6. CLARA:	yes
7. PEGGY:	you phone up and say whatever they /want to outside =
8. VITA:	/[laughs]\\
9. PEGGY:	= business hours\ but in business hours it's welcome=/
10. VITA:	/=[laughs]: where did that come from anyway: [laughs]
11. SMITHY:	just made that up

Clara has no hesitation in making a unilateral decision which simultaneously undermines the proposal of her second-in-command. He has no sooner suggested that they vote on the alternatives than she states the decision: 'oh it's welcome' (line 3). However, the rest of the excerpt illustrates how the other group members use humour to manage this bald disagreement. Smithy asks audaciously if Clara is sure (cf. the 'clear maybe no' from example 1) sparking a humorous sequence which is elaborated by Peggy and Vita. Peggy's argument that Smithy must kowtow to his seniors at work is clearly amusing to Vita, but can be seen as a further signal that overt power displays elicit a response. Smithy's downplaying of the issue, by designating one of the alternatives as something he just made up (line 11), can be interpreted as implicit acceptance of Clara's higher status. The fact that the other participants in this excerpt get involved in Clara and Smithy's disagreement seems to indicate their discomfort at the explicit display of power in this typically easy-going team.

In example 3, Smithy, in Clara's absence, takes on the role of the highest status participant and makes his own unilateral decision, albeit using different strategies. Again humour accompanies the point at which a decision is reached, namely that Clara ('Ms Banks') will be assigned the task of investigating 'the ongoing training needs' for the call centre.

Example 3

1. SMITHY:	[drawls]: um: + + and there's a new issue here
2.	which is ongoing training needs
3.	is this being examined in the career development project + +
4.	so we'll put that against + Ms Banks shall we
5.	who is running the + +
6.	train- er the career development project
7.	and is not here to defend herself + + + +
8.	jolly good

In line 4, Smithy's tone signals that his intention is to be tongue-in-cheek, as does the conspiratorial use of the tag *shall we*, and the use of a formal term of address, 'Ms Banks', in this informal team. In terms of structure, the humour again coincides with a decision: an acceptable solution has been reached. In this case someone has been nominated to take responsibility for a task.

This decision occurs in the form of a monologue, a somewhat unusual and marked discourse form for meetings where multiparty discussion is the norm. And in fact the frequent and long pauses at lines 1, 3, 4, 5 and 7 provide opportunities for a potential change in speaker. In making a decision on his own, Smithy highlights his status as the most senior member of the group present at the meeting. In example 1, Smithy indicated his own resistance to the instantiation of hierarchical structures when he drew attention to Clara's display of status. His use of humour in this example could be interpreted as an attempt to reduce the sharp power distinctions his behaviour is creating. By emphasizing his position as lower than 'Ms Banks', he could be seen as aligning himself with the others, i.e. as 'just one of the team'. His humour may be aimed at reducing potential ill feelings.

Another possible interpretation is that this humour challenges the dominance which is imposed upon the group through his status as meeting chair. It makes logical sense for Clara to take on the task because it relates to her responsibilities within the project, i.e. career development (line 6). This could provide an explanation for the lack of verbal participation from the other team members. It could be argued that if Clara had been present she too would have allocated the task in this way. As an apparently obvious conclusion, anyone facilitating this discussion might also have presented the decision outcome like this. However, Smithy still chooses to use humour, i.e. by emphasizing that they are allocating the task to a senior figure who is 'not here to defend herself'. His humour could signal the internal tension related to the appearance of a unilateral decision.

Humour, however, is only one possible signal of resistance. Example 4 illustrates other forms of resistance. In this extract Smithy is away and Clara is standing in as project manager. Here Renee challenges Clara's authority (as argued by Holmes and Stubbe 2003: 57, in their discussion of this extract as an example of a meeting opening). My interest here is not in Renee's attempt to subvert Clara's authority by suggesting that Clara fills the lower status position of minute taker rather than chair (line 3), or by attempting to disrupt the allocation of minute-taking duties (line 6). Rather, I draw attention to the humour introduced by Benny and supported by Clara (lines 10–12). After an uncomfortable section of dialogue between Clara and Renee, a normally reticent Benny not only volunteers to take on the role of minute taker, but also jokes about needing to keep his minute-taking skills quiet to avoid being called on in the future.

Example 4

1. CLARA:	okay well we might just start without Seth
2.	he can come in and can review the minutes from last week
3. RENEE:	are you taking the minutes this week
4. CLARA:	no I'm just trying to chair the meeting
5.	who would like to take minutes this week
6. RENEE:	who hasn't taken the minutes yet
7. BENNY:	I (have next) I will
8. CLARA:	thank you /Benny\
9. RENEE:	/oh Benny\ takes beautiful minutes too
10. BENNY:	don't tell them they'll want me doing it every week
11.	[general laughter]
12. CLARA:	it's a bit of a secret
13.	okay shall we kick off and just go round the room

Benny's unsportsmanlike suggestion that his talents as a minute taker should be kept hidden to avoid taking on the task permanently (line 10) is responded to positively by his colleagues and manager. After the laughter begins to ebb, Clara acknowledges the humour and expands it in line 12: 'it's a bit of a secret' (cf. Hay's 1996 humour support strategies).

Interestingly the humour follows a subversive act by another subordinate to trouble the organizational hierarchy (i.e. Renee's ongoing jibes at Clara's authority in lines 3, 6, and particularly line 9, where it could be argued that she attempts to assert herself as the participant with the authority to ratify the decision that Benny will take the minutes). A functionalist interpretation might suggest that Benny's humour aims to smooth the ruffled feathers and unsettled feelings within this team. Benny's utterance could equally be a signal of his unease at Renee's challenge to the organizational hierarchy which allows Clara to control the interaction. This analysis suggests that humour can draw attention to a challenge to the established and accepted hierarchy, as well as signalling awareness that legitimized power has been exercised (as described in the earlier examples).

In the final example, I take a closer look at the more traditional interpretation of humour as a solidarity device (e.g. Duncan *et al.* 1990; Vinton 1989). Example 5 is the kind of extract which could easily be analysed as the team having fun with each other, maintaining solidarity and developing group harmony. In the example, a decision needs to be made about how to deal with incoming miscellaneous calls to the call centre. The topic begins as Smithy raises the issue (number 49 in the groups 'issues register', a list compiled for discussion and follow up at the group's reporting meetings).

Example 5[9]

1.	SMITHY:	[quietly]: shooting on through: +
2.		[drawls]: er: training number forty nine
3.		[drawls]: um: is there a process for handling general
4.		inquiries from the public
5.		and I've got Ange down on this one +
6.		er it's where the public ring up and say
7.		um I want a job [in your industry] …
8.		we need to consider that there'd be there'll
9.		be regular things coming in that we could
10.	DAISY:	checklist on the [computer system]
11.	SMITHY:	yeah
12.	ANGE:	it's just like um like the what is it file …
13.	SMITHY:	or we could have just a like a regular gossip thing
14.	ANGE:	yeah there is there is a gossip file in there
15.	XM:	gossip and promotions and just new stuff um
16.	SMITHY:	is there like malicious gossip
17.	DAISY?:	[laughs] /[laughs]\
18.	XM:	/(it's up it was going to be)\ up to Ange
19.		[general laughter]
20.	ANGE:	no then we're not having any
21.	ALL:	[laughs]
22.	ANGE:	and there'll be no pornography in there
23.	SMITHY?:	oh (/liven it up)\
24.	ANGE:	/not at this point\ that's not a priority at this point
25.		/maybe later\
26.	SMITHY:	/right (okay)\ + + [drawls]: um:

The team negotiate a workable solution, starting from Daisy's suggestion of a checklist (line 10) and finishing with a regular and updatable *gossip* file. The seeds of humour begin with the use of this accurate but arguably frivolous term for the file of new miscellaneous information, a term not typically associated with serious business. The humour here and in the rest of the example demonstrates a team getting on well with each other, with many different team members contributing pithy and witty comments to a jointly constructed humour sequence. In terms of solidarity and team building, it is a convincing example. However, with a different set of spectacles, a darker interpretation of the humour can also be suggested.

The decision is to all intents and purposes finalized when Ange notes that a gossip file already exists (line 14). Smithy, cheekily asks if the gossip will be malicious (line 16) and a male participant comments that it will be up to Ange, the team member allocated the task of running the call centre, to decide (line 18). This humour is then expanded by others. Instead of moving to the next topic, a possible progression for the meeting, there is a humorous episode at a key structural point once again. As a strictly superfluous component of the decision, it is worth reflecting upon the significance of its occurrence.

Ange's responses (lines 20, 22, 24) match the authoritative and bald style of Clara's 'no screendumps' and 'oh it's welcome' from examples 1 and 2. This might suggest that this speech style is one that the group associates with authority; Ange's status as the appropriate person to make this decision has been explicitly stated. In adopting this style, she also takes on the style of a statusful role model within the group, potentially easing the acceptance of her dominant role in this particular decision (if not in others made by this group).

Interestingly it is Smithy, the highest status member at this meeting (since Clara is not present), who introduces the humour at this point in the decision. Could it be that this humour is acknowledging that the power base has shifted for this topic? Ange's responsibility for the management of this area has allowed her the opportunity to harness expert power, and simultaneously reduced Smithy's ability to exercise the legitimate power associated with his role of project manager or meeting chair. This dynamic nature of power is discussed below.

Discussion

The focus in this analysis on the relationship between humour and power is a natural outcome of the theoretical standpoint adopted; CDA holds the misuse and abuse of power as its central tenet (e.g. Fairclough 1989; Kress 1990; van Dijk 1996, 1998; Wodak 2001). However, in practice, the humorous element in decision-making challenges the exercise of different kinds of power and dominance. It is particularly important in the workplace context to distinguish *power* from the closely associated concept of *status* which relates solely to hierarchical position within the organization. Synthesizing the research in this area, including important contributions from Pateman (1980) and Fairclough (1989), Sollitt-Morris defines power as 'the ability of a person to influence the processes of the meeting and/or the behaviour of other meeting participants' (1996: 4). Thus, while the same participant may often have high power and high status, a participant of low institutional status may have high power if they are able to affect the way a meeting progresses (or does not progress). This is apparent in example 4 where Ange's power arises from her expert knowledge of how the call centre will be run on a day-to-day basis and her responsibilities in managing the call centre. Power is a complex and complicated phenomenon: as seen in examples 1, 2 and 4, Clara draws on her organizational position as the highest ranking participant in the meeting; in example 3, as meeting chair, Smithy plays the role of unilateral decision-maker; in example 5, Ange's responsibility as the person running the call centre means she has a major influence on the final decision. In other words, the location of power, or the ability to influence what is going on, changes subtly from context to context to within the interaction.

This changing nature of power is best addressed with a dynamic definition of power, one which acknowledges that power can shift within an interaction since it is language-bound and negotiated. Charles, who also acknowledges the significance of a dynamic understanding of power, notes that '[t]he conceptualisation of power depends upon assumptions about relationships and the stress laid upon various features of interactive situations' (1995: 151). Thus power is fluid and highly context-bound.

The challenge signalled by the humour in the examples also demonstrates that power is jointly produced. For the chair to have legitimate power to facilitate the meeting the rest of the group must regard this as appropriate, and behave discursively in ways which support this role construction. In examples 1 and 2, the power gap between Queen Clara and the rest of her team, including her second-in-command, was clearly on the table. However, when there is an overt challenge to Clara's hierarchical power, as in example 4, the humour from Benny can be interpreted as unease at an attempt to subvert the status quo, a status quo which only exists because the subordinates allow themselves to be dominated. And in the final example, the exercise of expert power by a hierarchically subordinate team member, Ange, is also challenged by humour, this time from someone who is high in status himself. In all five examples, then, humour indicates some tension arising from power inequalities.

The notion of markedness is a useful basis for interpretation here. The humour in the examples, as in any workplace talk, is essentially redundant to the task. If we accept that humour is superfluous to the task-related goals of decision-making (if not the relational aspects of interpersonal communication), we need to ask why humour seems to occur at the same structural point so frequently. Using the notion of markedness, I suggest that humour occurs as a result of the group *noticing* something which they find unsettling. In the key example discussed above, Clara acknowledges the discomfort such a display of status provokes in her otherwise cosy team when she asks rhetorically if the others feel 'disempowered'. For a group of New Zealanders who, according to global cross-cultural research, value equality (Hofstede 1997), and for a team with such a strong sense of collegiality, the recurrence of humour in this important structural position can be interpreted as indicating heightened awareness of power inequalities.

Conclusion

One of the particular aims of this book has been to move away from a functional approach to humour in organizations. This chapter has addressed this intention by avoiding an approach which considers humour as a discourse strategy for achieving a particular goal or as a strategy to be actively adopted by employees or managers within their communication repertoire. Instead, I have focused on the distribution of humour in decisions and argued that its recurrent position, at the end of the negotiation of a decision, highlights and challenges the power asymmetries inherent in organizational talk. Humour in this structural position draws attention to the power assigned to the powerful which allows them to influence decision outcomes, and conversely the reduced power available to subordinates to effect change in this process. Many of the examples could have been analysed as humour used to establish group harmony. The very need to address the issue of group harmony, however, may result from the imbalance created by the power exercised in reaching the decision. While this power inequality is imposed by organizational accountability, the impact it has on a philosophically democratic community troubles the negotiation process. If humour is strictly unnecessary at work, its occurrence and prevalence suggests it is worthy of careful examination.

In societies where democracy is an ideal, the workplace remains a site where dominance is organizationally sanctioned but socially unappealing. Humour, as an off-record feature of discourse, allows this dominance to be acknowledged and simultaneously challenged. It may appear to be an amusing distraction and signal a group's sense of team and coherence as has been argued, but there are many other ways of analyzing its effect. While the complexity of humour has always been acknowledged, at the very least a move towards considering its multifunctionality within interaction needs to be given more priority by researchers of organizational humour.

Notes

1 I wish to acknowledge other members of the Language in the Workplace team and especially Professor Janet Holmes who commented on a draft of this chapter.

2 Earlier in the process the research team supplied participants with cassette walkmans, but more recently we have used digital MiniDisc recorders.

3 I am particularly grateful to Clara Banks (pseudonym) and her team for their cooperation and support during and after the recording process. This data was collected with the help of funding from the New Zealand Foundation of Research, Science and Technology.

4 In his study of decision-making, Marshall Scott Poole notes that 'some researchers have argued that periods of conflict or tensions are followed by socioemotional expression' (1981: 20), certainly a good description of laughter if not of all humour.

5 Except for the greater level of buy-in which may be achieved from the group being 'involved' in the discussion.

6 This example has been analysed from many angles (see e.g. Holmes and Marra 2004). All names used in examples are pseudonyms. Other transcription conventions (following the Language in the Workplace Project) are as follows:

[laughs] : :	Paralinguistic features in square brackets, colons indicate start and finish
+	Pause of up to one second
… / … \ … … / … \ …	Simultaneous speech
(hello)	Transcriber's best guess at an unclear utterance
?	Rising or question intonation
-	Incomplete or cut-off utterance
…	Section of transcript omitted
=	Turn continues
=/ /=	Latching, i.e. next turn follows with no discernible pause
XM/XF	Unidentified Male/Female.

7 Maori are the indigenous people of New Zealand

8 The minor grammatical faults etc. represented in this transcript are indicative of naturally occurring speech as opposed to scripted speech and should not be considered errors.

9 This example has had minor editing for ease of reading

References

Ackroyd, S. and Thompson, P. (1999) *Organisational Misbehaviour*, London: Sage.

Austin, P. (1990) 'Politeness revisited: the dark side', in A. Bell and J. Holmes (eds), *New Zealand Ways of Speaking English*, pp. 276–95, Bristol: Multilingual Matters.

Bettenhausen, K. and Murnighan, J. K. (1985) 'The emergence of norms in competitive decision-making groups', *Administrative Science Quarterly*, 30: 350–72.

Blommaert, J. (2005) *Discourse: A Critical Introduction*, Cambridge: Cambridge University Press.

Boden, D. (1994) *The Business of Talk: Organizations in Action*, Cambridge: Polity Press.

Brown, P., and Levinson, S. C. (1987) *Politeness: Some Universals in Language Usage*, Cambridge: Cambridge University Press.

Brugman, C. (1995) *Communication and Context: A Guide to Issues in the Interactional and Transactional Uses of Language*, Dunedin: University of Otago Press.

Buzzanell, P. M. (1994) 'Gaining a voice: feminist organizational communication theorizing', *Management Communication Quarterly*, 7(4): 339–83.

Candlin, C. N. and Maley, Y. (1997) 'Intertextuality and interdiscursivity in the discourse of alternative dispute resolution', in B.-L. Gunnarson, P. Linell and B. Nordberg (eds), *The Construction of Professional Discourse*, pp. 210–22, London and New York: Longman.

Chan, A. (2006) 'Small talk in business meetings in Hong Kong and New Zealand', unpublished PhD thesis, Victoria University of Wellington, Wellington, New Zealand.

Charles, M. (1995) 'Organisational power in business negotiations', in K. Ehlich and J. Wagner (eds), *The Discourse of Business Negotiation*, pp. 151–73, Berlin and New York: Mouton de Gruyter.

Collinson, D. L. (2002) 'Managing humour', *Journal of Management Studies*, 2(3): 269–88.

Consalvo, C. (1989) 'Humor in management: no laughing matter', *Humor*, 2(3): 285–97.

Drew, P. and Heritage, J. (eds) (1992) *Talk at Work: Interaction in Institutional Settings*, Cambridge: Cambridge University Press.

Duncan, W. J, Smeltzer, L. R. and Leap, T. L. (1990) 'Humor and work: application of joking behavior to management', *Journal of Management*, 16: 255–78.

Edelsky, C. (1981) 'Who's got the floor?', *Language in Society*, 10: 383–421.

Fairclough, N. (1989) *Language and Power*, London: Longman.

Foucault, M. (2000) 'The subject and power', in J. D. Faubion (ed.), *The Essential Works of Foucault 1954–1984*, vol. 3, *Power*, pp. 326–48, New York: New Press.

French, J. R. P. Jr, and Raven, B. (1959) 'The bases of social power', in D. Cartwright (ed.), *Studies in Social Power*, pp. 150–67, Ann Arbor, MI: Institute for Social Research.

Fry, R., Barrett, F., Seiling, J. and Whitney, D. (eds) (2002) *Appreciative Inquiry and Organizational Transformation: Reports from the Field*, Westport, CT: Quorum Books.

Hammond, S. A. (1998) *The Thin Book of Appreciative Inquiry*, Plano, TX: Thin Book.

Hanak, I. (1998) 'Chairing meetings: turn and topic control in development communication in rural Zanzibar', *Discourse and Society*, 9(1): 33–56.

Hay, J. (1996) 'No laughing matter: gender and humour support strategies', *Wellington Working Papers in Linguistics*, 8: 1–24.

Hindess, B. (1996) *Discourses of Power*, Oxford: Blackwell.

Hofstede, G. (1997) *Cultures and Organisations: Software of the Mind*, New York: McGraw Hill.

Holmes, J. (2000) 'Politeness, power and provocation: how humour functions in the workplace', *Discourse Studies*, 2(2): 159–85.

Holmes, J. and Marra, M. (2002a) 'Over the edge? Subversive humour between colleagues and friends', *Humor*, 15(1): 65–87.

Holmes, J. and Marra, M. (2002b) 'Having a laugh at work: how humour contributes to workplace culture', *Journal of Pragmatics*, 34: 1683–710.

Holmes, J. and Marra, M. (2004) 'Leadership and managing conflict in meetings', *Pragmatics*, 14(4): 439–62.

Holmes, J. and Schnurr, S. (2005) 'Politeness, humour and gender in the workplace: negotiating norms and identifying contestation', *Journal of Politeness Research*, 1(1): 121–49.

Holmes, J. and Stubbe, M. (2003) *Power and Politeness in the Workplace: A Sociolinguistic Analysis of Talk at Work*, London: Pearson Education.

Iedema, R. (1999) 'Formalising organizational meaning', *Discourse and Society*, 10(1): 49–65.

Kress, G. (1990) 'Critical discourse analysis', *Annual Review of Applied Linguistics*, 11: 84–99.

Larrue, J. and Trognon, A. (1993) 'Organization of turn-taking and mechanisms for turn-taking repairs in a chaired meeting', *Journal of Pragmatics*, 19: 177–96.

Marra, M. (2003) 'Decisions in New Zealand business meetings: a sociolinguistic analysis of power at work', unpublished PhD thesis, Victoria University of Wellington, Wellington, New Zealand.

Morgenthaler, L. (1990) 'A study of group process: who's got WHAT floor?', *Journal of Pragmatics*, 14: 537–57.

Pateman, T. (1980) *Language, Truth and Politics: Towards a Radical Theory for Communication*, London: Jean Stroud.

Pennycook, A. (2001) *Critical Applied Linguistics: A Critical Introduction*, Mahwah, NJ: Lawrence Erlbaum.

Pizzini, F. (1991) 'Communication hierarchies in humour: gender differences in the obstetrical/gynecological setting', *Discourse in Society*, 2(4): 477–88.

Rodrigues, S. B. and Collinson, D. L. (1995) 'Having fun? Humour as resistance in Brazil', *Organization Studies*, 16(5): 739–68.

Sarangi, S., and Roberts, C. (eds) (1999) *Talk, Work and Institutional Order: Discourse in Medical, Mediation and Management Settings*, Berlin and New York: Mouton de Gruyter.

Scheuer, J. (2003) 'Habitus as the principle for social change', *Language in Society*, 32(3): 143–75.

Sollitt-Morris, L. (1996) 'Language, gender and power relationships: the enactment of repressive discourse in staff meetings of two subject departments in a New Zealand secondary school', unpublished PhD thesis, Victoria University of Wellington, Wellington, New Zealand.

Tannen, D. (1994) *Talking from 9 to 5*, New York: Avon.

Thomas, J. (1995) *Meaning in Interaction: An Introduction to Pragmatics*, London and New York: Longman.

Titscher, S., Meyer, M., Wodak, R. and Vetter, E. (2000) *Methods of Text and Discourse Analysis*, London: Sage.

Tracy, K. and Dimock, A. (2004) 'Meetings: discursive sites for building and fragmenting community', in P. Kalbfleisch (ed.), *Communication Yearbook 28*, pp. 127–66, Thousand Oaks, CA: Sage.

van Dijk, T. A. (1996) 'Discourse, power and access', in C. R. Caldas-Coulthard and M. Coulthard (eds), *Texts and Practices Readings in Critical Discourse Analysis*, pp. 84–104, London and New York: Routledge.

van Dijk, T. A. (1998) 'Principles of critical discourse analysis', in J. Cheshire and P. Trudgill (eds), *The Sociolinguistics Reader Volume 2: Gender and Discourse*, pp. 367–91, London: Arnold.

Vinton, K. L. (1989) 'Humor in the workplace: it is more than telling jokes', *Small Group Behaviour*, 20(2): 151–66.

Vuorela, T. (2005) 'Laughing matters: a case study of humour in multicultural business negotiations', *Negotiation Journal*, 21: 105–30.

Westwood, R. (2004) 'Comic relief: subversion and catharsis in organizational comedic theatre', *Organization Studies*, 25(5): 775–95.

Wodak, R. (1997) 'Critical discourse analysis and the study of doctor–patient interaction', in B.-L. Gunnarson, P. Linell and B. Nordberg (eds), *The Construction of Professional Discourse*, pp. 173–200, London and New York: Longman.

Wodak, R. (2001) 'What is CDA about – a summary of its history, important concepts and its developments', in R. Wodak and M. Meyer (eds), *Methods of Critical Discourse Analysis*, pp. 1–13, London: Sage.

Wodak, R. and Iedema, R. (eds) (1999) *Discourse and Society, Special Issue: Discourse in Organizations*, 10(1).

Part III

Humour of organizations

Chapter 9

Representing the d'other
The grotesque body and masculinity at work in *The Simpsons*

Carl Rhodes and Alison Pullen

At the beginning of François Rabelais's 1534 novel *Gargantua* there is a short poem dedicated to 'the reader'. The poem ends with a plea that the book contains only one lesson to which the reader should pay heed:

> [L]aughter's good for you.
> And that's the best of arguments, since few
> Advantages come from the grief and sorrow
> That harass you. Writing should laugh, not weep,
> Since laughter is of the man the very marrow.
> (Rabelais 1534/2003: 2)

Taken seriously, such an appeal might invoke woe in the heart of the social scientist with *his* dry treatises on, and proposals to, the lives of others. But it is not to such solemn souls that Rabelais claims to be writing. The readers who he dedicates the book to are categorized by him as being either 'distinguished boozers' or 'dearly beloved pox-sufferers' (p. 3). He offers such souls a book of wild and irreverent humour. This is a humour of exaggerated bodily imagery and language which stems from 'fertility, growth and a brimming-over abundance' (Stallybrass and White 1986: 9). Laughter is provoked by bodily excess and extremity, and by the body's continuity with the world as exemplified in drinking, feasting, fucking, pissing and shitting.

As young boys giggle at the mention of 'ratacuntarseing' (p. 13) and 'the dignity of codpieces' (p. 3), in the prologue to the book Rabelais distinguishes his endeavours from being only about surface hilarity of ribaldry (p. 4) – this is not just the 'Renaissance equivalent of knob-jokes, farts, potty humour and flatulent booziness' (Brown 2003: p. xii). The 'marrow' that Rabelais dares us to suck on is not something he has placed there as a 'secret' to be discovered – 'shit on him!' (Rabelais 1534/2003: 4) says Rabelais to anyone who might accuse him of such a thing. As the poem says, it is the laughter itself that is the marrow – Rabelais seeks the 'honour and glory ... of being called a real joker' (p. 5). The honour of such an endeavour is to be 'merry and bright' (p. 6); to laugh in the face of the self-serious 'monkish' knowledge of the 'Brother Boobius' and the 'bacon-filcher' (p. 6).

In his renowned study of folk culture and humour, Mikhail Bakhtin (1965/1984) celebrates Rabelais as providing 'the key to the immense treasury of folk humor' characterized by 'a boundless world of humorous forms and manifestations opposed to the official and serious tone of medieval ecclesiastical and feudal culture' (p. 4). This laughter is more than just frivolous. It is a mode of critique that sees the 'possibility of a radical transformation of the ways a culture sees and understands the relations amongst its subjects' (Bernard-Donals 1988: 113). It is a form of culture that can 'evade, resist, or scandalize ideology and social control' (Fiske 1987: 240). Such a Rabelaisian humour mocks and satirizes official culture. It sets such culture in stark relief against the grotesque other and, in doing so, exposes it, makes it all the more real, and renders it ridiculous and malleable.

In this chapter we explore work and organizations in relation to the way that the spirit of carnival folk humour is manifested in contemporary popular culture. In doing so, we might be located within a 'small, but growing trend in explaining topics of traditional academic interest through reference to artifacts in popular culture' (Dobson 2006: 45). In particular, we are concerned with what Lindvall and Melton (1997) called the 'cartoon carnival' where cartoons work, in a manner similar to the Rabelaisian novel of the Middle Ages, to provide a critical folk knowledge of work and organizations. In this culture, 'sex, violence, pain and power that permeate organizational life are permitted airtime through the carnivalesque representation of organizations' (Rhodes 2001). Our particular focus is on the animated television program *The Simpsons,* a show long heralded as a 'rich source for all academic disciplines to draw upon in elucidating their subject' (Dobson 2006: 64) and for the value of its satire of contemporary capitalism and its relation to work. *The Simpsons* has been characterized a form of oppositional culture (Alberti 2003) that attacks capitalism, celebrates the frailty of corporate power (Weinstein 1998) and offers a coherent and pungent critique of contemporary life (Marc 1997) in the modern urban space (Wood and Todd 2005). On the basis of such meritorious accolades, and inspired by Bakhtin's analysis of Rabelais, we take as our task to read the carnival in *The Simpsons.*

Since its inception as a prime time television program in 1989, *The Simpsons* has iconoclastically broken the rules of established expectations of television by 'boldly experimenting with subjects that have always been taboo for animated series' (Cohen 2004: 144). *The Simpsons* is also a clear example of how 'actions of political resistance are commonly played out within popular culture' (Street 1997: 13) that can draw attention to and critique the 'strong plots' that govern cultural understandings of work and organization (Czarniawska and Rhodes 2006). Indeed, it has been claimed by Hull (2000: 65) that *The Simpsons* 'offers the subjected, disciplined individual the easily accessible tool of humour and parody in acts of subversion that allow the subjected to gain even small degrees of leverage over the confines of modern power'. While we are perhaps less sanguine than Hull, we concur at least that, as a form of parody, *The Simpsons* destabilizes and defamiliarizes the commonplace by 'placing it under the microscope for scrutiny' (Gray 2005: 227). It is such scrutiny that we intend to reflect on – that is, the way that the culture of contemporary television carnival can supplement, challenge, destabilize, relativize and pluralize official versions of social reality (Docker 1994). As we explore below, the 'strong plot' we are concerned with relates to male bodies and the portrayal of masculinity at work – the assumption and dominance of masculine normalcy, security and potency. In doing so we laugh with *The Simpsons* and at some of its characters, both for its own sake, and also to show how humour in this iconic popular culture show can expose the frailty of work-based masculinity through a parody of the male body. It is the program's honesty, humour and 'uncompromising boldness in addressing the various hypocrisies of our culture' (Frank 2001: 97) that enables us to do this. If, as Rabelais says, 'writing should laugh, not weep', we will try to laugh along with *The Simpsons* and to revel in the carnival joy of that laughter.

A body of/at work

Although the body has been addressed in some studies of popular culture and organization (see Brewis 1998; Höpfl 2003), with few notable exceptions the cartoon body has received precious little attention (Rhodes 2001). More generally, even though the body has been under researched and theorized until the last decade or so, recent advances in sociological inquiry (Turner 1984; Featherstone *et al.* 1991; Shilling 1993) and organization theory (Hassard *et al.* 2000; Dale 2001; Morgan 1996) have radically questioned the assumed disembodiment of human beings in and at work. This research has challenged the Cartesian mind/body dualism that has informed the dominant strands of how people at work have been understood. For example, through Foucault's analysis of power (1981), the surveillance and control of the body (see Trethewey 1999) and the everyday embodied experiences of gender, sexuality and identity (Butler 1993; Grosz 1996; Davis 1997) have been thoroughly interrogated. Central to this is a consideration of how the meanings attached to bodies are products of social relations which are organized, regulated and normalized in ways that reinforce the dominant social order (Foucault 1981). For Foucault, the body emerges as the point where social regulation and practices of the self come together. Working patterns, organizational practices and disciplinary procedures inscribe themselves on the self and on the body. The inscription of the body is a gendered inscription. Understanding gender as a social construction inscribed on the body in and through work suggests that the material body can be read as a surface, a map, where gender is produced and reproduced, rather than a source of biological sex distinction (Gatens 1996). Inscriptions on the body and gender norms are products of dominant power structures that inform, control and suppress the practices of the body, and which in doing so, marginalize that which is other to them – the other as abject. For example, 'abnormal' bodies such as conjoined twins (see Shildrick 2002), disabled bodies (see Buurman 1997), transsexual bodies (see Garber 1992), the Victorian elephant man and the bearded lady at the fair are minoritized and in some cases mocked as spectacles. These are 'bodies out of place' (Ahmed 2000) that are not locatable within the culturally normal.

We are concerned here to expose the grotesque as other – the grotesque body as 'matter out of place' (Douglas 1968/2002). Moreover, as we also argue, the grotesque enables culturally normalized bodies to be rendered 'out of place' and abnormalized through critique. This overturning highlights how the body is a site of struggle – bodies that resist and fight their minority positions by displacing the majority. Literature that addresses 'neglected' bodies (see Cunningham-Burley and Backett-Milburn 2001) and 'vulnerable' bodies (Shildrick 2002) is testimony of how abject others resist their suppression. For example, whereas the Victorian elephant man was humiliated, laughed at and scorned because of his physical deformities, he resisted his marginalized, abject position and the limitations of his body by transgression, focusing not on the body but instead on the acceptance of his intellectual endeavours with the elite classes.

Carnival humour enables the body, in particular the male body, to become a site of laughter. This is a humour of the body's incompleteness and of its continuity with the world. By examining how the body is portrayed in *The Simpsons* we explore how humour surfaces from the body and how gender is central in the process. There is of course a long history of the significance and centrality of the body, and differences between bodies, in producing laughter. From the visual humour in the silent movies of Charlie Chaplin and *Mr Bean*'s body performances and exaggerated facial contortions, bodies that do not act as they are expected to have long inspired laughter. In *The Simpsons* we witness the depiction of diverse male bodies and their social relations. This is exemplified in *The Simpsons* by the character C. Montgomery Burns. He is one of the central characters and, as the owner and manager of the Springfield Nuclear Power Plant, one of the most powerful. He is an old money industrialist who runs his business empire with an iron fist and a crooked nose. As a physical character, Burns is emaciated, ancient and under-sized – precisely the inverse of the abundance of his wealth as a capitalist. The warts and blemishes that emblazon his body map the ugly and disdaining features of his personality – a personality that personifies a hyperbolized, amoral and vicious capitalism. This body is in stark contrast to that of *The Simpsons'* eponymous anti-hero Homer Simpson. Homer works at Burns's plant as a safety inspector. Without wealth or power, his industrial accolades are limited to holding the 'plant record for most years worked at an entry level position' (Richmond and Coffman 1997: 10). Physically he is opposite to Burns as well. He is the dumb worker and the working-class bread (and bacon!) winner, with his over-sized, excessive belly. Here we can see how Homer's body dominates and privileges the mind.

The bodies of Burns and Homer are a special source of humour in *The Simpsons* – each of which plays on the different ways they grotesquely exaggerate and parody masculinity. For Homer this means laughing at his bacon chewing habits, his beer guzzling obsession, his achievements in flatulence and his wobbling gut. For Burns the mirth stems from his physical inability (literally) to steal candy from a baby, the fact that he is as impotent as a Nevada boxing commissioner, and the irony that despite all of his evil ways he still clingingly hugs his childhood teddy bear Bobo. What interests us here is that Homer and Burns are presented in different ways as having exaggerated and grotesque bodies. So, even though, as we discussed earlier, until relatively recently sociology has neglected the body, it is something quite central to this example of popular culture – in the same tradition that Bakhtin identified in Rabelais. But, while the medieval carnival may have used the grotesque body in the context of a subversion of ecclesiastic and monarchical rule, in *The Simpsons* the dominant institution of contemporary themes is that which provides the context – organized work. The identity of the Burns character is premised on his status as a capitalist, and that of Homer on his role as a workaday suburban dad. It is in the context of such male imagery that much of the action in *The Simpsons* is played out.

Grotesque realism and the body

One of the key features of carnival folk humour that Bakhtin identifies is that of the aesthetic concept of 'grotesque realism' as a means of representing the material body. It is such a form of realism that can be located in Burns and Homer as examples of the carnival 'cultural mode' that is still dominant in examples of popular culture such as can be found in television (Docker 1994; Lindvall and Melton 1997). Following Bakhtin, '[t]he essential principle of grotesque realism is degradation, that is, the lowering of all that is high, spiritual, ideal, abstract; it is a transfer to the material level, to the sphere of earth and body in their indissoluble unity' (1965/1984: 20). Such degradation is achieved through vast exaggerations of the body in its material form and in its unity with the world. As Bakhtin goes to great length in demonstrating, Rabelais was historically grotesque realism's chief progenitor. So, when Rabelais's provincial character Gargantua went to Paris he expressed his views on the 'stupid, idle gawpers' when he 'undid his fine codpiece, and pulling his willy out, wee-wee'd over them so ferociously that he drowned 260,418 of them'. As one who escaped the flood of piss explained: 'this isn't what we meant by Paris in the Spring!' (Rabelais 1534/2003: 44).

The material body for Bakhtin is a carnival body – 'flesh conceptualised as corpulent excess – to represent cosmic, social, typographical and linguistic elements of the world' (Stallybrass and White 1986: 8–9). Grotesque realism portrays the human body as

> multiple, bulging, over- or under-sized, proturberant and incomplete. The openings and orifices of this carnival body are emphasized, not its closure and finish. It is an image of impure corporeal bulk with its orifices (mouth, flared nostrils, anus) yawning wide and its lower regions (belly, legs, feet, buttocks and genital) given priority over its upper regions (head, 'spirit', reason).
>
> (Stallybrass and White 1986: 8–9)

As Bakhtin (1965/1984) explains, the grotesque body was traditionally presented 'not in a private, egotistic form, severed from the other spheres of life, but as something universal, representing all the people'. As such, it is opposed to 'the severance from the material and bodily roots of the world' (p. 19). The material body then is not 'in the biological individual and not in the bourgeois ego, but in the people, a people who are continually growing and renewed. This is why all that is bodily becomes grandiose, exaggerated, immeasurable' (ibid.). The norms of the grotesque body are:

> impurity (both in the sense of dirt and mixed categories), heterogeneity, masking, protuberant distension, disproportion, exorbitancy, clamour, decentred or eccentric arrangements, a focus on gaps, orifices and symbolic filth ... physical needs and pleasures of the 'lower bodily stratum', materiality and parody.
>
> (Stallybrass and White 1986: 23)

Grotesque realism degrades the body and, as Bakhtin explains, it contrasts the upward as being towards heaven and the downward as being towards earth. The aesthetics of grotesque realism are ones where the body is seen in terms of its physical connections with the earth, and with the reality of its 'lower strata' – think of Burns's flaccid penis and Homer's exploding anus. For Bakhtin, however such degradation is regenerative – it is the becoming of the body through its ongoing destruction and rebirth. It is down to earth – but to a 'fruitful earth and the womb. It is always conceiving' (Bakhtin 1965/1984: 21). It was Gargantua's piss that brought down the 'haughty in speech' (Rabelais 1534/1984: 21) Parisians. Better face the world by laughing at exaggerated weaknesses than by fanatisizing about impossible virtues.

Although there are plenty of them to be had, grotesque realism goes beyond cheap laughs. This is because the Rabelaisian 'marrow' of the grotesque is its subversive laughter and its ability to dethrone established hierarchies and to overturn official orders of reality. Jung states that the grotesque can 'expose the "dirty bottom" of officialdom and the established regime' (Jung 1988: 104). But the grotesque body is not at all unrealistic – on the contrary it is an exaggeration of the reality of bodily imperfection and impropriety. It is one that 'contradicts the pretensions and ideologies of perfection in its defecation, sneezing, farting, belching and bleeding' (Hitchcock 1998: 85) – bodily functions that conspire against the rationality of the mind, and presumption of the perfectibility of being. It is through the 'profanation of the sacred' that the grotesque realism of carnival destabilizes the serious, gloomy, hierarchical, reverential and pious formalities of life (Bakhtin 1984: 129–30) – a function as much in play in the medieval culture of the Middle Ages carnival as it is in contemporary popular culture (Docker 1994). It is a culture that mocks 'on behalf of humanity those who proclaim authority, rules, binding conventions, received proverbial wisdom' (Docker 1994: 217) and in so doing vitalizes ambivalence, destabilization and becoming. It is here that 'the imaginative field of the grotesque, of the monstrous, of the excessively human, has its revenge on exploitative forms of rationality' (Hitchcock 1998: 81). The grotesque registers, not just as a form of depiction, but as a political term that 'can be used to indicate that phenomena – bodies, genders and sexualities – are not as self evident as we would often like to think' (Vänskä 2002: 154).

The grotesque manifests in two distinct forms. First, there is 'the grotesque as the "Other" of the defining group or self' (Stallybrass and White 1986: 193). This is the body of the abject and abnormal that defines the normal. In this first sense, the grotesque is part of the self. In its second meaning, the grotesque can be conceptualized 'as a boundary phenomenon of hybridisation or inmixing, in which the self and other become enmeshed in an inclusive, heterogeneous, dangerously unstable zone' (ibid.). The importance of isolating these two forms is articulated by Stallybrass and White:

> If the two are confused, it becomes impossible to see that a fundamental mechanism of identity formation produces the second, hybrid grotesque at the level of the political unconscious by the very struggle to exclude the first grotesque. That is to say, when the bourgeoisie consolidated itself as

a respectable and conventional body by withdrawing from the popular, it constructed the popular as grotesque otherness: but by this act of withdrawal and consolidation it produced another grotesque, an identity-in-difference which was nothing other than a fantasy relation, its negative symbiosis, with that which it had rejected in its social practices.

(Ibid.)

In other words there might be some of Homer's and Burns's masculinity in all of us and by considering their characters as cultural forms of the grotesque we might be able to question masculine social practices as they are located, in our examples, in the heart of organizations and at work. With management and organizing commonly being represented as an idealized rational myth (Czarniawska 2003) of order and cleanliness (ten Bos and Kaulingfreks 2001; cf. Douglas 1968/2002), images of grotesque realism in relation to work are not just oppositional to social expectations of behaviour in organizations, but also can be seen to represent the 'political unconscious' of work.

Brush with greatness

Having taken time to explore the character of grotesque realism as a cultural form and an aesthetic sensibility, we now consider in more detail the grotesque male body as it is represented in *The Simpsons*. To do so we turn to a 'classic' 1991 episode of *The Simpsons* entitled 'Brush with greatness' (production code 7F18).[1] We read this episode as a means of exploring some of the cultural meanings that the grotesque can invoke, with particular attention to the portrayal of the male body and its inferred parallels to the organizational body as masculine.

If the grotesque body is one that is 'disproportionate, exorbitant, outgrowing all limits, obscenely decentred and off-balance, a figural and symbolic resource for parodic exaggeration and inversion' (Stallybrass and White 1986: 9) then no better example of it can be found than in *The Simpsons* character of C. Montgomery Burns — or, as he is almost always addressed formally, Mr Burns. On one level Burns is the most powerful man in the town of Springfield, where the show is set. He is the owner of the town's main industry and employer, the Springfield Nuclear Power Plant, and is a person to be both feared and reviled. As an archetype of the capitalist robber-baron he is regularly involved in storylines that pitch him as an exploitative abuser of power. As Gray (2005) has described, Burns's

plant is in an awful condition, with luminous drops falling from overhead pipes; Burns addresses the workers as 'drones'; his parents died, he says, because they 'got in my way'; he pays $3 a year in tax; and due to his plant's emissions, Springfield fish have three eyes, and Homer is sterile. (p. 232)

The representation of his material body, however, is another matter. The power and brutality of his persona is located in the body of a frail old man – impossibly thin, perpetually bent over, physically weak, and constitutionally sickly. It is these features that are mercilessly parodied in the episode 'Brush with greatness', as we shall see.

The chief protagonist here is Marge Simpson, Homer's long suffering wife. Marge's character is very much based on the archetype of the American sit-com wife and mother. She is a 'homemaker' who provides the bedrock of stability for her family – husband Homer, and their children, baby Maggie, brainy Lisa and bad-boy Bart. Erion and Zeccardi characterize her as a 'stable touchstone of morality' (2001: 46) and even a 'Christian-flavored Aristotelian' (p. 57). As a character she is 'directly descended from a long line of saintly and long-suffering TV wives and mothers whose main dramatic function is to understand, love and clean up after her man' (Snow and Snow 2001: 131). The meaningfulness and the humour of her character, however, does not come from her stereotypification as a suburban mother. Although Marge's attempts 'to break out of the traditional female role is obviously funny, and a large number of Marge episodes trade on this kind of humour' (ibid.), there is much more to Marge than that. The laughter that we become entrapped in emerges when, through her acts of transgression, subterfuged under the mask of the mother, she brings dominant social and gender relations into question with satirical aplomb. The fragile construction of masculine power grotesquely depicted by Homer and Burns become the subject of Marge's satire and politics … Read on.

'Brush with greatness' starts with the Simpsons on a family outing to the aquatic fun park Mt Splashmore. In contrast to Burns's scrawny frailty, Homer's grotesque obesity is the immediate subject of ridicule. He dons an embarrassingly revealing swimming costume. When he squeezes into the driver's seat of the car his gross belly sets off the horn. Later when his enormous girth makes him get stuck in a water slide the technician says referring to Homer: 'it's too big to be human'. So, before the plot is even established we have the familiar grotesque imagery of the exaggerated, excessive belly which symbolizes man as animal. Back at home and worried about his fatness, Homer gets on the scales and declares 'I'm a big fat pig' – again invoking an animal imagery well established in the European low grotesque (see Stallybrass and White 1986: 44–59).

With Homer's male, competitive, yet insecure, position established in opposition to the grotesque non-human, the real plot begins to emerge as Marge takes centre stage. While Homer and Bart are in the attic of the family home looking for discarded fitness equipment (e.g. the Glutemus Maximizer), they discover a box of paintings of The Beatles drummer Ringo Starr created by Marge as a schoolgirl – including one of her and Ringo getting married. When quizzed about the paintings by Lisa, Marge explains that when Ringo never replied to her after she posted a painting to him, she decided never to paint again. This failure to attract male response to her talent is what is described by feminist Lisa as 'the particulars of how [Marge's] gift was squashed'. Against the forgotten fantasy of the rock star, Marge's life plays out in the reality of her husband Homer – a reality where his 'obese body codes him as obscene, as lacking perspective, as unable to exercise any consumptive constraint' (Ott 2003: 65). But he is still, at least to Marge, loveable.

Nevertheless, at Lisa's suggestion, Marge decides to try to rekindle her childhood talents by enrolling in an art class at Springfield Community College. Marge calls her first work 'Bald Adonis'. It is a picture of Homer asleep on the sofa with a beer can in his hand and spittle dribbling from his mouth on to his vest. Marge wins first prize at the Springfield Art Exhibition competition.

Meanwhile in another storyline from the episode, Mr Burns has fired yet another of his portrait painters and is looking for a new one. His assistant and lickspittle Waylon Smithers suggests Marge as the person who might be able to 'immortalize' Burns on canvas. As Smithers states, not only is she a prize winner but 'she's the wife of an employee, she'll be easily intimidated'. But will she? Burns and Smithers go to the Simpson home and commission her for the portrait. He says he will allow her to paint him if she answers 'yes' to his question: 'Can you make me beautiful?' Marge agrees on the basis that she believes he must have an 'inner beauty'. When Burns sits for the portrait he infuriates Marge with the arrogant, dismissive and insulting way that he treats everyone from her baby Maggie to his sycophantic employee Smithers. As the only person prepared to stand up to Burns, Marge sends him away, apparently having given up on finding any beauty in him – internal or external. But later, after recovering her confidence, Marge decides to go ahead and do the painting anyway. Armed with an image of Burns from when she accidentally walked in on him naked in her bathroom in a break of one of his sittings, she decides to paint this image with all the vulnerable grotesquerie that this entails. The result is a portrait of Burns's naked emaciated body. His head is turned down, his long nose points to the floor, his eyes peer sideways, and his arms are open as if wanting to reveal the nakedness of his body – his penis dangles for peer review. This is a pose that says 'look at me' and appears to reveal a narcissistic and masculine personal endeavour which may represent a mask of managerial perfection. But this is infused with vulnerability.

The painting is unveiled at the opening of the 'Burns Wing' of an art museum to a shocked audience. Burns is shuddering with embarrassment. Feeling the need to explain her work, Marge addresses the audience:

> I wanted to show that beneath Mr Burns' fearsome head with its cruel lips, spiteful tongue and evil brain, there was a frail withered body, perhaps not long for this world. As vulnerable and beautiful as any of God's creatures.

Then, a critic can be heard to say: 'He's bad, but he'll die. So I like it'. Seemingly unaware of the grotesque parody of his already grotesque cartoon body, Burns announces 'I don't hate this'. Then he says to Marge: 'Thanks for not making fun of my genitalia'. Marge turns to Homer and says in a soft tone: 'I thought I did'.

D'oh-ing masculinity

If, as Rabelais has told us, laughter is good for you, why then is it good to laugh at Marge's depiction of Burns as a frail and evil old man with a shrunken penis? We note here that, if we take this picture to be an example of grotesque realism, then the penis is not the only thing worth looking at. As Bakhtin (1965/1984) has argued, it is in fact the nose that is one of the most important parts of the grotesque image and, importantly, the nose 'always symbolizes the phallus' (p. 316). In Marge's portrait of Burns there is an immediate contradiction. It is stated that Marge's painting was intended to caricature Burns's penis – nevertheless, we never see this image, perhaps because such an image would not pass the censor's scissors. When the painting is shown, Burns's groin is always obscured by various objects – the feather in the hat of a woman attending the opening, an upheld wine glass or Marge's outlandish blue hair-do. This absent present is all the more visible by its disguise. Burns's face, however, is clearly visible and the nose noticeably phallic. While all of the Simpson family and most of the other characters have small button-like noses, Burns has a long pointy nose – a feature that appears exaggerated in Marge's portrait of him. Indeed, the contrast between his face and his unseen crotch is duly noticeable. His eyes bubble down – they are close together and the eyeballs are barely visible. From between the eyes the nose falls straight and long as if protruding out from his face. The obvious resemblance to male genitalia is stark.

While there is a classic part of folklore that suggests that there is a direct relation between nose size and genital size and potency (see Bakhtin 1965/1984: 316), Marge's portrait is more ambivalent and paradoxical. We have the shrunken, dysfunctional, weak penis, which stands in contrast to the nose which is phallic, erect and loomingly penetrative. Following Bakhtin this contrasts the lower with the upper body strata. What appears potent in the face is revealed as pathetic below the belt. We can read this to suggest that, just as in the carnival, evil is laughed at by focusing on exaggerated features of the official, Marge is laughing at Burns's managerial officialdom. She does so by subversively revealing that the phallic symbol (the nose) does not really represent that which is symbolized (the penis). This playful effervescence surrounding the interplay between official managerial power and weakness conjures excitement amongst the art gallery spectators.

Burns's warted, emaciated body is the source of humour – the ugliness and deformedness of the body being played with to illustrate capitalist normative masculine social relations. That is to say, Burns is used to portray the capitalist classes' wealth, power and position as well as the insecurity, frailty and vulnerability of that power as it is embodied within one frail, old and ugly man. Burns is no charming, heroic, handsome business tycoon. Rather, his narcissistic performances which focus on the reality of his business success, fuel the fantasy of his 'beautiful' image – an image that Marge tries to shatter. And yet at the unveiling of the portrait, Burns is at the brink of narcissistic collapse. As the scriptwriters provoke a carnivalesque situation, his fantasy-driven self-knowledge and confidence are subverted by others' reactions to the exposure of the truth of his manhood. His power is being subverted as it is turned upside down and temporarily rendered abject. Burns escapes his shattered narcissistic fantasy by revelling in the crowd's pleasure at the portrait and by taking up his 'I don't hate it' position. But the audience knows otherwise. Even more politically, masculinity is mocked and fractured by Marge's female position and power.

The mocking of organizational masculinity by analysing the body runs against many of the established currents of thinking about organizations. So, contra the storyline in 'Brush with greatness', organizations have by and large been considered as disembodied (Dale 2001). Management has long been thought of as synonymous with masculinity (Kerfoot and Knights 1993; Pullen 2006); masculine discourses being dominant. Hierarchy, a principal feature of bureaucracy (Bologh 1990; Morgan 1996; Du Gay 2000), is well documented as a masculine organizational form (Morgan 1996) which oppresses and denies difference (see Bologh 1990). Morgan (1996) raised two central issues which are worthy of our attention: first, that bureaucracies are major sites for the development of modern masculinities and second, that men are more than likely to be carrying out managerial functions in a bureaucratic office. But, in the portrayal of Burns we see a critique of how hierarchy not only 'ungenders' individuals (Morgan 1996: 57) but disembodies them too, in treating them independently of their bodily characteristics (Pullen 2006). While in practice the maleness of managers is seen as irrelevant (Kerfoot and Knights 1999; Lennie 1999), this is not so in *The Simpsons*.

In the cases of Burns and Homer, each in their own ways, their sense of self is closely associated with hierarchy and the bureaucratic capitalist organization. Burns reproduces and reinforces hierarchy both formally and socially but in doing so squeezes the life out of people to the point at which they lose the ability to be themselves either within or without it. Thus they must attempt to reproduce it in order to cling on to some sense of vitality and meaning. Take Homer, when he comes home to discover Marge painting Burns, he shrieks with desperate irony: 'Aaargh! ... isn't that wonderful, my work and my home life come together in such a nice way'. His sense of self is, in part, derived from a fear of his boss Burns. He pleads with frightful and pathetic anxiety to Marge: 'Honey, he's nuts, he thinks he's handsome. You gotta make him look handsome. Please, please, please, please, please ...'

But masculinity requires constant work to be maintained or else the 'masculine/managerial masks slip ... to ... reveal forms of dominant and hegemonic masculinities that deny the subjectivity of the "other"' (Moodley 1999: 215). Indeed, Burns and Homer always work hard to stay close to their masculine work identities. Burns, as the model of dominant male power, cannot fully hold on to his narcissistic male image when he becomes the subject of Marge's representational practices. Thus, his masculine concealment and containment of his vulnerabilities is shown when his body is exposed by Marge – the mask of his ever present green business suit slips and we see him reveal his frailties and vulnerabilities as well as the importance of his mask to him. Requesting Marge to paint the portrait was an attempt to mask his 'warts an' all' imperfections and replace then with a beautiful image – a task that is clearly not easy, given that he had already rejected the portraits painted by all of the other artists in Springfield. In the final portrait Marge resists by shrewdly deciding to expose and reveal what she sees as the 'real' Burns, the 'human Burns', the 'grotesque' Burns. As Höpfl contends: 'When the mask fails the performance is thrown into question: becomes ludicrous. For the actor, the extent of his/her degradation [i.e. the dissolution of self into the mask] is revealed' (2002: 266). In the end though, the naked truth of masculinity is unbearable and Burns seeks the easy way out – 'I don't hate it'. Although his masculinity has been challenged, his defence against anxiety permeates this masculinity.

Masculinity in and out of place

Through all of this, Marge paradoxically uses subversive humour to mock Burns – or more importantly his phallus – and further adds insult to injury by responding 'I thought I had' when Burns thanked her for not laughing at his genitals. In this sense we see Burns 'do masculinity' (after Morgan 1996) in traditional hegemonic style (Messner 1992; Kerfoot and Knights 1993; Collinson and Hearn 1996). This is where Homer comes in. Marge contrasts the evil Burns with Homer's virtue as breadwinner – a traditional form of working-class masculinity (Donaldson 1991), with Marge herself representing mother and housewife.

Homer stands in contrast to Burns – he is the other – the grotesque other to Burns who is repulsed by his unravelling body. Burns mocks Homer as the fattest man that he has ever seen. Indeed, we would not have to look far to find a description of Homer in Bakhtin – 'the gaping mouth, the protuberant belly and buttocks, the feet and the genitals' (Stallybrass and White 1986: 22) all characterize Homer as a long-established cultural archetype. Further in 'Brush with greatness', we can read both Burns's and Homer's male bodies, after Douglas (1968/2002), as being overturned from cultural normalcy (boss and dad respectively) to 'matter out of place', at least temporarily. The excessive Homer is out of place and stuck in place in the water slide at the water park. In contrast, Burns's emaciated, warty body was 'out of place' at the art unveiling. Although both bodies, extreme opposites of each other, are anomalies, they react very similarly to being exposed by defending their masculinity. Each is deeply insecure and vulnerable. Against Burns's 'make me beautiful' plea which pushed the pressure and responsibility onto Marge, the carefree Homer goes on a diet – or tries to on 'pork chop night'. It is this movement of the male body out of place where the subversiveness of *The Simpsons* is revealed – a move that takes the normalcy of different male cultural models and renders them both abnormal and absurd.

In watching *The Simpsons*, we not only laugh, but can simultaneously become witnesses to how social relations influence our own constructions of our own bodies and indeed our interpretations of what these bodies mean to us. It is not until we become *matter out of place* that we become aware of our bodies. Moreover, as Douglas argues, matter out of place disrupts the social order – in this case masculine power. But while, as described earlier, we laugh at the pathetic body of Burns, with Homer the narrative suggests a close association with more quotidian vulnerabilities. An audience is more likely to both identify and be repulsed by him simultaneously – he disrupts *us* and we laugh. To be stuck in the slide is awkward, uncomfortable, painful – our emotions and bodies react to Homer and simulate *déjà vu* of our own suppressed bodily humiliations. Whilst Burns is the other of the people, Homer is the man of the people – both are laughable but Homer more likely to provoke reflexive embarrassment and identification. Neither is comforting.

While we have focused our discussion on the images of masculinity, it is important to note, too, that the disruption of masculinity in *The Simpsons* is achieved by feminine subversion – the fluid feminine – which fuels the transgression of traditional gender roles. The events that ensue only do so when Marge, at the initial urging of her feminist daughter Lisa, transcends her role as wife and mother to become a painter – a painter of the capitalist Mr Burns. Burns, the self-aggrandizing, aggressive, mean and ruthless businessman, entrusts Marge with his insecurities. She has the powerful role of not only representing Burns but recreating him, for the better, for the eyes of others. In doing this she transcends her class and gender status as wife of a loser-employee, but she is still put in a position of the feminine who is both subordinated to, and reinforcing of, the masculine. Given confidence by masculine figure heads, Marge pursues her role initially based on the assurance she garners from the supportive comments of her art teacher Mr Lombardo, and later from the much delayed response from Ringo Starr at the painting she sent him. 'Thanks for the fab painting of yours truly', he writes to her.

But Marge's subversiveness in eventually painting the naked Burns takes her out of her role as the other to the various men in her life – Homer, Mr Lombardo, Ringo Starr and Burns. It is through this act of creativity that she takes on a new character as the subtle exposer of the 'dirty bottom' (Jung 1988) of official masculinity and, in doing so, mounts a challenge to his phallic masculinity. For her this means that, in rekindling her childhood dreams, she faces a masculine world whose dominant self-representations (as powerful and beautiful) don't make sense to her, and by providing her own representations she inadvertently interrupts masculine self-characterizations – the equally sexualized images of Homer as 'Adonis', and Burns as phallically 'powerful'. It is humour through which the pathetic and frail cover-up that enables these images to prevail is rendered visible and unstable. The show is funny because it uses the grotesque male body as a means to question the assumptions of masculine power in relation both to sexual and organizational potency. It is Marge – the feminine – who enables this to happen.

Conclusion: is laughter good for you?

We started this chapter quoting Rabelais – 'laughter is good for you'. So, while we do indeed laugh at *The Simpsons,* is it good for us? If, as Bakhtin suggested, the carnival was a site where social hierarchies became suspended and overturned, then in *The Simpsons* the employment of the grotesque representations of Homer and Burns work as a means to show how masculine organizational hierarchies can be overturned. Just as the medieval carnival offered a temporary liberation from the dominant ecclesiastical culture, within the boxed confines of the television screen we can find a similar temporary liberation. This is the liberation through laughter that enables alternatives to be considered and the dominant to be ridiculed and debased. *The Simpsons* is, in the Rabelaisian sense, a text that laughs rather than weeps, even though its exacting critiques of contemporary culture offer many a cause for tears. And laughing in the face of power – gendered organizational power – may well be a means of understanding that power better.

Of course this is not the stuff of revolutionary liberation. Grotesque realism in *The Simpsons* retains the essential carnivalesque feature of *ambivalence*. The grotesque is not merely a 'negation, and exaggeration pursuing narrowly satirical aims' (Bakhtin 1965/1984: 304). It is not merely negatively degrading and satirical, but rather regenerates such that the '[c]osmic catastrophe represented in the material bodily lower stratum is degraded, humanized, and transformed into grotesque monsters. Terror is conquered by laughter' (p. 366).

So then, we might ask a second concluding question: can *The Simpsons* provide a form of laughter that can conquer terror? The answer, of course, lies in the marrow of the laughter, and how much nourishment one gains from it. At least we might claim that the employment of carnival grotesque in popular culture such as *The Simpsons*

> provides a space for organizational critique without finalizing the critique fully for viewers ... [it] breaks the rules in order to make them more visible ... [and] opens a space where these rules can be interrogated and questioned ... The Simpsons does not promise a new organizational utopia but rather creates a new opportunity for critique.
>
> (Rhodes 2001: 382)

To suggest that such a critique might usher in a new form of inverted domination is clearly not the point. But perhaps surfacing and laughing at power with joyous and ambivalent glee can show the way that organized life can become a 'funny monster' that combines horror and comedy in order to play with and deny oppressive forms of social existence (Lindvall and Melton 1997). Carnival humour which employs the grotesque is funny because it parodies and violates the rules of what is expected – but, in order for this to be funny one must first be aware, or made aware, of the rule. 'Violation produces comic pleasure' (Eco 1984: 5) but only to the extent that the rule is known and recognized. The subversive possibility of such a humour is that by confronting characters located in frameworks of social expectations, we might just become aware that the contradictions that make us laugh might also make us realize that 'we are no longer sure that it is the character that is at fault. Maybe the frame is wrong' (ibid. 8). For some this might be a subversive and ambivalent laughter yet one that 'offers the chance to have a new outlook on the world' (Bakhtin 1965/1984: 34).

Note

1   The quotations used in our discussion are taken from our own transcription of the episode and from the 'episode capsule' available at *The Simpsons* Archive website, <www.snpp.com>, accessed 2 Jan. 2006. The episode was written by Brian K. Roberts, and directed by Jim Reardon.

References

Ahmed, S. (2000) *Strange Encounters: Embodied Others in Postcoloniality*, London: Routledge.

Alberti, J. (ed.) (2003) *Leaving Springfield: 'The Simpsons' and the Possibilities of Oppositional Culture*, Detroit, MI: Wayne State University Press.

Bakhtin, M. M. (1965/1984) *Rabelais and his World*, tr. H. Iwolsky, Bloomington, IN: Indiana University Press.

Bakhtin, M. M. (1984) *Problems of Dostoyevsky's Politics*, tr. C. Emerson, Minneapolis, MN: University of Minnesota Press.

Bernard-Donals, M. F. (1988) 'Knowing the subaltern: Bakhtin, carnival and the other choice of the human science', in M. M. Bell and M. Gardiner (eds), *Bakhtin and the Human Sciences*, pp. 112–27, London: Sage.

Bologh, R. (1990) *Love or Greatness*, London: Unwin Hyman.

Brewis, J. (1998) 'What is wrong with this picture? Sex and gender relations in Disclosure', in J. Hassard and R. Holliday (eds), *Organization/Representation: Work and Organization in Popular Culture*, pp. 83–99, London: Sage.

Brown, A. (2003) 'Introduction', in F. Rabelais, *Gargantua*, tr. A. Brown, pp. xi–xvi, London: Hesperus Press.

Butler, J. (1993) *Bodies that Matter: On the Discursive Limits of Sex*, New York: Routledge.

Buurman, G. (1997) 'Erotic bodies: images of the disabled', in K. Davis (ed.), *Embodied Practices: Feminist Perspectives on the Body*, pp. 131–4, London: Sage.

Cohen, K. F. (2004) *Forbidden Animation: Censored Cartoons and Blacklisted Animators*, Jefferson, NC: MacFarland.

Collinson, D. and Hearn, J. (eds) (1996) *Men as Managers, Managers as Men: Critical Perspectives on Men, Masculinities and Management*, London: Sage.

Cunningham-Burley, S. and Backett-Milburn, K. (eds) (2001) *Exploring the Body*, Basingstoke: Palgrave.

Czarniawska, B. (2003) 'Forbidden knowledge: organization theory in times of transition', *Management Learning*, 34(3): 353–65.

Czarniawska, B. and Rhodes, C. (2006) 'Strong plots: the relationship between popular culture and management theory and practice', in P. Gagliardi and B. Czarniawska (eds), *Management and the Humanities*, pp. 195–218, London: Edward Elgar.

Dale, K. (2001) *Anatomising Organization Theory*, London: Palgrave.

Davis, K. (ed.) (1997) *Embodied Practices: Feminist Perspectives on the Body*, London: Sage.

Dobson, H. (2006) 'Mr *Sparkle* meets the Yakuza: depictions of Japan in *The Simpsons*', *Journal of Popular Culture*, 39(1): 44–68.

Docker, J. (1994) *Postmodernism and Popular Culture: A Cultural History*, Cambridge: Cambridge University Press.

Donaldson, M. (1991) *Time of our Lives*, Sydney: George Allen & Unwin.

Douglas, M. (1968/2002) *Purity and Danger*, London: Routledge.

Du Gay, P. (2000) *In Praise of Bureaucracy*, London: Sage.

Eco, U. (1984) 'The frames of comic freedom', in T. A. Sebeok (ed.), *Carnival*, pp. 1–10, Berlin: Mouton Publishers.

Erion, G. J. and Zeccardi, J. A. (2001) 'Marge's moral motivation', in W. Irwin, M. T. Conrad and A. J. Skoble (eds), *The Simpsons and Philosophy*, pp. 46–58, Chicago, IL: Open Court.

Featherstone, M., Hepworth, M. and Turner, B. S. (1991) *The Body, Social Process and Cultural Theory*, London: Sage.

Fiske, J. (1987) *Television Culture*, London: Routledge.

Foucault, M. (1981) *Power/Knowledge*, Brighton: Harvester Wheatsheaf.

Frank, L. (2001) 'The evolution of the seven deadly sins: from God to the Simpsons', *Journal of Popular Culture*, 35(1): 95–105.

Garber, M. (1992) *Vested Interests: Cross Dressing and Cultural Anxiety*, New York: Routledge.

Gatens, M. (1996) *Imaginary Bodies: Ethics, Power and Corporeality*, London: Routledge.

Gray, J. (2005) 'Television teaching: parody, *The Simpsons* and media education', *Critical Studies in Media Communication*, 22(3): 223–38.

Grosz, E. (1996) *Space, Time and Perversion: Essays on the Politics of the Body*, New York: Routledge.

Hassard, J., Holliday, R. and Willmott, H. (2000) *Body and Organization*, London: Sage.

Hitchcock, P. (1998) 'The grotesque of the body electric', in M. M. Bell and M. Gardiner (eds), *Bakhtin and the Human Sciences*, pp. 78–95, London: Sage.

Höpfl, H. (2002) 'Playing the part: reflections on aspects of mere performance in the customer–client relationship', *Journal of Management Studies*, 39(2): 255–67.

Höpfl, H. (2003) 'Becoming a (virile) member: women and the military body', *Body and Society*, 9(4): 13–30.

Hull, M. B. (2000) 'Postmodern philosophy meets the pop cartoon: Michel Foucault and Matt Groening', *Journal of Popular Culture*, 34(2): 57–67.

Jung, H. Y. (1988) 'Bakhtin's dialogical body politics', in M. M. Bell and M. Gardiner (eds), *Bakhtin and the Human Sciences*, pp. 95–111, London: Sage.

Kerfoot, D. and Knights, D. (1993) 'Management, masculinity and manipulation: from paternalism to corporate strategy in financial services in Britain', *Journal of Management Studies*, 30(4): 659–77.

Lennie, I. (1999) *Beyond Management*, London: Sage.

Lindvall, T. R. and Melton, J. M. (1997) 'Towards a postmodern animated discourse: Bakhtin, intertextuality and the cartoon carnival', in J. Pilling (ed.), *A Reader in Animation Studies*, pp. 203–20, London: John Libbey.

Marc, D. (1997) *Comic Visions: Television Comedy and American Culture*, 2nd edn, Malden: Blackwell.

Messner, M. A. (1992) *Power at Play: Sports and the Problem of Masculinity*, Boston, MA: Beacon.

Moodley, R. (1999) 'Masculine managerial masks and the "other" subject', in S. Whitehead and R. Moodley (eds), *Transforming Managers: Gendering Change in the Public Sector*, pp. 214–33, London: UCL Press.

Morgan, G. (1996) 'The gender of bureaucracy', in D. Collinson and J. Hearn (eds), *Men as Managers, Managers as Men: Critical Perspectives on Men, Masculinities and Management*, pp. 43–60, London: Sage.

Ott, B. L. (2003) '"I'm Bart Simpson, who the hell are you?" A study of postmodern identity (re)construction', *Journal of Popular Culture*, 37(1): 56–82.

Pullen, A. (2006) *Managing Identity*, London: Palgrave.

Rabelais, F. (1534/2003) *Gargantua*, tr. A. Brown, London: Hesperus Press.

Rhodes, C. (2001) 'D'Oh: *The Simpsons*, popular culture and the organizational carnival', *Journal of Management Inquiry*, 10(4): 374–83.

Richmond, R. and Coffman, A. (eds) (1997) *The Simpsons: A Complete Guide to Our Favorite Family*, New York: HarperCollins.

Shildrick, M. (2002) *Embodying the Monster: Encounters With the Vulnerable Self*, London: Sage.

Shilling, C. (1993) *The Body and Social Theory*, London: Sage.

Snow, D. E. and Snow, J. J. (2001) 'Simpsonian sexual politics', in W. Irwin, M. T. Conrad and A. J. Skoble (eds), *The Simpsons and Philosophy*, pp. 126–44, Chicago, IL: Open Court.

Stallybrass, P. and White, A. (1986) *The Politics and Poetics of Transgression*, London: Methuen.

Street, J. (1997) *Politics and Popular Culture*, Cambridge: Polity Press.

ten Bos, R. and Kaulingfreks, R. (2001) *De Hygiënemachine: Kanttekeningen bij de Reinheidscultus in Cultuur, Management en Organisatie,* Kampen: Agora.

Trethewey, A. (1999) 'Disciplined bodies: women's embodied identities at work', *Organization Studies*, 20(3): 423–50.

Turner, B. S. (1984) *The Body and Society: Explorations in Social Theory*, Oxford: Blackwell.

Vänskä, A. (2002) 'A heroic male and a beautiful woman: Teemu Mäki, Orlan and the ambivalence of the grotesque body', *Nordic Journal of Women's Study*, 10(3): 154–67.

Weinstein, D. (1988) 'Of mice and Bart: *The Simpsons* and the postmodern', in C. Deglin-Espoti, *Postmodernism in the Cinema*, pp. 61–72, New York: Berghahn Books.

Wood, A. and Todd, M. A. (2005) '"Are we there yet?" Searching for Springfield and *The Simpsons'* rhetoric of omnitopia', *Critical Studies in Media Communication*, 22(3): 207–22.

Chapter 10

Heidegger's unfunny and the academic text

Organization analysis on the blink[1]

Damian P. O'Doherty

Seriousness is the only refuge of the shallow.

(Oscar Wilde)

There are different versions of humour; one could exercise, for example, Marxist, Freudian, deconstructive or Levinasian modes of analysis as a way of studying humour (see Critchley 2002; Lingis 2004), or one could deploy Marxist, Freudian, or deconstructive humour. We might arrive at the insight that humour is an opiate of the masses; or we could use humour to caricature the activities of the capitalist as the usurious conniving of a Mr 'Moneybags', as Marx famously does in Capital.

Both subject and object, humour clearly also occupies a funny place in the study of organization. Labour process analysis, for example, has long sought to explain the role of humour within a dialectic of control and resistance in organization (Collinson 1988; Ackroyd and Thompson 1999). Ethnographies of work rarely fail to note the centrality of joking, badinage and humour (Roy 1958; Lupton 1963; Collinson 1992; Kunda 1995). Indeed, humour has long attracted the serious attention of philosophy and political theory. Kant in his 1790 *Critique of Judgement* defined laughter as an 'affection arising from a strained expectation of being suddenly reduced to nothing' (1. 2. 54), and Bergson suggests that a character is usually comic in proportion to his degree of self-ignorance (1911: 16). Darwin (1872) and Spencer (1860) emphasize the importance of its purposelessness and, in their physiology of comedy, laughter is defined as a form of 'tickling of the mind'. Mary Douglas (1975), on the other hand, understands humour as an interruption and subversion of social order, which reminds us that what we find funny is always cultural and historical. Humour, it would appear, is an exceedingly accommodating topic, offering an infinitely malleable opportunity for application and exercise.

In this chapter we grapple with the idea that humour is becoming a new 'logic' of organization; but in order to open up its logic to analysis we must risk this 'being suddenly reduced to nothing' to which Kant alludes. In the first half of this chapter we trace a number of general definitions and understandings of humour and the comedic before thinking of the ways in which humour helps us to delimit and understand 'character'. Character can be understood as a particular arrangement of primitive and existential forces whose humour comes from a negotiation with the 'blockages', the limits, the fears and the unknown, of identity and self. The classic characters of twentieth-century film humour – one thinks of the Marx Brothers, Chaplin, Laurel and Hardy, Jacques Tati, Woody Allen – remind us that humour is close to existential tragedy, if not fate. We then consider and dismiss the idea that there are relative degrees of sophistication in humour, an understanding which would lead one to conclude that the development of character is related to the cultivated appreciation of 'highbrow' comedy. As the ancient Greeks knew, humour is a form of sickness caused by a disequilibrium in the four humours. Literally, it is to be wet (*umor*); hence, to wet oneself (as opposed to the *humus* – the dry of earth). And there is nothing dignified in wetting oneself.

The movement of the first half of the chapter arrives at an understanding of what we call the 'entropic logic' of humour, and in so doing opens up a strange space for thinking, that helps to provide some preparation for the material that follows in the second half. We begin truly to risk wetting ourselves, crying or otherwise, when we turn to an analysis of the so-called 'post-ironic' in contemporary political and social relations. Subject to the post-ironic we find ourselves confronted with the uncanny prospect that it is no longer possible to distinguish the funny and the serious, nor the intentional from the unintentional comedic. The US defence secretary Donald Rumsfeld offers a paradigm case study of this post-ironic (as we will illustrate); but in organization analysis it is Huczynski and Buchanan (hucbuc) who are the most important symptoms or representatives of this condition (see also Lilley 1998). Indeed, we might even say that the academic textbook in organization studies has fallen victim to comedy and has become in its own right an artefact of humour or despair. As the social realms of culture, politics and entertainment begin to lose their once distinctive identity, it is becoming increasingly difficult to work out what is intentionally meant as comedy and what is supposed to be serious. Organization has always had its funny moments; it may even be intrinsically or constitutively absurd. But what is perhaps most disturbing today is the prospect that humour has become 'out-of-bounds'. Following the success of 'comedians' like Steve Coogan, Chris Morris and Ricky Gervais, we are no longer sure where the comedic begins and ends, nor can we be sure who are the comedians, who are the funny guys and who the straight. We may be tempted to laugh at Huczynski and Buchanan, but it is in fact deadly serious.

Huczynski and Buchanan continue to publish one of the most popular introductory textbooks in organization studies, and it is widely admired for its comprehensive and accessible coverage of the subject area. However, all is not what it appears in this strange land of hucbuc: it seems we are going to have to either laugh or cry. Here, Rumsfeld begins to sound like Martin Heidegger, and 'real' work organizations start to adopt and mimic those fantastic elements of hucbuc explored in Buchanan and Huczynski (1985, 1991, 1997, 2003). Hucbuc is seriously *unfunny*. Earth is a distant memory in the realm of 'hucbuc' and its 'ORBIT',[2] but the rigours of its pedagogy do allow us, albeit strangely, to conceive of the possibility that humour in organization today renders management impotent and absurd. Huczynksi and Buchanan are the Laurel and Hardy of organization analysis and a careful attention to their texts helps to show that they teach us something that comes before what we routinely recognize as the humorous. Neither funny nor serious, this is the space of something we might call the Heideggerian 'unfunny'. It provides the condition of possibility *and* impossibility for the humorous, it brings organization to a standstill and opens up a space within which we can develop some understanding of the humorous as a possible new and perverse logic of organization. As the text becomes increasingly surreal and absurd, testing the very possibility of meaning and sense, its 'humour' becomes infectious and virulent, essentially unknowable, necessary but impossible. Our journey becomes increasingly delirious as we become the subject of this unfunny, a movement that takes us into a confrontation with (a) death (of sense, meaning, self, identity). In this opening the subject stands on the brink of dread and the suspense of consciousness: it is organization on the blink – and 'there's another fine mess you've gotten me into'.

Humour, comedy: repetition and organization

If we ask if humour can be 'learned', we must first recognize that the spectrum of humour ranges from the puerile and inane to the urbane sophistications of Oscar Wilde. Moreover, humour is only one version of comedy. Indeed, humour and irony are very distinctive in their purpose and comedic effect (Brown 2003). There are subtle gradations between satire, witticism, mimicry, parody, sarcasm, mockery, slapstick, farce, lampooning, the scatological and the ribald; there are also many comedic characters that are either vehicles for the expression of humour or its unwitting dupes: Harlequin, Columbine, and Pierrot in the Commedia dell'arte; but also the buffoon, the clown, the jester or prankster. These characters often strike us as strange and unsettling, and they tend to remain marginal or excluded from the social; on occasion they recall the character of the scapegoat. With their so-called 'intelligent' or 'alternative' humour, today's cast of British comedians – Chris Morris, Steve Coogan and Ricky Gervais (in a line that might be traced back to Chaucer through Monty Python) – seem to stand outside the everyday. It is a space that generates insight into the social, encouraging satire and social critique, but it is arguably a lonely and alien space. In fact, it is a commonplace that comedians might be the loneliest people of all.

Since Aristophanes, the West has been preoccupied with the staging and dramatic performance of comedy (Griffith and Marks 2006), and when considered in terms of 'theatre' (Mangham and Overington 1987) contemporary work organization soon reveals the persistence of its own comedic characters and routines. Indeed, with its administrative logic of routine and procedure, marked by extensive automation, mechanization, and alienation, organization is seemingly condemned to eternal repetition, repetition itself being one of the components of classic comedy. One form of repetition is especially evident in the humour we find in those characters who display a certain predictability and inability to learn from their past misfortunes. Those managers and workers who are seemingly addicted to their routines often make for considerable comedy in organization. In this sense organization and comedy are no doubt synonymous.

The comedians Laurel and Hardy with their burlesque pantomime of repetition and difference capture some of this comedy. Like managers and their subordinates the routines of Laurel and Hardy display the fate of those characters who tragically get sucked into a logic of interaction that typically ends in disaster and embarrassment. Chaplin, however, particularly in *Modern Times*, perhaps provides the archetypal character of modern alienation, a film routinely cited in the plethora of textbooks and handbooks on the organization and management of mass production. Charlie is funny because he doesn't quite work, he does not easily fit into the Taylorized mass production system; with his jerky and clumsy movements he is an awkward man-machine symbiosis, a becoming-machinic that is far from habituated or accommodated to the alien rhythms of machinery and industry (Bazin 1985). With his courageous efforts and exaggerations he lets us see the everyday in new ways. In this sense Charlie is a hero and an 'everyman'. He is funny because he lets us see that which normally remains hidden – we 'feel' for Charlie, and so we have to laugh. In his films Chaplin is really showing us what we are becoming, and his genius is that he makes us sense the alien-like estrangement that is our becoming minds and bodies subject to the pressures and strains of modern production systems. Benjamin (1936) was the first writer to identify the potentially restorative and sublimating qualities of modern cinema. These qualities helped to aestheticize and beatify the disturbing effects of 'shock' experienced in modernity, a world of ceaseless change, coupled with the monotony of quotidian work that constantly verges on meaninglessness and despair.

Like cinema, comedy comes close to displaced frustration, repressed anger and even sublimated aggression (Lorenz 1963). In many ways it seeks to avoid the tragic dimensions of human existence, but with its repetitions and routines, and particularly in the figure of the clown, comedy inevitably seems to return full circle, to become, once again, tragedy. It was doubtless Chaplin who first said that a comedian is the saddest person of all because he has nothing left to sell but his own humour.

Sickness, sex and transgression: through laughter we find out about ourselves

> Imagination is a quality given to man to compensate for what he is not, and a sense of humour is provided to console him from what he is.
>
> (Oscar Wilde)

To be 'humorous' was understood for many years to be actually a form of sickness, a condition that reflected the imbalance or misalignment in the four basic bodily 'humours', usually expressed as an excess of phlegm, bile, blood or choler. As an 'escape attempt' (cf. Cohen and Taylor 1978) humour might then offer only temporary reprieve, the depth of our suffering betrayed by how 'deep catalogue', idiosyncratic, sophisticated or obscure our tastes have become. Instead of a simple repetition of the same, in which the subject continues to find humour in the possible multiple variations on the same joke – the bawdy slapstick humour of Donald McGill's British seaside postcards, for example – (sick) individuals looking for humour might progress or evolve, deepening their appreciation of different styles of humour as their taste and sophistication develop. How you like your comedy, then, might be an indication of character, but also, as we shall see later in this chapter, tragic fate. What we laugh at might be more an indication of who we are than a register of the essential comedic value of a particular story or situation.

Humour, of course, plays on the tension of limits and their transgression. In laughter we momentarily display the limits that mark us out and define our being. The interruption of the everyday by jokes and laughter often allows something that is routinely disallowed to be seen or spoken of. Trading on stereotype, racist humour allows its practitioners some reassurance that their prejudice has some foundation in truth. The classic of this genre in the UK, 'What do you call a black man with a Mercedes Benz?', answer: 'A thief', captures many of these dimensions. The answer reveals the question to have set up an initial incongruity. The joke only works because the one who laughs harbours the thought that there is something surprising or not quite right about a black man in possession of a Mercedes Benz. It also trades on the prejudice that black people are thieves. The joke opens up and displays existential dimensions of character but also helps to confirm and consolidate subjectivity and identity – in this case it marks out someone as racist. In this way we might say that humour affirms and displays the outline of subjectivity.

Humour is socially and culturally contingent and specific but one common feature is that jokes allow us to 'speak' about that which normally we are not allowed to think or say. Sex is, for example, a perennial subject of humour, perhaps because it looms so large as a difficulty or problem in our societies (Foucault 1981). History helps us to see that different societies organize sexuality in different ways; but there are always limits and taboos that isolate what is allowed and what is disallowed, what can be spoken of and what cannot be spoken. It is around these limits that the frisson of transgression can be mobilized, or where shock or outrage can be produced. We might expect to find in those societies that exercise a particularly severe regime of control over matters of sexuality – the Catholic Church in Ireland, for example – a predilection for humour that deals with sex. It offers one way of treating the subject of sex, of speaking of that which is of such importance to the human, but is routinely denied and forbidden. The man who continues to laugh at stories of sexual escapades and its potential embarrassments reveals an individual who finds it difficult to talk about these areas of human life. In that sense, just as with racist jokes, sexual humour discloses those regions of being in which we remain ignorant, of which we have little understanding or tolerance. It affirms identity, then, at the same time that it *delimits* subjectivity to reveal the shadow of ignorance or underdevelopment. This is why accident and chance are always central ingredients in humour, in part because accidents and chance represent those phenomena which remain outside our control, around which we are vulnerable and insecure. It is an old adage that we laugh at that of which we are frightened. In this respect, if death is perhaps the most fundamental question or problem, there can be little surprise that it remains an important source for comedy and humour.

In its many ways humour helps to delimit character, exposing points of irresolution and their premature closure, revealing lines of tension and 'childhood blockages' (Deleuze and Guattari 1987) that potentially riddle the individual long into maturity. It shows up the type of disposition we enjoy, or, in another sense, the kind of make-up we suffer – the 'trap' in which we are stuck. We have noted that humour depends on limits and control, but for it to work as comedy these limits and controls must resonate with existential limitations. Humour is intertwined with subjectivity in ways that are complex, multi-layered and dialectical. Inhibition and anxiety, for example, are essential to humour. We might ask if by nature and temperament we are ironic? Or, are we a humorist, or a sarcast? Do we enjoy puerile forms of humour? Do we find ourselves acting as the clown, or do we laugh at the clown? Each form of humour might be considered to be different arrangements of anxiety and neurosis. If repression is an inevitable cause and consequence of the human condition then we are all fated to exercise or enjoy a certain degree of humour; humour offers one medium through which to channel and shape the energies associated with suffering and despair, but it is also double-edged: whilst humour can be understood to discharge tension it does not offer a permanent or stable subject position.

Humour offers a temporary discharge of tension, but it also stokes up energies that are likely to rebound with 'delayed effects', effects that Freud called 'Nachträglichkeit'. In one sense this means we will always need ever-greater dosages of humour. The old comedic routines no longer stimulate humour but they renew and recollect the lines of tension out of which the subject is forged. In another sense, energies stoked up by humour are not all discharged at the moment of humour but instead are postponed or 'invested' into the future. We laugh today but the more we laugh the more we will be crying at ourselves in the future as deferred energies seek their postponed expression. According to Freud (1925), the traces and lines of memory create 'furrows' that mark out and predispose the subject to a particular psychic management and negotiation of energy, which means that humour recalls the inscription of certain memory traces and allows them to be 'played out' again, a repetition of the same which is both reassuring and comfortable. Humour in this sense offers a kind of regression.

How the individual might respond to the stimulation of tensions that cannot find an outlet through humour is indeterminable, but potentially more extreme and violent. In addition, there is always the danger of boredom. In response to boredom the subject might seek satisfaction by means of more intense or more sophisticated forms of humour that tickle the new, as-yet unthought, boundaries of anxiety and insecurity. Where slapstick holiday postcard humour might have been interesting and satisfying for a time, the subject might develop in ways that mean the more existential wit of Woody Allen or the tart irony of Oscar Wilde becomes more attractive. The simple inhibitions of sexuality are here replaced by more philosophic worries and anxieties. Humour opens us up to parts of our selves we didn't know were there or did not want to acknowledge were there.

The entropic logic of humour: Woody Allen and the 'post-human' subject?

It is often noted how the comedic can become addictive, providing an anaesthetic to ward off the more troubling aspects of memory and subjectivity that haunt the subject. However, to stave off the danger of boredom, this addiction requires increased dosages. For humour to have continued comedic effect, it cannot become too predictable or routine. It must take a new angle on an old subject, offer a slight variation and it must in some way continue to surprise the listener to the tale. Forms of comedy that subjects once found funny will die off as the subject sheds old prejudices and acquires new ones. If we accept that there is a maturational logic to the human subject, that an individual progressively becomes or desires to become more 'rounded' and 'developed' over time, we might expect that in the biography of an individual life humour becomes progressively more sophisticated and complex. In this way humour might be thought of as a medium through which the human subject works through a series of 'blockages', or alternatively as a way of acquiring temporary relief to placate more deep-seated anxieties and questions. The entropic logic of boredom, however, cannot be so easily avoided. Comedy seems to produce its effects by working (on) the boundaries of our being so that, as insight into the fate of our human condition matures, different forms of humour are required to 'manage' insecurities.

With this talk of maturity we might be suspected of exercising a humanist and developmental logic. The accusation could be made that we have been mobilizing a conception of the subject that betrays conservative assumptions of evolution and linearity, of progress and development, a liberal-humanist prejudice that is somewhat naïve in its belief that subjects inevitably do mature, become more rounded or more sophisticated as time goes on, and that there is something universal that can be identified as 'mature'. These assumptions, then, by maintaining some commitment to a hierarchy of values and taste, risk being judgemental. We mature into more metaphysical and existential forms of wit as we leave behind the clumsy and more awkward humour associated with immature inhibitions associated with sexuality and its embarrassments. There is, in other words, highbrow humour, and there are forms of humour that are more lowbrow and base. However, this gravitation towards the boundaries of being – in terms of deep metaphysics and existential questions – is perhaps better thought of in more cyclical terms.

In brief, the subject in their quest is unlikely to find answers or solutions to questions of being simply because they have found a more philosophical terrain in which to pose their questions. They shape their questions with a different discourse, in perhaps more extended, refined and complicated ways, but the answers still remain partial and provisional. Ultimately, the answers will not satisfy, which suggests that it is perhaps the questions that are misguided. Consider, in this respect, Nietzsche's (1974) reflections on the Epicureans, whom he admired precisely because the development and refinement of their senses, pushed to such an extreme of sensitivity and understanding, meant that all they could bear of life was to sit on the beach and stare at the blue waves lapping against the shore. When the logic of humour is analytically studied, its logic understood, and the humour exhausted of its innocence or spontaneous surprise, humour is either lost, or all things become equal such that individuals become indifferent to the highbrow or lowbrow. Both can be dismissed – by recognition, by the 'I get it', or 'I see through that joke' – or both can be embraced as simply variations on a theme. Highbrow and lowbrow become undecidable. We can laugh at both. Recall that there are philosophers who have written the most erudite contributions to the history of philosophical thought but whose taste in humour remains simple and obvious, bawdy or even vulgar.

At the hinge of this undecidability, the distinction between sophisticated and simple humour becomes irrelevant, a distinction, moreover, that can easily be revealed to have been established by the existence of hierarchy, elitism and pretension. The puerile or bawdy is funny in the same way that the philosophical or learned wit stimulates humour. In this sense we might be outlining here what is tempting to call, for want of a better term, a 'higher order', or reflexive mode of humour: a volatile 'position' of humour in which the individual still laughs at the joke, but in a different kind of way. There is here the possibility of a different logic of humour beginning to open up. One of the more disturbing things about this disposition is the possibility that the teller of jokes begins to realize that it is largely impossible to determine whether someone is 'genuinely' laughing at the content of the joke, or whether the audience is merely laughing at the *telling* of the joke. It may be that the reflexive audience admires the style, the individuality or the performance of this particular telling of the joke; or, more innocently, that the humour in itself is authentically funny. On another level, the audience might be laughing at the attempt by comedians, as a representative of the all-too-human condition, to make light of social or personal issues. There is the added complication that the comedian is also telling the joke in a knowing way – that s/he too is laughing at the possibility that such a joke, its style or genre, could be found funny by anyone. In this case we arrive at the absurd possibility that everyone is laughing, but at the same time no one is laughing – and neither the comedian nor the audience knows what the respective other is laughing at, or whether they intend the joke to be humorous at all. Can there be anything more tragic? Or funny?

For the serious student of existentialism it may be impossible to laugh at the human condition. Mortality, the accident of birth, the fleeting ephemerality of life, the lack of ultimate meaning, etc., may not be a cause of humour, but instead the motivation for doom and despair (see Cooper 1990). However, philosophy and humour are not so very different. We would not have philosophy without death and the fear of death, and similar to humour – but perhaps more elaborate and demanding – philosophy seeks, in part, to stave off anxiety, to offer distraction and entertainment, while seeking answers to the most fundamental questions of being. But the history of philosophy teaches us that the answers discovered or invented by the great philosophers never really endure, indeed philosophy often fails to be translatable to different times and places. It is, then, perhaps the *questions* that are funny. Even the way in which we question what we call 'existence', and *what* we are able to question – that which strikes us as being worthy of question or available for question – is historically contingent (see Heidegger 1962). Given this ultimate subordination to Time, philosophy is also constitutively funny and regularly collapses into the comedic.

The pretensions of philosophy and particularly the doom and gloom of this existential seriousness is tackled by Woody Allen, perhaps most memorably in some of the dialogue and soliloquies in *Stardust Memories* (1980). Woody Allen illustrates the futility and irony of philosophical ambition when he tells us that 'I took one course in existential philosophy at … errr … *New York University*, and on … errrr … on the final, they gave me 10 questions, and … ugh … I couldn't answer a single one of them. You know? I left 'em all blank … got a hundred!' In a deeply ironic sense, and subverting the *telos* and logic of the classic existential narrative Allen demonstrates *both* his understanding of the kind of existential philosophies developed by people like Heidegger, Sartre, Camus *et al. and* his departure from it. The 'blank' is the perfect answer, empty is full, and nothingness is being. At the same time, however, this 'departure' is ambivalent. This blank hints at either the inevitable nihilism into which the human is plunged, once it is realized, as Nietzsche taught, that 'God is dead', or it suggests the inability of the human to answer the most fundamental questions they might pose about existence – indeed it is arguable that the very ability to articulate questions about meaning, purpose, etc., is evidence that answers will *not* be found.

Mimicking the plight of Pablo Ibbieta (Sartre 1939), and the paradoxical logic of existential insight and its style of argumentation, Allen wins (or loses) by accident (or fate). Allen, or his character, is still trapped, condemned to freedom and its cruel ironies. The fact that he couldn't answer the questions is proof either of his idiocy or genius, or, more worrying, the impossibility of deciding the difference between the genius and the idiot. There is an extremely fine line (and one perhaps ultimately impossible to draw) between knowing and not-knowing – and in these scenes from *Stardust Memories* Allen demonstrates that knowing and not-knowing perhaps amount to the same thing. Enlightenment and the 'idiot savant' are perhaps impossible to distinguish. The question then becomes to what extent the evident anxiety of Allen and his characters in the telling of this tale is authentic, or whether it is simply performance enacted to exaggerate and twist the already abundant irony and absurdity of the situation. If it is calculated performance we might wonder if Allen has in fact escaped the anxiety of the existential condition. If Allen is anxious, he is then – and ironically so – both teller of the tale and its victim. Teller of the tale and tale of the teller (so to speak), subject and object, character and its author, Allen here comes close to the classic position of the clown (Bratton and Featherstone 2006).

In telling the tale of being awarded 100 in his existential philosophy exam he is either laughing or crying, and it is a tale that appeals to those with some knowledge of the existential tradition in philosophy and literature. Without this knowledge, it is still possible to laugh, simply because of the skill in the timing and inflection of its delivery. On one level the paradox of getting full marks for doing nothing may in itself be funny. Yet the joke works much more effectively if the audience has some knowledge of the literature that Allen is citing and parodying. However, whilst the joke may require this sophistication, on yet another level, the joke is funny because it is self-defeating. It implies that for all our learning we still know nothing, or worse that we don't know we know nothing. It was claimed that only Socrates, perhaps the first Western comedian, was able to know that he didn't know anything – and his strategy of philosophical dialogue did little more than help his interlocutor to see that what they thought they knew has in fact no substantial philosophical validity. The paradox of this self-understanding is itself funny; it seems to cancel itself out in its claim to know that one doesn't know. Is this not, precisely, a form of knowledge? Allen's position is similar. By mistake Allen achieves full marks for his exam. His lack of understanding, his 'blank', is precisely all that can be known about the subject of existential philosophy, or philosophy more generally. However, from this excerpt we don't know if Allen knows this himself. He could be simply bewildered by this apparent paradox. But we suspect that Woody knows only too well what he is up to and that his bigger claim is that it is precisely learning, academic knowledge and philosophical sophistication, which are the real jokes: they are unable to answer any of the most vital questions of being. Instead they make it more complicated, perhaps interesting, but in making it interesting it causes us to risk losing ourselves in ever more abstract and arcane speculation. Philosophy becomes a distraction, then, something similar to entertainment, something to pass the time. In other words, a bit like comedy.

The importance of this kind of humour is two-fold. Its self-deprecating nature undercuts the pretension that knowledge and its accumulation is of any real value. Secondly, it reminds us that all humour is similar, and in one important respect, namely that it is about reminding us about limits while at the same time introducing the frisson of an idealized transgression. From this vantage we can now see why the liberal-humanist assumption of personal growth and development, which suggests that humour needs to become more sophisticated as the subject grows, does not necessarily hold. Allen's form of existential humour reminds us that the accumulation, or 'deepening' of knowledge and understanding, leads no nearer to some kind of solution to the dilemmas of being – indeed it may take us further away from resolution and understanding.

It is a common reflection that as one reads and studies one progressively learns how little one actually does know; as time goes on the modesty and insignificance of one's own knowledge and capacity for understanding is made ever more clear. In this sense, if there is a trajectory to the subject's evolution, it is equally – or undecidably – towards ignorance as it is towards growth, maturity or any self-actualization in the Maslovian sense (Maslow 1954). As we become ever more ignorant and we realize the futility of the pretension to knowledge, we begin to appreciate that there is no highbrow or lowbrow. Rather, comedy simply offers variations on a theme – and the more elaborate, complex or philosophical we need our humour to be, becomes simply a measure of our own regression and the agitation of our 'humours'.

Reflexive humour and the post-ironic: opening the unfunny

British comedian Tommy Cooper was funny precisely because of the simple-minded awkwardness of his routines and pranks. Similarly, the sheer stupidity and infantilism of comedians like Ricky Gervais or *Little Britain* (BBC 2003–6) is their sophistication. One laughs for one of two reasons. It is possible that one recovers or re-enters those realms of being where the puerile or infantile was experienced as first-order, 'authentic' comedy. Practitioners of the 'perspectivism' of Nietzsche (see Klossowski 1997) have nothing but role and performance: the experiment with being annuls itself to become the desperate plight of the performance artist. In the absence of any central authority or judge there is no way in which one can adjudicate or hierarchicize standards, role or humour; here, in 'perspectivism' *without* perspective, nothing matters – everything becomes simply a dress rehearsal, or rather an opening night of Shakespeare's theatre of life. Sophistication leads nowhere; there is nothing inherently more satisfying in so-called 'sophisticated' humour and so one might as well recall the humour that is/was there in what is typically judged as the puerile, base or stupid. Variations of humour are simply variations of nonsense and absurdity. Alternatively, one laughs at the possibility of laughter that resides within each particular genre of humour. One then laughs at the joke of the West African Mercedes Benz car owner joke. One laughs at it, but not in it, or with it; one is laughing here with absurdity, or at the absurdity of all humour.

For many this position reflects the possibility that we have now entered the stage of the post-ironic (Williams 2003). Here, divisions between the funny and the unfunny, the humorous and the serious, are becoming increasingly unclear. Many of us cannot decide if George W. Bush knows that he is a stooge of higher powers in American society and politics – and, moreover, a man out of his depth – or, whether he believes in what he does and says. We might say the same for Tony Blair. When George W. Bush tells us, in his search for Osama Bin Laden, that he is 'going to smoke him out of his cave and get him running and shoot him down dead or alive', it is unclear if he is deliberately acting out the stereotype of a 'southern hick' – and perhaps, cynically, to galvanize support among a certain Republican vote – or whether he is speaking without script or rehearsal and simply articulating his own thoughts in his own words. Recall that for Bergson individuals were funny in proportion to their self-ignorance. The fact that the head of state of the most powerful country in the world equates international relations with the equivalent of a 'good old boys' turkey-shoot should perhaps not come as a surprise. Donald Rumsfeld is perhaps the most intriguing example of this genre. To give a few examples of the sophistic wit of Rumsfeld (from Kurtzman 2005):

> I would not say that the future is necessarily less predictable than the past. I think the past was not predictable when it started.

> The absence of evidence is not evidence of absence.

> Reports that say that something hasn't happened are always interesting to me, because as we know, there are known knowns; there are things we know we know. We also know there are known unknowns; that is to say we know there are some things we do not know. But there are also unknown unknowns -- the ones we don't know we don't know.

Now, Rumsfeld, a scholarship student and graduate of Princeton University, is part of the East Coast American educated elite. The youngest US Secretary of Defense on record when he held the post between 1975 and 1977 under the Ford administration, he is clearly no fool. With these quotes we are possibly reading the thoughts of a man who might rival Martin Heidegger for sheer hermeneutic reflexivity and dialectical sophistication. So close are they that it is almost as if Rumsfeld is quoting the famous paradoxical epiphanies outlined in *Being and Time*. His reflections on time, empirical evidence, absence and knowledge, etc., rival the most erudite epistemological and ontological discussions of a Socrates or a Heidegger. On a second reading, one begins to grasp the way in which the quotes exhibit a subtle grasp of the Epimenidean paradox. On occasion we might be led to speculate that the parody appears to be Lacan, whose intellectual strategy is often to undermine or deconstruct the procedures of language, knowledge and thought in order to explore regions of being and knowing 'outside' of the limitations of habitual knowing and reasoning. When he arrives at his discussion of 'unknown unknowns' Rumsfeld has surely even trumped the deconstructive subtlety of Derrida; like the writing of Derrida his conclusion leaves us wondering about the status of his own claims to knowing that there are 'unknown unknowns'. Is it a fact that two negatives cancelling each other out become a positive? Or, as Rumsfeld seems to claim, these are things 'we don't know we don't know', which seems to suggest a different order of knowledge. The head begins to spin at this stage and not untypically in these situations one is forced into a kind of laughter that for Bataille (1994) held out the possibility of a mystical experience and insight not normally available within the confines of normal language use and the thinking it allows. This opening might well be the adumbration of that implied positive that comes when two negatives combine. But is it comedy or deadly serious? Perhaps Rumsfeld is surreptitiously deconstructing the authority of American politics and in his own way more subversive of American democracy than any Osama Bin Laden or Saddam Hussein.

When political press statements begin to sound like the arcane musings of continental philosophy we have surely entered an arena in which high politics has become an example of the sublime, but a sublime that is difficult to distinguish from comedy or farce. Perhaps we might want to call this the 'stuplime' (see Ngai 2000). The stuplime announces a condition of social relations that is difficult to take at face value. At the same time the quest to look behind the surface for some more fundamental or underlying Truth or explanation seems to be a futile adventure in a world that for many has become 'post-paranoid' (Wood 1998). In the 'postmodern' condition there is arguably nothing but surface, and subject to the same perverse logic that 'explains' humour, we might venture the suggestion that there is nothing behind, below or beyond the surface of the social; there is, in other words, no depth, no substance or foundation, and little ultimate meaning or sense behind different surface representations. When we tried to take the logic of humour to its end-point we discovered that there was no easily identifiable or discernible end-point, but rather an endless spiralling return to the beginning (end). Humour becomes a perpetual beginning. Seeking the Truth behind the surface, the Truth that reveals apparent lies or obfuscation, has left many questioners confused, disorientated and disappointed. Today, when it becomes impossible to separate the serious from the comedic, or the superficial from the deep, the profoundest depth of Heideggerian philosophy merges seamlessly with the improvisations of a court-jester in the guise of Donald Rumsfeld.

There is, nonetheless, some 'logic' of organization that is at work here, or more accurately, a *contagion* of logic that threatens to over-run meaning and sense: as a consequence the academic discipline known as organization studies, or organization behaviour, must perhaps learn to *give itself over* (Derrida 2005: 60) to the understanding and explanation of this logic. It would appear, then, that in recent years the subject of organization analysis is becoming *terribly* funny.

Tragedy or farce, we are beginning to lose our wits; and this remains necessary and preparatory for the understanding of contemporary organization where we discover some of the most bizarre and delirious manifestations of this condition of the tragi-farce.

Organizational behaviour: an introduction to the world of 'hucbuc'

The honorific title of 'Laurel and Hardy' in organization analysis is arguably claimed by the combined writing duo of David Buchanan and Andrzej Huczynksi (1985, 1991, 1997, 2001, 2003), who script one of the most popular, influential and successful introductions and primers in the subject area (cf. Lilley 1998). Now in its fifth edition the reader can begin to see the routines and tragic repetitions; each chapter follows the predictable pattern of 'key concepts', 'learning objectives' and the 'why study …' section, before entering the main body of the text and its cornucopia of colour pictures, multiple font styles, diagrams, cartoons, tables, highlights, the periodic 'stop and criticise' section, indents and definitions, which is followed by the summary punch line provided by the 'Recap', 'Revision', 'Springboard', 'Home Viewing', 'OB in literature' and 'Chapter exercises' sections. Humour is deliberately deployed as a pedagogic device by the authors, and in a number of ways. The cartoons are particularly voluminous, drawing on Calvin and Hobbes (Huczynski and Buchanan 2001: 7, 37, 123, 190), Alex (pp.116, 228, 329, 424, 525, 636), Scott Adams (pp. 390, 541, 660, 794), Oliver and Claire (p. 336), and other miscellaneous cartoons (pp. 18, 32, 55, 76, 98, 109, 143, 146, 197, 212, 245, 260, 276, 286, 312, 357, 359, 457, 458, 492, 495, 574, 589, 609, 647, 685, 695, 714, 745, 757, 779, 810). Humorous films are also used in the 'Home Viewing' section to illustrate various aspects of organizational behaviour: *Gung-ho* is recommended as a way of understanding organization culture; *I'm Alright Jack* helps explain the behaviour of 'individuals in groups'; Chaplin's *Modern Times* illustrates the issues and dilemmas around traditional job design; organization development and sensitivity training is explored through the 1969 film *Bob and Carol and Ted and Alice*; and *One Flew Over the Cuckoo's Nest* provides a study of power and politics in organization.

Huczynksi and Buchanan remind us, and help us to see how much of organizational behaviour is inherently funny. The Solomon Asch study of conformity to group norms (p. 363) is a classic, illustrating how individuals will, seemingly like lemmings, tragically elect to follow the decisions of the majority even when it flies in the face of all their better sense and judgement. Non-verbal courtship gestures (p. 192) consciously and unconsciously deployed by humans to organize mating rituals are also not without their humour. On a darker side, the Milgram 'electric shock' experiments (p. 365) suggest the fallibility of humans to suggestion and authority and the casual ease with which the majority of individuals succumb to sick and sadistic exercises. The Zimbardo prison experiments (pp. 471–2) are also both worrying and darkly comedic, showing how context and role can rapidly and easily transform personality through forms of experiment that seem to tap into or exploit something within the human that desires reward, power and control. Buchanan and Huczynski appear to have an infinite library of funny stories and asides to pepper and spice their material. They tell the ironic story (at least it is ironic for the prejudices of the English) of a German airline trying to turn its cabin crew into comedians (p. 650) in an effort by management to improve customer service and win back market share from competitors. Drawing on the work of Starkey and McKinlay (1994) they compare and contrast Disney Culture to the culture of Ford. Where Disney is all smile, pathos and emotion, the advice given by managers to each other at Ford is to 'look busy, even if you aren't', 'don't smile let alone laugh too much', 'if a colleague gets into trouble with this boss – don't help' and 'CYA (cover your ass)'.

The more we lose ourselves in the pleasure of reading Huczynski and Buchanan, the more we learn to read and navigate our way through organization in ways that allow us to see the proliferation of humour in organization. However, the medium and the message, the tool and its object – the text and its referent – soon begin to lose their distinction and opposition. On closer study of hucbuc we find that the word and the world begin to migrate and (dis)intermediate: the putative reality of organization, the world-out-there that is being referenced and talked about by Buchanan and Huczynski, starts to become difficult to disentangle from their text. With its textual strategies, techniques and ruses, its images, metaphors and stylistic motifs – indeed its very organization – we might be prompted to ask if the text and its authors are cause or consequence, agent or symptom, of contemporary organization? This confusion of text and context and the reversal of our usual expectations of cause and effect can be explained in the following way: before reading Buchanan and Huczynski we may not perceive or see the humour that exists in organization. As we read and study their text we begin to appreciate its ubiquity in workplaces and organizations and its multi-faceted nature. In work organization we then begin to respond to the comedic aspects of organization, and we may even learn to participate and even how to introduce and manage humour in organization. Even if we only laugh alongside others at a joke, we encourage its repetition; but as many have begun to recognize, the power of the text is more potent and extensive than this (see Westwood and Linstead 2001) – more like an agent of reality-making than a second order derivation that merely represents a well-formed reality that pre-exists textual enactment.

In many ways the text replicates a number of features that it intends to talk about; more specifically we can see how the text resembles a classic Weberian bureaucracy or a Taylorist mass production assembly plant. Knowledge is subdivided into highly discrete and specialized areas – or 'departments' – and with its endless definitions, summaries and bullet points, it turns knowledge into convenient 'nuggets of information' that can be easily stored and recalled for the highly instrumental purposes of examination and accreditation. At the same time, this iron-cage of bureaucracy seems to be a thinly veiled disguise for what is more evidently a gluttonous riot of multi-coloured textual and stylistic display that adorns and puts to work an assembly and juxtaposition of heterogeneous and even contradictory narratives of organization. Looking more like the stills of a movie rush or an internet website than an academic book, the text speaks in multiple voices and in places with a forked tongue, if not with its tongue firmly placed in the side of its cheek. With their seemingly infinite archive of text and resource Buchanan and Huczynski spin tales and perform routines like ringmasters of the fantastic. Combining citation and quotation, soliloquy and dialogue, the authors cut and paste, stitch and weave, parody and pastiche. There is something for everyone here. Although this is mass-market product one can find allusions and references to the work of Foucault and Derrida; there are conspiracy theories, cabbalistic intimations, mission statements and discussions of *Star Trek*, space invaders and the prospect that we might live in (an) alien/ation.

'That's another fine mess you've gotten me into'

Our suspicions that something is amiss are perhaps first raised when we encounter that abyssal moment when 'organizational behaviour' enters the text as glossary item, and, what is perhaps more worrying, summarized in little more than 1½ lines (Huczynski and Buchanan 2001: 884). The book seems to contain and reduce itself to only 19 words. 'Organizational behaviour' includes 'organizational behaviour' as one of its components. It is somehow subject *and* object, container *and* contained. At this moment the text seems to waver on the hinge of a possible self-reflexive or infinite regress. Like that fabled evening when Scheherazade begins to narrate the tale of a woman condemned to tell stories to the King in lieu of her own life (Borges 1941), the occurrence of the word 'dictionary' in the dictionary, or when Quixote begins to learn of the book that recounts the exploits of Quixote (see Foucault 1970), the opposition of container and contained begins to lose its stability, and the terms their definition. The text seems to want to contain itself – evident in those moments where the subject of organizational behaviour struggles or threatens to become a mere object of analysis, included as a subcomponent inventory of itself. There are other moments of self-reference, increasingly extreme and surreal. 'Organization behaviour' is a key concept seemingly contained within the prologue (p. 1), 'learning' is a learning objective of the chapter on learning and, most bizarre of all, the authors explain that the wearing of Buchanan's own bright red and yellow Scottish family tartan is an example of a personality type who is 'preoccupied with their own ideas and feelings' and 'worry more about their self-presentation than their performance' (Huczynski and Buchanan 2001: 164). At this stage we suspect that the codicil which tells us that the author does not wear the tartan is a case of he doth protest too much.

This boundaryless, all-consuming, self-consuming text is a marvel of *monstrous* proportions. The relatively well-known paradoxes of organization behaviour identified in the text – the Hawthorne effect (p. 283), or the curious 'pre-arrival stage of socialisation' (p. 634), for example – simply offer an apprenticeship into these more structural or profound, ontological paradoxes and confusions opened up and circulated by the text. It is perhaps little surprise, then, that subject to this structural dissemination, the text of Buchanan and Huczysnki becomes increasingly surreal and indulges in wild organizational misbehaviour. We read about Bandler and Grinder's *The Structure of Magic* and their publication of *Frogs into Princes*. Henry Alexander Murray's 'Thematic Apperception Test' introduces us to Blacky the dog and his family and friends, the mysterious 'CAT 1949', 'James Bond-like tasks' and the house-tree people (see O'Doherty and Case 2003). We are undoubtedly entering strange dimensions of organization: like those infamous Tlonists brought to our attention by Borges, we might henceforth suspect that the world of 'adhocracy', the 'anchor and adjustment heuristic', the 'availability heuristic' and 'balanced scorecards', 'superleaders', 'vertical loading factors' and 'communigrams' are all being willed into life by conspirators and agents of this shadowy planet of 'hucbuc' (O'Doherty and Case 2003).

One may also worry that there is no escape from this world-making conspiracy. Huczynksi and Buchanan are seemingly ubiquitous; hucbuc plans its conquest in a number of ways, some more surreptitious and covert than others. The text comes in a variety of shapes and sizes and can be customized to suit all needs – sold separately, part of a 'multi-pack' or 'value pack',[3] the text is variously published with a teacher's manual, instructor's handbook and overhead projector acetates. Students and lecturers are now provided with a website that includes downloadable PowerPoint slides, extra *Financial Times* articles, class exercise debriefs, something resembling an avatar who acts like a so-called 'syllabus manager' – someone, for example, 'that will build and host your very own course web page' (Buchanan and Huczynksi 2003: p. xvi) – and a 'user's club chat-room' (www.booksites.net/hucbuc). Adding to this lurking sense of paranoia and conspiracy, an online virtual newsletter called 'ORBIT' circulates, rather like the emails of a viral marketing campaign, from which it seems impossible to escape – or to escape and return to something we might recognize as earth. In tandem with user profiling, the extensive network of Pearson representatives (the publishers), the virtual surveillance performed by cookies injected in your hard-drive, and the rather shadowy and sinister activities of a 'syllabus manager', it might appear that, once sampled, you can never escape: the text infiltrates itself into your very being whilst becoming mutant, multiple and self-generating. It is possible that after this journey through hucbuc you may even forget who you were before you entered its sinister world; that there might be no escape seems to be confirmed by what the authors themselves say about the text:

> Eating a pizza in a restaurant, joining a queue at a theme park, returning a faulty product to a store, arguing with a colleague at work, taking a holiday job in a factory, watching a movie or reading a novel – are all experiences that can be related to the material in this book.
>
> (Huczynski and Buchanan 2001: p. xix)

Magnificent! A triumph. There is a subtle pedagogic strategy at play here, no doubt. The movement that takes the reader through humour, self-reflexivity and self-parody, to then gently introduce the absurd and the surreal, before developing the sense of paranoia and panic, is one of the most subtle textual orchestrations in organization behaviour today. Working with the 'logic of excess' (O'Doherty and Rehn 2006), it is a movement or transformation that ultimately takes us from behaviour to misbehaviour. By way of the burlesque, of exaggeration and the grotesque, our Laurel and Hardy of organization behaviour draw us into a veritable 'theatre of cruelty' (Artaud 1958) that provides a space (or, more accurately, a 'space-ing') within which we can most effectively seek understanding and participation in the work of contemporary organization. We are actually made to become characters in this absurd dramatization through a whole series of exercises that, despite appearances, amounts to a veritable regimen of self-cultivation equivalent to that sense of the ancient Greek art of stylization that Foucault identifies as the 'ascesis' (Foucault 1990). Consider the 'Ringelmann effect' exercise (Huczynski and Buchanan 2001: 373), for example, a 'chapter exercise' designed, apparently, to introduce the concept of 'social loafing'. Students are requested to come to the front of the class in order to 'produce some shouts (raaaaaah!)'. 'Shouters', as they are known, are asked to generate this sound for five seconds, and then again to complete the exercise in groups of one, two, four and six. Are they serious? The briefing for the chapter exercise, designed to simulate the assembly line (p. 444), is simply a delight of mischief and subversion.

In most cases the time allocations allowed for the class exercises are hopelessly inadequate. One can only imagine the confusion and disarray that descends the classroom as some new university lecturer attempts to arrange the students into 'syndicates with three to five members each' to 'design a practical, realistic behaviour modification programme' (p. 139). Behaviour modification! There is surely some irony here; but it is written with such deft and effortless grace that nothing seems amiss. Not only must the lecturer ensure that the students are prepared and have read the 'Making modifications' brief, that they are familiar with the 'behaviour modification' approach – and note that hucbuc offers no measurement tool or guidance so that the tutor might be in a position to make these assessments – but they must also assume responsibility for the normal pressures and strains of classroom management: what to do about absentees; late arrivals; those who have to leave early; special needs students who must have 25 or 50 per cent additional time; those students who don't have the text, etc. … it is simply a case of another fine mess you've gotten me into.

Conclusion

In this chapter we set out to explore some of the characters and situations of comedy and laughter and found that humour might be a safety valve in organizations, one that remains critical to the maintenance of routine and order. We also discovered that laughter marks the limits of subjectivity and identity. Through its transgressive qualities the comedic opens up a space in organization from where it is possible to contend with and understand important features of contemporary social relations including: the apparent absurdity and tragedy of much of the activity which takes place in organization today; the ambiguity and undecidability of phenomena that outline an edge between the serious and the ridiculous; and the despair that always threatens to eliminate a sense of purpose and meaning. There is also an entropic logic and tragic fate to humour where the comic is often found standing on the margins of the social – a lonely clown-like figure, a pariah or scapegoat.

As the text developed it seemed to get increasingly out of bounds, difficult to swallow or manage, but this seemed to coincide with the opening up of a zone of 'indiscernibility' where philosophy and humour began to merge in the very writing and where organization began to resemble the tragic fate of character. The 'funny bone' of organization we found was that the comedic exposes and *delimits* subjectivity to help reveal a shadow of ignorance or underdevelopment that remains a necessary aporia in the constitution of a 'modern subject', providing for the possibility of subjective consistency and identity but also rendering this integrity and consistency impossible. However, neither funny, nor serious, this is perhaps the terrain of the Heideggerian 'unfunny' – and the end(s) of the subject as we know it – a situation in which we might owe congratulations to Huczynski and Buchanan for their marvellous comedic subversion of organizational behaviour in which the modern subject has so far been incarcerated. As we tried to read this text we even began to resemble the figure of Charlie Chaplin – strangely articulated, shouting and dancing, on the brink of breakdown, and increasingly stressed in terms of our own organizational integrity – and as the chapter progressed we nearly wet ourselves as we discovered how laughter always threatens to over-flow, to over-run itself and become excessive.

The academic textbook has long been the butt of student jokes and humour, but today there is more serious comedy at play in the textual productions of the university scholar. It seems that we have all arrived in 'hucbuc'. With its retinue of impossible class and tutorial exercises, reading Huczynksi and Buchanan soon leads us to doubt the authenticity of all those fabulous inventions of theory (and) practice that circulate in organization behaviour. Who can now trust the so-called 'Minnesota Multiphasic Personality Inventory', 'PESTLE analysis', 'the transactional leader' or the 'Vroom-Yetton decision tree (group problem)'? At this stage, with delirium and vertigo setting in, we can no longer tell if these are genuine concepts, whether or how they are supposed to work in practice, or even if they are recognized as 'real', forming part of the official world of organization and management. Even the relatively well-accepted language of 'hard and soft human resource management', 'total quality management' or 'the learning organization' no longer sounds quite so innocent or convincing. Entering hucbuc we discover organization on the blink.

The sense of confusion and disarray generated as a result of completing the battery of tests and exercises provided by Huczynski and Buchanan suspends the student of organization behaviour somewhere between comedy and tragedy, between the scream of Munch and the tears of the circus clown. Through laughter we have gotten out of bounds. Our theoretical explorations of subjectivity and humour, however, seem clunky in comparison with the performative effects of Huczynski and Buchanan that we explored in the second half of the chapter. Huczynski and Buchanan provide an invaluable service to the student of organization and management today. With all their athletic and intellectual exercises, springboards, recaps, revisions, home-viewings and applications, we can at least be certain of possessing the necessary health and vigour required to navigate the absurdity, meaninglessness and despair of contemporary organization. Or at least, it will help us to fit right in, suddenly reduced to nothing, dissolved in the tears of laughter and crying in organization on the blink (wink, wink ☺): from blank to blink (and back again), in other words. It seems obscurity and the shallow meet in the last refuge of the serious, to paraphrase Wilde. And that's another FINE mess you've gotten me into.

Notes

1 Thanks to Peter Case and Theo Vurdubakis for the helpful suggestions in revising this paper. The editors of this volume have also been patient and understanding with the ambition and adventure essayed in this chapter.
2 Try getting off this online newsletter that circulates to users offering the latest add-ons and updates to the basic Huczynksi and Buchanan model!
3 See <http://www.amazon.co.uk/exec/obidos/ASIN/027367658X/qid%3D1142246441/202-8707255-8423050>.

References

Ackroyd, S. and Thompson, P. (1999) *Organizational Misbehaviour*, London: Sage.

Artaud, A. (1958) *The Theatre and its Double*, New York: Grove Press.

Bataille, G. (1994) 'The Labyrinth', in A. Stoekl (ed.), *Visions of Excess: Selected Writings, 1927–1939*, tr. A. Stoekl with C. R. Lovitt and D. M. Leslie Jr, Minneapolis, MN: University of Minnesota Press.

Bazin, A. (1985) *Essay on Chaplin*, New Haven, CT: University of New Haven Press.

Benjamin, W. (1936) 'The work of art in the age of mechanical reproduction', in *Illuminations*, tr. H. Arendt, New York: Random House, 1985 edn.

Bergson, H. (1911) *Creative Evolution*, New York: Henri Holt.

Borges, L. (1941) 'The garden of forking paths', translation of 'El jardin de senderos que se bifurcan'. Reprinted in Borges, L. (1962) *Ficciones*, pp. 15–104, New York: Grove Press,

Bratton, J. and A. Featherstone (2006) *The Victorian Clown*, Cambridge: Cambridge University Press.

Brown, C. (2003) 'Goodbye cruel world', *Guardian* (25 Jan.).

Buchanan, D. and Huczynksi, A. (1985) *Organizational Behaviour: An Introductory Text*, Hemel Hempstead: Prentice Hall.

Buchanan, D. and Huczynksi, A. (1991) *Organizational Behaviour: An Introductory Text*, 2nd edn, Hemel Hempstead: Prentice Hall.

Buchanan, D. and Huczynksi, A. (1997) *Organizational Behaviour: An Introductory Text*, 3rd edn, Hemel Hempstead: Prentice Hall.

Buchanan, D. and Huczynksi, A. (2003) *Organizational Behaviour: An Introductory Text*, 5th edn, London: Pearson Education.

Cohen, S. and Taylor, L. (1978) *Escape Attempts: The Theory and Practice of Resistance to Everyday Life*, Harmondsworth: Pelican.

Collinson, D. (1988) 'Engineering humour: masculinity, joking and conflict in shopfloor relations', *Organization Studies*, 9(2): 181–99.

Collinson, D. (1992) *Managing the Shopfloor*, Berlin: de Gruyter.

Cooper, D. E. (1990) *Existentialism*, Oxford: Blackwell.

Critchley, S. (2002) *On Humour*, London: Routledge.

Darwin, C. (1872) *The Expression of Emotions in Man and Animals*, London: John Murray.

Deleuze, G. and Guattari, F. (1987) *A Thousand Plateaus: Capitalism and Schizophrenia*, Minneapolis, MN: University of Minnesota Press.

Derrida, J. (2005) *The Politics of Friendship*, London: Verso.

Douglas, M. (1975) *Implicit Meanings: Selected Essays in Anthropology*, London: Routledge.

Foucault, M. (1970) *The Order of Things: An Archaeology of the Human Sciences*, New York: Random House.

Foucault, M. (1981) *The History of Sexuality*, vol. 1, *An Introduction*, London: Pelican.

Foucault, M. (1990) *The Care of the Self: The History of Sexuality*, vol. 3, Harmondsworth: Penguin.

Freud, S. (1925) 'Inhibitions, symptoms and anxiety', in *Standard Edition*, vol. 20, pp. 87–179, London: Hogarth Press, 1959 edn.

Griffith, R. D. and Marks, R. (2006) *A Funny Thing Happened on the Way to the Agora Today: A Study of Ancient Humour*, mimeo, Ontario: Queen's University.

Heidegger, M. (1962) *Being and Time*, Oxford: Blackwell.

Huczynksi, A. and Buchanan, D. (2001) *Organizational Behaviour: An Introductory Text*, 4th edn, London: Pearson Education.

Kant, I. (1790) *Critique of Judgement*, tr. J. Meredith, Oxford: Oxford University Press, 1952 edn.

Klossowski, P. (1997) *Nietzsche and the Vicious Circle*, tr. D. Smith, London: Athlone Press.

Kunda, G. (1995) *Engineering Culture: Control and Commitment in a High-Tech Corporation*, Philadelphia, PA: Temple University Press.

Kurtzman, D. (2005) 'Donald Rumsfeld quotes', at <http://politicalhumor.about.com/cs/quotethis/a/rumsfeldquotes.htm>, accessed 11 Dec. 2005.

Lilley, S. (1998) 'Wisdom and understanding? Would you like fries with that? A view from behind the counter', in D. Jary and M. Parker (eds), *The New Higher Education: Issues and Directions for the Post-Dearing University*, pp. 173–84, Stoke-on-Trent: Staffordshire University Press.

Lingis, A. (2004) *Trust*, Minneapolis, MN: University of Minnesota Press.

Lorenz, K. (1963) *On Aggression*, New York: MJF Books.

Lupton, T. (1963) *On the Shopfloor: Two Studies of Workshop Organisation and Output*, Oxford: Pergamon Press.

Mangham, I. and Overington, M. A. (1987) *Organizations as Theatre*, Chichester: Wiley.

Maslow, A. H. (1954) *Motivation and Human Personality*, New York: Harper & Row.

Ngai, S. (2000) 'Stuplimity: shock and boredom in twentieth-century aesthetics', *Postmodern Culture*, 10(2), available at <http://muse.jhu.edu/journals/postmodern_culture/toc/pmc 10.2.html>.

Nietzsche, F. (1974) *The Gay Science*, New York: Random House.

O'Doherty, D. and Case, P. (2003) 'Motorvation: chrysology, mutant offspring (hucbuc), and all that TAT', *Discussion Papers in Management*, 03/13, Exeter: School of Business and Economics.

O'Doherty, D. and Rehn, A. (2006) 'Organization/the logic of excess', *Culture and Organization* (special issue on excess), forthcoming.

Roy, D. (1958) 'Banana time: job satisfaction and informal interaction', *Human Organisation*, 18(1): 158–61.

Sartre, J. P. (1939) *Le Mur*, Paris: Gallimard; tr. publ. as *The Wall, and Other Stories*, preface by Jean-Louis Curtis, New York: New Directions, 1948.

Spencer, H. (1860) 'The physiology of laughter', *MacMillan's Magazine*, 1 (March): 395–420.

Starkey, K. and McKinlay, A. (1994) 'Managing for Ford', *Sociology*, 28(4): 975–90.

Weick, K. (1979) *The Social Psychology of Organizing*, Reading, MA: Addison-Wesley.
Westwood, R. and Linstead, S. (eds) (2001) *The Language of Organization*, London: Sage.
Williams, Z. (2003) 'The final irony', *Guardian* (28 June).
Wood, M. (1998) 'Post paranoid', *London Review of Books*, 20(3).

Chapter 11

The comedy of ethics

The New York four, the duty of care and organizational bystanding

Stephen Linstead

You cannot be a bystander and be guilty. Bystanders are by definition innocent. That is the nature of bystanding.

(Jackie Chiles, character in Seinfeld, #169: 'The Finale',
14 May 1998)

We should incidentally be unable to imagine what goes on in the secret depths of the minds of the bystanders if we could not call on our own personal ... experiences, if only childhood ones.

(Bataille 1986: 16, cited in Clarkson 1996: 30)

In the hour-long or two-part last episode of the record-breaking US sitcom Seinfeld (#169: 'The Finale', 14 May 1998) the four main characters – Jerry Seinfeld, George Costanza, Cosmo Kramer and Elaine Benes – are granted a trip to Paris in the NBC company jet. This treat is a compensation for the studio having kept the pilot of Jerry's show on the shelf for five years before accepting it, as a result of organizational politics. The plane, due to an onboard accident precipitated by Kramer trying to remove some water lodged in his ear whilst swimming, is forced to put down in a field outside the fictional town of Latham, Massachusetts. As they wait for the plane to be repaired they walk into the town and witness a fat man being robbed of his money and car at gunpoint on the other side of the street.

Kramer videos the event. Jerry comments: 'There goes the money for the lipo [suction]' and holding his cellphone as the car is stolen, says 'Aw, that's a shame' and calls NBC for news on the plane repair rather than the police for help. Elaine observes: 'You see the great thing about robbing a fat guy is the easy getaway. They can't really chase ya'. George opines 'He's actually doing him a favour. There's less money to buy food'.

When confronted by a police officer they discover that Latham has a 'Good Samaritan' by-law that requires anyone within the jurisdiction 'to help or assist anyone in danger as long as it is reasonable to do so'. The four are incredulous,

George inquiring, 'Why would we want to help someone? That's what nuns and Red Cross workers are for'. Even their lawyer is puzzled, arguing, 'You don't have to help anybody. That's what this country is all about'. Nevertheless, after a trial that involves the appearance of many minor characters from the previous seasons as negative 'character' witnesses, the four are found guilty of 'selfishness, self-absorption, immaturity and greed' and, as the judge hyperbolically comments, a 'callous indifference and utter disregard for everything that is good and decent' that has 'rocked the foundation on which this society is built'.

For some commentators (e.g. Epperson 2000: 164 n. 1) the final episode of the show 'struck a false note'. For such critics, for the four principal characters – christened 'the New York Four' by the media in the episode – to face a charge of moral indifference was false because throughout the series they had regularly involved themselves in others' lives, being anything but indifferent. They had frequently tried to help others in their relationships, personal dealings, businesses and commercial projects with inadvertently disastrous consequences, and had constantly consulted each other and debated about what constituted the right course of action in every new set of circumstances each faced, even if sometimes this discussion was about manners rather than morals. Self-absorbed, superficial, immature, greedy upper west side New Yorkers they might have been – but that wasn't all they were.

Fans of the show knew that all the characters were morally flawed, but not necessarily uncaring or indifferent towards others – this particular brand of eccentricity was one of the qualities that endeared them to their audiences and indeed each other (McMahon 2000: 106–8). But what this tragi-comic last episode did was turn some assumptions on their head in the way that comedy usually does in its customary redeployment of the everyday (Garcia 2000) and reveal that we are all deeply vulnerable to narrative. When our lives are rescripted by others, especially those in authority, how can we come up with a persuasive alternative story, especially when we were just improvising moral judgements from episode to episode and situation to situation, with no real moral compass? When this rescripting happens, how do you cope with being decentred from your own life-history, rendered a marginal and erroneous notation to a broader setting, even it's only temporary? For Jerry, the mere prospect of eating breakfast cereal with only half his usual serving of milk is appalling: 'This is the hardest thing I've ever had to do'.

Keeping these questions in mind, it's also worth reminding ourselves with respect to this episode that a) it is comedic fiction; b) it had to provide the producers with an excuse for running a 'clip show' from the whole series; and c) despite the way that the court case is constructed, character witnesses are generally not admissible in law and certainly for a whole case to be built round a series of them is absurd. We do need to suspend a good bit of our natural disbelief. But even though it might not be entirely fair in the real world to condemn individuals solely on the basis of character, and certainly not on the sort of evidence presented in the final episode, we can still profit from reflecting on whether and how far we *should* be condemned for our lack of positive action with regard to others. How far does and should criminality extend in social relations? Is it really a crime just to stand on the sidelines and not get involved? Does ignoring the other ultimately impose a cost on the self?

Humour, perhaps most pointedly since Bergson, has had an acknowledged moral dimension; indeed comedy can be considered a moral enterprise in itself. But as Buckley (2005) explores exhaustively, morality extends beyond comedy and laughter is not always morally defensible. What this episode of *Seinfeld* does is put a number of issues into play that question the relationship between comedy and morality in a way not really possible in any other medium with such economy nor with such resonances. If comedy is a language game, and it could be argued that most comedy is a play with language forms, then the four friends are certainly guilty of responding to the plastic possibilities of linguistic representation in the situation they witness. They play their inwardly focused game of comedy at the expense of the victim, preferring witticisms to witnessing. But whether they are callous or just coping with their anxieties, they themselves soon become the victims of language as they are arraigned in a jurisprudential argot they find difficult to understand. Their actions are then publicly constructed through the languages of others that run at variance to their own interpretations of their intentions, motivations and feelings. In this way, although the incident begins in irony, the snowballing comedy rapidly becomes post-ironic as the ironies are layered thick and fast and smart-ass implodes into sociopath (Linstead and Collinson 2005).

So this episode of *Seinfeld* illustrates how comedy, whilst suspending some of the constraints of reality within its frame, also accelerates aspects of that reality, and in doing so not only produces something funny, but something, I will argue, that is capable of engaging with moral questions that have troubled and indeed continue to trouble philosophy itself. One such issue is that of bystanding. But before we interrogate the nature of bystanding more deeply, we perhaps should establish what it has to do with organizations and how *Seinfeld* connects to any organized dimension of the problem. After all, isn't an organization of bystanders a contradiction in terms?

Moral harassment

It shouldn't be too hard to imagine the situation – let's say it's an academic department but it could be any kind of work unit really. One of the workgroup disagrees with a proposal of the Head of Department, and in group discussions everyone agrees that something must be done about it, and supports the member. This collective support is voiced on several occasions and individually colleagues are equally supportive, so the member decides on the strength of this to raise the matter at the next formal meeting of the whole department. Meanwhile, the Head of Department has had one-to-one discussions with all the rest of the group in their own offices and done a series of side deals – support for promotion, reduced workload, additional conference support or similar – as well as giving colleagues the impression that everyone else has already expressed agreement with his view, which they had not. Meanwhile, the one dissenter has not had a personal interview in this way but has occasionally been summoned to the head's office – to have career enhancing responsibilities reduced, to be discouraged from seeking promotion, to have their workload increased with time-consuming and unattractive tasks whilst attractive and interesting ones go elsewhere, to be given responsibility for a politically problematic and dead-end project, to have conference or research funding reduced or receive negative interpretations of acceptable performance feedback. On the day of the meeting, the member speaks up forcefully, but none of the group supports them, remaining silent. The member is totally exposed and feels betrayed as the HoD makes the most of the humiliation. The member may perhaps be further bullied over the coming months and will eventually leave the group, who still feel guilty and sheepish, but take the promotions and inducements on offer, probably within the year. If the member stays, he or she may be dismissed anyway if employment conditions allow it – and some organizations, including some academic institutions, are willing to pay an expensive settlement to get an individual to go, in order to reassert control.

Sound familiar? This scenario contains at least two phenomena that should be. The first has recently been termed 'moral harassment' by employment researchers and is argued to be on the rise in ways that evade those situations normally captured by anti-discrimination legislation. The term was first coined by French therapist Marie-France Hirigoyen who claims from her research that 8–9 per cent of people are affected by bullying at work (Hirigoyen 2005). What many researchers now also include in their definition and claim to be on the increase is what they term imposed 'inactive occupation' – starvation of work, information and interaction, and cutting out of all communication loops, which despite its subtlety can be as damaging to the psyche of the victim over time as more direct and visibly aggressive victimization (Fuller 2004: 11). Hirigoyen found that the initiating conditions for the behaviour frequently lie in the inability of the narcissistic and controlling employer to tolerate talented employees whose contribution is valuable to the organization but who make it clear that they have other options in the labour market and expect their voice to be heard and taken into account in the workplace.

While some employers treat their personnel like children, others treat them like things – to be used at will.... . [W]here creativity is involved, the attack on the person is even more direct: any initiative or innovation on their part is destroyed. Employers try to prevent the departure of useful or indispensable employees; they mustn't be allowed to think the situation through or feel capable of working somewhere else. They must be led to believe they're only worth their present job. If they resist, they're isolated. They are denied any kind of contact: eye contact, greeting in the hall, or a deaf ear turned to their suggestions. Hurtful and unkind remarks come next, and if these prove insufficient, emotional violence appears.

(Hirigoyen 2005: 73–4)

Whilst the above example illustrates the tendency for this behaviour to escalate, Hirigoyen found extreme examples of the behaviour going unchecked, being then exacerbated by the increased resistance of the employee, and producing even more intense vicitimization from the employer. This can stop short of nothing less than the psychological and, on occasion, even the physical destruction of the employee.

Outright hostility later replaces latent ill-will or malevolence if the victim reacts and tries to rebel. This is the phase of emotional abuse that has been called 'psychoterror.' At this stage, any means or methods will be used, sometimes including physical violence, to destroy the designated victim. This can lead to psychical annihilation or suicide. The attacker has now lost sight of any potential benefits to the company and focuses only on his victim's downfall.

(Hirigoyen 2005: 74)

This might seem somewhat exceptional, but evidence that it happens and extends to the highest levels can been seen from the case of Dr David Kelly, a specialist in nuclear weapons in the UK who had advised the United Nations on the possible presence of weapons of mass destruction (WMDs) in Iraq. Kelly made an anonymous statement to a journalist, Andrew Gilligan, who reported it briefly by telephone interview at 6.07 a.m. in the 29 May 2003 broadcast of the BBC Radio 4 *Today* programme. The reported comment was to the effect that in September 2002 the government appeared to have edited favourably, or 'sexed up', the Ministry of Defence dossier on WMDs that suggested that Saddam Hussein had the capability of launching an attack on Britain in 45 minutes. This had been one of the main public justifications for British intervention in the second Gulf War in February 2003. Hounded by the Government through the Downing Street office of the obsessive director of communications Alistair

Campbell, the MoD made public the source of the information, although Gilligan and the BBC had refused, thus exposing Kelly to intense political, media and personal pressure. Under extreme psychological stress, professional attacks from high level and attempts at discreditation, utterly isolated and abandoned by his employer, a despairing but innocent Kelly committed suicide on 9 July 2003 – a scandal that initiated the review that led to the *Hutton Report*.

From bystanding to organizational bystanding

The second phenomenon I have termed 'organizational bystanding', where we know and may even witness the sort of injustice or bullying entailed by moral harassment, but do nothing about it. The classic study of the social psychology of bystanding was undertaken by Darley and Latané (1968a, 1968b; Latané and Darley 1968, 1976) with their study of the murder of Kitty Genovese, a young woman who was brutally beaten to death in a public place in New York over a 30-minute period. Some 38 people either heard or watched from their windows but only one called the police, and then after some considerable delay. Darley and Latané (1968a, 1968b, 1969; Latané and Darley 1968, 1970) attempted an analysis of how the bystanders accounted for their non-intervention, although there was some controversy arising from the original newspaper report as to how many of the 38 could hear or see events sufficiently well to be fully aware of what was taking place. In subsequent studies and a book they explored 'bystander apathy' through laboratory experiments that collectively rank with Milgram's 'obedience to authority' studies in the exploration of non-intervention. Clarkson (1996) summarizes these and other studies and identifies a number of common rationalizations for non-intervention.

One of the key findings of this work appears to be that the presence of others makes it harder to take action or to define the situation as one in which action is required, especially where the rapid processing of information is critical. The relative unfamiliarity of the situation is also a factor. Perhaps oddly, this tendency seems to be reversed in decision-making groups where decisions to act are made and debated over time, where 'risky shift' indicates a propensity for more extreme decisions to be made collectively than by individuals. Significant is that there is a focal event that requires a time-critical decision, or one that can be made, or made to appear, so. Skilled moral harassers are accomplished in the informal manipulation of background discussions towards extremes, with key groups or subgroup members, whilst pressing for decisions formally that push non-key or non-involved group members into bystander apathy. 'What did we just do?' is a frequent comment after such meetings.

Drawing on the work of Latané and Darley and Clarkson we can identify differences between bystanding in an emergency and organizational bystanding.

First, bystanders such as those in the Genovese case and particularly those in the experiments are a collective only by virtue of being in the same place at the same time. They have no particular connection either to the victim, the perpetrator or each other. In an organization this is certainly not the case, although the strength, saliency and value of the connections will vary. Second, bystanding in an emergency is temporally bounded by one event; in organizations it is usually a series of often connected events that may escalate in seriousness. Where the consequences of bystanding in an emergency are discrete, in an organization they are continuous. Consequently, there is a greater degree of reflexivity implied in organizational bystanding. Third, events in organizations may be even less clearly defined than in emergencies, although the research demonstrates that even apparently straightforward situations can be problematic to define. Finally, bystanders are not a language community, and are likely to share no common argot, whereas organizational members to a greater or lesser degree will be co-participants in a language game of organizing. Clarkson (1996: 76–7) argues that gossiping, which is an inauthentic form of communication as it does not involve the subjects of the gossip, is a form of bystanding or non-engagement. Gossip and rumour, as Noon and Delbridge (1993) have demonstrated, are important means of both organizing and resisting organization.

The *Seinfeld* episode offers a useful bridge between bystanding in an emergency and organizational bystanding. First, the characters are known to each other and have close relationships, although neither the victim nor the perpetrator are known to them and the setting and situation are unfamiliar. Second, although the emergency is bounded as an event, the law sees such events as having connections and the prosecution seeks to make even further connections to the lives of the NY4, 'organizing' them into a text that is analogous to the continuous and motivated bystanding found in organizations. Third, when these extensions are made, the definitional problems are magnified, indeed the four are stunned by the unforeseen possibilities. Finally, the four characters are gossiping as they are bystanding. They are caught up in their own game of wit, and are not responsive to those outside their text but reflected in it, transposed and reorganized.

The cautionary notes sounded already notwithstanding, it is fairly easy to accept the argument that assault or murder is wrong and there is not too much difficulty in reaching the conclusion that one or the other of these things is taking place when we witness it. Yet whilst we could easily argue that moral harassment in organizations is wrong, it is not easy to capture and stop it – indeed it is perhaps only the intervention of colleagues that could truly be effective in these cases. So is it therefore wrong to be an organizational bystander? Is there a moral imperative to be an organizational Good Samaritan? Should members of the MoD have spoken up for Kelly?

The Kelly affair not only demonstrates moral harassment, but also illustrates how it is underpinned by bystanding. After the inquiry into Kelly's death was completed, the *Hutton Report*, widely and scornfully regarded as a whitewash, was critical of the BBC in not performing adequate checks on the quality of reporting by Gilligan. This the BBC Director-General, Greg Dyke, supporting the internal investigations carried out by the Corporation, denied. When the report was released (although slightly before it was published) in January 2004, again under pressure from Campbell's office, and although they had no need to do so, the BBC Governors led by the Deputy Chairman declined to support their Director-General, and indeed the Chairman, Gavyn Davies, who were forced to resign. Not everyone in the BBC was a bystander in this, although almost all the Governors were. They and the Government were publicly embarrassed when 6,000 BBC employees took to the streets in protest in an emotional show of support (Dyke 2004: chs 1, 10, 12, 13 and 14 for a full and fascinating managerial and organizational perspective on events). Yet although an unprecedented number of people chose not to remain bystanders in the face of this injustice, their action in this case was of no avail. The politics of hierarchy ensures that *parrhesis* – the speaking of truth to power – is never easy nor without risk, or necessarily effective, yet it is simultaneously a responsibility of both individuals *and* communities (Foucault 2001).

The reason for this is that bystanding was already endemic in the system that produced the harassment. We can go further: organizational bystanding is a necessary condition of a context in which moral harassment is successful and sustained. A similar observation has been used as a learning tool in the training of torturers where systematic acts of evil are to be performed. Inductees are taken through a process of desensitization and dehumanization in order to carry these acts out, and bystanding is the first step in their training. Enforced witnessing and enforced silence makes bystanders complicit in the acts witnessed and hence part of their legitimation (Clarkson 1996: 29; Conroy 2000; Staub 1990). Here, as in organizations, bystanding is not neutral, but reflects non-involvement as a form of involvement, a dissolution of any resolution to resist, and a prelude to active involvement. In the David Kelly affair, the consequences for Dyke, the bullying reported by Hirigoyen and our fictional case, bystanding is similarly a necessary condition for moral harassment to take place. In all these cases, people see something they know is wrong and do nothing about it, thus perpetuating it.

The moral questions of bystanding are raised explicitly in the last episode of *Seinfeld*. In what follows I will look at the context of legal approaches to bystanding and the questions occasioned by *Seinfeld*, both in the last episode and the series more generally, using contributions to Irwin (2000) as a guide. Whilst these authors present a rich view of the range of philosophical resonances of

Seinfeld the series, they do not engage with any of the more recent contributions of continental philosophers such as Foucault, Derrida or Lévinas and this chapter will attempt therefore to extend the discussion in this direction and bring the philosophy applied up to date – in ways which I argue are in fact already captured by the acute observations of the *Seinfeld* episode itself.

Good Samaritan laws

It was in the aftermath of the death in a car crash of the UK's Princess Diana that the idea of a Good Samaritan law was brought to the attention of those of us unaware that such laws existed. Indeed the Diana tragedy is cited in the *Seinfeld* episode as the inspiration for the fictional Latham law. Articles 223–6 of the French Penal Code were invoked against the paparazzi at the scene of the Paris accident for witnessing by photographing rather than assisting the injured. The Articles, first enacted in 1941, translate into:

- Anyone who, by their own actions, if there is no risk to themselves or another, can prevent a crime or physical harm and refuses to help shall be punished by five years imprisonment and a 500,000 franc fine.
- Anyone who refuses to come to the aid of a person in danger, if there is no risk to themselves or another, shall be punished by five years imprisonment and a 500,000 franc fine. (Translation in Schick 2000: 185)

Perhaps surprisingly, similar laws exist or have existed in several countries – notably those not based on English common law with its emphasis on the rights of the individual to act in their own self-interest. These include Portugal (1867), the Netherlands (1881), Italy (1889, 1930), Russia (1903–17), Turkey (1926), Norway (1902), Denmark (1930), Poland (1932), Germany (1935, 1953), Romania (1938), Hungary (1948, 1961), Czechoslovakia (1950), Belgium (1961), Switzerland (various) and in the United States Minnesota, Wisconsin and Vermont have them despite the basis of US law in English common law (Schick 2000: 185). The penalties may not be as severe as in the French system but the principle is clear – many parts of the developed world consider it not just a virtue to help one's neighbour, but consider not to do so to be a crime.

But helping to rescue another person from drowning, for example, is not the same as helping a person who is being mugged because there is a *social* dimension to the danger that the victim faces. The Other here is not solely the person in trouble, but a third person who has put the victim in their predicament, who has motivations of their own, and may even have the assistance of even more sinister others. We do not have the assurance that the situation as it presents itself is, in fact, the full reality of the situation: the bystander literature deals with some of these social dimensions (for example, the effect of the presence of others on intervention, the apparent social category of the victim, and the fear of looking socially foolish if a wrong interpretation has been made and acted upon). There is ambiguity over whether we have Weber's required adequacy with respect to meaning – is the mugger, for example, merely seeking to reclaim something that the apparent victim stole from them earlier, and thus redress a previous wrong? Most social situations unfold within streams of meaning that intersect and unless there are clear signs that a situation is self-contained we would naturally hesitate to make sure that we had grasped the correct potential stream of intentionality. The existence of an intelligible social system with formal and informal rules to help provide a grid of meaning for interpretation and options for action is therefore of critical importance. If the situation seems unfamiliar to us we might be puzzled as to what is happening; if it is horrible or surprising to us we might wonder whether what appears to be happening really is happening, and again hesitate in intervening; if we are naturally suspicious, we might expect a practical joke (given the number of comedy reality TV programmes currently in existence) or a criminal set-up of some kind. In all of these circumstances the right to assistance is rendered problematic because the definition of the situation is not clear, and a reasonable course of action in admittedly exceptional circumstances is not automatically generated nor easy to discern. The point is that victims, muggers and bystanders do not prepossess or announce their status unequivocally – they are part of systems that are both socio-legal and semiotic and need to be decoded and interpreted in the flow of action, and whose meaning emerges accordingly. Such situations may in fact only be accurately or adequately defined retrospectively some time after the event, which means that a reasonable course of action has to be determined in the light of the information available at the time and the anticipated consequences – a problem that is hermeneutic, sociological and political as well as moral and ethical. Time pressures may also mean that the window of possibility for helpful intervention may be far too small for even a fraction of the information to be processed anyway if the action is not to be too late.

Derrida (1997a, 1997b, 2000; Derrida and Ferraris 2001; Dufourmantelle and Derrida 2000) follows Lévinas in challenging the convention that selves can be viewed as atomistic, acting upon each other. For Lévinas self is only recognized as self at the moment of its distinction from the Other, which means that the existence of the Other, and the alien knowledge and experience that represents, is prior to the existence of self and occasions the definition of self as a response to its own existence. Potential power/knowledge differences are motivated at this point although not yet revealed, and for Lévinas in particular the choice of how to respond lies between generosity, or embracing the other as guest in a spirit of sharing, and hostility, where the object is to dominate if not destroy the other. Derrida formulates this as the problem of 'hostipitality' – host and hostility being terms derived from the same etymological root. The Other is thus simultaneously an inalienable part of self, in originating the mirroring recognition of self, and inalienably other, and different in a way that cannot be appropriated by self. Butler (2005) develops this idea in arguing that there is always part of the self that cannot be revealed, that cannot be accounted for, because we cannot know it – if Other is always inalienably other (radical alterity) and cannot be appropriated, then the possibility of a radical interiority (of the inalienable other within) cannot be discounted. This recognition is haunted by the fact, appreciated by modern thought at least from Kant onwards, that the possibility of radical evil has to be taken into account as 'one can presuppose evil to be subjectively necessary in every human being, even the best' (Kant 1996; Fenves 2001). There is therefore arguably some inalienable element of badness that is irrelevant to personal interest or benefit in all humans that cannot be exorcised entirely. This evil within is other to what self would want to perceive as self, though not identifiable with the social Other, and thus even when it could become an object of consciousness it is often denied or suppressed to the point that self fails to recognize it and cannot therefore reveal it even in a relationship of openness and honesty. Whilst we are familiar on an everyday level with the psychological risks of extending generosity and affection only to be rejected, the long-term risks of spiritual and material generosity being extended only to embrace a radical evil that will damage or destroy the host are far worse. The possibility of such a betrayal haunts all social relationships and is felt most keenly at the heart of our most intimate liaisons, although as Lévinas (1969, 1981, 1987) observes all relationships depend at some point on a leap of faith towards the other. This leap may not be fully blind, as a move towards the Other is always a move towards self, but because of the combination of radical alterity and interior alterity, always has at least a blind spot. As relations unfold, each party is interpreting the Other and adjusting their behaviour and potentially redefining the situation against changes both contextual and immanent, a relation that Habermas and Giddens (Giddens 1976, 1984; Habermas 1987) would regard as the 'double hermeneutic'. The encounter of the New York Four with a seemingly unremarkable street hold-up is therefore not quite so straightforward as it may seem. Although we have little evidence of the event unfolding and it is allowed to define itself as a simple mugging within the episode, it nevertheless introduces the possibility of a high degree of moral complexity that renders even more problematic the demands placed on a legal system that seeks to formalize the personal ethical requirements of dynamic yet systemic social relations, one that Continental philosophy with its indefatigable interrogation of the nature of self and other opens up. Furthermore, where Jerry and the others illustrate intertextuality through their interpretations of the event, they are themselves subjected to further and conflicting intertextualities in the courtroom, where their previous actions and motives are read and reread by others in ways that run quite counter to their own preferred readings of what happened and why in each different situation, cumulating in a rewriting of the character of the NY4 and a definition of their actions in regard to the mugging as immoral and ultimately criminal.

English common law and the right to be left alone vs Samaritanism and the duty to render assistance

As we have suggested, legal systems based on the particular individualism of English common law tend to underpin the principles of business ethics under Western free-market capitalism. Such systems emphasize the protection of individual liberty, the pursuit of one's own self-interest and the right not to be interfered with as long as one does not interfere with, harm others or force them to do something against their will. Individual subjects, in the eyes of the law, become legal agents, defined by a system of rights granted and associated duties imposed to ensure mutual observance and respect for these rights. There are different perspectives customarily taken on how this should be achieved. The libertarian view is that the state apparatus needs to be minimized in order to allow for the maximum exercise of individual freedom, so the right to be left alone must be paramount to allow individuals to exercise the will to choose to assist others or not. It is important to recognize that libertarians are not here arguing against altruistic intervention or assistance, which they might indeed advocate, but for the right to choose how to act without the compulsion of state legislation. In contrast the communitarian view springs from the assumption that a right such as the right to life carries with it the right to the means to live, and therefore carries an obligation from, and reciprocal to, the community that provides it. For communitarians the pursuit of pure self-interest is self-defeating. Nevertheless there remain questions as to whether the giving of assistance is a moral ideal or a moral obligation; whether it is in fact a practical necessity for an efficient and effective society; and the extent to which moral decency can be required of rather than simply desired from individuals.

First, if we defer to the original parable of the Good Samaritan as establishing an appropriate principle, commentators have argued whether Jesus' exhortation to 'go and do thou likewise' constituted an ideal to aim for or an instruction to emulate. Was the Good Samaritan an aspirational role model or an absolute requirement for our behaviour? Whilst it is clear from the parable that we owe others a duty of support that goes further than just simply leaving them alone, it is not clear where the line should be drawn in assisting them.

Second, a more secular argument is that societies simply cannot be successful without some sort of concept of collective interest and a duty of care. These are a practical necessity. As Etzioni (1993: 259–60, cited in Schick 2000: 188) puts it:

> [T]he exclusive pursuit of one's self-interest is not even a good prescription for economic conduct in the market-place: for no social economic political, economic or moral order can survive that way. Some element of caring, sharing or being our brother's keeper is essential ...

Even in libertarian economics, markets are not perfect. Similarly, in the pursuit of self-interest, people make mistakes. We often act against our own interests because we don't always know what they are until it's too late. Marx identified something similar in his concept of false consciousness, the inculcation of which was essential to obscure the inherent contradictions of capitalism and thus preserve belief in the system. Some degree of error in our judgement is inevitable. The right to an easy rescue if we screw up might, paradoxically, be in our long-term self-interest and give us greater freedom in planning for the future if we know we can count on the assistance of others when we really need it. It might also encourage greater inventiveness and entrepreneurship in the economy by promoting higher levels of trust, especially in making the first move in initiating new transactional relationships. Good Samaritan laws therefore might promote liberty and market freedom rather than curtailing it, in a truly social market.

Third, there is a difference to be made between acts that we are required and obligated to perform and acts that go above and beyond the call of duty. The original Good Samaritan was clearly carrying out the latter – he didn't simply call the authorities, he dressed the man's wounds and cared for his welfare, took him to accommodation and paid for it and undertook to pay any further bills until the man recovered even though he himself had to leave. Clearly this sort of behaviour was exemplary, was hard to perform, and we could not reasonably condemn anyone else for not performing in this way – it was *supererogatory* behaviour. On the other hand, for the others simply to pass by and not call any help or assistance for the injured man did fall short of standards of *minimal decency* – the least one could do to prevent unnecessary suffering or harm. Failure to act with minimal decency therefore does commonly attract social censure, and consequently could function as the basis for a Good Samaritan law. The New York Four, however, did not simply fail to act with minimal decency as they *did* act in relation to the incident – they ridiculed it. This raises a question as to whether this goes beyond a failure to act with minimal decency and constitutes something worse – does humour itself here become *immoral* (Buckley 2005)? Or does culpability cease at the boundaries of causality?

Are we only responsible for what we cause?

One objection to Good Samaritan laws states that we should only be responsible for what we cause, but the question of causality is complex. Elsewhere in commercial and employment law, for example, it has been established that causes and causal relationships may be of different types and may therefore be weighted differently. In organizations and business, for example, we may be required to anticipate problems and try to prevent them, as with the products we produce in relation to consumers' rights, and in providing a safe and healthy working environment, where the law requires everyone who works in the organization to carry some degree of specific and general responsibility. In addition, responsibility may be relative and not total in that causes may be direct, indirect or contributory. Doing nothing can therefore be doing something – for example, not causing something to happen, if that would have been desirable and would have been straightforward to achieve, does carry a moral responsibility. It's a situation commonly encountered at the end of adventure movies – the villain dangles by a thread over the edge of a cliff and only the hero stands between him and certain doom, although the hero would benefit by the villain's death (as the villain has usually been trying to kill the hero). Of course, the hero pulls the villain up because he sees no moral distinction between failing to pull him up (thus inevitably allowing him to fall) and pushing him off the cliff to his death. Let the criminal justice system arraign, sentence and punish the villain – the hero's role is only to bring him to justice and act morally as an individual in the service of the system in doing so. Again, here the system exerts a powerful symbolic presence even though no formal legal penalty applies. But it could be argued that, in cases such as the NY4 mugging, the perpetrator would be less likely to commit the offence if they had a high degree of confidence that others would rush to the aid of the victim. Bystanding then could be said to make a causal contribution in making it more likely that such offences would be committed in the future, even though not directly causing the specific offence in question.

The issue of responsibility has become central in recent Continental philosophy. As I noted earlier, Lévinas and the later Foucault (Smart 1998) place upon us the burden of responsibility towards the other. But as I have already implied, responsibility can be constructed differently. Clarkson (1996) identifies two major forms of construction of responsibility, and later discusses a third alternative construction of responsibility: fidelity. *Responsibility as liability* as already discussed is interest-based; has a fixed view of how that responsibility may be determined; sees that responsibility as finite and bounded, even proportionate; tends to be applied primarily to self and immediate family members; unless contractually specified tails off dramatically after that and may not even include friends; and psychologically engenders inauthentic or neurotic guilt. This form of guilt is essentially an overreaction, and prevents any practical steps being taken towards redress of the situation as it is a form of narcissistic response – the subject is paralysed at the realization of their guilt like a rabbit in headlights. *Responsibility as a relationship* in contrast to the first form is empathy-based; accordingly it remains in flux, to be determined situationally and relationally; rather than being finite, it is complex and may extend in many directions; it is not limited to existing kinship or social groupings; and is characterized by authentic or existential guilt. Genuine guilt involves a reparation for acts committed, but this may only result in situationally determined action rather than any change of life-position by the guilty. Existential guilt, on the other hand, is both a 'deep personal awareness of the suffering of others' coupled with a commitment to change, to use 'one's life and one's resources differently'. This involves 'celebrating opportunites with joy and gratitude without demeaning others or ourselves with false hypocritical protestations' of guilt, or claims of responsibility recycled for their social popularity value or academic currency, whilst having no effect on present or future behaviour (Clarkson 1996: 16).

Responsibility as fidelity is based on the thought of Gabriel Marcel but with a postmodern twist. Lévinas's great insight was that morality is situational and evolving and that it must therefore be determined by relationships. The relation with the Other, for him, was prior to the relationship with self, as self could only be discovered in relation to the Other and difference. So the Other places an imperative to respond upon self. Lévinas argues that ethics must therefore be the first move of philosophy, or first philosophy. But if this is so, it also follows that connectedness must be first *nature*. Disconnectedness, initiated at the first moment of differentiation, is ironically a part of sociability, a learned behaviour that is *second* nature, intervening at the very moment we become aware of the divisibility of individuality and sociability, of selves as *dividuals* (Backius 2005). Responsibility then is immanent in the relationship with others of which the awareness of structure, of interior and exterior as difference, robs us. As Marcel (1952) observes, discussed by Blackham (1961: 76, emphasis added):

> The concrete historical permanence that I give myself in fidelity cannot be derived from a universal law ... in fidelity I continuously inform myself from within ... in fidelity I am not merely cultivating an ideal, I am making a response: I am not merely being consistent with myself, but I am bearing witness to an other-than-me which has hold of me. Fidelity is not a mere act of will, it is faith in the presence of an other-than-me to which I respond

and to which I shall continue to respond. It is this continuous response in the bond of fidelity which is my life and my permanence.

Fidelity then is fidelity to the concrete other and fidelity to being-in-relation. It is, as implied here, intuitive; the relation is one of multiplicity and hence in constant evolution as a minor shift here requires an adjustment there.

The knowledge base for these adjustments is not based on principles nor does it form a cohesive whole – it is fragmented, and thus may have elements of logic and affect, is driven by desire in the sense of a generous exuberance to connect and can be irrational. Indeed, it embodies the possibilities for an ethics of irrationality, and an emergent logic of the fragment, which may be considered erotic in that it is passionate (Bataille 1986). The domain of such a responsibility is not totalizing nor is it bounded, but immanent within the dynamics of fidelity, and is thus processual. And when guilt is felt, it is not individual and isolated, but collective, in that we fail each other because of our mutual limitations. At these moments, we feel our absurdity, and we laugh together.

Who is my neighbour?

Desire to entertain the other may be desire to understand the other, desire for the other, or desire to incorporate and thus destroy the other.

(Derrida and Ferraris 2001)

	Responsibility as liability	Responsibility as relationship	Responsibility as fidelity
Motivation	Interest	Empathy	Intuitive
Ontology	Fixed Essential Universal	Situational In flux	Multiple Evolving
Epistemology	Finite Principled Contractual Rational	Complex Transactional Reciprocal Asymmetrical Negotiable	Fragmented Logical Affective Irrational Generous
Domain	Self and immediate family	Other – Not limited to localised groups	Immanent Processual
Guilt	Neurotic Unauthentic	Existential Authentic	Absurd Collective, shared

Figure 11.1 Three forms of responsibility (developed from and based on Clarkson 1996)

If we turn to the question that motivated the original parable of the Good Samaritan, it was in response to Jesus' commandment to 'love thy neighbour as thyself' that he was asked 'Who is my neighbour?' This invokes the question of the other and how the other is constructed, but also of how the boundary between self and other is to be managed, as I introduced earlier in my discussion. This may quickly become a political question, as it became for those who condemned Jesus, and as it remains for a political philosopher such as Michael Ignatieff. For Ignatieff (1984:15) my neighbour is other humans, and my responsibility is not to deny them what they need to be human, to help them realize the full extent of their potential. Such things as love, respect, honour, dignity and solidarity with others are therefore included in this responsibility that go far beyond basic survival needs and helping others when they are in difficulty, but they are also needs that are not easily satisfied and require sustained effort through the co-ordination of the efforts of both self and society in order to be delivered.

In this regard the New York Four may well represent a site of the tension between aesthetics and ethics, if we view these terms from the perspectives of Aristotle's virtue ethics (MacIntyre 1981, 1988; Skoble 2000), Kierkegaard's distinction between the two (Irwin 2000) and Foucault's attempt to produce an ethics through the aesthetic (Cummings 2000; Foucault 1997). For Aristotle, ethics was a matter of the character of the individual and the circumstances in which they find themselves working out their *telos*. The important question for Aristotle was not what is the right thing to do, but what sort of character is indicated by doing one thing rather than another – i.e. what sort of person would I be if I did *a* rather than *b*, and how would a wise person act in this situation? As Skoble points out, this is exactly the sort of question the characters in *Seinfeld* ask themselves, although they have been accused of asking them at the level of manners rather than that of morals. Comedy, in fact, excels as a medium for raising questions about the social order, including the moral order that is part of dominant reality and/or which we take for granted – which is why there has been so much philosophical speculation about the missing volume 2 of Aristotle's *Poetics* on comedy, and why for some medieval scholars the book was so potentially dangerous, as dramatized in Umberto Eco's *The Name of the Rose* (Eco 1983).

Character for Aristotle was not an absolute quality, but something that was dictated partly by the talents, qualities and circumstances of the individual and partly by what they made of it by their efforts to develop themselves. *Phronesis* was the practical wisdom bestowed by the combination of character and experience, and Aristotle urged each individual to choose a *phronemos*, a person of practical wisdom, as a role model, and to practise emulating them. Not only did this approach suggest an aesthetic dimension to morality in that character could be seen as a style of the person, but it also recognized an experiential or existential dimension to moral virtue whilst making the link to Ignatieff's idea of the social requirements of a welfare ethic through the following of role models.

Whilst emphasizing the existential and to some extent the social dimensions, Kierkegaard nevertheless denigrated the aesthetic dimension in a way that cast a long shadow into late modernity. He makes his argument across two linked books under the one title *Either/Or*, and assumes the identity of different characters in each – in the first, he is a seducer (A); in the second, a judge (B, or Judge Vilhelm, writing to A). The objective of the seducer is to avoid commitment whilst avoiding blame, to play and remain in play without attachment – an aesthetic rather than an ethical life, one that has lost its connection to the overarching idea of the good life that was paramount for Aristotle. Thus the seducer's skill is not in the winning of the affections of the woman, but in disentangling from the relationship in such a way that she breaks off the relationship and takes the responsibility for it, believing it is what she wants rather than he. From this argument the origin of the modern popular disapproval of the superficiality of the aesthetic can be traced. The judge advocates the ethical approach, but rejects a Kantian deontology, proffering an existential ethics. For him, the skill and the thrill of ethics is that one can never be sure what the right thing to do is because each set of circumstances is different and will unfold differently. Thus you need to work constantly on your abilities to make assessments of people and situations and even then can never be sure that you did not make a mistake – and it is this risk that provides the excitement of the ethical. This thrill is not the superficial excitement experienced by the seducer, where a game works out to their advantage, but the more profound one of having tried to do the right thing in a difficult situation and finding one's judgement vindicated. Kierkegaard thus makes a clear distinction between aesthetics and ethics because in the former the other is manipulated in order for the self to avoid responsibility. In rendering his account, Kierkegaard's fictional respondent A necessarily accepts that he can be rendered accountable by the other. His efforts to manipulate the other therefore occur through the shaping of accounts of the situation and feelings about the situation as it unfolds, in order that the other will begin to claim responsibility for the ending of the relationship and the final account of the affair will absolve him of responsibility for its failure.

Foucault seeks to restore the link between ethics and aesthetics, but rather than making aesthetics the route to the ethical life as in Aristotle or downgrading aesthetics as in Kierkegaard, that life itself is seen as an aesthetic object, the self and the life being created as works of art. This is echoed by Ignatieff in suggesting that any theory of human needs has to be based on what humans need to be human, which his discussion implies is a developmental project rather than a state of affairs. Foucault was, in his later work, energized by the prospect of challenging the modern dependence on normalizing rules and codes of ethics by a rediscovery of the Greek idea of the aesthetic existence, revitalized by a new context. The apparent self-obsession of the cast of *Seinfeld* could be seen therefore not simply in terms of the neuroses of contemporary post-Woody Allen New Yorkers, but as part of their stumbling attempts to create a 'beautiful life' in modern Manhattan, aesthetically sensitive to the efforts of others to do the same in the same social pressure-cooker. Of course, their choices of *phronemos* are frequently problematic, and it is in the flaws and failures of their attempts that the humour is generated, and through their friendship that the worst of their excesses are redeemed.

'Spectacting' and bystanding

It is also important to note that bystanders don't just stand by, they look on. They are audiences (Clarkson 1996; Latané and Darley 1970). Guy Debord (1994) argued that even before the spread of mass television we had become a society of the spectacle, and that events unfolded in relation to theatres of action. Since then Jean Baudrillard (1994) noted that the creation and transmission of simulacra had meant that it was becoming impossible simply to spectate, and that one was always incorporated in some way as part of the spectacle presented, the artifice of the situation. Spectating and acting became 'spectaction' (Sotto 1996) in the contemporary videocracy – a point that Baudrillard originally made well in advance of the rise of reality TV and its domination of prime-time, the growth of virtual reality gaming, and the internet. Gregory Ulmer has argued that literacy in the general population has been displaced by videocy – that young people in particular, but consumers in general, are now much more skilled at decoding visual messages than they are literary ones, and have a visual repertoire of a sophistication that exceeds anything that was historically available to them. Actors are much more conscious of being observed and of themselves observing even whilst being engaged in their performances, a degree of self-consciousness in performance that resonates with Kierkegaard's aesthetic mode of being.

Bystanding then begins in spectaction, where theatres of action, simulacra and the performances of others intersect. Bystanders could possibly be in a state of preparedness or readiness to act, on stand-by. But spectacle displaces action. Simultaneously as onlooking creates a spectacle of the other, framing action so as to keep actor and audience separate, bystanding without such anticipation of action comes to absolve the audience of the responsibility to act and suppresses the fact that even audiences have other audiences for their performance *as* audience. In the context of Good Samaritan laws, the bystanders create themselves as audience for the event, but forget that societal laws create a legal gaze that authorizes a higher audience to whom they may subsequently be held accountable – 'in the eyes of the law'. Just as the NY4 were an audience for the mugging, others had been audiences for their previous actions, and suddenly these audiences are given the power in the courtroom to bear witness and thus redefine these situations, resulting in the co-production of a legal gaze that 'sees' the actions of the accused as criminal.

The inverse of this situation is where the action dimension of spectaction requires moral-ethical decisions with real life-and-death consequences in the world of actuality to be made on the basis of the spectacle of virtual images on a computer screen – as with fighter and bomber crews in both Gulf Wars (Baudrillard 1995; Sotto 1996). The consequences of those decisions too become virtualized on screen. We see so much of the world in a stylized presentation via the media that turns the news format into performance art until human tragedy hardly seems real, as Ian McMillan (1994) puts it in his poem 'Bosnia Festival':

At 10.00 a.m. mime show
By The Shuffling Headscarves.
Nothing much happens;
Some shuffling, weeping.
Mimed weeping, that is

Jeanette Winterson argues even more forcefully that the constant exposure to things it is impossible to do anything about – the success of Live Aid notwithstanding – is pornographic in that it deadens our ability to feel.

Reportage is violence. Violence to the spirit. Violence to the emotional sympathy that should quicken in you and me when face to face we meet with pain. How many defeated among our own do we step over and push aside on our way home to watch evening news? 'Terrible' you said at Somalia, Bosnia, Ethiopia, Russia, China, the Indian earthquake, the American floods, and then you watched a quiz show or a film because there's nothing you can do, nothing you can do, and the fear and unease that such powerlessness brings, trails in its wash, a dead arrogance for the beggar on the bridge that you pass every day. Hasn't he got legs and a cardboard box to sleep in?
And still we long to feel.
(Winterson 1994: 13–14, cited in Clarkson 1996: 90)

In the last Seinfeld episode, both this visual dimension and the associated deadening of feeling are gestured to by the fact that Kramer not only witnesses but videos the event – not for the purposes of providing evidence for use in court, which could be classified as a form of action, but for entertainment. Yet here there are also echoes of the paradox of videocy, that we interpret the world so much through the lens on the camera or the on-screen simulation that we cannot understand what happens in reality until we see it virtually represented in this way. Kramer was not just recording reality, he was providing it with a grid of intelligibility in order to translate it into terms he could understand. Which is to say that so much in the way of representation and interpretation is interposed between self and reality and self and other in contemporary society that we are in effect bystanders to our own experience – not merely alienated from the products of our material or even symbolic labour but from our experiences themselves – until it is rendered back to us in more digestible form. We stand by not just others, but ourselves.

Following from this, we might make one observation as to the key characteristic of bystanding that renders it pernicious. That is to say, the real offence of bystanding is not in standing *by*, but in the effort to create the absolute separation of self and other necessary to find a place to stand outside of the situation and look *on*. This is not an offence so much against the other but reflexively acts against the self, because without the other, self is diminished. Indeed this last point has been made as an interpretation of the significance of the final episode by Jennifer McMahon (McMahon 2000: 106–8). But we can go further, whilst accepting this point, to say that what is created by this separation from both self and other is a simulated self, and it is from this doubly morally alienated position that Kramer videos the action whilst the others perform their wisecracks.

The New York Four then play a language game of distraction rather than rescripting. They technologically inscribe the separation between self and other by recording the action, not changing its course. They thus limit their idea of 'relationship' and 'responsibility' to their known circle. They could have made a difference, but didn't – they did not attempt to 'repair' the relationship that events had fractured.

Could minimal action have made a difference? Sometimes no action at all can have some impact. The United Nations relies on the fact that the presence of its 'observers' will make a difference to the actions of the military and law enforcement authorities in places where they are sent to help keep the peace. Television cameras may have a similar effect.

The 'bystander witness' may be an appropriate role in some circumstances. Clarkson (1996: 96–7) recounts an example in which just making one's presence fully known and felt can affect outcomes. A middle-class, middle-aged white woman made a point of standing observing with full attention while police stopped and searched a young Asian male. She made quite clear that she was watching them, that they realized it, that they knew who she was and what she stood for, and that she would be prepared to speak out if necessary. The police were careful not to breach any procedures and to be polite and use no unnecessary roughness or disrespect, and did not book him. After the search, the young man came over to the lady and shook her hand.

Philosophers such as Alain Badiou and Jacques Rancière would see this type of action, however modest, as a mode of being a subject – a form of subjectivation. This creative view differs from the more determined views of subjectivation in both early and later Foucault, as it entails more poeisis – an impressing of one's self on the world in rescripting it. In short, whilst the world might position us as subjects, we can still reach out to it and make it react to us. Just being there puts us in relation to the world, and constitutes the world as in being relation to us.

Further aspects of bystanding in organizations

When we extend the concept of bystanding into organizations, we find it acquires a distinctive texture. First, in organizations rather than society more generally, *selves and others are more formally interconnected*. This inevitably means that with greater interlocking sets of responsibilities and consequences of one's actions, plus the greater focus on action, more moral dilemmas are likely to be generated. They won't be of the type that moral philosophers usually use to illustrate moral issues, which tend to be stylised life-or-death sorts of considerations that we will rarely ourselves have to encounter in real life, but those that we have regularly to resolve in the ordinary interaction that characterizes both the whole Seinfeld series and our everyday existence. Remembering that the premise of the show was 'something from nothing' it stands as another example of how comedy makes the apparently insignificant become significant, in this case in a way that is organizationally illuminating (Garcia 2000).

If we turn to the idea of resolving individual and collective self-interest, we find that *self, collective, organizational, stakeholder and customer interest overlap*. They are neither always easy to distinguish, nor often not in conflict. Not helping one 'other' that one could reasonably help might in fact help a different other, and vice versa. So where interests interlock, theatres intersect and decisions need to be made that prioritize and thus make bystanding more difficult – we have to choose one action or another and inaction without consequence is not always an option. This opens up the recognition that we are presented with a *frequent need for paradoxical thinking*. Actions don't appear from nowhere, as I have noted above, and they have histories, are reconstructed in multiple narratives, the full range of outcomes of actions is not always obvious, there can be multiple unintended consequences of actions, and time and space – or timing and spacing – can be actants in these situations, as what is possible in one time and place may not be in another. Even when we might wish to act or be seen to act altruistically, because of the intertextual nature of accounts of action and history *sometimes it is hard not to be self-serving or to be seen as such*.[1]

A rough Australian translation of a Chinese proverb reads 'The higher a monkey climbs up a tree, the more you can see of its arse'. In other words, *power and knowledge are inseparable*, and we tend to conceal our vulnerabilities, or our less worthy motivations, or even just a few facts, until we feel we are in a position not to be harmed by their exposure. Knowledge, whatever its epistemological status, is therefore organizationally very far from perfect or evenly distributed. Robert Jackall's (1988) study of the politics of organizational knowledge and the moralities of managerial decision-making observed accordingly that moral dilemmas become 'moral mazes' – where dilemmas are multi-dimensional and interlocking and choices are complex and confusing. The idea that ethical and moral action are what reasonable men and women of good Aristotelian character would do in the circumstances were they in possession of all the facts offers no recourse here, because the facts can never all be determined, and probably contradict each other, regardless of the problematic status of what is 'reasonable'. Within these moral mazes *multiple conflicts of interest* occur – indeed often an individual may have more than one interest in conflict. Such conflicts may be subconscious, latent and subversive yet despite their relative lack of visibility exert an important influence on ethical decision-making.

In organizations that are committed to high reliability, high performance levels and/or excellence, *the supererogatory becomes a cultural obligation* (and sometimes it is even a contractual one) – and this can have some negative moral consequences. The requirement to act consistently above and beyond the call of duty becomes itself a duty: one that is culturally policed by concertive control, with surveillance exercised by colleagues on each other (see Smith and Wilkinson 1996, for a good example of this at work in a high performance culture). In such cases the supererogatory and the minimal decency poles may collapse into each other, the result being an imperative to act in a way that is oriented towards excellence without any acceptable minimum standards of performance other than to be 'excellent'. Of course, exhortations to excellence may or may not have a moral dimension, and frequently do not, so high performance cultures – such as that prevailing in NASA at the time of the Challenger disaster (Schwartz 1990) or Enron in more recent times – may behave collectively in an unethical, immoral and even evil manner (Darley 1992, 1994, 1996, 2001).

Finally, *there are many ways to define the terms 'unnecessary suffering' and 'risk to oneself'*, terms that commonly appear in related legislation, especially when the degree of risk or suffering is not specified, but these need to be applied to the organizational context. One might begin with the relatively unusual but obvious risk to life and limb, or health, but detriment and risk could be applied to financial matters, career, psychological well-being, opportunity cost, the consequences of offending the powerful, the consequences of being oneself exposed (the collateral disinterment of our own skeletons from the closet), fear of retribution, or the harbouring of grudges. All of these more minor, less visible but no less real possible consequences are perhaps the most relevant ones to the issue of organizational bystanding, where the offences are moral and psychological rather than physical. But moral harassment and organizational bystanding happen, and regardless of the difficulty of addressing them and the appropriateness of a legislative response, they are issues that demand our consideration.

Organizational bystanding redux

Distilling this discussion, we can, I think, discern three main features at the core of organizational bystanding, both tying it to bystanding in general and lending it particular distinctiveness.

To ignore what's going on around you – not to see

This can have almost limitless scope from the head in the sand general strategy, through turning the occasional blind eye to the 'banality of evil' of the Third Reich administrators who hid behind the orders that they were 'only following'. In between we can create narratives through which to defend, mask or divert attention away from our inaction. We can ignore the moral dimensions of a situation altogether and see each unfolding episode only in terms of technical or functional issues. This general focus on the minutiae of events entails a bigger refusal – the failure to connect means that it becomes impossible to sustain any meaningful definition of organizational citizenship (except in a very formal sense) or of collegiality.

To witness, but fail to recognize or make the effort to recognize what's really happening

Not everything we see is self-evident. We have to make an effort to understand it and often we doubt our interpretations of events if they seem to indicate shocking behaviour or terrible and unexpected consequences. There is a hermeneutic effort involved in comprehending that moral harassment exists and is being put into action in the events that we have witnessed – we don't want to believe in its truth, we don't want to be hypersensitive or over-react. But this is exactly why we must engage our critical faculties with our puzzlement, and we must make the effort to understand what is really going on, taking the issue of bystanding deeper than simply seeing and failing to act – the offence should include failing to interrogate, investigate and understand.

To witness, to recognize injustice and refuse to act

This is perhaps where we often find ourselves sitting, and where the introduction of inducements and preferments by moral harassers are most often felt. We have seen it, we have made our inquiries and we know that what was and is happening is wrong. We can no longer hide the truth from ourselves. Here we lack either knowledge (which in reality is unlikely to be the case) or courage or experience or, we believe, potential support from others (there but for the grace of God go I) and we choose not to act in accordance with what we know and believe to be true. Our excuse for not acting might be that we did not feel we could act without danger to ourselves – that we would be putting ourselves in peril – but this merely allows the abuses to roll on unchecked and neglects the fact that action, rather than simply attracting retribution, creates the possibilities for its own future.

The New York Four: the verdict?

So what of our criminal eccentrics languishing in Latham jail? Do we believe them to be guilty of a heinous moral crime? Clearly, on this occasion, they were guilty of not behaving with minimal decency – in other words failing at that moment fully to be human, fully to engage with their experience. But as we have seen, that in itself is not as easy as it sounds, so they were surely not guilty of social pathology – they might not have been fully human at that moment but they were not inhuman or anti-human. They failed to take responsibility, they fractured their relationship with the other humans, yet they reaffirmed their relationship with each other. So they remained human with flaws, just like the rest of us but with some arresting differences.

The New York Four then don't so much break the law as break the faith – the faith that we need to have in each other in order to make life, not only tolerable, but joyous. Neither Lévinas nor Solzhenitsyn in their torture and captivity lost that sense of joy, even when it dwindled to only a spark. Foucault may have at times lost sight of it in the byways of pleasure. But the fact that the Four are laughing with each other, *schädenfreude* notwithstanding, offers a glimpse of redemption. We are at our most human when we laugh with each other at ourselves, and shed all responsibility save to care for each other in our absurdity. This is the ethics of comedy. It is how we keep faith in our humanity. It is perhaps why we love.

For a final moment, let's take our eyes away from the four friends making what they can of a year in the jailhouse, and their relative innocence of such a serious crime, and recall the organizational scenario introduced earlier in this chapter, its parallels in our organizational lives and the issues it raises. I have argued that, contrary to Jackie Chiles's view, the libertarian view and the view taken by English common law, bystanding is not only a crime, but it is not a victimless crime either, and it enables further crime in the future. It is not singular but continuous and becomes cultural and contextual. It enables oppression, discrimination and harassment to hide themselves under the cloak of desensitized and dehumanized customary relations. As in the case of David Kelly, it can be fatal. Both those whom they fail to support and the bystanders themselves are diminished by the act of bystanding. In failing to keep our 'brothers', we lose something of ourselves.

So the New York Four were at least wrist-slappingly guilty. How about us?

> The retrieval of relationship has become perhaps the most important moral issue of our time. Of course, relationship is difficult, demanding, ambivalent, relative, de-centering, vertiginous, disturbing and disorientating as well as rewarding and delightful. But it is only in relation to others that I can begin to know who I am as a human being, and who I can be for others.
>
> (Clarkson 1996: 97)

Note

1   Ethics can be understood in terms of different Greek forms of love: altruism, which operates according to an *agapeic* ethic, gives requiring nothing in return; egotism, operating to an *erotic* ethic, has the self as its first and last consideration; mutualism, with a *philic* ethic will give as long as it receives and is the assumed dynamic behind most socio-economic thinking (Fletcher 1966: 109–10). However, Staub argues that behaviour may blur the boundaries between these ethics, identifying *pro-social* behaviour as that which has as its primary purpose helping others but does not exclude the possibility of self-gain. Perhaps this is a more charitable interpretation of the actions of many of the original participants in *Band Aid*, who have sometimes been accused of using the event cynically as means of reviving flagging entertainment careers.

References

Backius, P. (2005) 'The other: a dividual enterprise', in A. Pullen and S. Linstead (eds), *Organization and Identity*, pp. 182–96, London: Routledge.

Bataille, G. (1986) *Death and Sensuality: A Study of Eroticism and the Taboo*, New York: Ballantine.

Baudrillard, J. (1994) *Simulacra and Simulation: The Body, in Theory*, Ann Arbor, MI: University of Michigan Press.

Baudrillard, J. (1995) *The Gulf War did Not Take Place*, Bloomington, IN, and Indianapolis, IN: Indiana University Press.

Blackham, H. J. (1961) *Six Existentialist Thinkers*, London: Routledge

Buckley, F. H. (2005) *The Morality of Humour*, Ann Arbor, MI: University of Michigan Press.

Butler, J. (2005) *Giving an Account of Oneself*, New York: Fordham.

Clarkson, P. (1996) *The Bystander (An End to Innocence in Human Relationships?)*, London: Whurr.

Conroy, J. (2000) *Unspeakable Acts, Ordinary People*, Berkeley, CA: University of California Press.

Cummings, S. (2000) 'Resurfacing an aesthetics of existence as an alternative to business ethics', in S. Linstead and H. Höpfl (eds), *The Aesthetics of Organization,* pp. 212–27, London: Sage.

Darley, J. M. (1992) 'Social organization for the production of evil', *Psychological Inquiry*, 3: 199–218.

Darley, J. M. (1994) 'Organizations as a source of immoral behavior', *Global Bioethics*, 7: 53–63.

Darley, J. M. (1996) 'How organizations socialize individuals into evildoing in codes of conduct', in D. M. Messick and A. E. Tenbrunsel (eds), *Behavioral Research into Business Ethics*, pp. 13–43, New York: Russell Sage Foundation.

Darley, J. M. (2001) 'The dynamics of authority in organizations and the unintended action consequences', in J. M. Darley, D. M. Messick and T. R. Tyler (eds), *Social Influences on Ethical Behavior in Organization*, pp. 37–52, Mahwah, NJ: L. A. Erlbaum.

Darley, J. M. and Latané, B. (1968a) 'Bystander intervention in emergencies: diffusion of responsibility', *Journal of Personality and Social Psychology*, 8: 377–83.

Darley, J. M. and Latané, B. (1968b) 'When will people help in a crisis?', *Psychology Today*, 2: 54–7, 70–1.

Darley, J. M., and Latané, B. (1969) 'Bystander "apathy"', *American Scientist*, 57: 244–68.

Debord, G. (1994) *The Society of the Spectacle*, New York: Zone Books.

Derrida, J. (1997a) *The Politics of Friendship*, London: Verso.

Derrida, J. (1997b) *On Cosmopolitanism and Forgiveness*, London: Routledge.

Derrida, J. (2000) 'Hostipitality', *Angelaki*, 5(3): 3–18.

Derrida, J. and Ferraris, M. (2001) *A Taste for the Secret*, Cambridge: Polity Press.

Dufourmantelle, A. and Derrida, J. (2000) *Of Hospitality*, Stanford, CA: Stanford University Press.

Dyke, G. (2004) *Inside Story*, London: Harper Collins.

Eco, U. (1983) *The Name of the Rose*, New York: Harcourt Brace.

Epperson, R. A. (2000) '*Seinfeld* and the moral life', in W. Irwin (ed.), *Seinfeld and Philosophy*, pp. 163–74, Peru, IL: Open Court.

Etzioni, A. (1993) *The Spirit of Community: The Reinvention of American Society*, New York: Touchstone.

Fenves, P. (2001) 'Out of the blue: secrecy, radical evil and the crypt of faith', in R. Rand (ed.), *Futures of Jacques Derrida*, pp. 99–129, Stanford, CA: Stanford University Press.

Fletcher, J. (1966) *Situation Ethics: The New Morality*, London: SCM Press.

Foucault, M. (1997) *Ethics: Subjectivity and Truth – The Essential Works*, vol. 1, London: Penguin.

Foucault, M. (2001) *Fearless Speech*, New York: Semiotext(e).

Fuller, T. (2004) 'Bully them to make them leave', *International Herald Tribune* (8 Sept.): 11.

Garcia, J. E. (2000) 'The secret of *Seinfeld*'s humour: the significance of the commonplace', in W. Irwin (ed.), *Seinfeld and Philosophy*, pp. 148–60, Peru, IL: Open Court.

Giddens, A. (1976) *New Rules of Sociological Method*, London: Methuen.

Giddens, A. (1984) *The Constitution of Society*, Berkeley, CA: University of California Press.

Habermas, J. (1987) *Knowledge and Human Interest*, Cambridge: Polity Press.

Hirigoyen, M.-F. (2005) *Stalking the Soul: Emotional Abuse and the Erosion of Identity*, tr. H. Marx, with an introduction by Thomas Moore, New York: Helen Marx Books.

Ignatieff, M. (1984) *The Needs of Others*, London: Vintage.

Irwin, W. (ed.) (2000) *Seinfeld and Philosophy*, Peru, IL: Open Court Press.

Jackall, R. (1988) *Moral Mazes*, Oxford: Oxford University Press.

Kant, I. (1996) 'Religion within the boundaries of mere reason', tr. G. di Giovanni, in I. Kant, *Religion and Rational Theology*, A. Wood and G. di Giovanni (eds), Cambridge: Cambridge University Press.

Latané, B. and Darley, J. M. (1968) 'Group inhibition of bystander intervention in emergencies', *Journal of Personality and Social Psychology*, 1: 215–21.

Latané, B. and Darley, J. M. (1970) *The Unresponsive Bystander: Why doesn't he Help?* New York: Appleton-Century-Crofts.

Latané, B. and Darley, J. M. (1976) *Helping in a Crisis: Bystander Response to an Emergency*, Morristown, NJ: General Learning Press.

Lévinas, E. (1969) *Totality and Infinity*, tr. A. Lingis, Pittsburgh, PA: Duquesne University Press.

Lévinas, E. (1981) *Otherwise than Being or Beyond Essence*, tr. A. Lingis, The Hague: Martinus Nijhoff.

Lévinas, E. (1987) *Time and the Other*, tr. R. Cohen, Pittsburgh, PA: Duquesne University Press.

Linstead, S. and Collinson, D. (2005) 'Irony in a post-ironic world', in U. Johannson and J. Woodilla (eds), *Irony and Organizations*, pp. 381–90, Malmo: Liber/Copenhagen Business School Press.

MacIntyre, A. (1981) *After Virtue: A Study in Moral Theory*, London: Duckworth.

MacIntyre, A. (1988) *Whose Justice? Which Rationality?*, London: Duckworth.

McMahon, J. (2000) '*Seinfeld*, subjectivity and Sartre', in W. Irwin (ed.), *Seinfeld and Philosophy*, pp. 90–108, Peru, IL: Open Court.

McMillan, I. (1994) *Dad, the Donkey's on Fire*, London: Carcanet.

Marcel, G. (1952) *The Metaphysical Journal*, London: Rockliff.

Noon, M. and Delbridge, R. (1993) 'News from behind my hand: gossip in organizations', *Organization Studies*, 14: 23–36.

Schick, T. Jr (2000) 'The final episode: is doing nothing doing something?', in W. Irwin (ed.), *Seinfeld and Philosophy*, pp. 183–92, Peru, IL: Open Court.

Schwartz, H. S. (1990) *Narcissistic Process and Corporate Decay*, New York: New York University Press.

Skoble, A. J. (2000) 'Virtue ethics and the moral life', in W. Irwin (ed.), *Seinfeld and Philosophy*, pp. 175–83, Peru, IL: Open Court.

Smart, B. (1998) 'Foucault, Lévinas and the subject of responsibility', in J. Moss (ed.), *The Later Foucault*, pp. 78–92, London: Sage.

Smith, S. and Wilkinson, B. (1996) '"We are our own policemen!" Organizing without conflict', in S. Linstead, R. Grafton Small and P. Jeffcutt (eds), *Understanding Management*, pp. 130–44, London: Sage.

Sotto, R. (1996) '"Spect-action": technical control and organizational action', *Studies in Cultures, Organizations and Societies*, 2(1): 131–45.

Staub, E. (1990) 'The psychology and culture of torture and torturers', in P. Suedfeld (ed.), *Psychology and Torture*, pp. 49–86, New York: Hemisphere.

Ulmer, G. L. (1989) *Teletheory: Grammatology in the Age of Video*, London: Routledge.

Winterson, J. (1994) *Art and Lies: A Piece for Three Voices and a Bawd*, London: Jonathan Cape.

Part IV

The organization of humour

Chapter 12

Advertising
The organizational production of humour

Donncha Kavanagh and Don O'Sullivan

The focus of this chapter is on a particular aspect of the relationship between humour and organization, namely the deliberate production of humour by organizations through advertising. Our aim is to study humour in advertising and through doing so to investigate what it tells us about humour, organizations and the social context of advertising/consumption. Specifically, we are interested in explaining the nature and increasing use of humour during the period that has come to be known as late capitalism. While no data are readily available to allow a quantitative, historical comparison, Beard (2005) provides a recent and insightful account of the emergence of humour within advertising. Also, the anecdotal evidence suggests that the number of 'humorous' advertisements has increased over the last 20 years, to the point where humorous appeals are now endemic in advertising and television advertising in particular (Tomkovick *et al*. 2001). This is corroborated by Weinberger (1999), who has studied advertising humour extensively over the last 20 years.

Weinberger is one of a relatively small number of academics who has studied humour in advertising. Indeed marketing has had little to say about humour, save for a body of quite instrumental research aimed at measuring the degree to which humour helps an advertiser communicate his/her message (see e.g. Chattopadhyay and Basu 1990; Weinberger and Gulas 1992). What is especially surprising is that the postmodern moment – which emphasizes fun, play, parody and pastiche – has not inspired marketing scholars to theorize about humour more deeply. In particular, the marked and perceptible increase in the use of humour in advertising, which has occurred since the 1980s, has gone without comment or analysis by students of marketing. This chapter seeks to plug this gap a little.

As a way of anchoring our discussion, we focus on beer advertising campaigns from the USA, Britain and Australia as exemplars of humorous advertisements. Specifically we look at Budweiser's well-known and long-running series of reptilian advertisements, John Smith's 'No Nonsense' campaign, and recent Carlton Draught advertising from Australia. Beer advertisements are chosen for a number of reasons. First, beer and other forms of alcohol account for a significant portion of the advertising spend in most developed markets. In the UK, for example, £204 million (approximately 1/16th of total UK advertising) was spent on alcohol advertising in 2004 of which over 54 per cent was spent on beer advertising (UK Office of Communications 2005). Similarly, in Australia, beer advertising accounts for $A52 million or just under 50 per cent of total alcohol advertising spend (Miller and Mizerski 2005). By far the greatest spend takes place in the US, where $1.1 billion was spent advertising beer in 2002 (Nelson 2005).

Second, beer is a widely consumed product in most developed markets and therefore suitable for considering contemporary production and consumption. Finally alcohol, along with tobacco, has been the subject of progressively restrictive legislation in recent years. In particular, advertisers of alcohol are restricted with regard to the product claims that they can make, and many have consequently looked to humour as one means of promoting their product. Caillat and Mueller (1996) found that humour was the dominant appeal used in beer advertising in the UK while Pettigrew (1999) found that humour was also prevalent in Australian beer advertisements. In this regard, alcohol is a bell weather product for late modernity where distinct benefits and advantages are more and more difficult to isolate and defend. One concern we do have about beer advertisements is that, since they routinely make use of gender typecasting (Barthel 1988), our analysis may potentially promulgate such stereotypes.

We begin by summarizing the nature and content of each of the three campaigns.[1] We briefly review the literature on humour in advertising and the wider literature on humour generally. We then use a variety of theoretical frames and various aspects of postmodern discourse to interpret the advertisements and their consumption.

The no. 1 rule of marketing: frogs sell beer

In 1995, Budweiser began a successful series of advertisements featuring three animated frog puppets living in a swamp. The series revolved around a pun with each of the frogs in turn contributing to the 'Bud Weis Er' brand name. In 1997, a related series of advertisements was broadcast, featuring two Lizards, also in the swamp, looking on, jealous of the Frogs' success. By the end of the campaign, Budweiser had broadcast over 80 different television and radio advertisements featuring the Lizards. The Lizard advertisements were rated as America's most popular ad campaign ever in a survey by *USA Today*, and were deemed the most 'likeable' by those surveyed by Ad Tracking, which looked at over 170 ads broadcast during the Superbowls between 1995 and 1998.

Both the Frogs' and the Lizards' series rely heavily on comedy, and there is a clear development of storyline and characters, much like a sit-com. In the Frog series, the following events occur. Three frogs sit on lilies in a swamp outside a bar where Budweiser is for sale. The frogs croak out in turn giving effect to the Budweiser name. The three frogs are carried on the back of an alligator into the swamp bar where they disrupt the customers and leave with a case of Budweiser. One of the frogs attaches itself to a passing Budweiser van and gets taken from the swamp.

The Lizard series focuses on Frankie and Louie, two lizards that watch on from a distance at the frogs croaking out 'Budweiser'. The running gag is that they are lizards in a swamp *and also* out-of-work (New York) actors. The scene in front of them is both swamp *and* a film set for the previous advertisements. Frankie and Louie are jealous of the frogs' success in landing the Budweiser roles. Frankie is philosophical – 'Louie, frogs sell beer. That's it, man. No. 1 rule of marketing' – while Louie is more spiteful:

LOUIE: The Budweiser Lizards. We coulda been huge.
FRANKIE: Hey, there'll be other auditions.
LOUIE: Oh, yeah? For what? This was Budweiser, buddy. This was big.

Or later:

LOUIE: (to the Frogs): Hey! Your mother's an iguana!
FRANKIE: Hey! My mother was an iguana.
LOUIE: Sorry, I meant no disrespect.

In the late 1990s, Scottish Courage launched the first of its series of 'No Nonsense' television campaigns to promote the John Smith's brand. The campaign (www.johnsmiths.co.uk), which had a £20 million budget, featured outsized British comedian Peter Kay and ran from 2002 to 2005, coinciding with a 16 per cent increase in product sales. It received significant press coverage and industry awards such as the Creative Circle and Campaign Magazine's Campaign of the Year in 2002 and the Marketing Week Effectiveness Award 2004. Each execution of the campaign featured a less than glamorous Kay and his 'no nonsense' approach to parenting, care for the elderly, sport and consumption. In one advert Kay is the subject of a 'door step challenge', the common advertising ploy for detergent soaps. Indeed, the focus of the advert – John Smith's beer – is only revealed in the final frame. The advert begins with television personality Danny Baker (former spokesperson and doorstop challenger for Daz soap powder) walking through a working-class housing estate accompanied by a camper crew.

BAKER: Here we are in Bolton and me and the gang are in town to do another doorstep challenge.

Knocks on door of modest house and smiles to camera.

Door is opened by a bedraggled Kay who is continuing a conversation with an unseen other inside the house.

KAY: I don't care whose it is; it's floating!

BAKER: Hello! Would you swap these two large packets of ordinary powder for one packet of biological powder?

In keeping with his no nonsense approach (but contrary to the conventions of such adverts) Kay, quickly accepts the offer.

KAY: Yea … yea.

Swaps one pack of powder for two.

KAY: Tarra

Kay turns and closes door on a suitably bemused Baker

The advert closes with a picture of two cans of John Smith's beer on a washing machine and the tagline: No Nonsense

More recently, Australian brewers Carlton have attracted international attention for their 'Made from Beer' campaign which feature two executions – Big Ad (www.bigad.com.au) and No Explanations (www.Carltondraught.com. au). The first of these, Big Ad, is a parody of epic ads and films. The advert, which was shot in New Zealand, features stunning scenery, a large cast (over 300 actors and more than 20,000 computer-generated men) and a dramatic musical score (*O Fortuna* by Carl Orff, originally used in the Old Spice adverts in the 1970s). The advert builds to a climax as two armies march towards one another through a large valley, in a scene reminiscent of *Braveheart*. The armies sing (with the words subtitled for effect):

> It's a big ad. Very big ad.
> It's a big ad we're in.
> It's a big ad. My god it's big!
> Can't believe how big it is!
> It's a big ad! For Carlton Draught.
> It's just so freak … ing HUGE!
> It's a big ad! Expensive ad!
> This ad better sell some bloody beer!

In the second campaign, which parodies Budweiser's traditional Clydesdale based adverts, an earnest and serious voiceover describes the manufacturing and distribution process for Carlton Draught beer.

Carlton Draught, brewed with sun-ripened barley, individually picked hops and attractive yeast.
Poured down pipes and fermented in a big … metal thing.
Carlton Draught, admired by scientists, put in kegs and driven around … by horses. More horses!
Poured into frosty sideways glasses and drunk in pubs.
Carlton Draught, made from beer.

The campaign is a clear shift away from the traditional blokey beer advertising and has been described by the brewers as 'almost anti advertising' (quoted in Ligerakis 2004).

Now how is that supposed to sell beer?

We now return to our original questions of why the use of humour is so prevalent, and secondly what the prevalence of humour tells us about the nature of consumption. In an attempt to answer these questions, in this section we will briefly review the literature on humour in advertising and the literature on humour generally. We begin with the advertising literature.

Within the advertising literature – which is the only part of the marketing field that considers humour at all – humour is generally seen as a peripheral cue, an optional element (and very much a secondary element) in the sales package offered to rational, potential buyers. Thus, the research has been prescriptive and positivistic, focusing on the degree to which humour is related to gaining attention for an advertisement, comprehending an advertisement's message, being persuaded by an advertisement and believing/trusting/liking the source of an advertisement (see e.g. Weinberger and Gulas 1992; Cline et al. 2003; Geuens and Pelsmacker 2001; Chandy et al. 2001). In addition, all humour research is bedevilled by definitional difficulties, methodological enigmas and the reflexive conundrum common to all prescriptive research. So, for example, if research indicates that slapstick is positively linked to persuasion and this leads to a significant increase in the use of slapstick, then this increase is likely to result in slapstick being *negatively* linked to persuasion as viewers become used to and eventually bored with the genre.

A further difficulty with the research to date is that it adopts a rather naive view of the nature of advertising, of how advertisements are consumed and the degree to which consumers deconstruct advertisements. Thus, advertisements can no longer be interpreted solely – and one might say simplistically – in terms of their functional utility in communicating a message about a product with the intention of engendering sales (in his chronological taxonomy, Holt (2002) describes this as the 'modern branding paradigm'). On this point, it is interesting to note that sales of Budweiser have continued a ten-year decline despite the popularity of their Frogs and Lizards ads (Budweiser sales dropped by 13 per cent between 1999 and 2003, while the US beer market grew by 1.7 per cent in the same period[2]). Tellingly, one of the creators of the series, copywriter Steve Dildarian, is not too concerned about what happens at the cash register: 'Advertising', Dildarian says, 'can only be held so responsible for sales' (USA Today, 26 Jan. 1999). This reflects Holt's 'postmodern branding paradigm' which dispenses with the modern notion that a brand should articulate a specific value proposition: 'The postmodern branding paradigm is premised upon the idea that brands will be more valuable if they are offered not as cultural blueprints but as cultural resources, as useful ingredients to produce the self as one chooses' (Holt 2002: 83). Thus, Calvin Klein's comment that 'my ads are made exactly to have ambiguous readings' (quoted in Martins 1995: 81) sits easily within this postmodern paradigm that recognizes the sophistication of the advertiser *and* the consumer of ads. Holt describes other branding paradigms as well, so it is not surprising that interpretations will vary and intended messages will be lost in the noise. So, for instance, Jakki Mohr of Courage expected quite ambiguous responses to Carlton Draught's Big Ad: 'I wouldn't be surprised if people's response is "What the?" when they first see it' (quoted in Ligerakis 2004). In this context, it behoves us to understand advertisements more broadly. Ads are perhaps best seen as literary texts, artistically created by an author and aesthetically realized by a reader, who are both in continuous dialogue with other cultural, communicational and artistic texts (Holt 2002).

This suggests that postmodern discourse can help us to better understand the nature of contemporary advertising/consumption and also explain why the number of humorous ads has increased over the last 20 years. It seems clear to us that the selected beer ads 'work' because they tap into fashionable aspects of postmodern discourse – such as intertextuality, reflexivity, self-referentiality, parody, paralogy – which are recognized and appreciated by the postmodern consumer, even if s/he doesn't necessarily use or know these terms. The ads are littered with in-jokes that the viewer can enjoy getting because they are 'in the know' due to their media literacy. That is, they are not just watching an advertisement; rather they are sharing the parody of advertising, sit-com and film created by the advertisers. In this sense, these are not commercials trying to represent an external or social reality; instead they are representing media to a media-literate audience. For example the line, 'Number one rule of marketing: frogs sell beer', can be seen as a take on the use of models to promote products, or the representation of the idealized person in much advertising, or as a parody of simplistic representations of management knowledge. The line allows viewers to smile knowingly at the notion of this approach being applied to something like a frog as opposed to a beautiful person (or prince). Similarly, the Doorstep advert for John Smith's requires that we are clued into the conceit of the situation, from Peter Kay's opening line directed back into his unseen family as he opens the front door through to the final pay off as he accepts the offer of two boxes of his 'old powder'. Perhaps the best exemplar of this phenomenon is Carlton Draught's 'No Explanations', which is unintelligible other than as a parody of Budweiser's advertising. The inherent humour in each of these campaigns requires that we identify with the joker at the expense of those who fail to see that the hand of the advertiser is behind the idealized images in the advertisements.

Humorous advertisements can be seen as symptomatic of the romantic aspects of postmodernism (Brown *et al.* 1998). Romanticism, it is worth recalling, celebrates the emotional, the creative, the imaginative, the unreal, the fictive, parody and irony, and each of these features are present, to a greater or lesser degree, in the three campaigns under study and many other contemporary advertisements. Just as romanticism stands in opposition to classical realism, the three campaigns stand in opposition to more 'modern' ads (or what Holt (2002) would term pre-modern ads) that are framed within a paradigm based on information processing and communication (e.g. 'buy this dress because it is 20 per cent cheaper … NOW!').

The selected adverts are inter-textual to the nth degree, making innumerable references to other ads in the series, to advertising norms, to the advertising process itself and to well-known characters from film and television. Most notably, the advertising style and content in the Budweiser campaign reflect the more popular sit-coms of the 1990s, such as *Seinfeld* and *Larry Sanders*. *Seinfeld*, which was the decade's biggest prime-time sit-com in the US, was about a stand-up comedian and featured inserts from his shows. Towards the end of the show's successful run, the characters were played by characters written by characters in a sit-com. Likewise, the setting for *Larry Sanders* was a production team of a late night chat show with inserts again from the show. There is a self-consciousness about the Budweiser ads in the style of *Larry Sanders*, while the aggression and mean-mindedness of the ads is similar to both *Larry Sanders* and *Seinfeld*. Moreover, Louie's most notable attribute is his bloated self-concept, which underlies his attempts to get and expand his part in the commercials. In this respect much of the humour in Louie can be read as a play on the folly of ego and human endeavour. Again, this closely parallels the mood of *Seinfeld* and *Larry Sanders*, with Louie's character echoing the George and Hank characters in these shows. Some of the ads also take broader swipes at the media. For instance, in one 'episode' Louie does a parody of method actors, showing Frankie his 'look'. Also, Frankie attributes the Ferret's success ahead of the Lizards to the fact that he looks like a small European film director.

In essence, the selected adverts are a parody on advertising and various media genres. Parody is a pre-eminent example of intertextuality in that it relies on the addressee recognizing the original text in order to get the most out of the humour. Moreover, from the marketer's perspective, a comedic ad is the ideal format for a reflexive, intelligent, media-literate audience because it encourages and indeed requires deconstruction in order to be understood. This differs from a straight ad, which will fall apart when deconstructed.

One explanation for the increasing number of humorous ads is that humour effectively penetrates the contemporary media saturation without recourse to claims of superiority or differentiation, which may be difficult to fulfil when the product is purchased/consumed or, alternatively, may be neutralized by competitors. Thus, a significant feature of these campaigns is that there is little mention of the gratification or utility that the consumer will gain through buying or drinking beer. Accordingly, we can usefully categorize the campaigns as 'postmodern' in contrast to 'modern' advertisements where the reward or gratification for consuming the advertisement is deferred until the advertised product is consumed. Thus, 'modern' advertisements are structured within a *teleological* framework – 'listen to this ad now and you will benefit in the future' – where the temporal structure is the present during which the advertisement is being experienced *and* the future when the product will be consumed. Postmodern advertisements, in contrast, exist in an *ateleological* structure in so far as they are disconnected from the future consumption of the product. We could say that for the postmoderns there is no time like the present, or maybe no time other than the present. This privileging of the present is a common theme in postmodern discourse, which is axiomatically incredulous to teleological thinking, or the belief in some grand, over-arching narrative within which current actions are seen to be unfolding. Furthermore, the abandonment of linear time and teleological understandings of the present gives rise to a greater appetite for humour, since there is no longer a point to deferring gratification. Humorous advertisements fit well within this scheme since, in so far as they provide instant gratification, they are based on an *immanent* temporality, in contrast to modern advertisements where the temporal structure is best described as *imminent*. As Hesse (1961) argues in *Steppenwolf*, infinity is a moment, and if you only have a moment then it is a moment best spent laughing. Howells (no pun intended) makes a similar point in his aphoristic assertion that 'there will presently be no room in the world for things; it will be filled up with the advertisements of things' (quoted in Lears 1994: 286).

If belief was the byword for the moderns – belief in reason, belief in science, belief in progress – then scepticism is surely the enduring attribute of the postmoderns. This is not to say that contemporary, postmodern consumers are totally negative or cynical to the marrow. Far from it. Instead, they might best be described as 'sophisticated and literate sceptics', at least in relation to popular culture and its aesthetics and semiotics, who readily and reflexively deconstruct both advertisements and their consumption of products (Meadows 1983). In other words, the postmodern audience will critically interrogate an ad to see what its producers are trying to do, how they are trying to sell their wares, what meanings can be constructed from the advertisement and what texts the ad refers to (O'Donohoe 1997; Holt 2002). Moreover, as Mick and Buhl (1992) and others have shown, advertisements are idiosyncratically interpreted and experienced against the backdrop of the individual's life history and current life-world. Marketers, of course, are well aware of this phenomenon and it's possible that humour is used as a way of inhibiting the creative interpretation – or wanton deconstruction – of advertisements that an audience routinely engages in. To expand on this point, we draw on Umberto Eco's somewhat counterintuitive distinction between 'closed' and 'open' texts. *Closed* texts – like Superman comic strips and Ian Fleming's novels about James Bond – are immoderately 'open' to every possible interpretation, while *open* texts don't allow readers to decode the texts any way they want: 'You cannot use the text as you want, but only as the text wants you to use it. An open text, however "open" it be, cannot afford whatever interpretation' (Eco 1979/1984: 9). Humorous adverts are a good example of Eco's *open* texts since they try to create a particular kind of reading and reader – people who will respond with smiles, laughter and related feelings to the advert/text. This is because, for a joke to work, the addressee must understand the message and have the same assumptions the sender has. Or, in other words, they know that the greatest satisfaction will be derived from a particular reading – which will be adopted in an attempt to get the joke.

The conjunction of these phenomena has created a significant reorientation in the nature of advertising, as evidenced by ads like the selected campaigns discussed here, which now may be best interpreted as a form of sponsored programming. These are not so much ads, in our traditional understanding of adverts. Rather they are jokes 'proudly brought to you by the people from Budweiser/John Smith's/Carlton'. Thus, there is little substantive difference between (a) a comedy show which has product placements in it; (b) a sit-com that is sponsored (for example, Bailey's sponsorship of *Friends*); and (c) a comedic scene which is in a commercial break but which is clearly being paid for by a company (i.e. Budweiser). The distinction is even more blurred when the comedic scene is part of a series, as in the Budweiser (or John Smith's) case, which, in many ways, is a sit-com, sponsored by Budweiser, about reptiles in a swamp. Indeed, this approach could be seen as very appropriate to the contemporary viewing pattern of channel-hopping between a multiplicity of channels, since viewers can more easily follow a storyline that is delivered in short bursts, frequently and across a large number of channels. An advertisement comfortably fits this format.

Funny and free?

Thus far, we have examined and interpreted advertising humour as an important and neglected aspect of postmodernism. In this section we adopt an alternative approach by considering humour as a reaction *against* postmodernism. First, we can argue that humour is a viable *alternative* to – rather than just a by-product of – the postmodern, since it has an innate palatability and positiveness that is absent from much of postmodern discourse. The postmodern, which we understand as the cultural critique of modernity (Rosenau 1992), has no true existence save for its play on the incongruities of modernity. Thus, just as anti-structure (or post-structural) has no meaning without the existence of structure, postmodernism as anti-modernism has no meaning without modernism. In contrast, humour has no Other except the target of 'being funny', which provides it with an ontology that is always unattainable by the postmodern. Or, as Vasantkumar (1998: 229) has observed, 'the reality of jokes is more tolerable than the joke of reality that is the discovery of postmodernism'. In other words, postmodernism quickly leads into nihilism and despair – the joke of reality – while jokes, in contrast, create their own reality that is tolerable, happy and fulfilling (as well as reminding us of the fragile, arbitrary and tenuous nature of 'reality'). Furthermore, much of what passes for postmodernist writing is actually writing about postmodernity in a manner and style that conforms to *modern* mores covering discourse. Humour, however, while having conventional forms and structures, has to be different, surprising and incongruous if it is to work. Indeed to achieve its purpose (being funny) it has to play with form and expectations. In this regard, humour achieves an outcome that postmodernism (or more accurately the discourse about postmodernity) very often doesn't.

A further attribute of humour is that it gets us away from the relativism of postmodernism, since it's difficult to argue that humour exists merely and totally in the eye of the beholder. If humour was totally subjective how then could one explain the fact that large numbers of people laugh at the same time when watching a humorous play or film? Since humour is invariably shared with others – either real or imagined – it creates a link between the singular and the collective, effecting a transition from aloneness to togetherness, countering the Thatcherite notion that there is no such thing as the social. And uniquely, laughter is a powerful social contagion, triggering the release, in a collective, of great quantities of emotion. Along with sympathy and other emotions, humour is an emotional state in which 'the need is felt to behave as part of some real or imaginary entity that transcends … the boundaries of the individual self' (Koestler 1964: 54).

Humour also provides an interesting perspective on the postmodern (problematizing) of epistemology and consequent scepticism to *all* truth claims.

This is because humour provides what amounts to an alternative epistemology, because the transitions from humour (the 'Haha reaction') to discovery (the 'Aha! Reaction') to the delight of the aesthetic experience (the 'Ah … reaction') are continuous: witticism blends into epigram, caricature into portrait, art into science, beauty into truth. For example, a funny caricature works because even though there is no attempt to accurately represent reality, the basis of the humour is that it captures the essence or idealized concept of reality. Some jokes, therefore, are funny because they're true, and conversely, some truths are true because they're funny. Or, as Will Rogers once said, 'Give me the truth. I'll exaggerate it and make it funny' (Fadiman 1955: 227). In this sense, there is a humorous dimension to epistemology that has, unfortunately, got lost in much, if not most, of organization theory's epistemological debate (see Kavanagh 1994, for a summary).

A final approach to the study of humour is to consider the phenomenon at a different level of analysis, namely at the level of the capitalist *system* as first described by Marx. Here, we can draw on a long-standing argument — expounded by writers such as Marx, Durkheim, Schumacher and latterly in organizational studies by critical theorists like Alvesson — which asserts that as consumption increases and as the consumer society becomes more extensive, existential angst, anxiety, alienation and anomie will also increase. Marx's thesis was that this alienation could only be ameliorated through (proletariat) revolution, while Durkheim (1897/1970) posited that *deviant* behaviour, rather than social revolution, would be the outcome of the dysfunctions within capitalism. However, an interesting alternative is that the anxiety produced by the capitalist system is *released through humour*, and that advertising provides a convenient and appropriate process to effect this. This is because humour has a 'liberating' aspect, since it plays with our ideas of what's normal and abnormal. For example, the punchline in a joke leads us in a direction we had not anticipated and thus suggests that there is an element of freedom in our lives (it intimates at alternative realities by showing the arbitrary and tenuous nature of mundane, paramount reality). This, in turn, implies that changes are possible and that we need not be prisoners of habit, fixations, etc. Thus humour, which has an important function in providing release from tension, is of equal importance to the capitalist system as other, apparently more central, phenomena like alienation. From this systemic perspective, advertising responds to a need for humour within the capitalist system and, correspondingly, individuals will consume advertisements that satisfy that need. Here, it should be noted that, since the unit of analysis is the capitalist system, there is no interest in whether a particular advertisement is humorous or not, or whether the humour was useful in communicating the advertisement's message.

If we take a Baudrillardian rather than a Marxist perspective – i.e. if we centralize consumption rather than production – a similar, but somewhat different argument applies. Unlike Marx, Baudrillard saw no potential for a proletariat revolt and saw no possibility of the capitalist system being overthrown. In developing his ideas, Baudrillard centralized the concept of the 'code', which he understands as a controlling system of signs: 'one is permanently governed by a code whose rule and meaning-constraints – like those of language – are, for the most part, beyond the grasp of individuals' (Baudrillard 1998: 61). The 'code', which bears strong and explicit resemblances to the 'matrix' in the film *The Matrix*, is pervasive, ensuring that people participate, and participate actively, and in particular ways, in the consumer society. Thus, in a world dominated by the code, consumption no longer has anything to do with satisfying 'needs'. As Ritzer (1997: 81) explains, 'We do not buy what we need, but rather the code tells us we should buy. Further, needs themselves are determined by the code so that we end up "needing" what the code tells us to we need'.

Again, we can argue that humour's liberatory potential provides a means of escape, albeit temporarily, from the code, and, in addition, it gives individuals a feeling of superiority in an arena where they are constructed as receptacles. Moreover, in an age when postmodern discourse is characterized by scepticism towards great visions, advertising – and humorous advertising in particular – presents a utopian vision of a happy, imaginary world to the consumer and, through doing so, celebrates the continuing human ability to be creative and to transcend the mundane. As Martins (1995: 51) puts it:

> in the absence of stronger illusions, the public needs to invest its dreams somewhere. Replacing other vendors of illusions that progress has dislodged from their traditional positions, advertising appears at the right time to fill the vacuum.

Alternatively, however, we can see humorous advertisements as very much a central part of the code, acting to control and construct consumers (ah – as I interpreted it above). In Baudrillard's (1998: 80) opinion, 'consumerist man (*l'homme-consommateur*) regards *enjoyment as an obligation*; he sees himself as *an enjoyment and satisfaction business*' (original emphasis). Moreover, this interpretation suggests that in the selected advertisements what is being sold is not beer, but humour, since a feature of the code is 'that which was once thought to be inalienable is exchanged: "virtue, love, knowledge, consciousness"' (Baudrillard 1973/1975: 119). And so it is with humour. By selling humour, or more accurately by ensuring that consumers consume happiness – 'Happiness', as the ad used to say, 'is a thing called *Hamlet*' – the code ensures that consumers giggle or, in Neil Postman's (1985) phrase, 'amuse themselves to death', rather than rebel or destabilize the system.

Conclusion

The difference between a conclusion and a punchline is that a conclusion self-referentially connects with the storyline's narrative structure, in particular its beginning, so as to create a closed oneness between the beginning and the end, the alpha and the omega. A punchline, in contrast, deliberately eschews the narrative structure, creating a new meaning to the text that is in opposition to the prior sequence. Modern texts, like this one, have conclusions rather than punchlines. Maybe.

Notes

1 Given the difficulty of explaining the humour, we have where possible provided readers with the URLs of sites where the campaigns can be viewed.
2 Data obtained from industry report produced by Beverage Marketing Corporation of New York available at: <http://www.beveragemarketing.com/SelectTopline.doc>, accessed 19 Jan. 2006.

References

Barthel, D. (1988) *Putting on Appearances: Gender and Advertising*, Philadelphia, PA: Temple University Press.

Baudrillard, J. (1973/1975) *The Mirror of Production*, St Louis, MO: Telos Press.

Baudrillard, J. (1998) *The Consumer Society*, London: Sage.

Beard, F. (2005) 'One hundred years of humor in American advertising', *Journal of Macromarketing*, 15(1): 54–65.

Brown, S., Doherty, A. M. and Clarke, B. (1998) 'Stoning the romance: on marketing's mind-fora's manacles', in S. Brown, A. M. Doherty and B. Clarke (eds), *Romancing the Market*, pp. 1–20, London: Routledge.

Caillat, Z. and Mueller, B. (1996) 'Observations: the influence of culture on American and British advertising: an exploratory comparison of beer advertising', *Journal of Advertising Research*, 36(3): 79–88.

Chandy, R. K., Tellis, G. J., MacInnis, D. J. and Thaivanich P. (2001) 'What to say when: advertising appeals in evolving markets', *Journal of Marketing Research*, 38(4): 399–414.

Chattopadhyay, A. and Basu, K. (1990) 'Humor in advertising: the moderating role of prior brand evaluation', *Journal of Marketing Research*, 27 (Nov.): 466–76.

Cline, T. W., Altsech, M. B. and Kellaris, J. J. (2003) 'When does humor enhance or inhibit AD responses? The moderating role of the need for humor', *Journal of Advertising*, 32(3): 31–45.

Durkheim, É. (1897/1970) *Suicide*, London: Routledge and Kegan Paul.

Eco, U. (1979/1984) *The Role of the Reader: Explorations in the Semiotics of Texts*, Bloomington, IN: Indiana University Press.

Fadiman, C. (1955) *The American Treasury, 1455–1955*, New York: Harper.

Geuens, M. and De Pelsmacker, P. (2001) 'The role of humor in the persuasion of individuals varying in need for cognition', *Advances in Consumer Research*, 29: 50–6.

Hesse, H. (1961) *Steppenwolf*, New York: Holt Rinehart & Winston.

Holt, D. B. (2002) 'Why do brands cause trouble? A dialectical theory of consumer culture and branding', *Journal of Consumer Research*, 29 (June): 70–90.

Kavanagh, D. (1994) 'Hunt v Anderson: round 16', *European Journal of Marketing*, 28: 26–41.

Koestler, A. (1964) *The Act of Creation*, New York: Macmillan.

Lears, J. (1994) *Fables of Abundance: A Cultural History of Advertising in America*, New York: Basic Books.

Ligerakis, M. (2004) *B&T Weekly*, 54(2469): 3-3.

Martins, M. C. d. S. (1995) *Humor and Eroticism in Advertising*, San Diego, CA: San Diego State University Press.

Meadows, R. (1983) 'They consume advertising too', *Admap*, 18: 408–13.

Mick, D. G. and Buhl, C. (1992) 'A meaning-based model of advertising experiences', *Journal of Consumer Research*, 19: 317–38.

Miller, R. and Mizerski, D. (2005) 'Using the RCE scales for testing the effect of beer ads in underage teen intention to consume and reported consumption of beer', 8th Australian and New Zealand Marketing Academy (ANZMAC) Conference, Freemantle, Australia, 5–7 Dec.

Nelson, J. (2005) 'Beer advertising and marketing update: structure, conduct, and social costs', *Review of Industrial Organisation*, 26: 269–306.

O'Donohoe, S. (1997) 'Raiding the postmodern pantry: advertising intertextuality and the young adult audience', *European Journal of Marketing*, 31: 234–53.

Pettigrew, S. (1999) 'An analysis of Australian beer advertisements', Australian and New Zealand Marketing Academy Conference, Sydney, Australia, 30 Nov.–2 Dec.

Postman, N. (1985) *Amusing Ourselves to Death: Public Discourse in the Age of Show Business*, New York: Viking.

Ritzer, G. (1997) *Postmodern Social Theory*, New York: McGraw-Hill.

Rosenau, P. M. (1992) *Postmodernism and the Social Sciences*, Princeton, NJ: Princeton University Press.

Tomkovick, C., Yelkur, R. and Christians, L. (2001) 'The USA's biggest marketing event keeps getting bigger: an in-depth look at Super Bowl advertising in the 1990s', *Journal of Marketing Communications*, 7: 89–108.

UK Office of Communications (2005) *Young People and Alcohol Advertising: A Study to Assess the Impact of Regulatory Change*, London: Office Of Communications.

Vasantkumar, N. J. C. (1998) 'Being analog', in A. A. Berger (ed.), *The Postmodern Presence: Readings on Postmodernism in American Culture and Society*, pp. 212–38, London: Sage.

Weinberger, M. (1999) Personal communication.

Weinberger, M. G. and Gulas, C. S. (1992) 'The impact of humor in advertising: a review', *Journal of Advertising*, 11: 35–59.

Chapter 13

Grotesque humor regeneration of McDonaldization and McDonaldland

David M. Boje, Yue Cai-Hillon,
Grace-Ann Rosile and Esther R. Thomas

This chapter, written in a critical postmodern style, discusses and presents the script of a play entitled "Grotesque humor regeneration of McDonaldization and McDonaldland." The first act of the play introduces the story of Nan, a worker in a Happy Meal toy factory in China, who is pregnant as a result of an illicit affair with her direct supervisor. In the second act, the action moves between three zones of the main stage: stage left is a meeting of McDonald's board of directors; stage right, the Chinese factory; stage center is McDonald's Redlands restaurant. In the third and final act spectators are asked to select an ending informed by one of three literary theories: Brechtian tragic grotesque, Boalian resituated grotesque, or Bakhtinian carnivalesque.

The purpose of the play is to regenerate McDonald's business behavior and theories of McDonaldization, through a management education pedagogic performance with what we are calling "grotesque theater." Our play is purposely dialectic, creating oppositions between the grotesque laughter of Mikhail Bakhtin (1968, 1981), the satiric "Epic Theater" of Bertolt Brecht (1969; in Willett 1957) and the "Theatre of the Oppressed" of Augusto Boal (1979, 1992, 1995). All three have contributed to critical theory, with Boal being more affirmative, Brecht being more mocking, and Bakhtin being more grotesque.[1] The first half of the chapter explores each of these theories in relation to research into humor in organizations. On that basis, the second half of the chapter presents the script of the play itself and discusses the four occasions on which the play was staged in 2004.

Humor in organizations

Studies of humor in management and organization research have focused, more commonly, on the effects and influence of humor in the workplace. Workplace culture studies have found that humor in organizations has helped to improve workers' confidence towards their jobs (Gruner 1997), created a positive culture for employees, influenced culture change in organizations (Clouse and Spurgeon 1995), enhanced group cohesiveness and individual and group creativity (Duncan 1982; Csikszentmihalyi 1996; Holmes and Marra 2002), increased employee motivation (Crawford and Gressley 1991; Dienstbier 1995), and increased productivity (Clouse and Spurgeon 1995).

A second focus of studies on humor is in the area of leadership – especially in terms of how leaders and managers use humor (e.g. Duncan 1982; Clouse and Spurgeon 1995). Such studies have shown humour to be a positive tool for management (Collinson 2002). In another study, Avolio *et al.* (1999) found that humor was the moderator in the relationship between leadership style and individual and unit-level performance. It was found that active leadership, either in the form of transformational or contingent reward leadership, was positively related to the use of humor. Conversely, laissez-faire leadership was negatively related to the use of humor.

Examining some of the research conducted in management strategy, Boje and Cai (2004) found an inescapable link between humor and strategy in organizations. They explored the role of strategy within the realm of organizational life encompassing management decision-making, leadership, and consulting in the workplace. This covered growth strategies (e.g. Organ and Grover 1987), knowledge management strategies (e.g. Koch 2004), and hiring strategies (e.g. Raffoni 1999). Based on this examination, Boje and Cai (2004) identified humor as playing a role in the dramatic metamorphosis of descent to the netherworld and ascent and rebirth cycle which is the humorous strategy story. This humor dictates that a dethroning, descending, degradation, and grotesque dismemberment phase be followed by rebirth, renewal, and regeneration.

Humor can be defined as a comedic quality, sometimes ironic and sometimes satirical, that makes some event seem funny or at least amusing and can take on various forms. Our strategic use of humor in the play presented in this chapter is based on a theorization of organizations as systems of utterances (including humorous ones) that have complex historical dynamics reflecting the changes taking place within the corporation's socioeconomic, cultural, and technical environment. While we use the case of McDonald's to illustrate this, it should be realized that the implications go beyond this example. Indeed, the broader implication is that the understanding of humor in relation to work can deepen our knowledge of how corporate actions can be rewritten, respoken, and graphically reimagined in other idea systems and how, in this process, a taste of humor can play a significant and dynamic role. In this context, humor can no longer be separated from understanding organizations because it constantly manifests itself in this dynamic environment.

We use the grotesque humor theories developed by Mikhail Bakhtin (1968, 1981), Augusto Boal (1979, 1992, 1995), and Bertolt Brecht (1969/1932) to inform our work on the McDonald's corporation and our play. Bakhtin, Brecht, and Boal, our three central humor theorists, have laid out a ground path that enables us to seek connections between different genres of humor and corporate behaviors. To examine the implications of the work of these three scholars and their theories of humor in depth, we incorporate fictive examples of humor, and, through the play, interconnect them with the corporation's historical dynamics. For instance, without understanding Bakhtin's theory of grotesque humor combined with the understanding of the environmental context, it would be difficult to understand why McDonald's strategically decided to create chicken McNuggets in the shape of a chicken head in certain parts of the world. It would also be difficult to understand why, in the marketing videos, McDonaldland uses characters in the image of their own processed food products (chicken McNugget, Milk Shake, Hamburger). To begin making these connections, in the next section we present a detailed review of grotesque humor theories and their links to our play in the subsequent section.

Theories of grotesque humor

Grotesque humor is premised on exaggeration for the sake of humorous effect. This involves taking one element of reality and distorting it out of proportion. In the sixteenth century, François Rabelais wrote five books of satire and parody, where the literal grotesque came in the form of the giant, Gargantua, and descriptions of pre-Lent Carnival (1532/1873). This carnival involved the suspension of prohibitions at the expense of the upper class; sometimes literally tossing dung and urine at their caricatures. Carnival, however, is not entirely a relic of pre-modern medieval times. One of us (Thomas) is from the capital city Roseau on the island of Dominica. In Roseau, carnival is held at the traditional pre-Lenten time. It begins a month before the two days (Monday/Tuesday) of "jump-up". This ritual is called this because people dance in the street and "jump up" to the beat of steel band music. People wear grotesque masks that exaggerate their facial expressions. In such festivities, grotesque humor has two contemporary Dominican forms. The first is the presence of grotesque masks, and the second are the calypso songs, with lyrics of social commentary, and accompanying theater skits where people dress up in costumes to parody various issues. Calypso songs are a parody of the economic, political, and social situation. The topics of these parodies include government policies, the behavior of politicians and government ministers, the treatment of workers in public and private sectors, IMF policies, the spread of AIDS, the increase in crime, and the deterioration of morals and social values. Unlike sixteenth-century Rabelaisian carnival, people in Dominica do not throw dung (or anything else), and there is no nakedness, or sexual abandon (as one finds in Bakhtin's (1968) reading of Rabelais). People in Dominica do, however, get drunk and disorderly. There is, in Dominican carnival (important to our performance) the use of grotesque humor for social and economic commentary.

Grotesque humor can also be found in the activities of the McDonald's corporation, although this official humor is more conservative than the sixteenth-century Rabelais or twenty-first-century Dominican carnival. Even though McDonaldization (Ritzer 2000) can be regarded as the triumph of systemic rationalism, it also contains a definite humorous element. Ronald McDonald and McDonaldland characters (Hamburglar, Mayor McCheese, Grimace, etc.) that feature in McDonald's advertising and promotions have a history of clown-humor, and an important interplay with grotesque humor. The more literal grotesque humor that is displayed in relation to McDonald's (i.e. the tossing of dung and urine) is present in public protest, most particularly the mud-slinging that McDonald's corporation endures from the counter-globalization, slow food, vegetarian, and animal rights movements. José Bové, of France, for example, covertly dismantled a McDonald's restaurant one night, and deposited it on the front lawn of a government official. In other examples carts with dung were tossed onto McDonald's franchise lawns, and women wearing nothing but bikinis of lettuce have burlesquely protested animal rights for PETA (People for the Ethical Treatment of Animals). The grotesque humor of Ronald and his representation of McDonald's have also been brought into real-life representations. Activists have related the image of Ronald to President Bush, called McBush. There are grotesque mask characterizations of all the McDonaldland characters, and grotesque humor in parody and satire on the internet. For example, a 2003 UK website featured a bronze casting called *Last McSupper* showing Christ and company eating a McMeal. *Unholy Trinity* shows Ronald McDonald crucified, flanked by also-crucified Hamburglar and a Big Mac. In sum McDonald's rational systems of post-Fordist global production contends with grotesque humor every day both through its self-representations and those representations reformulated in public protest.

Our study of McDonald's is not just about the grotesque humor of mockery. Instead we contrast such mockery with two forms of much more affirmative grotesque humor. First, as in the Dominican carnival, there is a time set aside for social commentary, for the people to express, in mask, theater gestures, and song, what are the ills of the economy, social life, and government. Second, there is a grotesque real, within official McDonald's humor – this is a tamer grotesque humor, a more romantic grotesque (as Bakhtin calls it). Our purpose is therefore to exhibit a theater that unleashes the dialectic forces of a variety of critical, affirmative, and transformational grotesque humor aesthetics. As we introduced earlier, our play ends with the audience being asked to select one of three endings, each informed by a different theory of grotesque humor. Next, we present a brief overview of these three theories as they are represented in the work of Bakhtin, Boal, and Brecht.

Mikhail Bakhtin

Bakhtin's (1968) study of Rabelais is a critique of Enlightenment rationality, and a careful genealogy of the history of grotesque humor from antiquity, through the Middle Ages, into the Renaissance, and into modernity. Enlightenment rationality denies grotesque humor, in favor of the abstract realism that is modernity's signature. Countering such a logic, Bakhtin sees in grotesque humor a very affirmative ethos. Bakhtin introduces his 'grotesque' method to focus on the regenerative and revitalizing power of the people's festive-carnival, during those temporary times and places when official spectacle of religious and courtly life prevailed. Bakhtin theorized that during carnival, the people could lead the reform of the social and economic spheres normally dominated by hierarchy and dogmatism. Bakhtin's affirmation of the regenerative power of the carnival is cast against those critics (e.g. Coleman 1971; Schwartz 1990; Prescott 1998) who argue that people of the low classes are bound by social prohibitions and suggest that while in carnival they may act out a little, they do so within hegemonic bounds. Such critics have also charged Bakhtin with over-emphasizing what he referred to as 'the lower bodily stratum' – this suggests that carnival in the sixteenth century was not all about hurling dung, peeing on caricatures of officialdom, or engaging in sexual abandon. In short, the role of grotesque humor in festive-carnival, and how it accomplishes social and economic transformation is hotly debated. Nevertheless, it remains central to Bakhtin's theorization of the carnival, that folk-humour can perform an important role in the transformation of society through parody and critique.

Augusto Boal

Like Bakhtin's carnivalesque, Boal's (1979) *Theatre of the Oppressed* is also a critical and affirmative method of parody and satire. Again like Bakhtin, Boal is a critical theorist influenced by Marxist theory who believes that people can and should overcome the oppression of class hierarchy. Boal's theater workshops are conducted in countries around the world. Indeed, in our own teaching practice, Boal has provided a critical pedagogy incorporated in the curricular options for management education. In teaching, we use Boal's (1992) exercises in image, invisibility, and forum theater, as explained below.

Image theater allows a person who has experienced oppression to create a physical image of how they experienced that oppression by creating a tableau or short skit. For example, an operating room nurse created a scene where she knelt and bowed before a man who represented a surgeon. The nurse instructed the "surgeon" to stand with arms folded, looking angry. The nurse repeated a litany of apologies for not having the surgeon's preferred chair available in the operating room. One particular version of image theater employs the practice of "body sculpting." This is an improvisation of story construction that involves participants engaging in silent bodily expression of social and economic conflicts. The intended effect of image theater, like all of Boal's theater techniques, is to put the person who has experienced oppression into the powerful position of recreating that situation. The physical, theatrical recreation puts all participants in the role of spect-actors; that is, being both spectators and actors in this theater. Spect-actors experiment with ways to revise the original scene to make it less oppressive.

Image theater can also be considered to be an appreciative inquiry in terms of what Boal terms the "rainbow of your desire." There are, however, differences between Boal's theatrics and the field of study known as appreciative inquiry (Cooperrider and Srivastava 1987; Srivastava and Cooperrider 1990).[2] Boal assumes there is a "cop in your head" that limits your power in a situation, by the internalization of oppression. Through acts of awareness, the spect-actors are able to move into a more appreciative stance of their own position in society.

Invisibility theater exercises use body gestures and dialogue, in juxtapositions of multiple zones of the stages, to show center-stage what the spectators see in official spectacle. Invisibility theater takes that which is normally hidden or off stage and brings it on stage to show its more grotesque and burlesque aspects. In our case, it can do so in the halls of power, or in some scene (such as a factory floor) that customers and non-factory employees do not normally see.

Forum theater allows the spect-actor audience to yell "stop" and suggest ways to change situations portrayed on stage. Such changes are intended to enable people to imagine and invent courses of events where they try out a solution to their disempowerment. Game rules can be modified, but they still exist – this ensures that the players are involved in the same enterprise of power, yet facilitates the generation of serious and fruitful attempts at developing solutions (Boal 1992: 18).

In the classroom, we have used Boalian theatrics to present case material on Enron, McDonald's, and other large and small businesses. Such theater sets up a game of conflict between antagonists and protagonists. We invite participants to rescript the protagonists' roles, to better counter or what we call 'resituate' the drama. In our grotesque theater play presented in the second half of this chapter, the character of Nan is based upon research by one of the co-authors of the chapter (Yue Cai-Hillon). The dialogue is adapted from her research in China that investigated factory communication. This research is adapted in the form of Boalian invisible theater by juxtaposing the McDonald's board of directors and a

Redlands McDonald's restaurant with a Chinese factory subcontracted to make Happy Meal toys. This is also informed by a similar incident that happened in a Vietnamese contract factory.[3]

Bertolt Brecht

Discussions of Brecht's epic theater can be found in the collected works of Willett (1957) and in his own plays, such as *Saint Joan of the Stock Yards* (1932).[4] Brecht's humor is something many critics find entirely negative – it is a blatant mockery of forms of exploitative capitalism and fascism. Brecht parodied the official capitalist spectacle such that the audience members could be infused by revolutionary spirit – they would laugh, but they would do so intelligently and with a view to action.

Brecht (in Willett 1957: 71) distinguishes between the dramatic and the epic spectator. If we assume people are socialized in the dramatic aesthetic, then the task of epic theater is to defamiliarize such an aesthetic. There is a dialectic relation between two spectators, as summarized in Figure 13.1.

Brecht did not promote dramatic grotesque humor for its own sake, he wanted the audience to take the role of an epic spectator and, leaving the theater, to go and change the world. In this sense epic theater invites the spectator to take a critical and intelligent (epic) role. The actors and the script purposely do not invite an empathetic viewing that one finds in Aristotelian drama (i.e. as comic entertainment or cathartic relief from fear and pity). A key concept in epic theater is defamiliarization. Its purpose is to take a "common recurrent universally-practiced operation and try to draw attention to it by illuminating its peculiarity" (Willett 1957: 145).

All three of the scholars introduced above are important to our play. Our purpose is to make the familiar in McDonald's appear strange and remarkable.

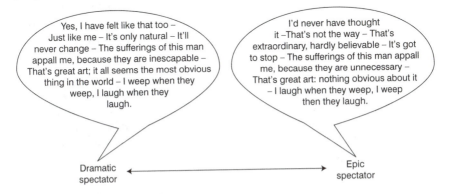

Figure 13.1 Dialectic of dramatic and epic spectator

We do this in two ways. First, we invite spectators to be epic spectators, to use the Brechtian "A-effect" (alienation-effect) to break out of empathy with characters and the dramatics of storyline (see Willett 1957). Second, we interrupt the dramatic view, by showing "factoids" (i.e. some pieces of social research) on a back screen. One example of this is *The Economist's* "Big Mac index" – an index that seeks to make exchange-rate theory more digestible. This is arguably the world's most accurate financial indicator to be based on a fast-food item. It shows how, for example, the cheapest burger is in China, at $1.23, compared with an average American price of $2.80. This implies the yuan is 56 per cent undervalued.[5]

In sum, our play combines the work of two more appreciative grotesque theorists, Bakhtin and Boal, with the more mocking grotesque approach of Brecht. Our thesis is that this will set up a transformative and regenerative dialectic that can defamiliarize McDonald's and leads to its metamorphosis using what we are calling "grotesque theater." We turn next to the activities and script of the play after which we present a summary of the reactions of conference participants to the actual staging of the play.

Staging McDonald's

The script provided is designed as a minimal framework that involves no memory work on the part of those involved. Volunteers are asked to get acquainted with their characters, and if possible meet with their respective stage groups (left, center, right) to discuss themes they want to portray beyond the basic script. First, we introduce the casting call.

The characters who appear in stage left are Jim Cantalupo (McDonald's CEO), Larry Light (McDonald's Global Chief Marketing Officer), Ronald McDonald (McDonald's Chief Happiness Officer), Juergen Knauss (CEO of Heye and Partner, the Munich, Germany, advertising agency), and Charlie Bell (McDonald's President and COO). Unlike the actual people being portrayed, the volunteers/actors do not have to be white men – in our play there can be female and non-white board members. The lead actor plays the role of Ronald (costume included), and roves between stage left, right, and center.

On stage right the main role is that of Nan, a 16-year-old, pregnant Happy Meal toy factory worker. She also moves between stage center and stage right. We call on between three and six volunteers to play other Chinese factory workers: Ling, Bing, and others that volunteer. There is also a role for a Chinese factory supervisor (reputed father to Nan's unborn child, played by another volunteer).

We do stage-center casting two ways (discussing this with the volunteers). First, we can use the more cartoonish characters of McDonaldland. Second, we can keep Ronald as the central clown symbol-image and the players stage center wear their conference attire playing roles as customers, employees, and manager. For our purposes here, however, we elaborate the first option in the script that follows.

In total, we use a minimum of fifteen volunteers/actors – three for stage left (Board); three for stage right (Factory); and nine for stage center (McDonald's restaurant).

The script of Regenerating McDonaldland play

Act 1 – scene 1 – stage right

The spotlight directs your attention stage right to the Happy Meal factory in China. Several workers are gathered around an assembly line. The supervisor is nowhere in sight. Dialog is just above whisper, with a few explicative much louder glee comments. The workers assemble toys as they chatter.

WORKER BING (*whispering*): Nan, are you pregnant? I can see the change in your body.

WORKER NAN (*face red, shocked with embarrassment*): You can tell (*Exhibiting the protruding belly, with a deep and long sigh*).

WORKER LING: Nan, you better suck it in. Supervisor sees that, you are definitely fired.

Enter Supervisor stage left.

SUPERVISOR: You girls act like old women. Shut up! Get back to work! (*He taps the work table and glares at the workers.*)

Worker Bing slowly looks up into his face.

SUPERVISOR: That's it! You are docked half a day's pay.

Worker Ling slowly looks up and stares at him; pauses her work.

SUPERVISOR: A day's pay is docked for you! Anybody else want to play? *He looks at them for a long while, then smiles creepily at Nan and gives her a sly nod.*

Exit Supervisor – stage left.

WORKER LING: He's the one. Admit it Nan. Tell us all the details.

The players can improvise the scene from here.

Spotlight fades to black

Act 2 – scene 1 – stage left

The spotlight directs your attention stage left to the McDonald's International Board meeting in Lyon, France. Several Board members and Ronald are gathered around a conference table. There is a commotion outside that will be interrupted by a phone call.

Left to right are seated: Larry Light, McDonald's Global Chief Marketing Officer; Ronald McDonald, Chief Happiness Officer; Juergen Knauss, CEO of Heye and Partner, the Munich advertising agency that developed the creative approach; and Charlie Bell, McDonald's President and COO, etc. (between three and six OBTC volunteers).

On the backstage wall, an image is projected of José Bové, a French activist in the slow food movement, who is dumping a tractor trailer load of dung on the lawn of the McDonald's restaurant across the street. The image shifts to Lettuce Lady by PETA (People for Ethical Treatment of Animals).

CEO CANTALUPO: What is all that racket?

LARRY (*looking out the window*): It's Lettuce Lady, she looks cold today; I cannot believe how PETA accuses us of animal exploitation. Isn't what they do sexual exploitation of the female body?

RONALD: They also have Cucumber guys. They have protruding cucumbers. At least they are wearing vegetables.

LARRY: I don't believe this (*still looking out the window*) a crowd is cheering on José Bové; he just got released from prison by the president of France, and he is at it again. I don't believe it. He is actually dumping a trailer full of cow dung onto the lawn of that McDonald's restaurant.

ADMAN JUERGEN: And they say grotesque carnival is dead.

RONALD: A hoodlum, tossed a McCoke container full of urine on me. (*Board members lean away.*) Don't fret it was yesterday. I changed, but that urine messed up my white-face makeup.

Ring, ring, ring.

ADMAN JUERGEN: It's a call from the ad firm Heye and Partner, I'm CEO there. It is a press release coming out of China, on our fax, from an activist group . . .

CEO CANTALUPO: Read it. We got dung and lettuce girls outside, and now China.

ADMAN JUERGEN: It says: On June 1st, we issue this exclusive report. A woman named 'Nan' (no last name) is pregnant. Says she was raped by her supervisor on the McDonald's Happy Meal toy assembly line . . .

LARRY: Why do they say McDonald's assembly line, that is a subcontract job to a factory in China, we do not own that.

COO CHARLIE: Continue, what else?

ADMAN JUERGEN: Just says that a protest is planned in Beijing for tomorrow. What do we do about it?

RONALD: I know. I can go to the factory and put a Happy Face on our Happy Meals.

LARRY: That's ridiculous! Ronald you have to stay away from rape and sex of any kind.

CEO CANTALUPO: Maybe not. Ronald, you go to China and offer to put the child in a Ronald McDonald House, and see if the girl, what's her name? ['Nan', *the others yell in unison*] will sign an agreement not holding McDonald's responsible.

RONALD: Maybe she could be a spokesperson, and say how happy she is to work at factory making all those Happy Meals.

COO CHARLIE: We will see. Keep in mind she makes 18 cents an hour, and she was raped, so she will need your best smile face.

OBTC players can improvise from here, and adapt the scene to their tastes. Spotlight fades.

Act 2 – scene 2 – stage right

The spotlight directs your attention stage right to the China Happy Meal factory. Ronald makes his happy entrance, but the workers are too scared to look up at him. Ronald does his best clowning to get them to smile. They are not smiling. Ronald gets desperate and does something strange.

WORKER BING: Now what? Who is this clown?

NAN: Keep working. Keep quiet, supervisor will see you.

WORKER LING: Right.
Enter Ronald stage left.

RONALD: I think I see a Hamburglar in that box. (*Ronald is McMagic; he does not need a translator; but no worker looks up; they stay busy assembling.*)
Enter Supervisor stage left

SUPERVISOR: You lazy old hags. Get back to work! McDonald's will pull our contract. (*He taps the work table and glares at the workers.*)

RONALD: No worries. We are happy to renew the contract. (*Ronald wonders if he has made a mistake.*)

SUPERVISOR: OK, then. Pay attention to this clown!

WORKER LING: He's not that funny.

SUPERVISOR: OK, you are docked half a day's pay.

RONALD: I think I see a Hamburglar in that box. (*This time all the workers laugh; all in unison.*)

WORKERS: Ha Ha; Ha Ha; Ha Ha.

WORKER BING: I know you. You are "McDonald Shu-Shu."

RONALD: What does that mean in English?

WORKER LING: It means something like Uncle McDonald.

RONALD: OK, call me Uncle McDonald. Who is Nan?

WORKER NAN: Me!

RONALD: When are you due?

WORKER NAN: Four months, I think.

RONALD: Want to go to the United States?

NAN: My parents are poor, they need the money I earn here.

RONALD: We have money for you if you will be our McDonald's spokeswoman.

NAN: How much?

RONALD: More than you get here!

NAN: I cannot. I need to find a father for my child.

RONALD: I thought he [*pointing to the supervisor*] is the father.

NAN: Watch it, we can all be fired.

SUPERVISOR: You got that right.

RONALD: McDonald has authorized me to put your baby in a Ronald McDonald House in the USA.

NAN: No, I need to find a father. Who will be the Father?

RONALD (*without thinking*): I am the Uncle, wait, the Daddy of all the children in Ronald McDonald Houses throughout the world.

LING: You are going to be the Father of her baby!

RONALD: I said Uncle.

BING: That is great. Say "yes" Nan.

NAN: OK, I agree only if you marry me. I want a proper father, not an Uncle.

Ronald pauses – does not know what to do, scratches the top of his head, taps his clown feet – decides to make a phone call.

Act 2 – scene 3 – stage left

The spotlight directs your attention stage left to the international McDonald's board of directors. They are always meeting. All are present, except Ronald.

ADMAN JUERGEN: It's a call from Uncle McDonald in China, he has a question for us.

CEO JIM: Who? I cannot hear anything with all that racket.

LARRY: That noise is José Bové. He is dressed as Professor Wrench, and is dismantling our McDonald's and putting it in a trailer pulled by his farm tractor.

CEO JIM: Call the police.

ADMAN JUERGEN: It's Ronald on the phone. Uncle McDonald is what the Chinese call him; cannot pronounce Rs.

CEO JIM: Put him on the speaker phone.

RONALD: Can you hear me?

ADMAN JUERGEN: We can hear you. What is your question?

RONALD: Nan and I want to get married. At least she wants to. Is that OK with the Board?

ADMAN JUERGEN: I'm not sure about this. It could backfire in terms of PR. That girl is only 16 years old.

LARRY: Wait it could be just what we need. Ronald marries Chinese factory girl, and becomes father to her child. That is taking responsibility. Ronald, how old are you?

RONALD: In clown years, Uncle Ronald was born 1963, that makes him 40, no 41 years old. But as I am the 3rd Ronald, I am on the job for 18 years; I am technically 18, the first uncle in China.

COO CHARLIE: Wow. I don't know! Ronald, you are both young; did she sign the agreement not to hold McDonald's responsible.

RONALD: She will if I marry her; Do you think she will look good in White-face? Do I call her Aunt McDonald?

ADMAN JUERGEN: I say marry her.

LARRY: Me too. China is a big market.

RONALD: I want a pre-nup.

Act 3 – scene 1 – stage center

The spotlight directs your attention stage center to the McDonald's in Redlands. Board of directors is seated at one table. Nan's worker friends (even the supervisor) are at another table. The McDonaldland characters are playing pranks on the McDonald's OBTC employees and manager. Mayor McCheese is about to call them into some kind of order. They are waiting for Ronald and Nan. A group of reporters are flashing cameras and asking silly questions.

REPORTER: Was Nan raped? Who is the father? Is Ronald the father?

SHERIFF BIG MAX: No more questions. Mayor McCheese has an official McDonaldland statement.

MAYOR MCCHEESE: We are gathered here today to have a marriage in McDonaldland.

REPORTER: So Ronald is the father!

CAPTAIN CROOK: No, dummy, Uncle McDonald is his name.

REPORTER: So Uncle McDonald is the father.

BIRDIE: You got it all backward.

REPORTER: So Nan raped Uncle McDonald. Who is Uncle McDonald?

PROFESSOR: That's what they call Ronald in China; something about pronouncing Rs.

GRIMACE: Where is the bride and groom?

HAMBURGLAR: What are you looking at me for. I did not eat them.

CAPTAIN CROOK: Me neither.

BIRDIE: They'll be here. I'll fly around and see if I can see them.

PROFESSOR: I brought this wrench as a wedding gift.

BIRDIE: They are here. Everyone get ready!

SHERIFF BIG MAX: Make way, form an aisle [*pointing for them to separate at center stage*].

Ronald and Nan (in her white-face) dance onto center stage, entering from stage right. By now Nan is nine months pregnant and does she show. Nan's friends Bing and Ling accompany her as bridesmaids.

The audience cheers (there is a applause sign to help them with the cue).

GRIMACE: I hope it's a girl.

RONALD: We're having ultrasound at Ronald McDonald House after the wedding.

BING: Who is that woman dressed in Lettuce bikini?

LING: I don't trust her. She shows her body, nude in public.

NAN: Uncle McDonald, why is this woman without clothes? This is very embarrassing!

RONALD: Its just protestors – they treat women like sides of beef!

LING: I heard they throw dung and urine.

RONALD: Listen! Don't ever use words like that in McDonaldland. Why do you think we have Grimace?

HAMBURGLAR: Cause he's got no body!

The McDonald's Board approaches the Happy Couple.

COO CHARLIE: On behalf of the International McDonald's Board we welcome you Nan to the McDonaldland family.

REPORTER: Is this a real marriage?

LARRY: Ronald, have you got the contract she signed?

There is a commotion, and Nan faints on the stage. The Board is clueless. None of the McDonaldland characters know what to do. They all call for the Manager.

MANAGER: I'm no doctor. Get the Professor to deliver. He has a white smock.

PROFESSOR: I'm not that kind of doctor. I just carry wrenches.

MANAGER: Is there a doctor in the house. (*Pause, looking across the audience.*) No, a real doctor – Why me?

Nan's work buddies crowd around her, pushing everyone out of the way. Nan is parallel to the audience, stretched out on a McDonald's table. Her legs are spread, but not so the audience can see.

BING: Push Nan. Push.

LING: I think it's coming out.

Pop. With a furious push, and a scream by Nan, the baby flies out in an arch across the stage, and is caught, thank goodness, by Hamburglar.

HAMBURGLAR: This is not mine. (*He tosses the child to Captain Crook.*)

CAPTAIN CROOK: Not mine either.

RONALD (*always ready to be Superman and save the day*): I'll take that child. I'm the
legal father. Well, I will be after the ceremony. (*A relieved Nan embraces the baby.*)

NAN: It's a girl.

BING: Better here than in China.

At this point Ronald approaches the audience, the non-acting spectators and poses the question: which ending?

RONALD: That concludes Act 3, scene 1. The audience has a playbill. It
summarizes three endings. They are: Brechtian tragic grotesque, Boalian
resituated grotesque, and Bakhtinian carnivalesque. You the audience must
choose. You have 60 seconds to review, and I will call for your vote.

Pause for 60 seconds as people read the playbill (see appendix).

RONALD: What is your choice? Brechtian tragic grotesque, Boalian resituated
grotesque or Bakhtinian carnivalesque.

Questions from the audience:

BACK ROW: Can we have more than one?

RONALD: No, just one.

FRONT ROW: Ok, we want the carnival.

MIDDLE ROW: Not carnival, the whole thing is carnival. Let's try tragic.

RONALD: I am calling the question. Cast your vote by raising your hand only
once.

The audience makes its choice. You will have to attend the play to find out the ending.

Debriefing

After the play is staged, we usually devote 15 minutes for the participants to discuss the experience. The directors and spect-actors sit on the edge of the stage, and hear the commentary from the non-acting audience.

Our play was presented at four academic conferences during 2004. The first showing was at the International Academy of Business Disciplines (IABD) in San Antonio, TX, on 26 March 2004; the second was at the Organizational Behavior Teaching Conference (OBTC) in Redlands, CA, June 2004; the third at the Standing Conference on Organizational Symbolism (SCOS) in Nova Scotia on 9 July 2004; and the fourth at the Academy of Management (AOM) conference in New Orleans, LA, on 9 August 2004. At all four conferences the play script presented here was used. However, for the fourth presentation (at the Academy of Management) this script was used more as a starting point for improvisation. This more improvisational approach yielded equally good follow-up discussion, and had the advantage of being a more active and participative process overall. At all conferences participants were afforded the opportunity to play one or more of three roles; the role of actor, the role of spect-actor (Boal 1992), and the role of spectator/audience. The actor roles involved active engagement in the training and preparation sessions and in the performance sessions which followed; these participants presented their roles during the play. The role of spect-actor was primarily linked to the performance sessions and the transformation of the play's ending. In their roles as spect-actors, participants were engaged in presenting a transformation; their roles and the scenes performed emerged during the debriefing sessions when the audience was asked to transform the endings of the play. The role of the audience included passive and active involvement; passive in their roles as interested viewers of the performance, and active in their roles as evaluators of the performance where they discussed their reactions and thoughts during the discussion and commentary (debriefing) sessions.

In their role as actors many participants expressed gratitude for a positive, first-time experience in which they were required to portray roles assigned to them after having received very little training. Initial apprehension turned to relief as these actors became engrossed in the objective lesson of the performance and the excitement that was created as the scenes unfolded. In the script-based performances actors had a harder time getting the feel for the play. Being tied to their scripts, at least for the preparatory sessions, helped their self-confidence. However, when the script was removed the actors described initial feelings of inadequacy and confusion, which they indicated dissipated as they acted out their various roles during the actual performance. In the theme-based performances, the actors were more fluid and felt less restrained by a script; their 'script' was a theme from which they had to decide a real-time action performance. The actors expressed amazement at being able to see beyond the façade presented by corporations; the visual portrayal increased their awareness of the management issues faced by McDonald's Corporation and the links to the topics discussed in their classrooms.

The spect-actor role was a new experience for many and a common reaction was for the audience to shy away from that role. Participants who finally volunteered for that role described being able to feel the actions as the play unfolded on stage: a truly remarkable experience. Many of the spect-actors found their roles easy to attend to and were remarkably enthusiastic about participating once they realized that no real script was required for their participation. Being able to participate in what they initially thought was the best ending for the play was an exciting and revealing experience. For some of the participants it revealed the extent of variations in perception and understanding of issues among groups, and the importance of respecting these variations to allow for better world views. For other participants the ending, once presented, somehow did not live up to their expectations of the chosen ending; now they wanted to see the other two endings described in their instructions presented as well for comparison.

In their role as the audience, participants were presented with the challenge of recognizing the management principles and concepts being brought to the fore, and identifying the applications for the management classroom. In most of the cases, we found the audience fully engaged and attentive as they enjoyed the humor presented in the scenes. The result was active participation of all audiences during the debriefing sessions. Discussions included suggestions from the audience on ways to improve the scenes to better highlight the issues, to selecting an ending that would fit what they had seen and their interest in the ideas of any one of the three theorists presented. For the audience, the experience of seeing the ending portrayed, and relating it to the previous performances was powerful. The opportunity to explore the theorists' view of humor through the chosen endings was of profound significance as it provided a view into the realm of possibilities for engaging management students in theater as a learning tool.

In sum, we think there is more to McDonald's than the four abstract rationality dimensions our friend and colleague Ritzer (2000) poses: efficiency, calculatability, predictability, and control via nonhuman technology of Taylorist and Post-Fordist production. This is a global spectacle and there is a role here for a variety of grotesque humor. The audience through a live action interactive play is able to play with these forms of grotesque humor; as posed by Bakhtin, Boal, and Brecht. They are able to experience critical theory's three humorists in our grotesque theater.

Appendix – the distributed playbill

Regenerating McDonaldland: a play of grotesque humor

Brief clown history

Speedee was the first clown symbol-image of McDonald's from 1948 to 1960; Bozo the Clown was lead humorist from 1960–3; Ronald McDonald appeared in a parade in 1963 and has been super-clown (Chief Happiness Officer) ever since. Ronald actually has an office down the hall from McDonald's CEO Jim Cantalupo.

Ronald has trouble fitting into clown history. Does he fit with the grotesque whitefaces common in twentieth-century American circus history? Ronald is a neat whiteface, not a grotesque one; nor with the 'auguste clown' category, a clown who "stumbles, performs pratfalls, slaps and is slapped, and often is the butt of jokes."[6]

In the play you are about to see performed. Keep in mind that there are no professional actors. The volunteers are improvising from barebones script.

On stage you will see three zones of action: Stage Left, Stage Center and Stage Right. At left is the International McDonald's Board meeting in Lyon, France. Stage Center is the McDonald's restaurant in Redlands, California. Stage Right is a factory in China where young girls (15 to 20) are making Happy Meal toys. A spotlight (if not available, a flashlight) will direct your attention to the scenes.

The purpose

The purpose of our play is to let students and faculty experience what sociologist George Ritzer (2000) calls McDonaldization. McDonald's represents and exemplifies the triumph of Fordism and Taylorism in the fast food industry and is an icon for an organizational system of production and supervision in many industries that has now diffused globally. We want to let the audience experience efficiency, calculatability, predictability, and control by nonhuman technology in the McDonald's restaurant (and in more pre-Taylorist form in the Chinese factory). We have two very special roles for the audience.

First, we will be introducing you to three forms of grotesque humor: those of Bertolt Brecht, Mikhail Bakhtin, and Augusto Boal. Second, you will be asked to choose and ending to the play that will emphasize one of the three Bs.

Choose the play ending?

Choice one – Brecht tragic ending to the play

Brecht's humor is the *Epic Theater*, and we ask you to experience it in two ways: (1) there will be a series of slide facts and images shown on the back wall; their purpose is to keep you from falling into the role of passive spectator; we want you to be aware of the contrast between being engaged and passive, between being a critical audience and one that is here to be entertained; (2) the actors are not actors, this will help you to see a distance between their person and their character. Brecht is a very mocking grotesque. The play is part Brechtian. For example, in the play you will see that Nan (our heroine) is recruited to be spokeswoman to quell the activist protests: activists use grotesque characterizations of Ronald and McDonaldland characters. Her recruitment as spokesperson is also quite Brechtian. Choose Brecht and you will get a very tragic ending. Nan will be run over by a Speedee drive-thru motorist. Never fear the Board will name a McNanaise sauce after her; she will be martyr to the greater good, the McDonald's cause.

Choice two – Boal affirmative ending to the play

Boal is more affirmative than either Brecht or Bakhtin. Boal works with oppressed people around the world and helps them express their various oppressions. Choose this ending and you will see the spect-actors (his term for spectator who is also actor) ask you the spectators to become spect-actors, and suggest ways to rescript the ending. Of course Nan still dies, but this time from choking on a McNugget; no blood no mess at all. The good news is that Nanette (Nan's baby) lives! She becomes the symbol of animal activists in China; she heeds the dying words of her mother and is not immodest about it like Lettuce Lady. The volunteers on stage turn the tables on you; they will certainly ask members of the audience to try out the solutions they suggest, to play the role of one of the protagonists and see how effective their strategy really is. It won't bring back Nan, but you can suggest an ending that gets McDonald's board to understand martyrdom.

Choice three – Bakhtin carnivalesque ending to the play

Bakhtin plays the middle. Nan still dies, but in childbirth. Bakhtin views abstract rationalism, in the Enlightenment, what he calls modernity, as a taming of grotesque laughter. He relished Rabelais's passages about dung and urine, and bare nakedness; this Bakhtin influence you have seen in the play. Bakhtin would view Ritzer's dimensions (efficiency, calculatability, predictability, and control via nonhuman technology) as abstract rational systems theory. Bakhtin would wonder why people teach management without a philosophy of grotesque humor; he would be keen to look at the grotesque humor in McDonald's, what he calls the lower bodily stratum of festive-carnivalesque humor that opposes the upper stratus of official spectacle. Bakhtinian elements in the play have already focused on the regeneration of Ronald into Uncle, through grotesque laughter into the ambassador who marries the factory girl. And Nan represents the festive-carnivalesque transformative powers. In her death, she gives birth to Nanette. Choose this ending and you will see some kind of rejuvenation of the people's carnival in the McDonald's production and global system.

You the audience members will, after Act 3, scene 1, be asked to which of three endings to select. So be ready.

After the play, we will ask you the audience for your commentary. We are not concerned about your dramatic enjoyment or your entertainment. We want to know if you see the three B's (Brecht, Boal and Bakhtin) in action in our play. We want to know why you selected the ending we performed at your request. We want to hear your commentary about the relation between types of grotesque humor and their enactment (or not) in our performance, and in the global stage of McDonaldization. We want to know if management education has a place for grotesque humor.

Notes

1   Bakhtin is accused by numerous Rabelaisian scholars of being both too grotesque and too positive in his reading of François Rabelais (1532). While there is not space to present that debate see Gardine (1995); Gauna (1996); Schwartz (1990).

2   There are key differences between Boal's appreciative perspective and the field of Appreciative Inquiry begun with Srivastava and Cooperrider's (1987, 1990). We leave these nuances for the audience to decipher. We do contend that AI does not indulge more negative and mocking forms of grotesque humor. Boal's oppression, for some AI enthusiasts, may be unappreciative.

3   "Seventeen year old women were forced to work 9 to 10 hours a day, seven days a week, earning as little as six cents an hour in the Keyhinge factory in Vietnam making the popular giveaway promotional toys, such as Disney characters, for McDonald's Happy Meals." See http://flag.blackened.net/revolt/ws/ws51_vietnam.html; site visited 12 Jan. 2004.

4   The term Epic Theater, used by Brecht for the first time in 1926, did not originate with him, although it is generally applied to his work today. It was already in use in 1924 when Brecht moved from Munich to Berlin and was first used in connection with revolutionary experiments by director Erwin Piscator. Many playwrights and composers produced plays and musical compositions in the 1920s which have been since been labeled epic (Stravinisky, Pirandello, Claudel), and others have followed

in their footsteps (Wilder, Miller, Becket). See Oregon State University, <http://oregonstate.edu/instruct/ger341/brechtet.htm>, accessed 15 Dec. 2003.
5 See *The Economist* website at: <http://www.economist.com/markets/Bigmac/Index.cfm>; accessed 12 Jan. 2004.
6 Cited from LaVahn G. Hoh, <http://www.all4funchgo.bizland.com/clowns/msg5.htm>, accessed 1 Dec. 2004.

References

Avolio, B. J., Howell, J. M. and Sosik, J. J. (1999) 'A funny thing happened on the way to the bottom line: humor as a moderator of leadership style effects', *Academy of Management Journal*, 42(4): 219–27.

Bakhtin, M. (1968) *Rabelais and his World*, tr. H. Iswolsky, Cambridge, MA and London: MIT Press.

Bakhtin, M. (1981) *The Dialogic Imagination: Four Essays*, tr. C. Emerson and M. Holquist, Austin, TX: University of Texas Press.

Boal, A. (1979) *Theatre of the Oppressed*, tr. C. A. McBride and M. L. McBride, New York: Theatre Communications Group.

Boal, A. (1992) *Games for Actors and Non-Actors*, tr. A. Jackson, London: Routledge.

Boal, A. (1995) *Rainbow of Desire: The Boal Method of Theatre and Therapy*, New York: Routledge.

Boje, D. M. and Cai, Y. (2004) 'McDonald's: grotesque method and the metamorphosis of the three spheres: McDonald's, McDonaldland, and McDonaldization', *Metamorphosis Journal*, 3(1): 15–33.

Brecht, B. (1969/1932) *Saint Joan of the Stockyards: A Drama by Bertolt Brecht*, tr. F. Jones, Bloomington, IN and London: Indiana University Press.

Clouse, R. W. and Spurgeon, K. L. (1995) 'Corporate analysis of humor', *Psychology: A Quarterly Journal of Human Behavior*, 32(1): 53–67.

Coleman, D. G. (1971) *Rabelais: A Critical Story in Prose Fiction*, London and New York: Cambridge University Press.

Collinson, D. L. (2002) 'Managing humor', *Journal of Management*, 39(3): 269–88.

Cooperrider, D. L. and Srivastava, S. (1987) 'Appreciative inquiry in organizational life', in W. Pasmore and R. Woodman (eds), *Research in Organization Change and Development*, vol. 1, pp. 129–69, Greenwich, CT: JAI Press.

Crawford, M. and Gressley, D. (1991) 'Creativity, caring context: women's and men's accounts of humor preferences and practices', *Psychology of Women Quarterly*, 15: 217–31.

Csikszentmihalyi, M. (1996) *Creativity: Flow and the Psychology of Discovery and Invention*, New York: NargerCollins Publisher.

Dienstbier, R. A. (1995) 'The impact of humor on energy, tension, task choices, and attributions: exploring hypotheses from toughness theory', *Motivation and Emotion*, 19: 255–67.

Duncan, W. J. (1982) 'Humor in management prospects for administrative practice and research', *Academy of Management Review*, 7: 136–42.

Gauna, M. (1996) *The Rabelaisian Mythologies*, Cranbury, NJ and London: Associated University Presses.

Gruner, C. R. (1997) *The Game of Humor*, New Brunswick, NJ: Transaction.

Holmes, J. and Marra, M. (2002) 'Having a laugh at work: how humour contributes to workplace culture', *Journal of Pragmatics*, 34: 1683–710.

Koch, C. (2004) 'Can knowledge management become global? Consulting engineering companies in the knowledge economy', *Journal of Construction Research*, 5(1): 107–24.

Organ, D. W. and Grover, R. A. (1987) 'The management of service organizations', *Academy of Management Review*, 12(3): 558–61.

Prescott, A. L. (1998) *Imagining Rabelias in Renaissance England*, New Haven, CT: Yale University Press.

Rabelais, F. (1532/1873) *The Works of Rabelais*, London: Chatto & Windus.

Raffoni, M. (1999) 'Use case interviewing to improve your hiring', *Harvard Management Update*, 4(7): 10–11.

Ritzer, G. (2000/1993) *The McDonaldization of Society* (New Century Edition), Thousand Oaks, CA: Pine Forge Press.

Schwartz, J. (1990) *Irony and Ideology in Rabelais: Structures of Subversion*, New York and Cambridge: Cambridge University Press.

Srivastava, S. and Cooperrider, D. L. (1990) *Appreciative Management and Leadership*, San Francisco, CA: Jossey-Bass.

Willett, J. (1957) *Brecht on Theatre: The Development of an Aesthetic*, New York: Hill & Wang.

Chapter 14

The staging of humour
Organizing and managing comedy

Robert Westwood

That's the biggest joke of all, that the very best material never makes it past a fleeting moment in your head while you're queuing in the post office.

(Dan)

The role of a comedian is to make the audience laugh, at a minimum of once every fifteen seconds.

(Lenny Bruce)

His hand briefly drifted up towards his eyes, palm facing outwards about five inches from his face. The gesture signaled a shading of the eyes from the harsh spotlight, but also perhaps signified a defense against the heckler taking potshots from the back of the room. Beads of perspiration studded the comedian's forehead and his eyes began an eccentric scanning of the room. There were less than 35 people in the room, but it was hot. The set was not going well. There had been laughs and giggles in fits and spurts, but the crowd weren't really with him.

'Hunh ya, hanwa slee ya blunja.'

From the back of the room the heckler's words were loud but incoherent. It was obvious that his libations had penetrated his animal brain and tripped him into aggressive mode. It was also clear that ignoring him was not going to work. The comic decided he had to draw on one of his stock responses:

'Mate, this is my work, I'm working here. I don't come to your place of work and knock the toilet brush out of your hand.'

[small titter in the room]

'Huwah cass … Yer grunh al mushta. Ya fickwa…. . pishwa ya grundya, Smurfit ya cracknya.'

The mates had joined in now.

He tried returning to his routine, but the bellicose barrage continued from the gaggle of lads at the back. They had decided that was more fun than listening to the comic. He realized he should have reacted earlier. He escalated the putdowns:

'Oh it's you again … real attention seeker. Jeez, just got a good look at you … is that really your face or did your neck just throw up?'

'Huuh ya cronnska hadj … FICKWA.'

'Oh mate, listen, you're ugly, your dick is short, no one likes you, shut the fuck up.'

There was silence in the room, he knew he had gone too far and now the rest of the crowd identified with the heckler and did not find the putdowns funny. He struggled on, but knew he would not get the crowd back. There were a few faint giggles from the more polite, but mostly there was no response and some of the crowd began their own conversations. Oddly, the hecklers had shut up too, perhaps dredging up the clichéd ethic of 'don't kick a man when he's down'. He made it to the end of his set and walked off to faint applause.

'Fuck me, that was shite', he said as he passed the MC backstage, 'I don't know why I rock up for this crap everynight.'

This is the stand-up comedians' nightmare. It is not incidental that the argot of the profession refers to such an experience with the language of death – the comic has 'died' on stage. Conversely, if things go really well, the comic wins over the audience and gets a very positive response, it might be referred to as 'killing' the audience. The language of death is pervasive and apparent throughout the performing arts, but it is commonly acknowledged that comedic performance, and especially stand-up, is the most precarious and exposing. It is just the comedian and an audience – the comic places him/herself in a position of great vulnerability. If, like the comedian above, you find yourself 'dying' on stage, there is nowhere to hide, no escape. Comedians work to manage this vulnerability; they work to manage their material and performance, but also to manage themselves. They also work with an audience to co-create a positive experience, to have comedy produced and avoid the 'death' of an unfunny show.

Of course, all work performances need to be managed in multifaceted and multidimensional ways. This includes not just management of the task, but also of the self – including identity work and impression management (Goffman 1969) – management of others and of relationships, and management of context. Additionally, it is not just the immediate situation that needs managing, but also the socio-cultural and discursive context in which it is embedded. Performance requires consciousness of and alignment with the discourses that frame it and determine its meanings and parameters of legitimacy. Such management will primarily be a matter of alignment, but in some circumstances it may actually be shaping or even challenging the discourses. Every performance will either produce, reproduce or challenge the discourses that frame it. Given the vulnerabilities of stand-up comedic performance, it offers perhaps an acute or heightened case of performance management – particularly in terms of the management of self and of others – that we all face in our work.

Researching comedians

Based upon observation and interviews, this chapter examines the organization and management of comedic performance. Observational work was conducted at comedy clubs, primarily in an Australian metropolitan centre, but also in the UK and Ireland. In addition, face-to-face interviews were conducted with professional/semi-professional comedians in the Australian city, plus comedians in the UK, the USA and other parts of Australia were 'interviewed' via a three-phase email interview schedule. A total of 22 comedians were interviewed.[1] The email interviews were structured around 48 questions; apart from basic demographic information, the questions were open-ended. The face-to-face interviews were conducted in a naturalistic, conversational mode, but were guided by the same questions. These interviews were digitally recorded and subsequently transcribed.

'Scant scholarly writing has focused on stand-up comedy' (Mitchell 2001). What writing there has been tends to focus at the individual level with a large number of biographies (e.g. Anthony and Edmonds 1998; Williams 1991) and numerous autobiographies (e.g. Allen 1994; Berger 2003). There is also a notable popular literature about comedy and comedy performance as a practice (Berger 1985; Borns 1987; Double 1997), including instructional texts on how to become a comedian (e.g. Ajaye 2002; Schwensen 1998). Scholarly theoretical or empirical work is scarce. One exception is Fisher and Fisher's (1981) attempt to examine the background, particularly family background, of comedians and identify common psychological profiles. A popular assumption has been that the personalities of comedians are somehow different, often characterized as melancholic or depressive – something not confirmed in this study. In addition to Fisher and Fisher, the personality of comedians has also been assessed from a psychoanalytic perspective (e.g. Janus 1975). Other work has discussed stand-up comedy in relation to society and community, with interpretations of comedians as fulfilling the roles of critics, moralists or anthropologists who comment upon, interrogate or mediate social, cultural and political aspects of society (Greenbaum 1999; Koziski 1997; Mintz 1985; Stebbins 1993).

There have been even fewer studies of the comedic process, and especially of stand-up. Exceptions include Rutter's (2000) analysis of the role and function of comedy club comperes and Puliam's (1991) account of the jargon deployed by the comedic community. Of particular note in the context of this limited theoretico-empirical work are studies dealing with audience–performer dynamics (Pollio and Swanson 1995; Rutter 2001). A comedic performance obviously depends upon that dynamic, upon the reception of humour. Indeed, it can be argued that comedy is always a co-performance in which humour co-evolves between audience and comedian within a setting. For comedy to work there has to be a communion within the audience. A combinatorial audience reaction amplifies humour and functions as a signal for audience members to participate: we are all aware, for example, of the infectious nature of laughter and how rarely we laugh in isolation. Such co-dependency adds to the vulnerability of the comedian since he/she is not fully in control of outcomes.

Both the popular and scholarly literature acknowledge that comedy performances are probably the most difficult and exposing of the performing arts. From the days of the jester down to today's stand-up comedian the role and position of the comedic performer has been precarious and fragile, the comedic performer exposed and vulnerable. This is so for a number of reasons. First, humour and comedy are intensely subjective and indeterminable, thus the comedic performer can never be sure that his/her actions will generate the desired response. Second, as noted, comedy is socially constructed in the dynamic interplay between comedian, audience and context. The comedic performer is not directly in control of outcomes and any outcome may not necessarily be related to his/her performance competence as they often are in other modes of performance. Furthermore, whilst the outcomes are somewhat indeterminate and nebulous, the absence of desired outcomes is immediately and painfully obvious. A silent audience is a key performance indicator and a devastating signal of failure – so devastating that it is referred to as 'dying'. A comedian's credibility and capacity to keep performing depends on the ability to generate these nebulous outcomes – every time they perform. Third, comedy is inherently risky since fundamentally it attempts to construct an alternative world that is fresh and original and to present that to an unknown audience. The material must always be fresh (or appear to be so); there is little mileage in old, tired and already shared jokes and humour. More radically, the comedic process works by constructing an alternate reality that at some psychological level is threatening and incongruous vis-à-vis normal, mundane reality. It is resolution of the incongruity and the realization that the alternate world constructed is not a real threat but 'just a joke' that generates the humorous response (Berger 1997; Westwood 2004). In this elemental sense comedy is precarious because it challenges mundane reality and walks a line between reality and the fantastic, the mundane and the absurd, the funny and the frightening. Fourth, the stand-up comedian is typically working on his/her own and confronting an unknown audience. This is a lonely and exposing position. Finally, stand-up comedy often deals, in content terms, with the conditions and issues of human existence that are often unpalatable, even taboo, and as such frequently repressed or swept under the carpet in normal social discourse. Comedy surfaces these and allows us to scrutinize them from within the palatable frame of comedy. The comedian will often be the personal vehicle for this, surfacing these subterranean issues as manifest in their own lives and experience, thereby engaging in even more confronting self-disclosure and revealing even greater vulnerabilities. In this sense stand-up comedy, and to some extent the stand-up comedian, invoke the abject and in some senses the management of a comedic performance is the management of abjection, of which more subsequently.

In staging a comedic performance comedians must be mindful of all of the above and manage the associated dynamics. Significant work precedes on-stage performance and the preparations are not just in terms of sourcing and preparing material, but also organizational and management work to secure gigs and prepare the performance space. More importantly, the comedian must prepare for these solo acts of self-disclosure, of confrontations with alternate realities and encounters with the abject. There is also significant impression management, identity work, audience management and emotional labour actually during performance. It is this performance management work that is the concern of this chapter. Research on organizational humour and comedy has focused on the nature of comedic acts and the effects of humour on people and assorted organizational and work processes (see Chapter 1); there has been very little on the organization and management of comedy and humour itself.

In exploring these aspects of comedic performance Burke's dramaturgical pentad (Burke 1945, 1950) will be heuristically adopted to frame the discussion, but in doing so the opportunity is taken to interrogate the limits of a dramaturgical perspective and problematize the dramatistic pentad. The Burkean pentad was developed as a device through which motives, and particularly the grammar of motives embedded in people's accounts of what they think they do, could be examined. It consists, apparently simply enough, of Scene, Actor, Act, Agency, Purpose. The dramaturgical perspective has been a feature, albeit as a minority paradigm, of sociological and organizational analysis since Burke, deployed, for example, in analysing social and organizational processes, most notably in the work of Goffman, but also latterly in organizational studies (Mangham 1988, 1990; Mangham and Overington 1987; Harvey 2001; Oswick et al., 2001). Unlike Goffman, whose dramaturgical analytic is metaphorical, Burke takes the dramaturgy of life as literal. It has been criticized for disconnection from wider structures and discourses of power which might at least be considered as framing the elements of the pentad and shaping what transpires between its elements. It has also been criticized for sustaining the humanistic imperative of the human agency and of engaging in a kind of hermeneutic interpretivism. Nonetheless, it is a useful device for framing the discussion here. To look at the organization and management of comedy in terms of these dramatistic elements may appear somewhat simple and perhaps a little trite – but it is the dramatistic arrangement and enactment of them that enables people to frame a piece of behaviour and to construct meanings and interpretations. Comedians marshal these elements to manage their performance, but also to frame the meanings of their actions in an attempt to manipulate the interpretations of an audience. Indeed, before embarking of the application of the Burkean pentad, it is useful to introduce the notion of 'frame'.

Frame

A concept used by Goffman (1974), Burke (1972: 23) reflected that 'many times on later occasions' he 'regretted' not adding 'Frame' to his pentad. Frame establishes context through and within which a situation can be interpreted; it provides the basis for a general cognitive and conceptual view of a particular situation. It is a shared understanding that frames the meanings that are likely to be accepted and legitimated when constructed within a particular situation (Goffman 1969, 1974). For example, there are certain discourses, institutional arrangements and symbolic and physical features that frame a particular event at a particular location as a 'marriage ceremony'. Being thus framed, there are certain dramaturgical enactments and their resultant meanings that can be constructed and which pass as appropriate and legitimate for that context – such as the decorous singing of religious songs – and other acts and meanings considered as inappropriate – such as drunkenly belching and farting whilst reciting bawdy limericks (that might come later in something framed as 'the reception').

In that sense the very notion of 'comedy club' is a frame (and not just a physical location) within which particular dramatistic ratios are likely and in which certain meanings will be legitimated. There is already a dynamic tension here though since comedy, almost definitionally, constructs odd, alternate, even subversive meanings relative to mundane reality. Nonetheless, broad meanings are framed such that, for example, 'comedy clubs' specifically house 'stand-up' comedy and not other kinds of comedic performance. In that sense it needs to be noted that stand-up comedy clubs are a relatively recent phenomenon. They have their roots in vaudeville and burlesque, but modern 'stand-up' comedy proper dates back only to the early 1970s, emerging in the US, and then in Australia in the late 1970s. 'Stand-up' is a particular type of comedic performance different from other forms of performed comedy such as vaudeville. Comedians themselves make a distinction between joke-telling/gag-telling and stand-up. Stand-up is characterized more by the production of narrative and commentary, and by observational comedy, than by formally structured jokes or gags. However, it was noted that stand-up routines might have gags or jokes embedded within them. It is also, at least for the purist, a performance free of props and typically performed solo. In the broadest terms 'comedy club' is a frame in which the presentation and reception of stand-up comedy is legitimated. However, there is a discourse around stand-up comedy that has shifted and altered over time, providing a tighter frame and greater specificity about what kind of comedy is legitimate in a 'comedy club'. For example, through the 1990s 'alternative' comedy was legitimated, and sexist, racist and blue comedy delegitimated. There are then, situational expectations framed by the known, expected or experienced context of the 'stand-up comedy club'.

Scene

The 'scene' is basically concerned with when and where something is performed. It is the background of the act, the situation in which it occurred including the physical, geographic and cultural environment or setting. Here we are dealing with the physical location of a comedy club but also the cultural specificities that surround them. In this sense it is important to realize that there are specific dynamics within specific comedy clubs impacting on how comedic performances are delivered and received, and on the dynamics between the other dramatistic elements. At a broader level it should also be noted that the comedy scene in Australia is not the same as in the UK – on a number of dimensions – and even the comedy scene in Melbourne is different from that in Sydney.

I am going to assume most readers' familiarity with the physical setting of a typical stand-up club and focus on scene at a different level, on the particular way that a comedy scene is organized within a specific geographic and socio-cultural location. To do so I will focus on one Australian metropolitan scene.

The organization of comedy in this city has some distinctive features. First, it is dominated by one 'producer' who manages most of the venues within the metropolitan area and surrounding districts: there are only one or two other players. This producer/promoter runs a 'room'[2] that is the prime stand-up club in the city and is a joint venture with the venue owners. It is operated such that the venue management takes all the revenue from the sale of food and drink while the producer has the 'door take' as his source of revenue. The producer also manages several other 'rooms' around the city and metropolitan area – mostly in pubs, hotels and various social or sporting clubs. In some the arrangements are as for the chief venue, in others the venue owners/managers pay a fee for the 'show'. Of particular interest is the fact that this producer runs these 'rooms' in a kind of developmental hierarchy. Some are run as 'open mike' venues in which amateurs and beginners 'try out' on stage. Often the promoter makes these into competitions, but more importantly he uses this opportunity to spot talent and people displaying talent are migrated to mid-level managed venues. They receive a low fee, but it is an opportunity to develop and hone their skills. They may finally progress to the main comedy club where only well received professional or semi-professional comedians perform. This producer told me that within the metropolitan area there were about 70–90 would-be or amateur comedians, 15–20 who were developing and at stage 2, and only about 10–12 at the professional or semi-professional level who have the potential to earn a livable amount and who would perform two to three times a week.

In addition to work in these 'rooms', many stand-up comics also perform on a burgeoning corporate scene – performing for companies at various functions. This has been a major area of growth in the last 10–15 years. There are some comedians for whom corporate work is now their main or sole form of performance – often basing their comedy on corporate material and functioning as hoaxers. A typical performance would mean entering a company as a character – a favourite being 'the bastard' manager from head office, or some management guru – and then conducting a performance as that character (see Westwood 2004). Such performances typically attract bigger fees than club performances. Interviews with local stand-up comedians revealed that many had to supplement their comedy income from other sources.

As well as the comedians themselves there are other key players in the stand-up scene: producers, impresarios, agents and venue managers. Whilst not uniform, and most knew of or had heard of bad promoters, most of the comedians interviewed reported their experiences with promoters and venue managers to be mostly reasonable. It is worth noting that there are a number of key comedy venues that are run by comedians or ex-comedians and this may explain a fairly sanguine, even supportive relationship. Many comedians are self-managing, but attitudes towards agents and managers were generally not, however, positive:

> on the whole they can be full of self importance, which is a reflection on the fact that they can't do comedy so they try and lord it over other comics.

The relationships among comedians themselves appeared diverse with attitudes towards other comedians showing something of a split among the interviewees. A small majority (just) was favourably disposed and saw the relationships as positive and the community as mutual and supportive, but a significant minority saw the relationship more negatively and as characterized by competitiveness, talking behind backs, jealously. 'It's bitchy' was a comment made on more than one occasion.

A Burkean analysis directs attention to a specific scene in which a particular act occurs. However, a difficulty here is that scenes are not sensibly detachable from the wider context and analytically it might be important to consider the embeddedness of scenes. The interpretation and meanings in a specific scene remain indeterminate without cognizance of the dynamic relationship to the wider context of which they are a part. Scenes are constituted by, and produce, reproduce or challenge, discourses. That discursive location and the dynamics engendered therein are typically absent from a dramaturgical analysis or are merely taken-for-grated. There are discourses about comedy of a cultural political, ideological and even institutional nature that bear upon the meaning of any comedic act in any particular scene. Indeed, a scene is itself already framed by and partly constituted by such discourses.

Agent

Obviously central to a dramatistic perspective is the question of agent – of who performed, of what kind of person performed the act? Given the analytic focus here it is the comedians who would appear most obviously as the agents of concern. However, it is not that simple since, as noted, a comedic performance is in a very real sense a co-production. Thus when a comic act is performed is the agent the comedian or the audience, or even somehow a combination? Perhaps it is not sensible to differentiate and separate out an agent from the complex and dynamic context – implying another critique of a pentadic dramaturgical analysis. That notwithstanding, I will explore the comedians as agents in what follows, focusing, after providing a capsule demographic overview, on some of the processes of self-management they engage in.

The comedians interviewed were a heterogeneous group. Of those interviewed 12 were Australian, 9 British and 1 was from the USA. All but three described themselves as professional, but almost half had other sources of income – some related (e.g. acting), some not (e.g. hairdresser). Experience as a comedian ranged from 2 to 23 years with a mode around 12; the average age was 35. Only two were female, but that would probably match the gender structure in the field. This was an educated group with more than 50 per cent possessing at least a university degree.

Managing self: pragmatic

Most stand-ups operate on their own, manage themselves and pursue a somewhat independent, detached existence. The nature of what they do and of the profession engenders a considerable amount of vulnerability, insecurity and precariousness. There are aspects of the management of the self that are pragmatic and mundane, but other aspects that concern the managing of the psychological self and identity. In terms of the former, there were wide variations in levels of organization and disorganization. This ranged from one, specializing as a corporate comedian, who was extremely well organized, maintaining an extensive computerized data base in which were entered and cross-referenced details of all performances categorized according to character, accent, role, core topic/theme, core material, source for the booking, fee structure and a self-rating scale! For others it's a diary, a mobile phone and memory. Some presented and defined themselves as 'professionals' – in the sense of this being their job, their being properly organized, and serious about delivering their 'service' – almost in a defensive manner. Others were somewhat diffident about the whole thing.

The fulsome responses to the question 'How many hours per week do you spend on work related to comedy?', and the elaborations provided, are perhaps indicative of this concern with the practicalities of organizing themselves for performance. In response, many suggested that work on comedy was ongoing, always occupying their observations and thinking if not actual activity:

> Every time I see something or hear something, I am thinking about comedy. Either what is funny about a situation or topic or how it can be, 24/7. I can't stop, it gets annoying sometimes.

The intimation is that being a comedian means working all the time. Actual performance time is, naturally, very limited and rarely more than one hour per day. Some claimed to be working 60–80 hours a week, but it was unclear exactly what was meant by 'working'. Certainly travelling to gigs constitutes a significant portion of time:

> If a gig is a three hour drive away, I'll start packing at midday, leave at 2, set up, do an hour of comedy after dinner, pack up, drive home, unload equipment – 4 a.m. There's 14 hours straight for one gig.

Preparation time appears to be limited, especially for the more established and experienced comedians. In face-to-face interviews comedians often admitted spending little time writing and preparing material. Many had a stock of material – perhaps an hour's worth – and they would call selectively on that to compose a particular set, a bit like a musician with a repertoire. For perhaps half the group this material would at some point have been written out and more or less fully scripted, others relied either on notes or developed a routine without a script. Many spent little time in preparation. It was more often a case of running through a set in their heads, or perusing notes relating to their repertoire and working out a particular running order, on the day of the performance or just immediately beforehand. Some admitted to barely any preparation, feeling confident enough in their routine and/or their improvisational capabilities.

Management of self: identity

Stand-up is a performance, it is acting, but it is different from formal, dramatic acting, such as in a theatre. Normally stand-up comics are not acting out a character nor performing a script written by somebody else. In discussion the working comedians were unanimous in asserting that they were 'themselves' when performing. They held this to be so even in those situations where they assumed something of an onstage persona, an apparent paradox accounted for by the notion that their onstage persona was a mere exaggerated or modified version of their real self – half of those interviewed expressed a view along these lines:

> I go off script an awful lot, so it needs to be me at root because I'll have to deal with all kinds of spontaneous moments, and need to know very quickly exactly where I'm coming from logically and emotionally.

> I normally assume the identity of a weirdo for my act, but as I carry on performing it is becoming more and more like me.

This is precisely what provides the edge of vulnerability for comedians: unlike actors they are not cloaking themselves in a character, not assuming the role of Other; they remain somehow elementally Self, and that self is onstage, alone, and usually self-disclosing to a roomful of strangers. But then, the very setting has an artificiality, a frame, which clearly denotes this as a particular and unusual social setting. It is a frame within which a particular relationship between the comedian and the audience is constructed and within which certain mutual expectations about that relationship pertain. It is also a frame for the comedian-as-self and for other possible self–other relations to emerge and be seen as appropriate and legitimate.

There is a fundamental tension in the identity work of the stand-up since he/she is both trying to present self and other in a performance. The comic is 'onstage' and performing; this is not a 'normal' presentation of self in a 'normal' everyday interaction. It is staged, premeditated, performative and intentional. But wait, is that so different from the way much work-related performance is conducted? Is not much work-related performance of this type – especially, but not only, in the service sector and in those roles requiring emotional labour. Still, comedic performance is not mostly spontaneously constructed, but rather is already crafted. Nonetheless, the comic wants the performance and the material to be received and read as fresh and original. The comedians commented on the need for the performance to be received as authentic, and mostly they meant that the ideas and sentiments were read as authentically derived from the comedian and were not mere artifice for the purposes of entertainment. There is a tension, then, between the presentation of an authentic self and the careful construction of a performance making use of previously determined, crafted and even rehearsed material and modes of presentation.

Certainly a clear majority recognised the self-exposure inherent to a comedic performance. However, about 60 per cent saw comedy as involving both self-exposure *and* self-defence when asked which was present:

> Both. You want to show that you're vulnerable, but by getting up there you show that you have bigger balls than anyone there.

Both parts of this statement reflect vulnerability, but also give recognition to the courage and the distinctiveness of those prepared to get on the stage and make themselves vulnerable. It is recognition of the risks involved, risks leading to the type of calamitous experience symbolized at the start of the chapter. Given the self-exposure, the fact that they are not shielded behind an assumed persona, together with the immediacy and appalling obviousness of the feedback, a failed performance can be devastating. Many interviewees acknowledged that and pointed to various coping strategies to deal with the situation. As one comedian said, reflecting on how they felt about and dealt with 'dying' on stage:

> Normal depression for 3 days – kick the dog, over analyse every word that you said – nothing helpful but all part of the process!!

The more experienced comedians know that failure is inevitable and furnish themselves with the rationale that 90 per cent of the time they are received as funny and so can parcel off the failure as an exception or aberration, often attributing something to that particular audience. When such defensive rationales are in place the comedians can then take the chance to analyse and learn from the failure.

A significant difficulty in a dramatistic analysis focusing on the agent element of the pentad is identifying who the agent actually is. This is compounded by the dangers of an analytic that considers agent in a disconnected and decontextualized manner. As has been noted, a comedic performance is a relationship, a dynamic interaction between a comedian and an audience, but also including often other comedians, an MC, venue staff. A comedic performance is very much a *collective accomplishment*. Furthermore these various 'agents' are acting within a scene, but also in a scene framed by certain discursive, institutional and ideological parameters.

At issue here, in terms of the dramatistic analytic is, when we consider the agent, who or what precisely is under scrutiny? Of most concern given the above discussion is the issue of whether, in considering agent, we are considering an objective, embodied entity, a purposive autonomous person, a coherent and stable identity or a stable and coherent personality? All of these notions are problematical, and made more problematical within the postmodern turn within social philosophy and social science. Those wider issues notwithstanding, one issue arising from this study is that when we consider the agent in a comedic performance we are again faced with the problem of the co-construction of comedy and the lack of clarity regarding who the agent is. We also need to note the potential for artifice in mounting a comedic performance. Is a comedian, as part of his/her identity work, constructing a situated identity through the performance? Is the comedian on the stage because they desire to construct, present and have validated a certain identity, one which they find difficulty having validated offstage? Or looked at differently, when we seek for the agent in staging a comedic performance, are we locating or able to locate an authentic self, an actor, an ego defence, a liberated self, a mask of identity, or something else? The situated identity and indeed, the subject position of 'stand-up' is enabled, but also constrained by a wider discourse and so any notion of agent perhaps needs to be considered as a subject position within a discursive location. These are no longer surprising questions, but if we want to invoke the notion of agent we are confronted by its indeterminacy, dispersal and fragmentation. As an analytical device it might still have merit, as an ontological category it is certainly problematic.

Act

On the Burkean pentad, 'act' refers to what was actually done or performed, in thought or deed, in the designated scene and by the identified agent(s). Considering this most straightforwardly, the act in the context of the issues being examined here is the actual comedic performance. Once again, applying this analytically is not as simple as this description might suggest.

In line with the main intent of the fieldwork, the interviews focused less on the performance itself and more on how comedians prepared for and managed their performances. They were asked what they did to prepare for a performance, particularly on the day of the performance itself. A surprising number said they did nothing or very little, mostly relaxing. Preparation mostly consisted of running through the intended set for that night's performance. About half did this mentally, some used notes and only a small minority actually had a script and rehearsed. This reflects the general mechanics of stand-up where experienced performers have an already developed and tried-and-tested repertoire that they know works. The following quote is from one of the minority who has a script, but even he admits it's more ritualistic than an operational necessity, and the overall tone reflects a laissez-faire attitude:

> I always write my set down – always – its a superstition – in my sacred book, get my gig clothes on, drive to gig, look over set list, be funny, go home.

Given the vulnerability that has been spoken of and the pain of a failed performance, it is a perhaps surprising that about 40 per cent claimed that they did not get nervous before a performance. Only a couple said they still got very nervous, and one of those was a relative newcomer and amateur. The remainder said they became mildly nervous and engaged in a bit of pacing or similar. A minority had small rituals they performed prior to going on – one always ties his shoes tight, another practises his golf swing.

The audience–comedian dynamic and the co-production of comedy has been emphasized: managing the audience is a critical process in staging a comedic performance. It is especially acute in the context of stand-up given the vulnerabilities and the identity work at stake.

Managing the audience

The comedians were asked first about their general attitudes towards the audience and responses showed variability. For some the relationship with the audience was absolutely critical and establishing a good relationship fundamental to a successful performance. The majority certainly asserted that they respected an audience and acknowledged their dependence upon them. While for some this was expressed in terms of positive affect, for others it was an instrumental calculation:

> I try to respect them by assuming they will go with me, and usually that respect is reciprocated.

More importantly, given the concerns of this chapter, almost all attempt some assessment of the audience before the performance begins. They scan for information that bears on the type of audience – and they are seeking indicators such as class, gender composition, levels of intelligence, as well as specific features such as the presence of groups of lads, hen parties, drunks, potential trouble spots. In addition, they are trying to assess how responsive the audience is and what sort of material they are likely to find resonance with. Only one (relatively inexperienced) person said they were unable to read an audience. The extent of assessment varies – from a quick look to a multifaceted evaluation. For the more experienced it was an intuitive process that they found difficult to articulate. When following other comedians onto the stage they would use that time to make the assessment; a method that has the added bonus, of course, of providing an opportunity to see how responsive they are and the sort of material they are responding to. A significant minority would identify groups or persons in the audience that they would try and communicate with directly once they had begun performing. Some worked for and greatly prized this direct communication and the ad libs it gave rise to. Some used it at the outset to establish rapport with the audience and to 'get them onside'.

Comedians attempt to 'read' the audience during the performance and use that to monitor their own performance, making adjustments to the material and mode of presentation accordingly. Experienced performers do this intuitively. When a reading suggests that the comedy is not working they invoke some standard strategies. One is to dip into their repertoires and pull out stock material that they 'know' will work. Another is to directly engage the audience, talking to them, feeling for what else might work, but also generating connection and empathy. Mood is everything; if they can establish rapport, get the audience to like them and create a positive mood, people will be more inclined to laugh. Otherwise they may simply continue; working to retain a confidence in their performance and imply it is a problem for the audience for not 'getting it'. As one comedian put it:

> You have to try and bring them up to your level. Don't go down to theirs.

A typical feature of stand-up that often requires explicit audience management interventions is the practice of heckling. It seems to have become part of the interpretation of stand-up comedy from some sections of the audience, and some part of the 'frame' of stand-up, that the audience is at liberty, indeed expected, to heckle. Comedians, in fact, do not typically find this helpful, although some do find it offers additional source of material and interaction.

> Yeah, you always get some spotty youth coming up after the show … sidling up … and saying 'That was me … helped you out a bit there mate didn't I.' Like, yeah mate, thanks a bunch, that was just what I needed. You know, they really think they are … you know, adding something.

Every comedian has methods for dealing with hecklers; it is something they learn very quickly, often from seeing how other comedians handle them. Some will deal with it by the, apparently contrary, methods of either going and standing right over the heckler (circumstances permitting), or by turning away and addressing another part of the audience. However, the most common response to persistent hecklers is some form of a 'comeback' and 'putdown'. There are some well-known 'stock comebacks' known among and shared by comedians, although some develop their own and others ad lib them. Comedians will escalate comebacks depending on how irritating/intrusive the heckler becomes. Here are some favourite/stock heckler putdowns from the interviewees:

> Hey, I'm working here, I don't come down to your place of work and knock the toilet brush out of your hands [or (to a persistent female) knock a dick out of your mouth].

> You're the reason there are lesbians [to a rowdy male].

> I'm sorry, I need a translator, I don't speak fuckwit.

> Who here believes that birth control should be retrospective?

> You look really pissed off, disappointed and fed up. Could you not have waited until I'd fucked you first?

> Hey, man, I like doing my act the way you like having sex — alone.

In applying the pentad, there is again a difficulty in identifying and isolating the act and, indeed, risks in doing so. As with all analytics, what constitutes the point of analytical focus is a matter of choice or is theoretically determined. So we might decide that the comics' actual performance is the 'act'. That seems straightforward enough, but what actually constitutes that performance? Is it merely what he/she does whilst on stage, or do we need to include all that precedes that including many of the issues addressed in this chapter? The boundaries and parameters of a comedic 'act' are indefinite and hard to specify. This is further complicated by the co-production of a comedic performance in which successful performance is co-dependent on both comedian and audience. Audiences are not mere passive recipients, and even heckling is part of the comedic situation – whether it is part of the comedic 'act' is a moot point. It might be argued that all work performances have this complex and co-productive quality. The performance of a service and the quality of that, for example, is an interaction and a co-production between a service worker and a customer. It is less an act of service than a service interaction. Performance management systems rarely address this aspect of performance directly.

Agency

The agency of a dramaturgy refers to how something is done, to the methods, technologies, behaviours and instruments deployed by agents to accomplish acts. In the context of this research we are primarily concerned with the agency through which comedians construct an appropriate comedic performance. In particular, the concern is with the nature of the comedic material comedians bring to and construct in performance. The technology of a comedic performance consists primarily of the material the comedian develops and brings as well as the methodology and style of delivery. In a real sense the comedian him/herself is the technology. There may in some cases be props, although most do not and, as noted, many view the use of props as not proper stand-up and prop-dependent and musical comedy as a lesser form. There may be other bits of incidental technology such as lighting and microphones. Again, I do not focus here on the content of comedy performance, which is in any case extremely varied, but rather on the sources of material and management of it.

For the majority the main sources for material are derived from their own life and experiences, from observations and interactions in normal life (about 50 per cent said this was the prime or only source). Only a couple of them used materials from written sources or other media. This is in keeping with the way they tend to define stand-up comedy and distinguish it from comedy using 'gags' or formal 'jokes'. Stand-up provides much more of a narrative structure even though sometimes interspersed with gags. The comedians stressed the importance of making the material and the delivery of it seem natural, as if it had just been experienced or observed and the comedians were sharing for the first time with this particular set of people. This is establishing the connection, the resonance and intimacy with the audience that most think is vital for the success of the comedy. Banter and extemporization, especially when it includes the audience, adds to this sense of immediacy and shared fresh experience.

The comedians were virtually unanimous in condemning using other comedians' material and it was clearly something of a taboo within the business:

> NEVER – had my material stolen once and was not pleased – be original or be gone!!!!

> Never. The merest idea is incomprehensible to me. It is not a part of my job. Comics who do this are disgusting.

The notion of presenting something fresh appears somewhat at odds with comedians' practices regarding renewal of material. About a third of the interviewees said they had a developed, standard stock of good material and did not change it very often. As noted, this amounts to an hour or two of material. Most sets are not that long, more likely 20 minutes to half an hour, so they can draw on the full repertoire to construct a particular performance of a particular duration. The repertoire is also there to call on if things start to stall. Most of the remaining two-thirds would change at least portions of their act quite frequently – most adopted a kind of roll-on/roll-off practice with new material being added and older material dropped out. In this sense the development of new material, but not a whole act, was an ongoing process. There was much variability, with some having material in their repertoire they had used for years, others would expect to have, bit-by-bit, replaced the whole act within two to three years. One changed his whole act in August every year!

Comedians acknowledge that there are shifts in style and fashion, and whilst some are very anxious about becoming outmoded, most said that if their work remained anchored to everyday life it would remain relevant. The trends they spoke of were more to do with either issues of immediate topicality or general trends in the framing of stand-up and the wider discourses about what was appropriate and legitimate for stand-up comedy and comedy in general:

> Comedy grows and changes with time – terrorism is a hot topic here with many angles to view it. Mother-in-law jokes are out ... but then, you get retro comedians.

It has already been noted that comedians do not frequently use scripted material. Only about a third said they had a primarily fully scripted set, but even that did not mean that a script was prepared or even rehearsed for every show. Surprisingly, this group comprised people at the extreme ends of the experience continuum. As one senior comedian put it:

> It's fully scripted. I deliver a product intended to get the best result, this means eliminating risk. It's polished. Sometimes I chuck in an adlib. You do more adlibbing early in your career when you need material.

For the majority it was a mixture. Many had a core (or sometimes a start and a finish) of well-prepared, possibly scripted, material, but would either extemporize on that or improvise at least a portion of the set. Some had no written script at all, others a partial script, others just some outline notes. Tactically, many said they would seek to improvise but would revert back to stock material if the improvisations were not working. Some appeared to have no set material and improvised on the night, but even then they would often have a structure and some material that they knew and would draw on for each performance. Again, it's worth repeating that many emphasized that stock and scripted material needed to appear improvised and fresh, and that was part of the craft of the stand-up. There is clearly a tension in the performance of comedy between the security of scripted or known material – a reliable technology and methodology – and the imperative that what is performed appears as fresh, unique and constructed just for that audience. There is also a tension between the security of scripted and known material and the risk, exposure and vulnerability, but also exhilaration, of extemporized and ad libbed material. This is another balance many people face in their work-related performances – teachers might be one example here. The technology and methodology of a comedic performance is subject to the dynamics of the moments of its production, and those moments are not fully under the control of the comedian given the co-production issues already addressed. Once again with a dramatistic purview the delineation of agency is problematic. The agency is primarily, but not solely, in the hands of the producer. Comedy is a social accomplishment of a multiple of agencies as reflected in the comments of one comedian:

> The individual makes part of a bigger group of individuals who form a synergy – when they realise that as a group they are laughing louder than they would individually – that is when the magic happens – it is the experience as a whole that effects the individual audience member – not just the fact that they are one person at a comedy event.

Purpose

The final element in the pentad is 'purpose', which references the 'why' question. This is at the heart of Burke's project – the investigation into motives and how we might discern motive from people's performances, but especially from their accounts. It deals with the intended effect or outcomes of action. In terms of this research, *purpose* is taken to be concerned with what the comedians believe they are doing and achieving through their comedic performances: the purposes it may serve – for themselves, their audiences and for the community and society at large.

The function, role and purpose of humour are much debated philosophically and across other disciplines – as has been made apparent in other chapters in this book. Not surprisingly, there was much variability among the comedians, reflecting this wider diversity. Some see comedy merely as a form of entertainment, but many see other purposes and functions and I will focus on some of the more salient ones.

Purpose: general

Professional comedians are, amongst other things, trying to make a living and are, broadly speaking, part of a massive entertainment industry that has ballooned in the age of spectacle. It should come as no surprise therefore that some comedians see the purpose or motive for what they do in terms of simply providing entertainment, as simply making people laugh. Such a motive can, naturally, exist alongside others – motives are not mutually exclusive. One of the comedians who worked as a corporate hoaxer, and saw the purpose of his work in terms of undermining and usurping the power and authority of the managerial 'expert' and the pomposities and vacuities of senior management, also acknowledged that comedy was his job, that clients had to be satisfied and that sometimes it was 'just entertainment'. Another, more bluntly: 'There is no obligation on Comedy to perform any function other than to amuse. That's why we are there, that, in essence, is the job: to be funny.'

For some that was a valid and noble enough purpose, elevated perhaps by the valorization of humour within the wider culture. The majority, however, do see a wider role for comedy, particularly in its capacity to provide different viewpoints on society and to offer a challenge and critique of the status quo. As one eloquently suggested:

> The Hopi clowns had their one day of misrule. The Frecj boufinades [sic] drew a circle around themselves in the dust and could be as offensive as they liked within it. This was their holy clown-shaman task – to relieve society of the duty to misbehave, and show them what would happen if they did.

Such comments resonate with the western history of comedy, going back to the Dionysian bacchanalia of ancient Greece, the long and varied history of the fool and the jester, the Feast of Fools in Middle Ages Europe, and on to the Harlequin, and vaudeville (Davidson 1996; Westwood 2004; Willeford 1969).

Other purposes of comedy discussed included the notion that it is an expression and interpretation of human experience that can be brought into the open and shared – a way of connecting and showing the commonality of experience. A significant point of focus was the function of humour and comedy in surfacing and saying things that would otherwise not be said, to breach taboos and to reduce people's fears, anxieties and sense of isolation by raising such issues in a public domain and under the protective guise of humour. Others pointed to the healing capacity of humour, its ability to help people cope with the pain and suffering personally or socially present. For still others comedy provided a release from the travails of mundane existence or provided a balance to the serious, the calamitous and the painful. These are important and lofty aspirations and instill a burden of responsibility on the comedian and imbue comedy with a social and moral weight. This adds to the risks of comedy, to the vulnerability. The weight may explain the depiction of humour as *just* entertainment, perhaps a defensive move that lifts the responsibility somewhat.

There is an additional tension in a comedic performance and in the management of self in so doing, one that goes to the very heart of stand-up comedy. In many, but not all, cases stand-up comedians are presenting through their comedy, issues, ideas, events, circumstances and material in general that is often not addressed in mundane, everyday interaction. As noted, often the comedy consists of material that is taboo or repressed or sublimated in normal society. However, it is not completely repressed; otherwise it would not resonate with people and would require something more like psychotherapy to surface it. Limon (2000) argues that what stand-up deals with and manifests is abjection; indeed, for him stand-up comedy is an art form that is defined by its association with the abject. His opening premise is that 'what is stood up in stand-up comedy is abjection' (Limon 2000: 4) He draws on Kristeva's (1982) notion of abjection as those aspects of self that are antithetical or challenging to one's preferred, presented and valued sense of self-identity, but which cannot be fully repressed or masked. Limon suggests that abjection is the condition that comedians find themselves perpetually engaged with. We might take this at the personal and individual level to imply that comics are actually using comedy to play out their own struggle with abjection. This sense of personal struggle and connection to notions of self and identity is reflected in Kristeva (1982: 4) when she says 'Abject. It is something rejected from which one does not part, from which one does not protect oneself as from an object. Imaginary uncanniness and real threat, it beckons to us and ends up engulfing us.' The abject is something that is both repellent to and repelled by the person, but which, in the end, cannot be dispatched and has to be incorporated and somehow responded to. More usefully, perhaps, we can think of the relation of stand-up to the abject in a broader way by suggesting that the stand-up, by acting as a personal vehicle for the display of the struggle with abjection, almost by proxy as it were, is realizing the confrontation with the abject present in all of us and present in all our engagements with our social worlds. The abject is a kind of in-between category; neither one thing nor the other, neither filth nor purity, neither fully repressed nor fully integrated. It is material that is not fully rejected but nor is it openly acceptable either. In this liminal place it irritates the system. This, it might be argued, is precisely what stand-up comedy does; it trades in this twilight world between the ordinary and the weird, between the taboo and the mundane. It compels a confrontation with abjection. Linstead sees the abject as 'essentially denied experience which cannot be fully suppressed by the subject' (1997: 1116). Perhaps the purpose of stand-up, ultimately, is this confrontation, which is made manageable through the proxy of the comedian and palatable and accessible through being located within the comedic space.

Purpose: a message

The comedians were asked if they intended to impart a 'message' through their comedy. The responses suggest something of a paradox. A clear majority commented on the social function of comedy and its value to the audience, but around 35 per cent denied they were imparting any sort of 'message' in their comedy; others said that comedy could convey a message but its first job was to entertain. Some spoke of the importance of irreverence, of undermining authority and expertise, of easing the harsh truths of reality. One suggested his message was to

> Get over it. I don't think anyone responds to preachy art, but I think the best comedy tends to be a celebration of human frailty and foibles and individuality, and as such has a message whether it is explicit or not.

Perhaps, as the above response implies, the question was not specific enough; it did not really explore the difference between a specific message intentionally put into the comedy by the comedian and idea of a 'message' being inherent to comedy per se. It is clear, however, that for the majority comedy has important social functions beyond that of mere entertainment.

Purpose: a moral activity

There has been theoretical discussion about the moral role played by humour and comedy in society (e.g. Berger 1997; Morreall 1987). The interviewees were asked if they thought that comedy was a moral activity. It was again a frankly ambiguous question which unsurprisingly generated variable responses, often overtly with many saying 'it depends'. Most viewed comedy as a relatively moral profession and practice, but did not necessarily see that there was a personal obligation to be moral in one's comedic practice. On the other hand about half did also envisage a clear moral dimension in comedy. This was variously expressed, but most often in the form of comedy's moral obligation to satirize and critique, and expose the inconsistencies, flaws, inequalities and weaknesses of society. Responding in terms of this generalized moral quality in comedy one declared:

> Absolutely. More moral than any religion. Instead of a string of THOU SHALT NOTS, it asks WHAT IF THOU DIDST?

The subversive potential of comedy is much to the fore here: comedy representing an alternative moral order to society's dominant ones. For others the moral purpose was more personal and individualized:

> Yes, it is moral education. It is a series of insights into broken people, who are the same as whole people on the inside, but their cracks allow audiences to view themselves more clearly.

For some this revelation via comedy of the damage society inflicts on people is embodied in the person of the comedian. Some argued that comedians themselves were often 'damaged goods', psychologically scarred or in other ways impaired by life's experiences or the machinations of society. Comedy's purpose then becomes one of the displaying this damage as manifest in the comedian as everyman. This melancholy and psychotic clown motif is somewhat mythical and clichéd and was certainly not the majority interpretation among the comedians interviewed.

Purpose: subversion

Just as the moral function or capacity of comedy has been debated so has the extent to which humour and comedy can be subversive. Again this perspective has long, not to say ancient, roots and continues to be debated (e.g. Westwood 2004). Much of the research and conceptualizing on humour has stressed its functionalism, even utility, and this has been especially true of studies of humour in organizations as has been made clear elsewhere in this book (e.g. Chapter 1; see also Crawford 1994; Duncan 1982). But there has also always been a line of thinking from Plato onwards that sees humour as at least potentially subversive.

By a ratio of 2:1 the comedians held to the view that comedy was, could be, or should be, subversive. For some this meant that comedy was able to raise repressed or taboo issues and challenge dominant perceptions and structures that positioned them thus. As one comedian put it:

> Comedy is, even when it isn't explicitly political, about reversing or changing the expected nature of things.

This is the more common meaning of subversive when conceptualizing humour. Of course, humour has been deployed directly in relation to one subversive political or ideological agenda or another, but there is a more subtle form of subversion implied by this comedian's statement. This goes to, what for some, is the essence of humour, that it offers an alternate conception or image of reality, that it challenges, or as this person says, reverses the typical and taken-for-granted view of reality (see e.g. Berger 1997; Westwood 2004).

Purpose: relieving pain and suffering

Again, the conceptual literature has sought to make a connection between pain and comedy and to signal the adjacency of comedy to tragedy. Almost all the comedians recognized a close relationship between pain, tragedy and comedy. Indeed, a number repeated the now clichéd 'Pain and/or Tragedy + Time = Comedy'. For some (about a quarter) this was personalized, so that the role of the comedian is to reflect on his/her pain and depression and, through making comedy of it, provide some kind of salve for the pain and suffering of 'everyman'. For others it was more generalized so that comedy was treating of the pain and suffering inherent to human existence and by surfacing it, rather than hiding or repressing it, and turning it into humour, offer a palliative, helping everyone else to cope with and deal with it better.

Purpose: personal rewards

Finally, there are, naturally enough, outcomes from a comedy performance that the comedians themselves seek that are personal to them. When asked what they got from performing comedy – other than income[3] – the vast majority referred both to the acclamation and the pleasure of an audience response and also to the buzz or the adrenalin rush of live performance. This was sometimes expressed quite starkly:

> I'm a laugh whore.

> I love the buzz of it, the rush of being on stage and getting that reaction.

A minority made reference to the intensity of the experience and the immediacy of the feedback (good and bad). It is this that, as noted, is a clear source of vulnerability, but by the same token, if things go well the immediacy and obviousness of the feedback is a source of instantaneous gratification. This is not typical of most people's work-related performance where often the positive outcomes and feedback, if present at all, are often delayed or deferred. The instant and clear gratification, the affirmation that they have managed a comedic performance well and generated the laughter that is craved, is a major source of motivation for comedians. One expressed it in cathartic terms:

> It's an excuse for the damaged goods of society to get love for being damaged goods.

The flip-side is that when the comedy has not worked and laughter doesn't come, then the same clear and immediate feedback does not bring instant gratification but death ... which is where we came in.

Conclusion

This chapter has focused, in the first instance and somewhat prosaically, on the pragmatics of organizing and managing a comedic performance. In doing so, however, it has also revealed the complex dynamic of such a performance and in particular the need to manage self and identity. Whilst it is the performance of stand-up comedians that has been the focus for this consideration, it has been intimated that performance in many other work-related contexts is subject to similar dynamics and imperatives – they are perhaps simply more acute and intense in the case of stand-up comics. Stand-up comedians can be considered as being amongst that group of workers who are involved in positions of 'high visibility, high contact with the public, [and dealing with] the need to maintain a particular "face," and the need to manage one's self' (Höpfl and Linstead 1993: 81). As we have seen, such performers may, if the performance goes awry, be exposed to intense and immediate negative feedback, experience an assault on their very sense of self and identity, and suffer from a psychological strain that stands being labelled 'corpsing', which Höpfl and Linstead (1993: 90) describe, appositely, as 'not a failure of technique but a failure of the mask'. The extent of the management of self and of intense identity work amongst other groups of workers is increasingly being recognized. The parallels to the dynamics surrounding, for example, teachers, sales people and other service workers are apparent.

The extent to which comedians are donning a mask is a moot point and was addressed in this research and commented on earlier. Comedy is an act – is acting. However, stand-up comedians are not acting through a character, in an important sense they are 'themselves' – or at least that is how they depict themselves – and there are indications of a need for this, a need for the audience to sense some authenticity. This raises difficult questions about the notions of identity and authenticity, not only in the arenas of performance but more widely. Nonetheless, it is still a performance and is often a well-rehearsed or at least practised and crafted performance that masquerades as spontaneous and naturalistic social engagement – as the comedians involved in this study make apparent. This constitutes a tension at the heart of comedic performance and represents not just ambivalence about performance, but ambivalence about self – to be seen as doing something authentic and to self-represent as genuine, whilst obviously performing. Once again, I do not see this as unique to the performance of comedy but as present in many other work-related performance situations, and perhaps a dynamic that is becoming more pervasive in the context of the fragmentations and simulacra of the postmodern. There is another ambivalence or lesion in comedic performance, one reflected in Kaufmann's (1997) notion of the comedian as confidence man. In what he classes 'irony fatigue', Kaufman points to the internal conflict experienced by comedians as they struggle to deal with the juxtaposition of an aspired to identity position as 'social critics' who want to be taken seriously with the identity of 'comedian' who never can be taken seriously. But this is also a dynamic at the heart of comedy itself – that it works through interposing alternate realities and acts to subvert the status quo, but does so within the confines of that status quo as a permitted and contained interruption to the dominant order, a challenge but not a serious one since it is 'only comedy'. One response to this, and one that the comedians in this study had recourse to, is to disavow the social critic/subversive role, and just claim to be an entertainer.

A final tension concerns the relation of comedy to the abject. Part of the aspiration of the stand-up comedian to be perceived as social critic, to be taken seriously, rests on the capacity of comedy to surface those things that are more commonly repressed, marginalized and silenced in society. As discussed above, the comedian may do this by personally confronting and embodying these issues, reflecting on their own experiences and behaviours and sharing them with the audience. The audience can, from the safety of a vicarious position, confront such issues in their own lives. This relation to the taboo and repressed has led Limon (2000) to suggest that at the heart of stand-up comedy is a confrontation with the abject. Comedians are struggling to deal with those aspects of either their own lives, or aspects of all our lives, that we want to push away and mask, but which cannot be fully evacuated and that must be held within us and somehow dealt with. The comedian is perpetually confronted with abjection – perhaps we all are.

Notes

1 Nineteen completed all phases. A total of 35 comedians were contacted, giving a 63 per cent response rate.
2 This promoter and other people in the business referred to the venue in which stand-up was performed as 'rooms' as in 'I run a room at the Marmaduke hotel'.
3 I will not focus on extrinsic rewards. The financial rewards for the vast majority of working comedians are not high, and given the risks, the competition and the uncertainty seem unlikely to be the prime motivator in the vast majority of cases.

References

Ajaye, F. (2002) *Comic Insights: The Art of Stand-Up Comedy*, Berverly Hills, CA: Silman-James.

Allen, T. (1994) *Don't Stand Too Close to a Naked Man*, New York: Hyperion.

Anthony, B. and Edmonds, A. (1998) *Smile When the Raindrops Fall: The Story of Charley Chase*, Metuchen, NJ: Scarecrow.

Berger, A. A. (2003) *The Hero's Journey: A Reflection on Becoming a Comedian*, Burleigh: Poseidon Books.

Berger, P. (1985) *The Last Laugh: The World of the Stand-Up Comics*, New York: Limelight.

Berger, P. L. (1997) *Redeeming Laughter: The Comic Dimension of Human Experience*, Berlin: Walter de Gruyter.

Borns, B. (1987) *Comic Lives*, New York: Fireside/Simon & Schuster.

Burke, K. (1945) *A Grammar of Motives*, Englewood Cliffs, NJ: Prentice Hall.

Burke, K. (1950/1969) *A Rhetoric of Motives*, Berkeley, CA: University of California Press.

Burke, K. (1972) *Dramatism and Development*, Barre, MA: Clark University Press with Barre Publishers.

Crawford, C. B. (1994) 'Theory and implications regarding the utilization of strategic humor by leaders', *Journal of Leadership Studies*, 1: 53–67.

Davidson, C. (1996) *Fools and Folly,* Kalamazoo, MI: Medieval Institute Publications, Western University of Michigan.

Double, O. (1997) *Stand-Up: On Being a Comedian*, London: Methuen.

Duncan, W. J. (1982) 'Humor in management: prospects for administrative practice and research', *Academy of Management Review*, 7: 136–42.

Fisher, S. and Fisher, R. (1981) *Pretend the World is Funny and Forever: A Psychological Analysis of Comedians, Clowns, and Actors*, Hillsdale, NJ: Lawrence Erlbaum.

Goffman, E. (1969) *The Presentation of Self in Everyday Life*, London: Allen Lane-Penguin Press.

Goffman, E. (1974) *Frame Analysis*, New York: Harper Books.

Greenbaum, A. (1999) 'Stand-up comedy as rhetorical argument: an investigation of comic culture', *HUMOR: International Journal of Humor Research*, 12(1): 33–46.

Harvey, A. (2001) 'A dramaturgical analysis of charismatic leader discourse', *Journal of Organizational Change Management*, 14(3): 253–66.

Höpfl, H. and Linstead, S. (1993) 'Passion and performance: suffering and the carrying of organizational roles', in S. Fineman (ed.), *Emotions in Organizations*, pp. 76–93, London: Sage.

Janus, S. (1975) 'The great comedians: personality and other factors', *American Journal of Psychoanalysis*, 35: 169–74.

Kaufman, W. (1997) *The Comedian as Confidence Man: Studies in Irony Fatigue*, Detroit, MI: Wayne State University Press.

Koziski, S. (1997) 'The standup comedian as anthropologist: intentional culture critic', in Joseph Boskin (ed.), *The Humor Prism in Twentieth-Century America*, pp. 86–116, Detroit, MI: Wayne State University Press.

Kristeva, J. (1982) *Powers of Horror: An Essay on Abjection*, tr. L. S. Roudiez, New York: Columbia University Press.

Limon, J. (2000) *Stand-Up Comedy in Theory: or, Abjection in America*, Durham, NC: Duke University Press.

Linstead, S. (1997) 'Abjection and organization: men, violence, and management', *Human Relations*, 50(9): 1115–45.

Mangham, I. (1988) *Power and Performance in Organizations: An Exploration of Executive Process*, Oxford: Blackwell.

Mangham, I. (1990) 'Managing as performing art', *British Journal of Management*, 1: 105–15.

Mangham, I. and Overington, M. A. (1987) *Organizations as Theatre*, Chichester: Wiley.

Mintz, L. E. (1985) 'Standup comedy as social and cultural mediation', *American Quarterly*, 37(1): 71–80.

Mitchell, R. (2001) 'Review of Limon, J. (2000) Stand-up Comedy in Theory; or, Abjection in America. Durham: Duke University Press', *The Drama Review*, 45(3): 172–4.

Morreall, J. (ed.) (1987) *The Philosophy of Laughter and Humor*, Albany, NY: State University of New York Press.

Oswick, C., Keenoy, T. and Grant, D. (2001) 'Dramatizing and organizing: acting and being', *Journal of Organizational Change Management*, 14(3): 218–24.

Pollio, H. R. and Swanson, C. (1995) 'A behavioral and phenomenological analysis of audience reactions to comic performance', *HUMOR: International Journal of Humor Research*, 8(1): 5–28.

Puliam, G. J. (1991) 'Stock-lines, boats-acts, and dickjokes: a brief annotated glossary of standup-comedy jargon', *American Speech*, 66(2): 164–70.

Rutter, J. (2000) 'The stand-up introduction sequence: comparing comedy compares', *Journal of Pragmatics*, 32: 463–83.

Rutter, J. (2001) 'Rhetoric in stand-up comedy: exploring performer-audience interaction', 'Stylistyka Dziś/Style and Humor', a special issue of *Stylistyka*, 10: 307–26.

Schwensen, D. (1998) *How to Be a Working Comic: An Insider's Guide to a Career in Stand-Up Comedy*, New York: Back Stage Books/Watson-Guptill.

Stebbins, R. A. (1993) 'Social roles of the stand-up comic', *Canadian Theatre Review*, 77 (Winter): 4–7.

Westwood, R. I. (2004) 'Comic relief: subversion and catharsis in organisational comedic theatre', *Organisation Studies*, 25(5): 775–95.

Willeford, W. (1969) *The Fool and his Scepter: A Study of Clowns, Jesters and their Audience*, Evanston, IL: Northwestern University Press.

Williams, J. A. (1991) *If I Stop I'll Die: The Comedy and Tragedy of Richard Pryor*, New York: Thunder's Mouth Press.

Index